World Economic and Financial Surveys

Global Financial Stability Report

Market Developments and Issues

September 2005

International Monetary Fund
Washington DC

Production: IMF Multimedia Services Division
Cover: Phil Torsani
Photo: Padraic Hughes
Figures: Theodore F. Peters, Jr.
Typesetting: Choon Lee

ISBN 1-58906-450-X
ISSN 0258-7440

Price: US$49.00
(US$46.00 to full-time faculty members and students at universities and colleges)

Please send orders to:
International Monetary Fund, Publication Services
700 19th Street, N.W., Washington, D.C. 20431, U.S.A.
Tel.: (202) 623-7430 Telefax: (202) 623-7201
E-mail: publications@imf.org
Internet: www.imf.org

recycled paper

CONTENTS

Preface vii

Chapter I. Overview 1

Balance of Risks, Current Assessment 1
The Search for Yield 1
Potential Triggers for Market Corrections 2
Trends That Could Enhance Financial Stability 4
Policy Measures to Mitigate Risks 4
Global Asset Allocation Framework 5
Corporate Bond Markets in Emerging Market Countries 6

Chapter II. Global Financial Market Developments 8

Low Bond Yields, High Equity Earnings Yields, and the Recovering Dollar 9
The Search for Yield in Credit and Mortgage Markets—The Credit Cycle 19
Increased Resilience of Emerging Markets 28
Emerging Market Financing 32
Balance Sheet Developments in Major Mature Economies 35
Market and Credit Risk Indicators for the Mature Market Financial System 50
Banking Sector Developments in Emerging Market Countries 58
References 63

Chapter III. Aspects of Global Asset Allocation 65

Module 1. Global Asset Allocation 66
Module 2. Investment Fund Industry 77
Module 3. Home Bias 85
Module 4. Financial Stability Considerations Related to Trends in Accounting Standards 94
References 100

Chapter IV. Development of Corporate Bond Markets in Emerging Market Countries 103

Recent Trends in Local Corporate Bond Markets 104
Demand and Supply Factors Driving Corporate Bond Markets 110
Market Structure and Obstacles to Growth of Corporate Bond Markets 124
Challenges and Policy Issues 136
References 140

Glossary 142

Annex: Summing Up by the Chairman 148

Statistical Appendix 153

Boxes

2.1 U.S. Auto Companies and Losses in the Credit Derivatives Market 21
2.2 Emerging Market Borrowers Intensify Liability Management Operations 30
2.3 Foreign Investment in Local Currency Instruments: A Cyclical or Fundamental Phenomenon? 40
2.4 Collective Action Clauses 44
2.5 Foreign Direct Investment to Emerging Market Countries: An Asian Perspective 45
2.6 Impact of Correlation Assumptions on Multiple Default Probabilities and CDO Tranche-Specific Default Risk 57
3.1 A Sample Calculation of Potential Gains from International Diversification 92
4.1 Corporate Bond Market in Russia 116
4.2 High-Yield Bonds 120
4.3 Islamic Bonds in Malaysia 126
4.4 Demand and Supply Factors Driving Corporate Bond Markets in China and India 132

Tables

2.1 Global Financial Balances by Sector 12
2.2 U.S. Sector Financial Flows 26
2.3 Emerging Market External Financing 36
2.4 Emerging Market Countries: Selected Bank Financial Soundness Indicators 59
2.5 Countries with High Credit Growth in 2004 by Region: Financial Soundness Indicators 62
3.1 Assets Under Management by Institutional Investors 67
3.2 Major Industrial Countries: Assets of Institutional Investors 68
3.3 Assets Under Management of Mutual Funds 78
3.4 Assets of Exchange-Traded Funds 80
3.5 United States: Growth and Net Assets of Life-Cycle Funds 82
3.6 European Mutual Fund Distribution in 2002 84
3.7 United States: Mutual Fund Distribution 85
3.8 Share of Foreign Bonds from Inside and Outside Euro Area 91
4.1 Outstanding Domestic Debt Securities, Stock Market Capitalization, and Bank Credit, 2004 105
4.2 Corporate Issuers: Outstanding Domestic Debt Securities 107
4.3 Securitization: Selected Emerging Markets 110
4.4 Local Institutional Investor Base for Corporate Bonds 111
4.5 Assets Under Management by Insurance Companies 112
4.6 Pension Fund Investment in Corporate Fixed-Income Instruments 113
4.7 Emerging Market Mutual Funds: Total Net Assets 114
4.8 Cost of Domestic and International Bond Issues 130
4.9 Annual Turnover Ratios of Listed Bonds and Equities on Exchanges, 2004 134
4.10 Annual Bond Turnover, 2004 135

Figures

2.1 U.S. Yields 9
2.2 Inflation-Indexed Bond Yields 10

2.3 U.S. Real Yields and Inflation Expectations 10
2.4 U.S. Yield Curve Steepness and Real Short-Term Rates 11
2.5 Yield Curve Steepness 11
2.6 Global Equity Yields Versus Real Bond Yields 12
2.7 Corporate Financial Balances 12
2.8 Path for Real U.S. 1-Year LIBOR Discounted in the Term Structure 13
2.9 International Reserves 13
2.10 Earnings Yield in Major Developed Markets 14
2.11 Earnings per Share, Actual Minus Forecast 14
2.12 Earnings Yield Minus 10-Year Bond Yield 15
2.13 Implied Volatilities 15
2.14 S&P 500 Price and Difference Between Implied and Actual Volatility 16
2.15 U.S. Current Account Balance 16
2.16 U.S. Dollar Performance 17
2.17 U.S. Dollar Index: Net Noncommercial Positions 17
2.18 Net Foreign Purchases of U.S. Assets by Type 18
2.19 Chinese Renminbi Nondeliverable Forwards 18
2.20 Corporate and Agency Bond Issuance 19
2.21 Corporate Spreads 19
2.22 Credit Default Swap Spreads 20
2.23 Standard & Poor's Speculative-Grade Default Rates 24
2.24 High-Yield Debt and the Credit Cycle 24
2.25 Corporate Actions of Top 150 U.S. Corporations 25
2.26 Surveys of Bank Lending Standards 25
2.27 Global Merger Deal Value 26
2.28 Slope of the Corporate Credit Spread Curve 26
2.29 Foreign Net Purchases of U.S. Agency Securities 27
2.30 U.S. Home Mortgages and Financing Instruments 27
2.31 U.S. Mortgage Debt and Equity Extraction 28
2.32 Adjustable Rate Mortgages 28
2.33 EMBIG Sovereign Spreads 29
2.34 Emerging Market Credit Quality 29
2.35 Cumulative Net Flows to U.S.-Based Mutual Funds 33
2.36 Asset Class Risk-Return Performance 33
2.37 EMBI Global Performance, 2005 to Date 34
2.38 U.S. Corporate, EMBIG, and Auto Sector Spreads 34
2.39 Cumulative Gross Annual Issuance of Bonds, Loans, and Equity 35
2.40 Quarterly Net Issuance 35
2.41 Cumulative Gross Annual Issuance of Bonds 37
2.42 Emerging Market Bond Issuance by Currency 37
2.43 Equity Placements 38
2.44 Syndicated Loan Commitments 38
2.45 FDI Inflows into Emerging Markets 39
2.46 Japan: Capital-to-Asset Ratio of Corporate Sector 46
2.47 Japan: Corporate Debt and Cash Flow Relative to GDP 46
2.48 Japan: Business Conditions 47
2.49 Euro Area and United Kingdom: Ratio of Nonfinancial Corporate Debt to GDP 47

2.50 Selected Countries: Return on Equity 49
2.51 VaR With and Without Market Effects (VaR-Beta) for the Full Portfolio of Financial Institutions 51
2.52 VaR-Betas for LCFIs Versus Commercial Banks 52
2.53 Market Implied Correlation on CDX 5-Year Investment-Grade Tranches 52
2.54 VaR-Betas for Portfolios of Life Insurance Companies 54
2.55 Probability of More Than One Default Among the Portfolios of Financial Institutions 55
2.56 Spread Levels on 5-Year CDX Investment-Grade Index 56
3.1 Asset Allocation of Institutional Investors 69
3.2 Global Asset Allocation of Institutional Investors by Country 70
3.3 Equity and Bond Holdings of Pension Funds and Life Insurance Companies 72
3.4 Holdings of Foreign Assets by Type of Institutional Investor 73
3.5 Foreign Asset Acceptance Ratios for Portfolio Assets 87
3.6 Foreign Asset Acceptance Ratios 88
4.1 Size and Composition of Local Bond Markets Outstanding, 2004 106
4.2 Local Corporate Bonds Outstanding 108
4.3 Corporate Bond Market and Money Market Interest Rates in the Czech Republic 108
4.4 Domestic Government Bond and Money Market Rates 109
4.5 Pension Fund Assets Under Management and Corporate Bonds Outstanding 112
4.6 G-7 Corporate Bond Issuance by S&P Rating 119
4.7 Distribution by Size of the Corporate Bond Issues 131

The following symbols have been used throughout this volume:

. . . to indicate that data are not available;

— to indicate that the figure is zero or less than half the final digit shown, or that the item does not exist;

– between years or months (for example, 1997–99 or January–June) to indicate the years or months covered, including the beginning and ending years or months;

/ between years (for example, 1998/99) to indicate a fiscal or financial year.

"Billion" means a thousand million; "trillion" means a thousand billion.

"Basis points" refer to hundredths of 1 percentage point (for example, 25 basis points are equivalent to ¼ of 1 percentage point).

"n.a." means not applicable.

Minor discrepancies between constituent figures and totals are due to rounding.

As used in this volume the term "country" does not in all cases refer to a territorial entity that is a state as understood by international law and practice. As used here, the term also covers some territorial entities that are not states but for which statistical data are maintained on a separate and independent basis.

PREFACE

The *Global Financial Stability Report* (GFSR) assesses global financial market developments with a view to identifying potential systemic weaknesses. By calling attention to potential fault lines in the global financial system, the report seeks to play a role in preventing crises, thereby contributing to global financial stability and to sustained economic growth of the IMF's member countries.

The report was prepared by the International Capital Markets (ICM) Department, under the direction of the Counsellor and Director, Gerd Häusler. It is managed by an Editorial Committee comprising Hung Q. Tran (Chairman), Elie Canetti, Todd Groome, and Ceyla Pazarbasioglu, and it benefits from comments and suggestions by Axel Bertuch-Samuels and Charles R. Blitzer. Other ICM staff contributing to this issue include Geoffrey Bannister, Nicolas Blancher, Marcelo Carvalho, Peter Dattels, Michael Gapen, François Haas, Anna Ilyina, Andreas Jobst, Herman Kamil, John Kiff, William Lee, Pipat Luengnaruemitchai, Carlos Medeiros, Christopher Morris, Shinobu Nakagawa, Hiroko Oura, Michael Papaioannou, Lars Pedersen, Jorge Roldos, Paul Ross, G. Edwin Smith III, Laura Valderrama, Christopher Walker, Mark Walsh, and Luisa Zanforlin. Jonathan Fiechter, Kalin Tintchev, and Kal Wajid from the Monetary and Financial Systems Department (MFD) contributed banking sector developments in emerging market countries. Martin Edmonds, Ivan Guerra, Silvia Iorgova, Oksana Khadarina, Yoon Sook Kim, Ned Rumpeltin, and Peter Tran provided analytical support. Caroline Bagworth, Rosemarie Edwards, Vera Jasenovec, and Elsa Portaro-Cracel provided expert word processing assistance. Archana Kumar of the External Relations Department edited the manuscript and coordinated production of the publication.

This particular issue draws, in part, on a series of informal discussions with commercial and investment banks, securities firms, asset management companies, hedge funds, insurance companies, pension funds, stock and futures exchanges, and credit rating agencies, as well as regulatory authorities and academic researchers in many major financial centers and countries. The report reflects information available up to July 22, 2005.

The report has benefited from comments and suggestions from staff in other IMF departments, as well as from Executive Directors following their discussions of the *Global Financial Stability Report* on August 29, 2005. However, the analysis and policy considerations are those of the contributing staff and should not be attributed to the Executive Directors, their national authorities, or the IMF.

OVERVIEW

The global financial system has yet again gathered strength and resilience. As before, this trend has been fueled by continued balance sheet improvements in the financial and corporate sectors in most countries. The continuing global economic expansion, together with determined efforts to restructure and cut costs, has enabled many financial institutions and corporations to generate substantial, or even record, profits over the past three years. As a result, their balance sheets have strengthened to the extent that the financial and corporate sectors can absorb a significant degree of financial shock before coming under systemic stress. With global growth most likely to continue, inflation under control, and financial markets generally benign, we expect the resilience of the global financial system to improve even further. This improvement provides an important cushion in the event that any of the more medium-term risks discussed below were to materialize. This cushion against risks and vulnerabilities in the medium term may have expanded, but risks have not disappeared altogether.

Balance of Risks, Current Assessment

Hence, in the short term, the current configuration of solid growth, low inflation, as well as low bond yields, flat yield curves, and compressed credit risk premiums provides the global financial system with a favorable environment. At the same time, growth and interest rate differentials in favor of the United States, and consequently private investors' current appetite for U.S. dollar assets, allow for a smooth financing of global imbalances.

The same benign forces underpinning continued growth and buoyant financial markets, however, have also created larger global imbalances and built up higher levels of debt, particularly by the household sector. Consequently, the potential for a substantial adjustment of investor preferences for asset classes and currencies in the medium term has grown. In short, recent economic and market developments have reduced risks in the near term, but they are storing up potential vulnerabilities for the future.

When assessing the balance of risks, however, experience shows that even at times of sharp asset price movements, countervailing forces tend to mitigate such developments before long. This report sheds light on a few trends that could act as "buffers" in times of stress.

The Search for Yield

The search for yield emerged about two-and-a-half years ago, when very low short-term interest rates, rather steep yield curves, and sizable risk premiums triggered a larger amount of carry trades. The search for yield first took the form of directional bets on lower yields and tighter credit spreads, and more recently took the form of relative value trades using complex and leveraged instruments such as credit derivatives.

Carry trades and market expectations of contained inflation have exerted downward pressure on bond yields. In addition, increased secular demand for long-term bonds by institutional investors such as pension funds and life insurers has contributed to low bond yields and flat yield curves in the United States and Europe. In the case of the United States, the yield curve has flattened despite tightening moves by the Federal Reserve. While it is difficult to quantify precisely the influence of various factors leading to low bond yields and flat yield curves, their implications are clear.

Low bond yields and flat yield curves have encouraged investors to move out on the credit curve, compressing credit spreads, including those in emerging bond markets. Tight credit spreads have helped borrowers—sovereign and corporate—to engage in extensive liability management, which we have advocated as an important step to improve the structure of their debt, thus reducing their balance sheet vulnerability. In addition, low bond yields, and therefore low mortgage rates, have helped sustain activities in the housing market, and more generally the economy, of the United States and other countries.

While the search for yield has benefited emerging bond markets, the improving fundamentals of many emerging market countries have also attracted investors' interest. Specifically, many emerging market countries have experienced strong growth with moderate inflation, improved their current account and fiscal performance, and accumulated substantial reserves—even though many countries have adopted flexible exchange rates. Although total debt remains high, active debt management has reduced the share of foreign currency debt to total debt, and the average maturity of the debt stock has lengthened. Furthermore, most emerging market countries have prefinanced their 2005 borrowing requirements, and several have begun to prefinance 2006. The improvement in fundamentals and superior long-term risk-adjusted returns have convinced institutional investors such as pension funds to make strategic allocations to the asset class. These flows have served as a stabilizing factor for emerging bond markets, despite mature credit market corrections and growing political noise in several emerging market countries facing a heavy election calendar in 2006.

Low yields and tight credit spreads, in turn, have focused the search for yield on relative value trades, using complex and leveraged instruments such as credit derivatives and collateralized debt obligations (CDOs). Reflecting this trend is the recent phenomenal growth of credit derivatives and of hedge funds, which tend to be active in these investment strategies. Overall, these are positive developments that help improve market efficiency and liquidity.

Potential Triggers for Market Corrections

The current low bond yields and tight credit spreads, and low risk premiums more generally, have made financial markets vulnerable to corrections, if fundamentals deteriorate and/or investors' risk appetite diminishes for other reasons. After examining some of the risk factors that might trigger market corrections going forward, we will analyze some of the trends that, in our view, create self-stabilizing forces in the financial markets.

In cyclical terms, the most important question for financial markets is the extent to which the current global expansion will be sustained. Recently, the rise of crude oil prices to record highs has lowered bond yields and equity markets—partly triggered by expectations that high oil prices would slow economic growth. If growth slows only moderately, bond yields would stay low, yield curves would remain flat, and the search for yield would continue, thus supporting generally benign financial markets. If, however, growth decelerates more significantly, balance sheets will start to weaken again. But even in this "worse case" scenario, the financial cushions described above would support the global financial system and lessen its resilience in a gradual manner.

Related to the question about growth prospects is the assessment of where we are in the credit cycle. This in turn will determine if, and to what extent, currently tight credit spreads are likely to be corrected. While current indicators of credit quality are excellent—very low default and loan delinquency rates, and low loan loss provisioning by banks—the credit cycle may be peaking. Corporate earnings growth is likely to slow from the robust rate in the past few years. Default rates of subinvestment-grade borrowers are likely to increase, partly because of the wave of high-yield issuance in the previous years. Future credit quality could be weakened through increased corporate leverage, be it through higher dividend payments, share buyback programs, or more active merger and acquisitions activities. Reflecting market concerns about credit deterioration in the medium term, the U.S. credit curve has steepened: spreads on longer maturity corporate credits have increased, while spreads at shorter maturities have hardly changed from their low levels at the beginning of the year.

The earnings outlook for banks and other financial institutions traditionally suffers when there is less scope for traditional carry trades in a flat yield curve environment. Moreover, the process of releasing provisions to improve earnings has meanwhile run its course given current low provisions to loan ratios in most lending institutions. Stock markets have anticipated this trend; banks have slightly underperformed market indices in major equity markets so far this year. In a nutshell, a slow but persistent weakening of corporate credit quality could lead to a widening of credit spreads, causing market corrections and losses for those investors who warehouse credit risk.

While this is all true, such risks need to be seen in perspective. Corporations would cope with eventual cyclical challenges from a position of financial strength—their balance sheets are at present quite healthy and liquid, and serve as a long fuse to delay a general credit downturn. Individual credit events—such as the downgrading of General Motors (GM) and Ford—have been seen by market participants as idiosyncratic, rather than as a general trend. Hence, credit spreads could, and probably will, correct, but they might do so gradually and moderately from their currently tight levels. In addition, the corporate sector in a number of mature markets is no longer taking up credit, but on a net basis, it has become a net investor. If this trend persists, a number of corporations will be increasingly exposed to the same type of financial risks as traditional institutional investors.

Compared with the risk of a sharp widening of credit spreads, corrections in credit derivatives and CDO markets are more likely to occur. These complex and leveraged instruments are used in the relative value trades, which tend to be crowded trades (with many investors putting on similar strategies). These instruments also depend on relatively untested models and default correlation assumptions for pricing. As such, they are vulnerable to corrections that could be aggravated by liquidity disruptions—similar to the market disruptions and losses triggered by the downgrading of GM and Ford in May 2005.

In contrast to the corporate sector, the household sector, especially in the United States, has become a net borrower of funds, accumulating a record level of debt. Similarly, in a number of other countries, household sectors have also increased their indebtedness. However, their net worth has also risen because of asset price increases, mainly in the housing market. On balance, these developments increasingly expose the household sector to the performance of asset markets.

Most likely, substantial asset price declines would undermine consumer confidence and reduce personal consumption. However, as in the corporate sector, the accumulated increase in household net worth can also act as a long fuse to soften the immediate impact of any adverse development. At present, there are signs that the credit cycle is peaking in the household sector as well. In the United Kingdom, the personal delinquency rate has risen from very low levels, and some U.K. banks have reportedly begun to raise their provisions. In the United States, marginal homebuyers have been attracted by mortgages designed to minimize interest payments in the first few years by pushing off the debt service burden into the future, and also by a relaxation of credit standards. The U.S. regulatory authorities have rightly expressed concerns about these trends, and it is important to monitor them in the foreseeable future.

Increasing growth and interest rate differentials in favor of the United States more recently have generated private capital flows to the United States and more than financed the U.S. current account deficit while supporting the dollar. Once again, the growing global imbalances turn out to be a medium-term issue, while in the short term, deep and liquid U.S. markets and the fundamental factors described above seem to be sufficient to attract the necessary capital inflows. In other words, investors' willingness to smoothly finance global imbalances today reduces the sense of urgency for policymakers to take corrective actions and increases the potential for a "snap back"—a sharp reallocation of assets away from dollar assets—some time in the future. Such a snap back may not have a high probability, at least not in the near term. It would, however, entail large costs in terms of sharply falling dollar exchange rates and rising dollar interest rates, thus causing disorderly financial markets and depressing global economic growth.

All in all, while the near-term outlook is favorable, the increasing potential for a sharp correction in financial markets in the medium term makes it all the more important to address global imbalances and contain other risk factors, such as protectionist trends and/or "event risks" in emerging markets.

Trends That Could Enhance Financial Stability

In addition to the more cyclical factors discussed above, two observable trends could help enhance financial stability over time, especially to protect against the risk of abrupt and indiscriminate reversals of capital flows.

- Demographic changes and ensuing pension reforms increase the size and importance of institutional investors such as pension funds and life insurance companies relative to more short-term-oriented investors. To the extent that these long-term institutional investors need to match their assets to long-term liabilities, their corresponding asset liability management has shown a strong commitment to strategic asset allocation; such allocation is largely guided by long-term fundamentals as opposed to day-to-day noise in the markets. This type of investor is usually very large and can, by definition, move markets, especially if the markets are small and narrow. In addition, institutional investors' reallocations are typically infrequent and implemented at a rather deliberate speed. In short, the fast growth of assets under management of this type of investor will probably have a stabilizing effect on financial markets.
- A much enhanced transparency and disclosure in financial markets, including on the part of emerging market borrowers, together with a much more sophisticated investor base can reduce the likelihood of contagion risk, at least the "knee-jerk" contagion seen some years ago. Specific credit events or country problems may occur, but judging from market reactions to such events in the recent past, there is reason to expect that, in the foreseeable future, these events would be regarded as specific rather than generalized, further containing future market volatility.

Policy Measures to Mitigate Risks

As explained above, the short-term outlook for global financial stability is rather benign because of solid growth and favorable financial conditions. Traditional countervailing forces in financial markets, but also some of the more recent trends explained in the previous section, add to this benign assessment. As always, the ongoing risk management by and prudential supervision of individual market participants are the most important line of defense.

With regard to vulnerabilities of the relative value trades using credit derivatives and

CDOs, financial supervisors must ensure that regulated institutions maintain robust counterparty risk management practices, not the least to contain the spillover effect of market corrections should they occur. Given the complexity of these financial transactions and instruments, regulators need to upgrade their skill sets, where necessary, to be able to effectively perform their supervisory functions.

In this context, we welcome the release of the recent report of the Counterparty Risk Management Policy Group II that highlights, from a private sector perspective, counterparty and other risks and calls for action by financial institutions to deal with them.[1]

Financial supervisors also need to ensure—as they have begun to do in the context of household indebtedness—that lending institutions do not relax credit standards, which would in turn lead to tomorrow's nonperforming loans.

More generally, some monetary authorities face the challenge of gradually removing monetary stimulus, so as to contain excessive risk taking, without strangling financial markets or the economy as a whole. The Federal Reserve's program of "measured" tightening moves appears to have struck the right balance in this regard and should be continued.

For the medium term, the risk of growing global imbalances has to be addressed by a cooperative effort from the major countries, with each country adopting policies appropriate for its circumstances. As explained in various issues of the IMF's *World Economic Outlook,* these policy measures include efforts to raise national savings in the United States—both public and private—structural reforms and supporting measures to raise the trend growth rate of Europe and Japan, and financial sector reforms and greater currency flexibility by many Asian countries. Progress in implementing these mutually reinforcing policy measures can go a long way in maintaining investor, business, and consumer confidence, which in turn underpins the current configuration of benign economic and financial developments. In this context, the recent moves by China and Malaysia to alter their currency peg regimes are welcome steps in the right direction.

Emerging market countries have benefited greatly from benign financial markets over the last two or three years. They should not only continue to use the current favorable environment for further liability management operations, including debt buybacks but, even more importantly, they should consolidate their macroeconomic performance and persevere with structural reforms.

Global Asset Allocation Framework

As already mentioned above, the global asset allocation is driven not only by cyclical considerations but also by secular changes in financial markets. Chapter III provides insight into some of the structural trends that shape this process as well as their relevance for the IMF's multilateral surveillance.

Global financial assets held by nonbank institutional investors have more than doubled in the past 10 years, and more than tripled in the past 15 years to reach about $45 trillion (in the OECD countries), and they are expected to continue growing at a rapid pace. Demographic trends necessitate pension reforms that are expected to create more and larger "asset gatherers." The investment fund industry (comprising mutual funds, hedge funds, and so on), with the exception of those in the United States and the United Kingdom, is less developed in many mature and emerging market countries, and is likely to expand in the future. Consequently, the volume of financial assets under management by institutional investors such as pension funds, insurance companies, and investment funds will continue to grow.

[1]Counterparty Risk Management Policy Group II, 2005, *Toward Greater Financial Stability: A Private Sector Perspective,* July 27. Available via the Internet: *http://www.crmpolicygroup.org/docs/crmpg-II.pdf.*

Previous issues of the GFSR have examined in detail how the various nonbank sectors have—over the last decade or two—assumed a lot of credit risk previously held by the banking sector. These relatively new developments have increasingly put institutions such as pension funds and insurance companies more and more at the center of the financial system. Indeed, it is now virtually impossible to conduct multilateral surveillance in financial markets at large and not to understand the intricacies of nonbanks' investment decisions and their motivation.

Changes in the asset allocation decisions by these institutional investors will have an increasingly important impact on capital flows across asset classes and across national borders, as well as on asset prices. Both institutional and individual investors will seek to maximize risk-adjusted returns in an increasingly globalized financial system by diversifying their holdings to uncorrelated assets. In the process, a relatively small change in the asset allocation of funds—given their enormous size—may affect global financial stability and, by way of example, have a significant impact on the cost of external funding for emerging market countries.

To monitor and safeguard global financial stability, the supervisory community must understand and anticipate the systemic implications of the evolving global asset allocation. It needs to reflect seriously on developments that have taken place in the past decade. More importantly and looking ahead, private capital flows are likely to become ever more influential. As emerging market countries mature and open up their capital accounts over time, financial market integration will intensify, and these countries' financial sectors will increasingly compete for, open up to, and receive flows from the global pool of capital.

In Chapter III, a series of short modules explains the global asset allocation process and its various aspects. These modules examine the role of the key institutional investors, their decision-making processes, and factors that influence such processes. The modules analyze in greater detail recent developments and future trends in the investment fund industry, the changes in home bias and their implications for international portfolio diversification and capital flows, and the influence of accounting standards on the behavior of institutional investors.

These modules show that the investment of institutional investors, such as pension funds and life insurance companies, is increasingly shaped by their long-term liability structures. Partly because of regulatory and accounting changes. The resulting diversity in investment behavior and the growing importance of pension funds and life insurance companies—with their long-term orientation as opposed to short-term players such as hedge funds—have contributed to financial stability. Consequently, financial regulators should pay attention to preserving this diversity, as well as the long-term orientation of important institutional investors, in considering regulatory and accounting changes.

Corporate Bond Markets in Emerging Market Countries

Chapter IV builds on previous work in the GFSR related to corporate finance in emerging market countries. The domestic supply of credit to the corporate sector in most emerging market countries is channeled through the national banking system. In a number of cases, the corporate sector is unable to receive such bank credit with long tenors and moderate levels of interest rates, especially when the country in question has just weathered a period of high inflation. Typically, under such circumstances, corporations have tapped the international financial markets for long-dated finance, while being exposed to foreign exchange risk.

Recent work by the IMF on the use of the balance sheet approach to detect vulnerabilities in emerging market countries has highlighted the importance of corporate sector vulnerabilities and their linkages to other sectors and markets. In this context, the April 2005 edition of the GFSR demonstrated the importance of having alternative sources of financing for the corporate sector, both to finance growth and to reduce balance sheet vulnerabilities. Continuing this line of work, Chapter IV focuses on the development of corporate bond markets in emerging market countries. It highlights lessons from the experiences of mature markets as well as from a small group of emerging markets that either have large corporate bond markets or have seen them grow rapidly in recent years.

In terms of development issues, a thriving corporate bond market needs several sets of conditions to be in place:

- First, a country should have sufficient macroeconomic stability, so that market inflation expectation is anchored and bond yields are low enough to induce borrowing.
- Second, demand and supply factors have to be conducive to the use of corporate bonds. The development of local institutional investors such as pension funds, insurance companies, and mutual funds is crucial in generating demand for corporate bonds and other credit products. Local companies have to see the benefit of having access to an alternative funding source besides bank lending.
- Third, an appropriate legal and regulatory environment needs to be built up, so as to foster a credit culture in the local economy.
- Last, but not least, infrastructure for the primary and secondary markets for corporate bonds needs to be developed.

In terms of financial stability considerations, local corporate bond markets can help reduce the maturity and currency mismatches on balance sheets of corporations, minimizing their vulnerabilities to international capital markets and to cutbacks in lending by local banks. However, regulators need to monitor corporate bond markets that are growing quickly to guard against the risk of accumulating bad credits that can prompt market corrections and turmoil.

CHAPTER II GLOBAL FINANCIAL MARKET DEVELOPMENTS

In the April 2005 *Global Financial Stability Report* (GFSR), we noted that financial conditions were quite positive, leading risks to be skewed on the down side. Financial market developments since then have reduced risks somewhat, at least for the near term. However, the same forces that have supported buoyant financial markets have also created larger global imbalances and higher levels of debt, thus storing up potential vulnerabilities for the future.

Financial conditions have remained broadly positive over the past six months, but some market developments diverged from consensus expectations of market participants.

First, long-term interest rates, instead of rising, as expected by some investors, have moderated, leading to a further flattening of global yield curves. This reflected cyclical factors, as market participants seemed to expect more moderate global growth and inflation, and structural factors such as a secular portfolio shift toward long-term bonds (and away from equities) by pension funds and life insurance companies. With interest rates remaining low in both real and nominal terms, still-ample global liquidity continues to drive the search for yield, which has reduced credit spreads, including in emerging bond markets, to low levels.

Second, low bond yields, flat yield curves, and tight credit spreads have led market participants to seek returns through "relative value" arbitrage trades and through the leverage embodied in complex financial derivatives, such as credit derivatives. Potential risks in these derivatives surfaced in May 2005 when hedge funds experienced losses from such trades, following a breakdown in expected default correlations in corporate credit markets. As the losses were largely confined to specific hedge funds engaged in these trades, this episode may have served to remind market participants to avoid complacency and to strengthen counterparty risk management, thus helping enhance financial stability. Nevertheless, risks of corrections in these markets are likely to surface again, demanding vigilance by market participants and supervisors alike.

Third, the U.S. dollar appreciated in the first half of 2005, as market participants focused on growth and interest rate differentials in favor of the United States, rather than on the growing U.S. current account deficit. So far, ample capital flows have accommodated the deficit, although growing global imbalances constitute a growing medium-term vulnerability.

We have probably reached the peak of the credit cycle as corporations have begun to increase the leverage of their balance sheets in a variety of ways. In the mortgage sector, debt levels have continued to rise amid signs of a relaxation of lending standards to attract marginal borrowers, particularly in the United States. Nevertheless, sound and highly liquid corporate balance sheets and accumulated increases in household net worth are likely to delay a general worsening of credit quality. Emerging markets have remained particularly resilient, reflecting ample global liquidity, as well as improving fundamentals and a maturing and broadening investor base. Although risks are on the horizon (including a heavy election calendar in 2006), emerging markets are cushioned by well-advanced external financing, in some cases even including prefinancing for 2006, and self-insurance in the form of large holdings of international reserves.

Against this background, this chapter addresses three key themes:

- the cyclical factors and structural trends that have led to lower long-term bond yields, flatter yield curves, high equity earnings yields, and a strengthening dollar;

- the implications of this for the continued search for yield and leverage in credit and mortgage markets, and the possible triggers for market corrections as the credit cycle seems to be peaking; and
- the growing resilience of emerging markets attributable to the maturation of the asset class, and the extension of the search for yield into local markets.

The chapter also examines recent improvements in the balance sheets of key sectors of the major mature economies. Using indicators of market and credit risk, as well as financial strength indicators, the resilience of the banking and insurance industries in mature and emerging markets is underscored.

Low Bond Yields, High Equity Earnings Yields, and the Recovering Dollar

Low Bond Yields and Flat Yield Curves

The search for yield remains a dominant theme in financial markets. This has had several effects, including a narrowing of credit spreads, a focus on relative value trades using leveraged credit derivative products, and a flourishing appetite for alternative investments. An important element sustaining the search for yield has been the low level of long-term bond yields. Even as monetary policy rates have increased in some major economies, long-term bond yields have declined, leading to yield curves flattening across mature markets. Moreover, long-run expectations for long bond yields have also declined (Figure 2.1). This section examines the cyclical and structural factors thought to have caused long bond yields to decline and yield curves to flatten, including developments in global savings and investment, the influence of monetary policy, perceptions of inflation risks, and other term premiums, as well as the impact of the asset allocation process.

Figure 2.1. U.S. Yields
(In percent)

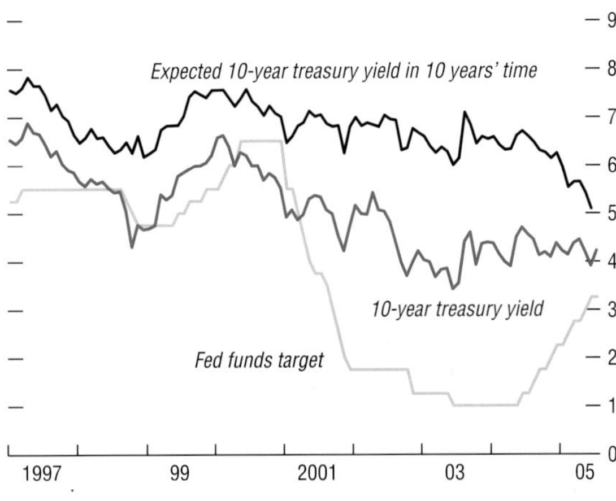

Sources: Bloomberg L.P.; and JPMorgan Chase & Co.

Figure 2.2. Inflation-Indexed Bond Yields
(In percent)

Source: Bloomberg L.P.

Figure 2.3. U.S. Real Yields and Inflation Expectations
(In percent)

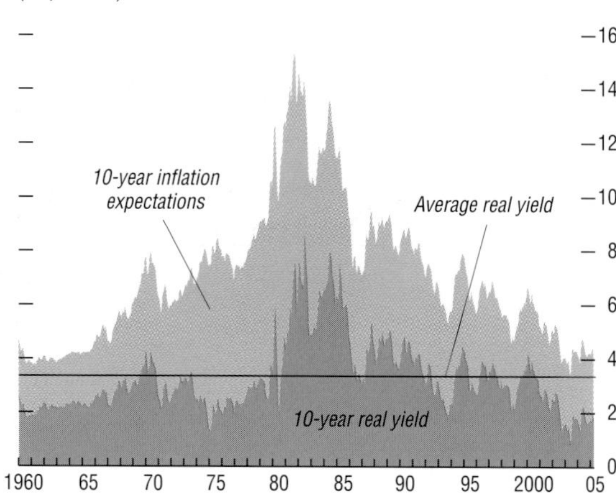

Source: JPMorgan Chase & Co.

By most standard criteria, long-term government yields have been surprisingly low over the past few years:

- Real bond yields are low relative to historical levels. Global real yields declined after the equity bubble burst in 2000 and are now near their lowest levels since inflation-indexed bonds were introduced (Figure 2.2). Euro area inflation-linked bonds have fallen in terms of real yields from about 3.5 percent since the end of 2000 to below 1 percent in mid-2005. Measured over a longer period, U.S. real yields are less than half their long-run average—currently 1.6 percent versus 3.3 percent since 1960 (Figure 2.3).[1]
- U.S. real bond yields are low relative to economic growth. Looking at the past two decades—which includes periods of both abnormally low real rates (marked by unexpected and rising inflation in the 1970s) and periods of high real rates (during the U.S. Federal Reserve's campaign to drive inflation down during the 1980s)—long-term equilibrium real yields consistent with stable rates of inflation have been estimated to be about 25 basis points less than real GDP growth.[2] Thus, real GDP growth of approximately 3–3.5 percent and stable inflation expectations of 2 percent, as seen over the past 12 months, would imply a 10-year nominal U.S. treasury yield of about 4.75–5.25 percent, some 100 basis points higher than at mid-2005.
- U.S. long bond yields are low relative to short-term interest rates—that is, the yield curve is relatively flat. The historically strong correlation between the slope of the yield curve and real short-term rates—reflecting the influence of monetary policy—broke down in 2005 as the spread between 10-year and 2-year bonds narrowed by more than would be expected by the

[1]The real yield is calculated as the nominal yield less inflation expectations derived from the Philadelphia Federal Reserve's survey of professional forecasters.
[2]See Hooper and Beceren (2005).

modest rise in real short-term rates, also suggesting that long bond yields are low (Figure 2.4).[3] The flattening of yield curves is also apparent in other major bond markets (Figure 2.5).

- In addition, long-term bond yields appear low relative to equity yields. Since 2000, real bond yields have declined while equity earnings yields have increased (Figure 2.6). As a result, the gap between bond and equity yields is wider now than at any point over the last 20 years.

Policymakers and market participants alike have been seeking explanations for the relatively low yields on long-term global bonds, which has been characterized by U.S. Federal Reserve Chairman Alan Greenspan as a "conundrum."[4] The answer is important not only for macroeconomic management but for financial stability, since the sustainability of low yields has significant implications for the pricing of credit, the appetite of investors for leverage and risk, and the allocation of capital. Understanding the causes of low long-term yields also sheds light on potential triggers for financial market corrections.[5] Accordingly, work has focused on the fundamental drivers of global long-term yields.

- In the wake of the 1997–98 Asian crisis, investment in emerging markets collapsed, capital flows reversed, and large current account surpluses led to a buildup of reserves. Emerging markets moved from an aggregate current account deficit in 1996 to a large surplus in 2004 (Table 2.1). In mature markets, an investment slowdown in the wake of the bursting of the equity bubble in 2000 has resulted in substantial net savings by the corporate sectors in several countries, most notably in the United States and Japan. The U.S. corporate sector

Figure 2.4. U.S. Yield Curve Steepness and Real Short-Term Rates
(In percent)

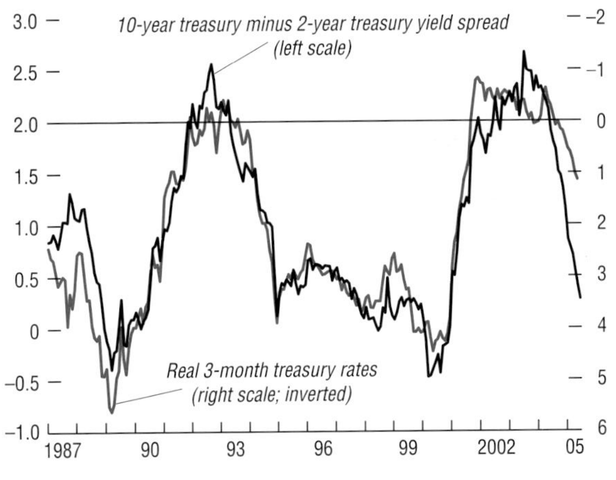

Source: Deutsche Bank.

Figure 2.5. Yield Curve Steepness
(10-year minus 2-year; in percentage points)

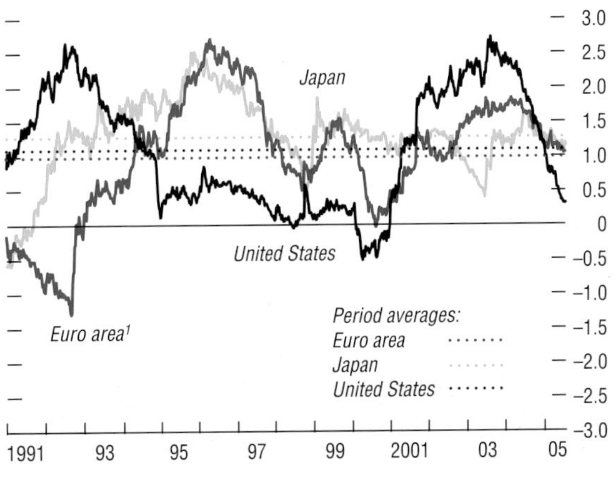

Source: Bloomberg L.P.
[1]Deutschemark before 1994.

[3]Real short rates calculated using core inflation.

[4]See testimony of U.S. Federal Reserve Chairman Alan Greenspan to the U.S. Congress on February 16–17, 2005.

[5]See IMF (2005b, Box 1.2, p. 18).

Figure 2.6. Global Equity Yields Versus Real Bond Yields
(In percent)

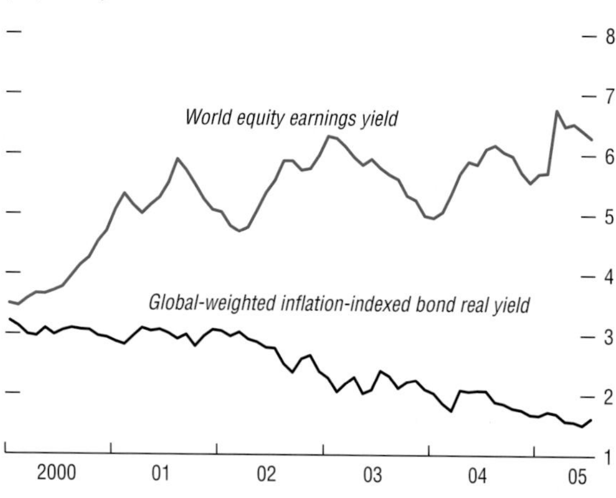

Source: Barclays Capital.

Table 2.1. Global Financial Balances by Sector[1]
(In billions of U.S. dollars)

	1996	2000	2004
G-6 economies[2]	4	–368	–504
Government balance	–795	–114	–1096
Household savings	594	271	26
Corporate savings	206	–525	566
of which:			
United States	39	–442	176
Euro area	50	–201	47
Japan	127	228	271
G-6 current account balance	4	–368	–504
of which: United States	–117	–412	–669
Emerging markets current account balance[3]	–88	129	337
Emerging Asia	–40	86	193
Latin America	–39	–48	16
Middle East	11	70	113
Africa	–5	7	1
Eastern Europe and Russia	–15	14	14

Source: JPMorgan Chase & Co.
[1]The financial balance for each sector is the difference between gross savings and gross investment.
[2]The G-6 is Australia, Canada, euro area, Japan, the United Kingdom, and the United States.
[3]The change in net savings for the G-6 economies does not equal the change in net savings for emerging market economies because the data presented for G-6 countries are based on national accounts estimates while data for emerging market economies are derived from balance of payments statistics.

Figure 2.7. Corporate Financial Balances

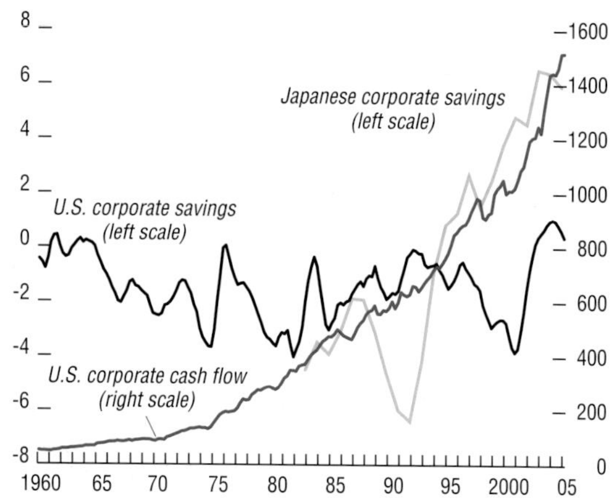

Sources: JPMorgan Chase & Co.; and IMF staff estimates.

shifted from being a net borrower to a net saver in 2003, leading to a sharp fall in the supply of bonds from the nonfinancial corporate sector (Figure 2.7). The Japanese corporate sector also deleveraged during this period. Some have termed the combination of rising global savings and declines in corporate investment a "global savings glut."[6]

- Risk premiums may have declined as investors appear more certain that inflation surprises and macroeconomic volatility of previous decades are much less likely to occur. Determined central bank action to combat inflation during the 1980s and 1990s, coupled with the adoption of inflation targeting monetary policy regimes in many OECD countries, have contributed to hard-earned inflation-fighting credibility by leading central banks. Expected real inter-

[6]See Bernanke (2005); Loeys and others (2005); and Cassard and Mayer (2005).

est rates implied in the yield curve of inflation-linked bonds indicate that market participants expect real short-term rates to stay low well into the future (Figure 2.8). U.S. Federal Reserve Chairman Alan Greenspan has argued that a significant portion of the decline in expected term rates over the past 12 months owes to falling risk premiums as investors appear to be encouraged by a perceived increase in economic stability, marked by significant declines in measures of expected volatility in equity and credit markets.[7]

- Foreign central banks, particularly in Asia, have accumulated sizable reserve positions as they have sought to stem appreciation pressures from current account surpluses and inflows of foreign direct investment (Figure 2.9). The accumulation of international reserves, historically held in bonds, has been similar in magnitude to net government bond issuance in the main markets during 2003–04. Foreign private and official investors together now hold close to 65 percent of all available U.S. treasuries from 1- to 10-year maturity.
- Partly in response to regulatory changes, pension funds and insurance companies are increasing their holdings of long-term fixed income securities and reducing the share of equities in their portfolios to match their assets more closely to long-term liabilities. For example, OECD pension funds have increased their holdings of fixed-income securities from 24 percent of total assets in 2002 to 26 percent in 2004, while reducing the share of equities from 55 percent to 42 percent of total assets over the same period (see Chapter III, Module 1, for more details).

Estimating how much each factor has contributed to the decline in long bond yields is of course difficult since the direct impact of each is not observable in yields. Going for-

[7]See testimony of U.S. Federal Reserve Chairman Alan Greenspan to the U.S. Congress on July 20, 2005.

Figure 2.8. Path for Real U.S. 1-Year LIBOR Discounted in the Term Structure

(In percent; as of July 28, 2005)

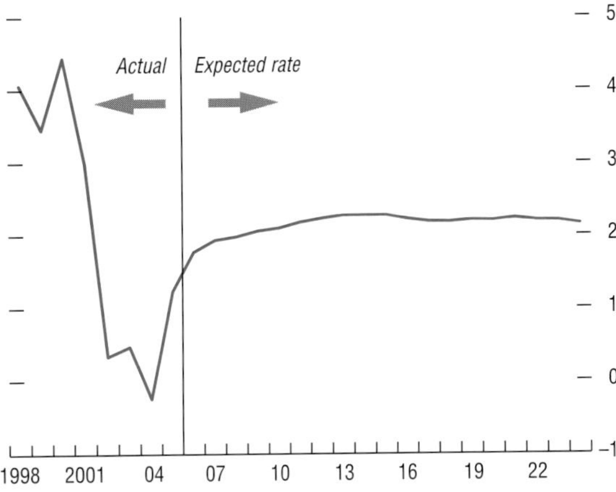

Source: Goldman Sachs.

Figure 2.9. International Reserves

(In billions of U.S. dollars)

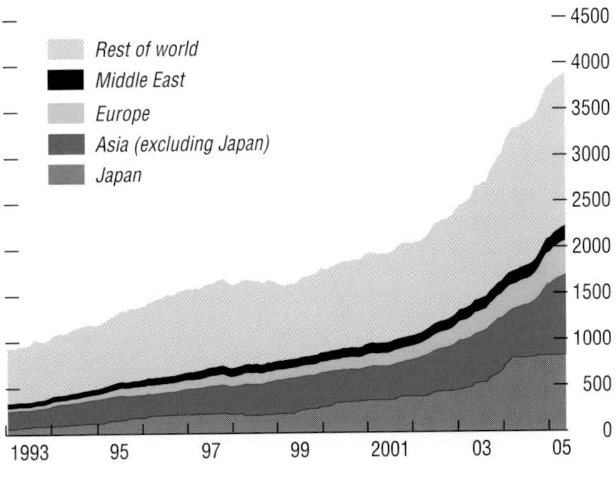

Sources: IMF, *International Financial Statistics*; and IMF staff estimates.

Figure 2.10. Earnings Yield in Major Developed Markets[1]
(In percent)

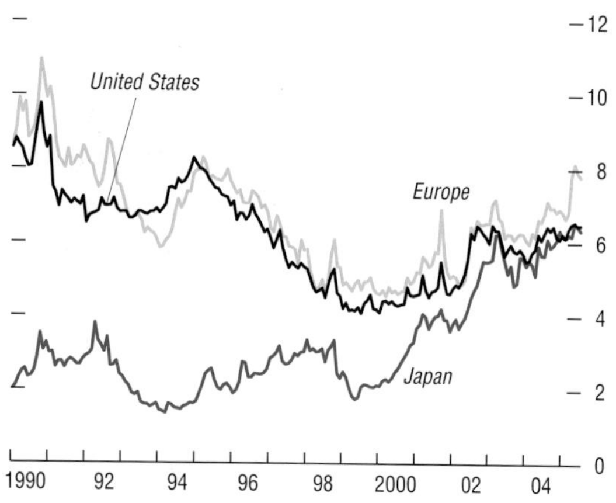

Sources: I/B/E/S; and IMF staff estimates.
[1]Based on 12-month forward earnings.

Figure 2.11. Earnings per Share, Actual Minus Forecast[1]
(In percent of forecast)

Source: I/B/E/S.
[1]Actual data refer to 12-month trailing earnings, while forecast are 12-month forward earnings provided 12 months previously.

ward, cyclical factors, including sustained growth and an increase in investment spending, could bring about a rise in long-term yields. In addition, changes in China's exchange regime, and increased flexibility of Asian currencies more generally, could eventually lead to reduced accumulation of foreign reserves, reducing the downward bias that reserve accumulation has exerted on long-term bond yields.

However, longer-lasting developments could act to cap or moderate the increase in long bond yields, keeping yield curves relatively flat. In particular, reduced premiums demanded by markets for inflation volatility may have reduced term premiums reflected in long-term real yields and expected long-term rates. Furthermore, the continuing trend of major institutional investors to increase portfolio holdings of longer-term fixed-income securities is likely to remain a feature of financial markets for many years. For instance, pension funds in the Netherlands are estimated to require some €255 billion of long-term bonds to lengthen the duration of their assets in line with liabilities. More work is needed to ascertain the influence of institutional investors on long-term bond yields.

Equity Earnings Yields Remain High

The shift in asset preferences since the bursting of the equity bubble in 2000 continues to weigh on equity valuations. Earnings yields indicate that equities are still valued relatively conservatively, with high prices reflecting particularly strong earnings expectations. Earnings yields have continued to rise across major markets, and now stand at or above historical averages (Figure 2.10).[8] Earnings have continued

[8]Earnings yields are measured as the ratio of 12-month forward earnings estimates to share prices. Historical averages are 6.9 for the S&P 500 (January 1985–June 2005), 3.7 for the Topix (February 1988–June 2005), and 7.8 for the FTSE Europe (December 1987–June 2005).

to surprise analysts on the upside in the United States and Europe, though the extent of those positive surprises has been diminishing in the United States (Figure 2.11).

The difference between expected earnings yields on equities and risk-free government bond yields widened during 2000–02 and has remained wide since then (Figure 2.12). This is particularly surprising as the implied volatility of equity prices, derived from option markets, has continued to fall since early 2003. Relatively conservative equity valuations therefore may reflect a shift in investors' preferences for reasons other than risk aversion, including changes in asset and liability management of major institutional investors (see Chapter III).

Looking forward, analysts are expecting earnings growth to slow moderately. For the financial sector, the flattening of the yield curve is likely to pose a more difficult earnings environment, and losses from second quarter disturbances in credit markets may also play a role. For example, in the United States, actual 2005 second quarter earnings for financial companies fell more sharply than for other sectors.

Figure 2.12. Earnings Yield Minus 10-Year Bond Yield
(In percent)

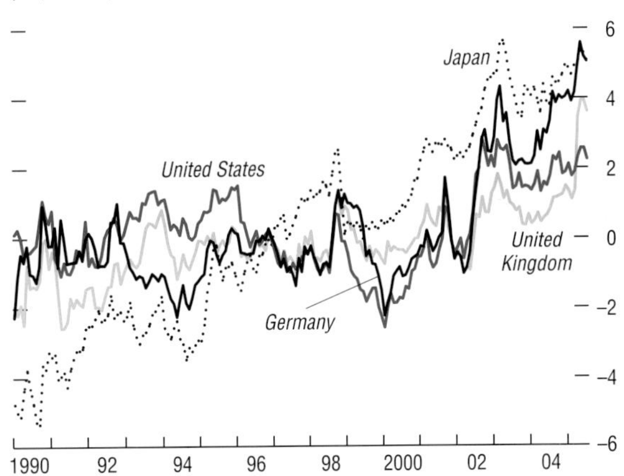

Sources: Bloomberg L.P.; I/B/E/S; and IMF staff estimates.

Figure 2.13. Implied Volatilities
(In percent)

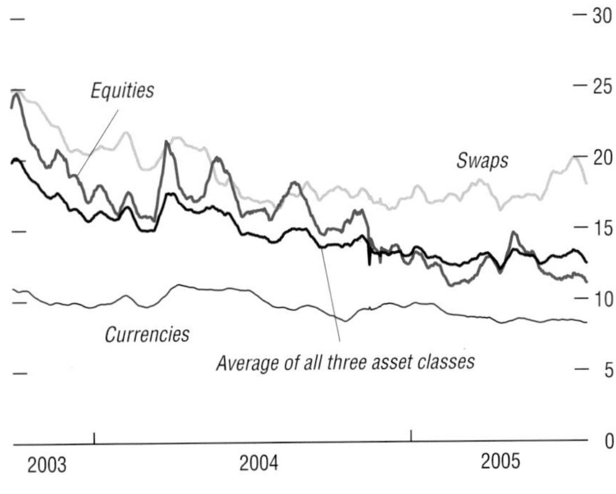

Sources: Bloomberg L.P.; and IMF staff estimates.

Market Volatility Remains Low

The search for yield has been given added impetus by subdued volatility. Despite the turbulence in the credit markets and large macroeconomic imbalances, investor complacency appears entrenched. As examined in the April 2005 GFSR, structural and cyclical features—including broader market integration and lower macroeconomic volatility—have enabled investors to better diversify risks, have contributed to reduced option premiums, and have reduced implied volatility. Where volatility has picked up, the spikes have been mostly short-lived and confined to specific asset classes (Figure 2.13).

For example, equity implied volatilities picked up briefly in mid-April after turbulence triggered by several high-profile earnings disappointments and the sudden emergence of disruptive developments in credit markets—as well as concerns about the pace of U.S. Federal Reserve policy tightening. However, the pickup in implied equity volatility was modest relative to the rise in actual volatility (Figure 2.14). That is, market participants did not fully incorporate the sudden jump in actual volatility into a new estimate of forward-looking implied volatility as a permanent factor. In the event, equity prices continued to recover and actual volatility stabilized. Another minor surge in implied volatility followed the emergence of uncertainty over the direction of the European Central Bank's (ECB) interest rate policy in June, which also turned out to be short-lived. As with the equity market turbulence in April, the impact of fixed-income volatility was localized to the euro swaptions markets, and did not affect swaptions volatilities in other major currencies.

Figure 2.14. S&P 500 Price and Difference Between Implied and Actual Volatility

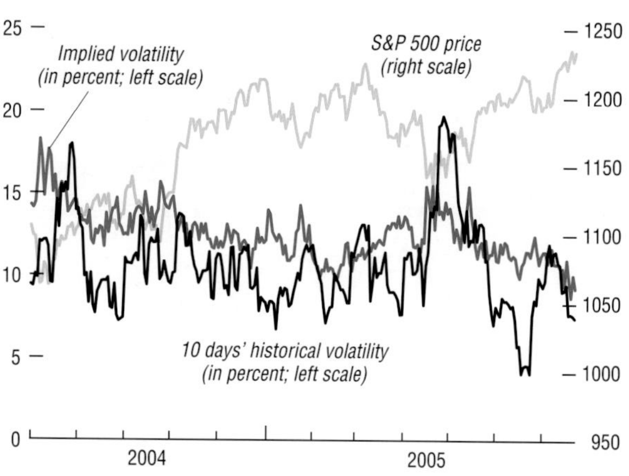

Source: Bloomberg L.P.
Note: A similar pattern following the mid-April turbulence is observed in German and Japanese markets.

Dollar Rebounded Despite the Widening U.S. Current Account Deficit

Despite the growing U.S. current account deficit, the U.S. dollar rebounded against major international currencies, particularly the euro, throughout the first half of 2005 (Figure 2.15). The move broadly reversed the dollar's weakness during the fourth quarter of 2004 (Figure 2.16). Widening interest rate and growth differentials in favor of the United States supported the dollar, while recurrent speculation that persistent economic weakness could induce the ECB to ease monetary policy weighed on the euro. The euro was also under pressure from market concerns over weak growth, flagging reforms, rising political uncertainty because of the rejection of the new EU constitution in French and Dutch referenda, and weak fiscal discipline of some countries in the euro area. However, the dollar was little changed against a trade-weighted basket of key emerging market currencies, as appreciations by several Latin American cur-

Figure 2.15. U.S. Current Account Balance
(In percent of GDP)

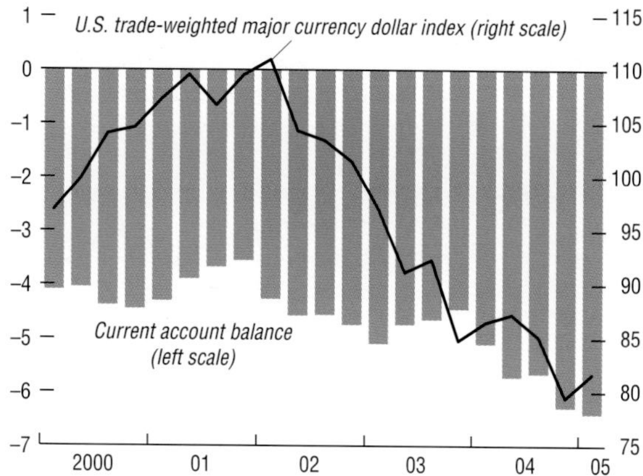

Sources: Bloomberg L.P.; and IMF staff estimates.

rencies were largely offset by weakness among certain Asian currencies.

In June, speculative positioning for continued dollar appreciation reached record levels. Futures market data from the U.S. Commodity Futures Trading Commission indicated that speculators had assumed the largest net-long position on record (Figure 2.17), although the position subsequently moderated. Currency options markets indicated similar expectations, as the skew in implied volatilities reached extremes in favor of continued dollar appreciation, especially against the euro.

The global appetite for U.S. assets has remained strong. Official reports of private sector foreign investment in U.S. securities—mostly bonds—roughly matched the pace of monthly trade deficits, which averaged close to $55 billion a month between January 2004 and May 2005 (Figure 2.18). Private purchases of fixed-income securities picked up as central bank purchases subsided in 2005, after monetary authorities—particularly in Asia—had aggressively increased their holdings of U.S. treasury securities throughout 2004. In the 12 months through May, official buying of U.S. securities came to $156 billion, compared with $131 billion from Caribbean countries, and $608 billion from all other private investors.

Market analysts have been debating the impact of recent U.S. legislation on the dollar during 2005, but the net effects are difficult to determine. The American Jobs Creation Act, passed in 2004, allows U.S. companies to repatriate profits previously held abroad at a 5.25 percent corporate tax rate during 2005, rather than at the 35 percent rate that would otherwise have prevailed. At issue is whether these tax advantages are leading to substantial flows in favor of the dollar as corporations convert funds held abroad in local currencies into U.S. dollars. During the first half of 2005, repatriation flows were reported to be light in advance of the U.S. administration's clarification of important procedural details in May.

Figure 2.16. U.S. Dollar Performance
(December 31, 2003 = 100)

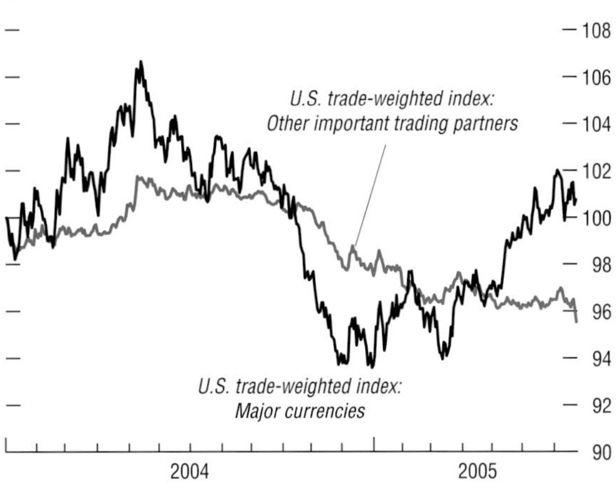

Sources: Bloomberg L.P.; and IMF staff estimates.

Figure 2.17. U.S. Dollar Index: Net Noncommercial Positions

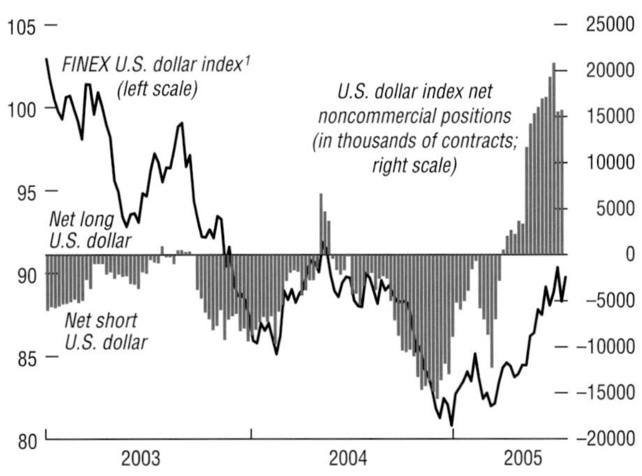

Sources: Bloomberg L.P.; and IMF staff estimates.
[1]The U.S. dollar index is an exchange-traded contract on the New York Board of Trade representing an average of six major international currencies against the U.S. dollar.

Figure 2.18. Net Foreign Purchases of U.S. Assets by Type
(In billions of U.S. dollars)

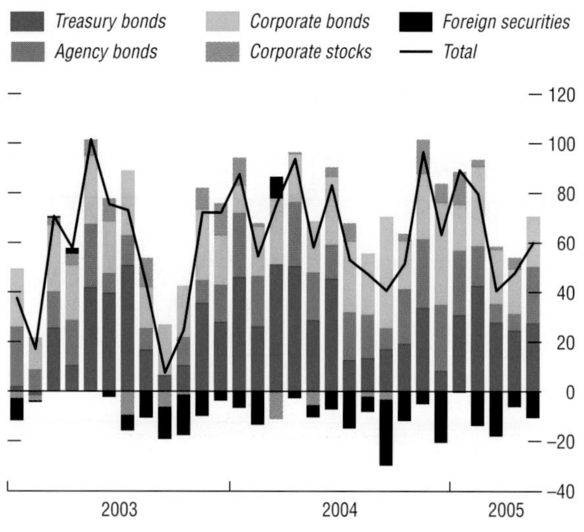

Sources: U.S. Treasury Department, *Treasury International Capital System*; and IMF staff estimates.

Figure 2.19. Chinese Renminbi Nondeliverable Forwards
(In renminbi per U.S. dollars)

Source: Bloomberg L.P.

As long anticipated, in July, the Chinese authorities announced a change in their exchange regime, including a one-off 2.1 percent revaluation and a peg to a new basket of currencies (Figure 2.19). The Malaysian authorities announced a similar change on the same day. Since the change of regime was announced, exchange rate movements have been more modest than some in the markets had expected. Perhaps more important than the immediate financial impact has been the view that the change of regime has defused to some extent growing protectionist pressures in the mature economies, which is seen as positive for global trade and growth prospects.

The Chinese authorities have continued to manage the renminbi tightly, and the appreciation of other Asian currencies has been modest. The nondeliverable forwards market is still signaling expectations of moderate appreciation of the renminbi against the dollar over coming months. The initial, but short-lived, impact of the announcement was to push up yields on U.S. fixed-income securities, as it was thought demand for dollar-denominated bonds might fall if Asian central banks no longer needed to intervene as heavily to prevent their currencies from appreciating, and if Asian current account surpluses were to diminish. It also pushed down yields on euro area bonds as market participants conjectured that the Chinese authorities might seek to increase nondollar holdings among their reserves. Although this impact on yields waned quickly, it does serve to demonstrate the likely direction of market moves should more substantial adjustments in Asian exchange rates be forthcoming.

Exchange rate volatility combined with rapid reversals in capital flows and a related spike in U.S. bond yields has been one of the vulnerabilities overhanging the stability of the global financial system over recent years. That threat has not been removed, but market developments have pushed it further into the medium term.

The Search for Yield in Credit and Mortgage Markets—The Credit Cycle

The influence of the ongoing search for yield remains strong in credit markets, supporting continued low credit spreads. With spread compression having left little scope to extract returns from betting on further spread narrowing, market participants are increasingly using leverage in various ways to enhance returns, including through relative value arbitrage using structured credit products. The proliferation of such investment positions, relying on relatively untested models and default correlation assumptions for pricing, has made these markets vulnerable to corrections that could be aggravated by liquidity disruptions, as shown by the credit market disturbances in April and May 2005. Such corrections in credit derivative markets could be triggered by a worsening in the credit quality of specific companies. In the mortgage market, recent developments may be raising credit risks as well—which could also trigger corrections of the tight spreads in mortgage-backed securities markets.

Corporate Credit Markets

The environment for corporate credit remains broadly supportive across mature markets. Continued global economic recovery and relatively low policy rates have allowed corporations to continue to generate profits and improve balance sheets. Strong demand for credit products and limited corporate bond supply have caused spreads to remain close to their recent historic narrow levels, and any widening of spreads has proved temporary as the quest for yield has swiftly reasserted itself (Figures 2.20 and 2.21).

The corporate bond market was only briefly roiled by declines in the creditworthiness of two major corporate debt issuers and subsequent disturbances in credit derivative markets. Announcements by Ford and General Motors (GM) of reduced earnings, combined with the companies' high cost structures, cul-

Figure 2.20. Corporate and Agency Bond Issuance
(In year-on-year percent change)

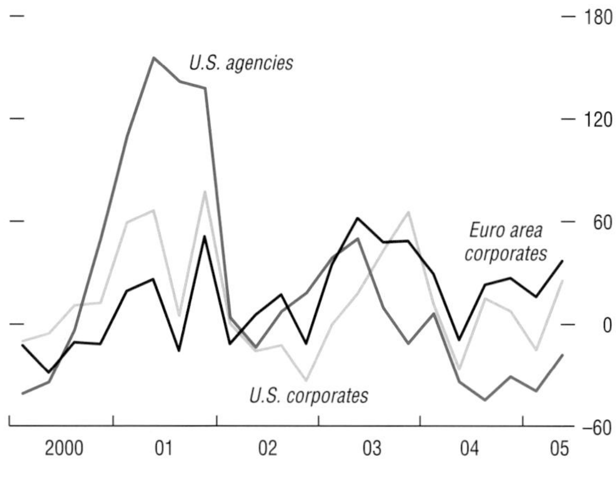

Source: Bloomberg L.P.

Figure 2.21. Corporate Spreads
(In basis points)

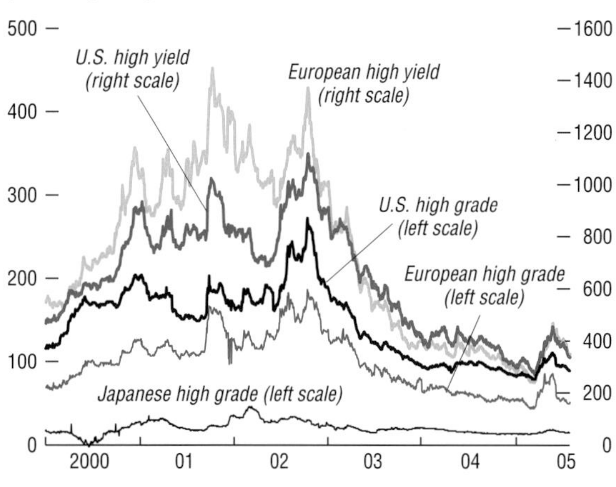

Source: Merrill Lynch.

minated in ratings agency downgrades to below investment grade in May. Market concerns initially centered around the ability of the much smaller subinvestment-grade bond market to absorb the hundreds of billions of dollars of bonds to be transferred from the investment-grade bond market.[9] Furthermore, these concerns were amplified as the effects of the credit deterioration rippled through credit derivative markets. This spoiled trading strategies that were designed to arbitrage perceived mispricings in the capital structures of these companies and the seniority structure of collateralized debt obligations (CDOs) (Box 2.1). As a result, several hedge funds and banks' proprietary trading desks were rumored to have suffered significant losses.

The disruptions in the credit derivative markets were, however, relatively short-lived, partly because of the continued search for yield. The cost of protection against default in the credit default swap market for Ford and GM jumped sharply in March when the probability of ratings actions first arose. The size of the move partly reflected the need to find new investors to hold the substantial amount of bonds then held by dedicated investment-grade investors. Although the cost of protection on those two companies remained elevated, the impact on the broader credit default swap indices was more muted (Figure 2.22).[10]

Figure 2.22. Credit Default Swap Spreads
(In basis points; 5-year)

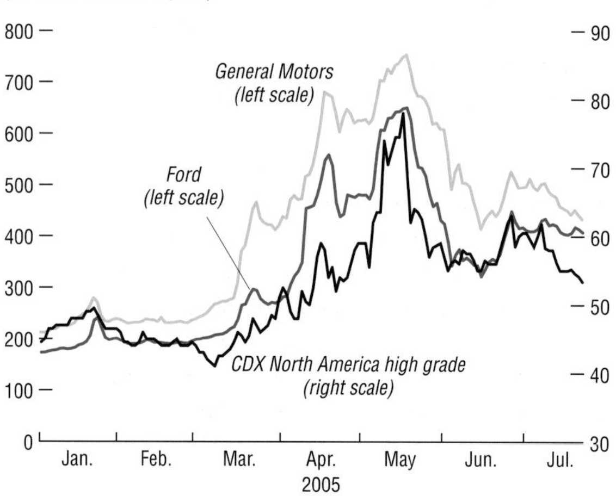

Sources: Bloomberg L.P.; and JPMorgan Chase & Co.

[9]A recent change by Lehman Brothers in the composition of the major investment-grade indices required that two out of the three major rating agencies (instead of one of either Moody's or Standard & Poor's (S&P)) downgrade a company toward subinvestment grade before it was moved out of the investment-grade indices. While General Motors received such a downgrade from two of the agencies, Ford was downgraded only by S&P. However, Ford temporarily entered the subinvestment-grade indices in June, before Lehman's rule change took effect, only to reenter the investment-grade indices in July.

[10]A commonly used index of credit default swap spreads for the U.S. investment-grade corporate sector—the JPMorgan North America CDX high-grade index—rose some 40 basis points, but by June fell back nearly to its level prior to the disturbances (see Figure 2.27, p. 26).

Box 2.1. U.S. Auto Companies and Losses in the Credit Derivatives Market

The emergence of sector-specific credit risks, particularly within the U.S. auto sector, prompted unexpected shifts within the pricing structure of collateralized debt obligation (CDO) markets. CDOs have helped to redistribute risk and provide arbitrage opportunities, while creating highly leveraged exposures to credit spreads that have proven to be unexpectedly volatile. Some hedging strategies designed to limit losses on these risky exposures appear to have failed, amplifying losses and sparking a substantial shift to new hedging transactions.

The use of credit derivatives—which include credit default swaps (CDSs), indices of CDS, cash CDOs of corporate bonds, and "synthetic" CDOs based on CDS indices—has expanded rapidly in the last few years.[1,2] The global credit default swaps market has grown quickly, from $3.8 trillion in the first half of 2003 to $8.4 trillion in the second half of 2004, according to a survey by the International Swaps and Derivatives Association. Cash CDOs in U.S. markets have been relatively static, growing from $235 billion outstanding at the end of 2002 to $283 billion in the first quarter of 2005. Additionally, the growth of the synthetic collateralized debt market has been much faster, though data on this market are difficult to come by.

CDOs reallocate the risk of default for a pool of securities into different tranches. The most subordinated tranche, termed the "equity tranche," bears all the initial losses stemming from defaults in the basket backing the CDO up to a prespecified percentage of the total portfolio. Investors in the mezzanine and more senior (and safer) tranches are progressively more insulated from loss. Because the initial losses are borne by the investor in the equity tranche, that investor is compensated with the lion's share of the total spread on the underlying securities.[3] The more senior tranches typically are rated up to the highest investment grade—that is triple-A—thus earning only a small premium over benchmark (Libor) rates.

The concentration of losses and returns in an equity tranche creates leverage. For instance, an equity tranche investor with a commitment of capital equivalent to only 5 percent of the underlying portfolio is in a risk position equivalent to a highly leveraged investor who buys the entire portfolio with 5 percent cash, borrowing the rest at the benchmark rate. In both cases, the investor has effectively leveraged 20 times. The difference is that the investor in the traditional leveraged case must be able to borrow at the benchmark rate to earn the spread over that rate, whereas an equity tranche investor need not borrow in his own name at all. Hence, equity tranches give access to substantial amounts of leverage to investors that may not have access to benchmark-rate funding.

In the spring of 2005, a series of negative news announcements about, and rating agency downgrades of, Ford and General Motors emerged. These raised market perceptions of the eventual probability of default, leading to spread widening on the equity tranches of corporate-backed CDOs. These equity tranche securities were reportedly bought largely by hedge funds and bank proprietary trading desks, which incurred rapidly increasing losses.[4] Moreover, many investors in the equity tranches had hedged with short positions in the mezzanine tranches of the same CDOs on the expectation

[1]Credit default swaps are securities that effectively insure investors against the possibility of predefined credit events, such as default, by reference entities such as corporations and sovereign issuers.

[2]Synthetic CDOs combine credit default swaps into notional indices; payouts on them are then arranged according to the default behavior of components of these standard indices.

[3]This concentration of expected losses and spread has typically earned investors returns of about 15 percent annually, comparable with historic returns in equity markets.

[4]Or, equivalently, and in practice more important, the same residual risk was borne by bank trading desks that had sold highly rated tranches backed by synthetic products to investors demanding high-quality fixed-income products but had chosen to retain the equity tranche on their own books.

Box 2.1 *(concluded)*

Collateralized Debt Obligations: Historical CDX Synthetic North American Investment Grade Equity and Mezzanine Tranche

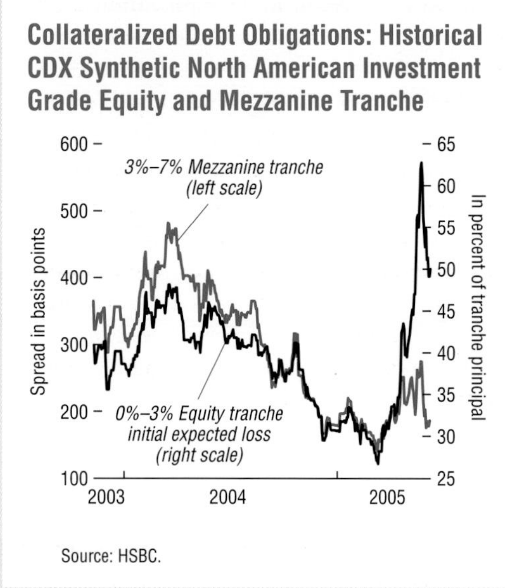

Source: HSBC.

Collateralized Debt Obligations: Changing Tranche Behavior
(CDX North American, investment-grade synthetic CDO tranches)

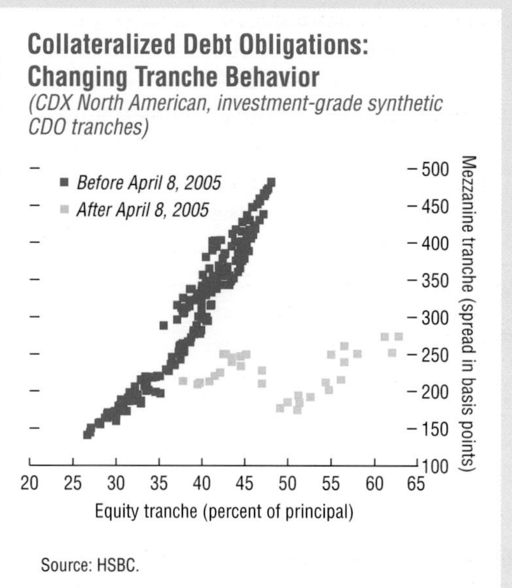

Source: HSBC.

that the values of these tranches would move together (i.e., be highly positively correlated). This appeared to be an attractive hedging approach, since no effort was required to ascertain which company was subject to changing default risk as would be required with sales of company-specific securities or default contracts.[5] The investor merely had to estimate the proportion of expected additional losses likely to spill over from the equity tranche to the next least protected tranche—the "mezzanine" tranche. Then the investor could sell short the appropriate amount of the mezzanine tranche that, if expectations of default rose, should have allowed the investor to recoup his or her losses on the equity tranche.

Market pricing through early April 2005 reflected relatively stable assumed correlations of default risk among the first two risk tranches in the CDO portfolio. In other words, changes in default risk were expected to affect the equity and mezzanine tranches in stable proportions (see first figure).[6] After early April, however, those correlations broke down as it turned out that Ford and GM proved to be subject to specific, idiosyncratic rises in default expectations that ended up concentrating losses in equity tranches, instead of spreading to mezzanine tranches as had been expected (see second figure). In fact, mezzanine tranche spreads were quite stable during this period, actually falling at some points. This may have led some tranche hedgers to lose money on both legs of their trade.

Market participants who held equity tranches may have been provoked by the failure of their model-based hedges into sudden portfolio adjustments to contain their losses. Some reacted by buying more protection on the underlying reference credits, which added to

[5]This "delta hedging" involves buying and selling securities of firms in the portfolio for which default risk is changing, but can be extremely expensive and imprecise. Alternatively, investors can also buy back all tranches and reconstitute the underlying securities that can then be sold back into relatively liquid markets.

[6]By market convention, equity tranches are priced in terms of cash paid to cover the initial expected loss for the portfolio, while mezzanine tranches are priced in terms of interest spreads, which compensate for the small expected loss.

the existing upward spread pressure on Ford and GM bonds.

Another reportedly widely used strategy was to arbitrage the capital structure of the auto companies by taking long positions in auto company bonds and financing them with short equity positions in the same company. This strategy also led to losses when the prices of GM bonds fell after the company was downgraded, but a surprise share bid by a prominent investor led to rises in GM's share price, thus again leading investors using this strategy to lose on both legs of the trade.

In the end, while a number of shorter-horizon investors (i.e., hedge funds, proprietary trading desks, and bank dealers) are thought to have suffered material losses, the events proved not to be of systemic importance for the financial system. Indeed, by alerting investors to the dangers of relying on specific assumptions underlying modeled risk, the episode may have had some salutary impact. It also points to the need for careful scrutiny of counterparty practices, to ensure that difficulties at individual hedge funds do not have wider repercussions for the financial system.

Meanwhile, the expected losses for the most volatile first-loss (equity) tranches of synthetic collateralized debt securities that contained the U.S. automakers doubled from about 30 percent at the beginning of this year to more than 60 percent by mid-March—reflecting the highly leveraged character of these securities—although such expected losses had fallen back to some 45 percent by the summer.

The search for yield swiftly reasserted itself. In the cash bond market, corporate spread widening proved very limited and short-lived, both in Europe and in the United States. U.S. high-yield spreads initially rose nearly 200 basis points, but the market began to improve steadily from the end of May as it became apparent that any damage to hedge funds and their prime brokerage banks was not systemic. Moreover, there was little, if any, spillover into other sectors. Market participants appear to have overestimated the scale of forced selling that might take place if a downgrade occurred and underestimated the ability of the high-yield market to absorb the debt of "Fallen Angels." One possible explanation for both misjudgments is the waning importance of benchmarking within the asset management industry over recent years. More funds are now managed on an absolute return basis, and even benchmarked funds now have greater flexibility to deviate significantly from their benchmarks. In addition, the credit difficulties at Ford and GM were relatively well telegraphed. In some cases, prior arrangements had been made to transfer the bonds from one fund to another within the same fund family, thus reducing the need to sell on the open market.

The difficulties at Ford and GM do not appear to signal broader problems in the corporate sector. Corporate default rates remain near historical lows, having fallen substantially over the past few years in all regions (Figure 2.23).

However, marking the turn in the credit cycle, rating agencies suggest that default rates have likely troughed and may start to turn back up, particularly in view of the recent pickup in high-yield issuance (Figure 2.24). Indeed, default rates have already edged up in Europe. S&P, which estimates that global subinvestment-grade default rates fell to 1.7 percent by May 2005, forecasts default rates to average just 2.1 percent over the next year, while Moody's expects rates to remain at about 2 percent through early 2006, and then to trend upward.

Credit risks, more generally, could also increase as corporations have begun to

Figure 2.23. Standard & Poor's Speculative-Grade Default Rates
(In percent)

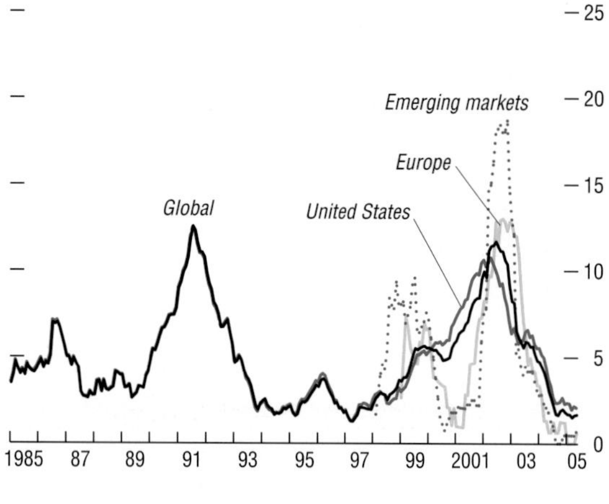

Source: Standard & Poor's.

Figure 2.24. High-Yield Debt and the Credit Cycle
(In percent)

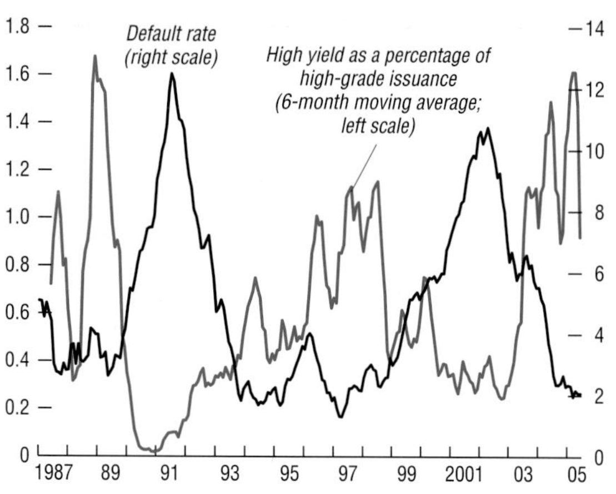

Sources: Board of Governors of the Federal Reserve System; and Standard & Poor's.

increase leverage of their balance sheets (see sections on Corporate Balance Sheets and Bank Balance Sheets, pp. 43–50, for a detailed discussion of recent balance sheet developments). The massive deleveraging of recent years that lowered default risks to very low levels has benefited bondholders. But companies now appear to be paying more attention to the interests of shareholders than they were over recent years, allowing indebtedness to stabilize or rise slightly in order to maintain high dividend rates and, in some cases, to fund share buyback programs. The number of companies increasing dividends has generally trended up over the past few years, although cash balances also continue to grow (Figure 2.25).

Moreover, encouraged by low default rates and solid corporate creditworthiness, lenders have been easing their standards, suggesting that credit quality is likely eventually to deteriorate. Lending standards have eased over the past few years across mature mar- kets (Figure 2.26). Banks in Europe and the United States report that the primary reason for easing standards was concern about competition from other sources of business credit.

Global credit demand is also being supported by mergers and acquisitions activity. As stock prices have risen and profit growth from cost cutting and productivity improvements has become harder to achieve, firms have increasingly been looking to other sources of growth to boost profits. Thus, global merger activity in 2004 reached almost $2 trillion, the highest in four years, and this pickup has continued into 2005 (Figure 2.27).

By raising the degree of leverage in the corporate sector, the resurgence of mergers and acquisitions activity—including leveraged buyouts—increases the risk of a deterioration in creditworthiness. In addition, this increase in leverage heightens the risk of specific corporate credit events, which have the potential for spillover effects into credit derivative markets. More generally however, sound and liquid corporate balance sheets suggest any such credit deterioration likely has a long fuse. Sustained profitability has led to a broad improvement in balance sheets in most countries. Thus, in the foreseeable future, corporate credit problems will likely be viewed, initially at least, as company specific, rather than indicative of broader credit difficulties in the corporate sector. Nevertheless, market participants have shown concerns about credit deterioration in the medium term. The U.S. credit curve has steepened: spreads on longer-maturity corporate credit have widened, while spreads at shorter maturities have hardly changed from their lows at the beginning of the year (Figure 2.28). In Europe, corporate credit curves have flattened since the beginning of the year. This may reflect the higher average quality of European bonds compared with U.S. bonds, and Europe's less advanced position in the credit cycle.

Figure 2.25. Corporate Actions of Top 150 U.S. Corporations
(In number of companies)

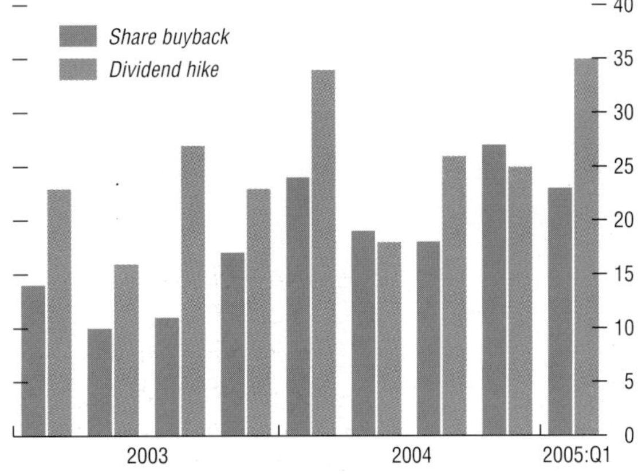

Sources: Lehman Brothers; and IMF staff estimates.

Mortgage Markets

The search for yield is also manifest in the shrinking spreads in the market for mortgage-backed securities. The growing appetite of international investors, together with U.S. investors, for new issues of mortgage-backed securities had shrunk the margin of 30-year mortgage rates over 5-year swap rates from 250 basis points in early 2003 to about 125 basis points in June 2005 (Figure 2.29). Spreads are low by historical experience, as a wider margin is normally demanded by investors to compensate for the right of mortgage borrowers to refinance. Direct foreign buying of U.S. agency debt and mortgage pools insured by the mortgage agencies has been running at an annual rate of $200 billion since late 2004. Foreign central banks have been buying this debt, albeit in small amounts.

Meanwhile, low mortgage financing costs have induced household borrowing in the United States, and, to a lesser extent, in Europe, providing a growing supply of mortgage-backed securities. U.S. households have accumulated net debt equivalent to 3.3 per-

Figure 2.26. Surveys of Bank Lending Standards
(In percent)

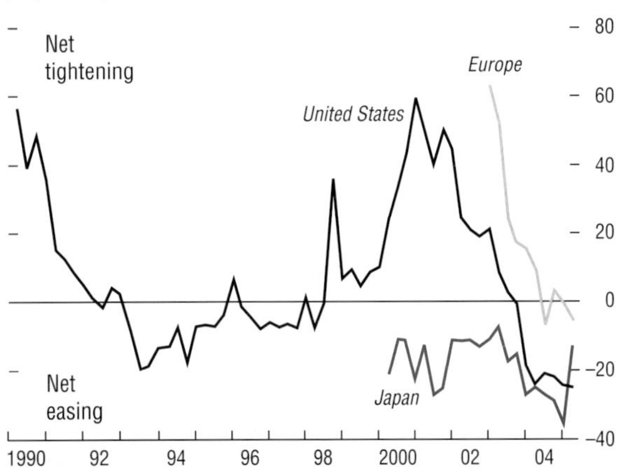

Sources: Bank of Japan; European Central Bank; Board of Governors of the Federal Reserve System; and IMF staff estimates.

Figure 2.27. Global Merger Deal Value
(In billions of U.S. dollars)

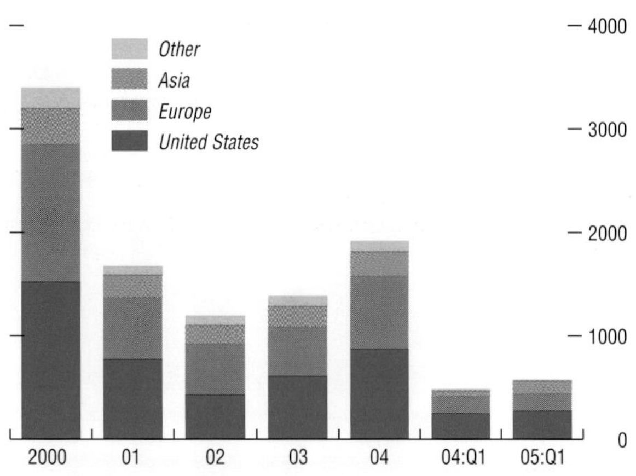

Source: Standard & Poor's.

Figure 2.28. Slope of the Corporate Credit Spread Curve[1]
(In basis points)

Sources: Merrill Lynch; and IMF staff estimates.
[1]Defined as 10–15-year investment-grade less 1–3-year investment-grade option-adjusted spreads.

Table 2.2. U.S. Sector Financial Flows
(In percent of GDP)

	1952–82	1986–87	1952–2000	2004Q2–2005Q1
Rest of world	–0.4	3.1	0.5	5.8
Household[1]	4.1	5.3	3.8	–3.3
Corporate[2]	–1.7	–1.1	–1.3	1.7
Federal, state, and local government	–1.9	–5.3	–2.5	–4.2
Other	–0.2	–2.0	–0.4	0.0

Source: Board of Governors of the Federal Reserve System, *Federal Reserve Flow of Funds.*
[1]Households and nonprofit organizations.
[2]Nonfarm, nonfinancial corporate business.

cent of GDP during the last year, whereas, in the past, they have been net savers, averaging 3.8 percent of GDP during 1952–2000 (Table 2.2).[11] The increase in household indebtedness thus constitutes a large counterpart to the growing U.S. current account deficit (or financing flows to the United States from the rest of the world).

Mortgage markets have adapted to the rising demand for mortgage financing and securities. In the United States, the highly developed mortgage lending industry coupled with sophisticated capital markets have quickly aggregated and transferred mortgage risk into the bond market. A rising share of mortgage lending is being financed by commercial banks and asset-backed credit structures that can facilitate flexible and innovative loans (Figure 2.30). In Europe, mortgage lending is rising and is increasingly securitized. In the second quarter of 2005, $84 billion in Pfandbriefe-type securities in euros were issued, up from $53 billion a year earlier. Net European bank lending was about $80 billion for home purchases in the three months through May 2005.

Substantial U.S. mortgage borrowing has accumulated amid easier lending terms. One indicator is the large amount borrowed

[11]See the discussion on household sector in the section on "Balance Sheet Developments in Major Mature Economies."

relative to the value of new construction.[12] The difference may be used by households for consumption or investment in other assets. A related measure of equity extraction for possible consumption spending is the rising level of home equity loans (Figure 2.31).

Lending innovations have allowed more borrowers to obtain larger mortgages. For instance, homeowners are increasingly borrowing at adjustable rather than fixed rates, which lowers their initial monthly payments at the expense of incurring the risk of larger payments later when the mortgage may readjust to higher interest rates (Figure 2.32).[13]

Additionally, holders of adjustable-rate mortgages are increasingly paying only interest, instead of the conventional interest plus principal. Other mortgage innovations include mortgages that allow borrowers to pay less interest than is accrued, thus leading to rising loan principal balances (negative amortization loans), as well as loans with various combinations of initially reduced rates and rapid reset conditions. If rates rise, the combined effect of higher rates on higher debt balances may create a strain for some borrowers. There has also been increasing use of nonconventional loans, including some with weaker standards of documentation and to low-income borrowers and those with poor credit histories. As a consequence, a rising share of mortgages is now pooled by private firms, some of which do not apply the same documentation standards as the traditional

[12]If anything, this measure may understate risk because it implicitly ignores the possibility of overbuilding. New mortgage lending net of new construction has been 2.5 percent to 3.0 percent of GDP in recent quarters, compared with a previous range of –1.5 percent to 1.0 percent.

[13]Adjustable-rate mortgages here also include hybrid-mortgages, which have specific fixed-terms at the beginning of the mortgage, generally of up to seven years. However, estimates are that the interest rate on some $1 trillion of these mortgages may adjust in 2007.

Figure 2.29. Foreign Net Purchases of U.S. Agency Securities

(In billions of U.S. dollars; 12-month cumulative rate)

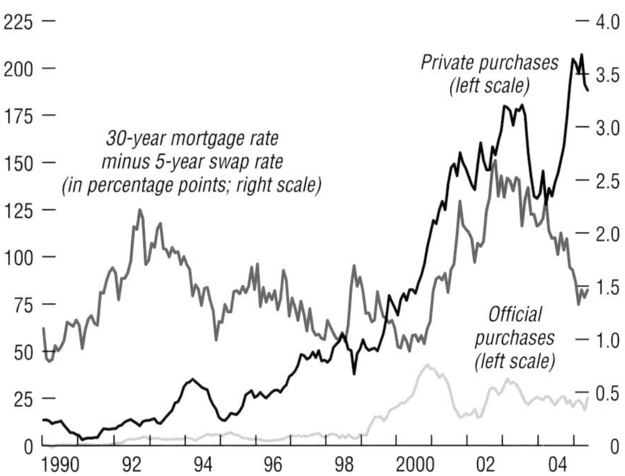

Sources: Bloomberg L.P.; U.S. Treasury Department, *Treasury International Capital System*; and IMF staff estimates.

Figure 2.30. U.S. Home Mortgages and Financing Instruments

(In billions of U.S. dollars; quarterly flows annualized)

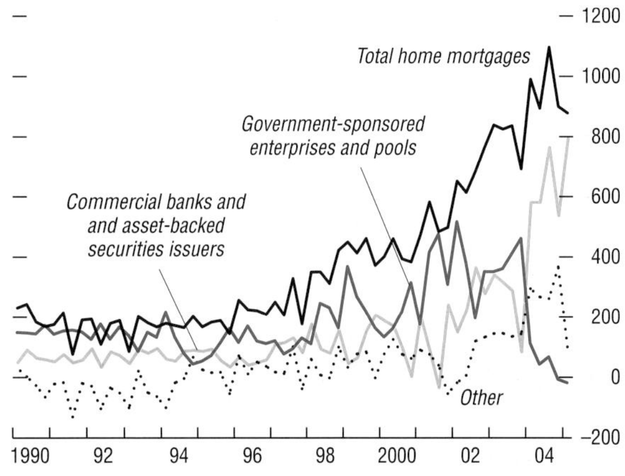

Source: Board of Governors of the Federal Reserve System, *Flow of Funds*.

Figure 2.31. U.S. Mortgage Debt and Equity Extraction
(In percent of GDP)

Sources: Board of Governors of the Federal Reserve System; and IMF staff estimates.

Figure 2.32. Adjustable Rate Mortgages
(Share of the dollar volume of conventional, conforming purchase originations; in percent)

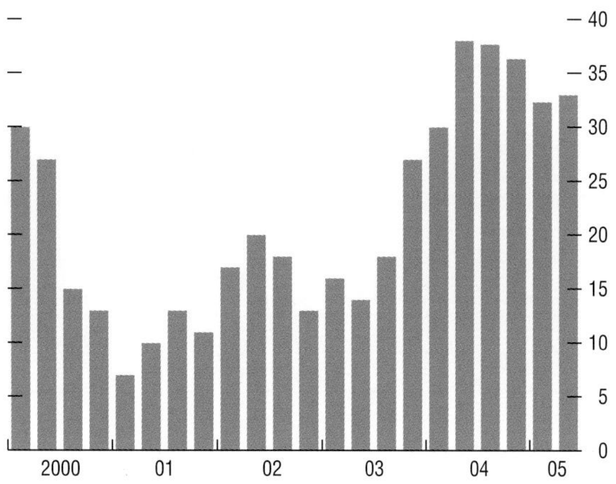

Source: Federal Housing Finance Board Monthly Interest Rate Survey.

agency pools.[14] Some borrowers may have been allowed to take out loans for which they would not otherwise be qualified under conventional mortgage standards.

The relaxation of credit standards and the growing use of payment reduction features in mortgages have increased the credit risk in the mortgage market. Regulatory authorities in the United States have rightly expressed concerns about these trends, and regulators must monitor carefully ongoing developments to ensure that risks arising from such activity are being well managed.

In sum, the household sector, especially in the United States, has become a net borrower of funds, accumulating a record level of debt. However, as discussed later in the subsection on the household sector, household net worth has also risen because of asset price increases, most importantly in the housing sector. Growing evidence suggests that it is the marginal borrowers with a smaller cushion of equity that have been most attracted by mortgages that minimize interest payments and therefore are the most exposed to rises in interest rates and/or declines in housing prices.

Increased Resilience of Emerging Markets

Ample global liquidity and low yields in mature markets have encouraged investors to look to emerging markets in their quest for higher returns. In addition, many institutional investors have made strategic investments in emerging markets, adding to the share of emerging market investments in their portfolios. As a result, emerging markets have become more resilient to market disturbances. Despite the turbulence in corporate debt markets and bouts of political uncertainty in

[14]Traditional agency mortgage pools include securities produced by GNMA, FNMA, FHLMC, FAMC, and the Farmers Home Administration.

emerging markets in the first half of 2005, emerging market bond spreads have remained within a narrow range and near all-time lows (Figure 2.33). This resilience also reflects improved fundamentals across the asset class. Nevertheless, the positive global economic environment, especially in commodity-exporting countries, may mask some of the underlying vulnerabilities in emerging markets.

After falling to record lows in March, emerging market spreads, particularly of lower-rated credits, corrected on the concern that U.S. interest rates might rise further and faster than previously anticipated. Eventually these concerns dissipated and spreads retightened. Survey evidence suggests that the April market correction reduced leveraged positions in the market, thus lowering the risk of a more disorderly adjustment in the future.

Emerging market countries have continued to build up cushions against adverse developments, including by accumulating additional reserves, and by early financing of external needs. Furthermore, several countries have conducted debt management operations to reduce the vulnerability of their debt structures to external shocks by lowering the debt service costs and lengthening the average maturity of borrowing, as well as by reducing currency exposure (Box 2.2). Near-term risks to financial stability are declining as credit quality improves and as an increasing number of emerging market commodity producers shift to net international creditor status, reflecting, in large part, the benefits of higher oil and other commodity prices.

The improvements in credit quality continue to be acknowledged by credit rating agencies. The average credit quality of the benchmark EMBIG index has risen further, exceeding a BB rating this year—a new high (Figure 2.34). Upgrades have outpaced downgrades by a wide margin. S&P, for example, upgraded 24 sovereigns in the 12 months through June 2005, while downgrading only nine sovereigns.

Figure 2.33. EMBIG Sovereign Spreads
(In basis points)

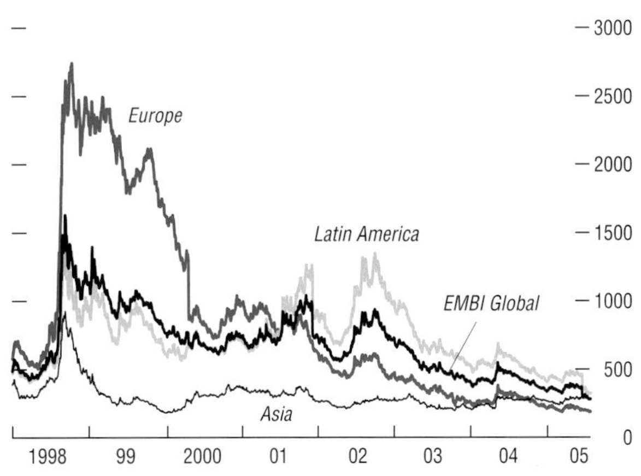

Source: JPMorgan Chase & Co.

Figure 2.34. Emerging Market Credit Quality

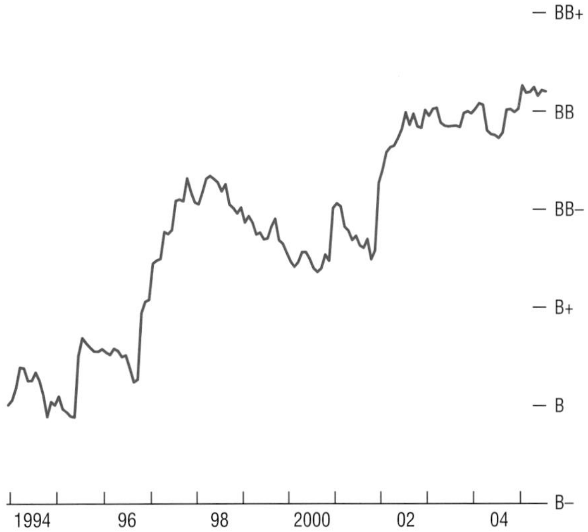

BB+
BB
BB–
B+
B
B–
1994
96
98
2000
02
04

Sources: JPMorgan Chase & Co.; Moody's; Standard & Poor's; and IMF staff estimates.

Box 2.2. Emerging Market Borrowers Intensify Liability Management Operations

Emerging market countries have continued to improve their debt structures in an effort to reduce their vulnerability to external shocks.[1] To this end, emerging market sovereign borrowers have carried out active liability management operations aimed at meeting their financial requirements, while minimizing the cost of debt and its risks. These operations have undoubtedly benefited from a favorable external environment. In the first half of this year, emerging market countries have focused on operations aimed at meeting domestic and external obligations and lengthening maturities. Some countries have taken further steps to develop their local markets. In this box we review the liability management operations of five major emerging market borrowers—Brazil, Mexico, Poland, Turkey, and Venezuela.

Brazil

Amid the favorable external environment, Brazil has completed its financing requirements of $6 billion for 2005 by tapping debt markets with five issues, including some reopenings. It also exchanged $4.4 billion of C-bonds (capitalization bonds) for new A-bonds (amortization bonds) with a participation rate close to 80 percent. As a result of the exchange, the authorities swapped the call option embedded in the C-bond for a maturity extension of 3.75 years on the new, non-callable bonds. The maturity extension shifted amortizations that would have taken place during the period 2005–14 to 2009–18, thereby smoothing the amortization profile of public sector external debt.

In domestic markets, Brazil has made significant strides in reducing the amount of dollar-linked domestic debt, while gradually improving the maturity profile. While actively tapping external markets, Brazil has continued its policy of reducing the share of domestic debt indexed to the exchange rate. The reduced rollover rate (see figure), a policy first put into place in June 2003, combined with the steady appreciation of the domestic currency throughout this period, caused the share of foreign-exchange-linked debt (including foreign exchange swaps) in total domestic public sector debt to fall from about 10 percent at the end of 2004 to approximately 4 percent in May 2005. The withdrawal of foreign-exchange-linked domestic debt has been offset primarily by an increase of fixed-rate local currency debt and inflation-indexed debt.

The maturity profile of domestic debt has improved as Brazil has sought to lengthen gradually the maturity of newly issued debt, while simultaneously increasing average size and addressing gaps in the domestic yield curve. The average maturity of newly issued debt increased from about 18 months at the end of 2004 to 23 months in May 2005. As a result, the share of domestic debt maturing in the ensuing 12 months fell to about 44 percent of total debt from more than 46 percent over the same period.

Brazil has also continued to strengthen domestic liability management practices by implementing new arrangements for primary and secondary dealers and by expanding the domestic investor base. The aim of the new primary and secondary

Rollover Rate of U.S. Dollar-Indexed Federal Domestic Debt
(Including swaps; in percent of total principal coming due)

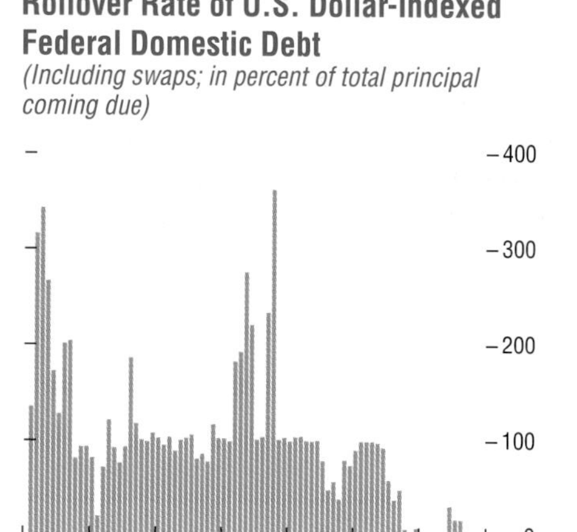

Sources: Brazil Ministry of Finance; and the central bank of Brazil.

[1] IMF (2004, Box 2.3).

dealer arrangements is to increase both liquidity and competition in domestic debt markets.

Market participants note that Brazil is expected to proceed with a $3 billion external prefunding for 2006 before the end of this year. They believe that Brazil will continue its strategy of boosting the liquidity of its bonds at selected benchmark points along the curve.

Mexico

Generally favorable market conditions and increased investor confidence have allowed Mexico to borrow at relatively low cost. Mexico issued three external bond issues in the first half of 2005, amounting to some $2 billion. Reflecting in part the resources provided by these issues, and the decision to purchase the international reserves from the Bank of Mexico to service principal obligations, Mexico completed by the end of July its funding operations for both 2006 (an election year) and 2007.

As part of the authorities' strategy to issue debt in various international markets, the nation's second issue was a seven-year 250 million Swiss franc bond in mid-May and the third was a 10-year 750 million euro bond issued in early June. These issues have not only helped Mexico to meet its debt refinancing program but also to lengthen the average maturity of its debt.

Mexico is taking steps to upgrade its debt management system to achieve a more integrated approach. This involves developing models that evaluate Mexico's domestic and external debt as part of a unified approach, which analyzes currency composition and duration, and establishes quantitative targets for liability management. The authorities also aim to reduce further the foreign exchange component of the sovereign's debt.

Poland

Poland embarked on an aggressive external debt issuance program this year, so far raising $9.6 billion. This program reflects Poland's status as the new European Union member with the largest gross external borrowing needs and its stated objective to repay its Paris Club debt in 2005. In meeting increased financing needs, Poland borrowed in several currencies, and was one of the most active sovereign issuers in international capital markets.

Total issuance has exceeded Poland's original 2005 target of 3 billion euros. However, the original target did not include prepayments of Paris Club debt of 12.3 billion euros, due between 2005 and 2009, that Poland decided to make in 2005. The majority of Paris Club creditors accepted the prepayments, with approximately 7.4 billion euros of Paris Club debt still left to be repaid. The prepayment resulted in the large-sized funding activity, which was also easily accommodated by the strong demand for Poland's foreign bonds.

Turkey

Favorable external market conditions allowed Turkey to almost complete its financing for 2005 by midyear. Turkey has issued four international bonds so far this year, raising around $5.6 billion. This brings Turkey close to its international bond issuance target for 2005. Market participants expect Turkey to tap international markets several more times by the end of the year, allowing it partly to prefinance 2006 requirements.

Market participants anticipate Turkey will engage in other liability management activities involving external obligations. In particular, this year or early next year, they expect Turkey to exchange short-dated, high coupon bonds for longer-dated bonds, carrying lower coupon rates to match rates on the yield curve more closely.

Venezuela

Under favorable conditions, Venezuela has issued two external bonds to cover its 2005 external financing requirements of $3 billion. The second bond was available only to local investors, who could purchase the bond with domestic currency at the official fixed exchange rate. Strong domestic retail demand reflected expectations of receiving foreign exchange at a favorable rate, in view of existing capital controls, and selling the currency for a capital gain

Box 2.2 *(concluded)*

in the black market. Locals could obtain foreign exchange by buying bonds at the official rate of 2,150 bolivares per dollar, compared with a black market rate of about 2,800 bolivares. Since locals could sell the bond abroad to obtain hard currency, they could make capital gains by selling their proceeds at the black market rate.[2]

The new issue also offered corporate investors a dollar hedge, helped the government mop up liquidity in the local market, and served to prevent capital flight. The sale of the bond helped bring down the black market rate, at least initially.

[2]However, in May, a judge ordered the Caracas Stock Exchange and all securities brokerage houses to halt stock and bond transactions designed to obtain dollars and skirt capital controls. President Chavez had earlier announced tougher punishment for those conducting transactions in the foreign exchange black market.

The improvement in credit quality has contributed to the ongoing broadening of the investor base. Emerging market countries that achieve investment-grade status gain access to a considerably wider pool of potential investors. At the same time, the search for yield continues to support higher-yielding, subinvestment-grade emerging market bonds. In the six months to end-June 2005, strategic asset allocations to emerging markets from such institutional investors as pension funds reached $7.3 billion; this represented a 73 percent increase over the year-earlier period, itself already a strong year for such flows. As pension funds continue to assess their asset allocation policies, further "buy and hold" investment flows will likely enter emerging markets. In addition, dedicated U.S. emerging market debt and equity mutual funds have continued to enjoy net inflows during 2005 (Figure 2.35) and may have benefited from the outflows from high-yield corporate bonds when conditions were disturbed by the credit downgrades of U.S. auto makers (see discussion in the previous section).

A strong record of risk-adjusted returns in recent years has also encouraged investor inflows into emerging market assets. Since 2001, emerging market bonds have been one of the best performing asset classes, while emerging market equities have generated higher risk-adjusted returns (ex post) than mature equity markets have generated (Figure 2.36). Returns in 2005, to date, remain attractive (Figure 2.37).

The larger and deeper pool of investors appears to have discriminated better between asset classes. Although typically exhibiting a positive correlation, emerging market and U.S. high-yield corporate debt markets somewhat decoupled during the turbulence that affected the high-yield market in April and May (Figure 2.38).

The search for yield has extended increasingly into local currency emerging market instruments as yields on emerging market external bonds have declined. However, more fundamental factors have also played an important role (Box 2.3).

Emerging Market Financing

As demand for exposure to emerging markets grew, external gross issuance by emerging market countries of bonds, equities, and loans reached a record high in the first half of 2005 (Figure 2.39 and Table 2.3). Bond issuance increased, supported by solid demand for emerging market assets and low global bond yields, and notwithstanding the brief spike in emerging market spreads during April when most issuers chose to stay out of the market.

By early July, emerging market sovereigns had already completed more than three-quarters of their planned external issuance for 2005. In Latin America, some issuers have brought forward placements planned for 2006, against the backdrop of a full election calendar in that year. By July, Brazil had already fully met its 2005 financing needs, Venezuela had begun prefinancing for 2006, and Mexico had already covered its financing requirements through the end of 2007. Of note, the inclusion of collective action clauses has become standard market practice in the issuance and documentation of sovereign bonds under New York law (Box 2.4).

As the U.S. dollar strengthened in the first half of 2005, issuance in nontraditional currencies rose, in part reflecting issuers' efforts to diversify funding sources. Emerging market issuance in euros rose through 2004 to a peak in the first quarter of 2005, but moderated in the second quarter, while issuance in yen, though picking up, remains modest. In some cases, countries extended their maturity spectrum, with Poland's recent issue of a 50-year bond providing the most striking example.

Equity issuance was also strong, predominantly in Asia, but also in the Europe, Middle East, and Africa (EMEA) region. Robust economic growth in emerging market economies, particularly Asia, combined with rising investor interest in local currency exposure, encouraged equity issuance. Syndicated lending was sizable, although down from the high levels seen in the second half of 2004.

Total net issuance rose in the first half of 2005 from a year ago, supported partly by lower amortization, but remained below the previous high in 1997 (Figure 2.40). Latin America's low share of total net external issuance (about 10 percent in the first half of 2005) is because many of the main issuers have privileged the development of and emphasized funding in their local markets. Mexico, for example, has had negative net issuance in external bonds since 2000. Another factor has

Figure 2.35. Cumulative Net Flows to U.S.-Based Mutual Funds
(In millions of U.S. dollars)

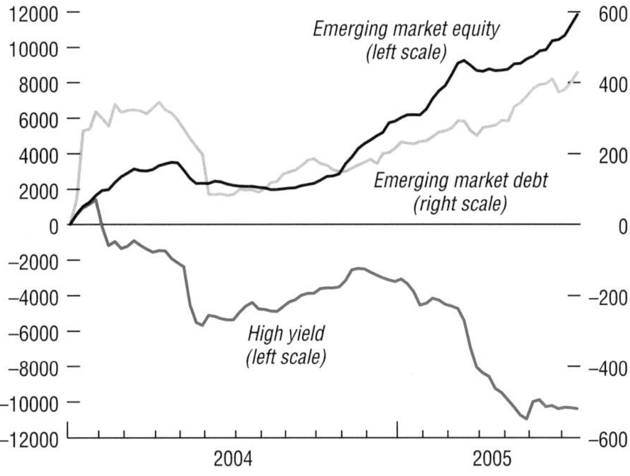

Source: AMG Data Services.

Figure 2.36. Asset Class Risk-Return Performance
(In percent)

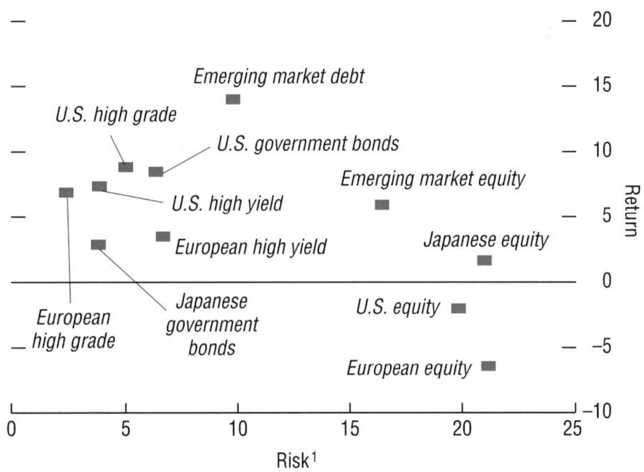

Sources: Bloomberg L.P.; Merrill Lynch; and IMF staff estimates.
[1]Five-year average of annualized standard deviations of total returns from 2001 to 2005.

Figure 2.37. EMBI Global Performance, 2005 to Date[1]
(In percent, through July 22, 2005)

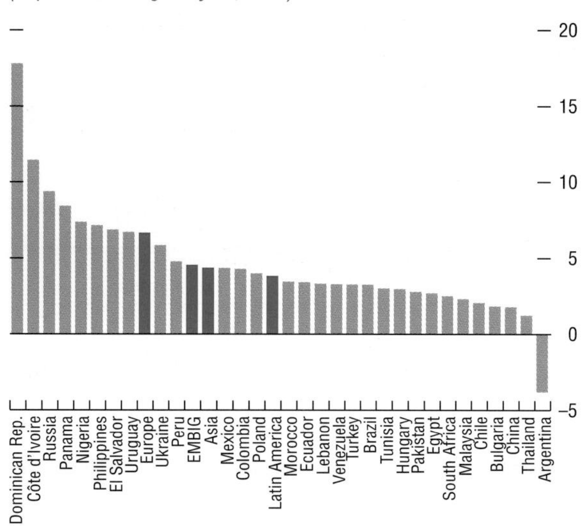

Sources: JPMorgan Chase & Co.; and IMF staff estimates.
[1]The EMBIG index so far this year has reflected changes in the composition of bonds used for Argentina and the Dominican Republic that have undergone debt restructurings.

Figure 2.38. U.S. Corporate, EMBIG, and Auto Sector Spreads
(In basis points)

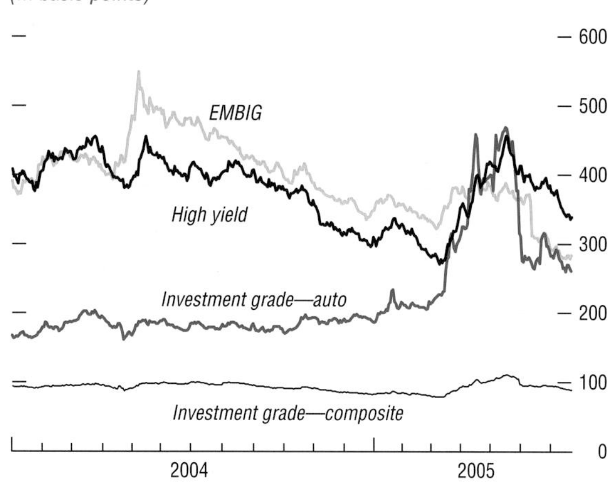

Sources: Merrill Lynch; and JPMorgan Chase & Co.

been the continued absence of Argentina from the market since 2001.

Bond Issuance

Bond placements by emerging market issuers remained strong in the first half of 2005, compared with the first half of 2004 (Figure 2.41). While issuance increased across the board, that by the EMEA region rose particularly strongly, accounting for 48 percent of total emerging market issuance. The composition of debt issuance changed little compared with a year ago: sovereign issuance accounted for roughly half of total bond issuance, corporate issuance represented about four-tenths of the total, and public sector corporate debt accounted for about a tenth. Currency composition notably changed in the first half of 2005, with increased issuance in nontraditional currencies—including Swiss francs and sterling, which rose to above 10 percent of the total—reflecting issuers' desire to diversify their sources of financing (Figure 2.42).

Equity Issuance

Asia continued to dominate equity issuance in the first half of 2005, accounting for about 75 percent of total issuance (Figure 2.43). By contrast, equity issuance in Latin America remained close to historically low levels—representing 6 percent of the total—in keeping with the Latin American practice by corporates of financing out of either retained earnings or borrowing.

Syndicated Lending

Syndicated lending in the first half of 2005 declined from the particularly strong pace seen in the preceding six months (Figure 2.44). The private sector received the lion's share of the lending, taking about two-thirds of the total. Loans to public sector companies were about a third of the total, with syndicated lending to sovereigns close to zero.

Foreign Direct Investment

After two years of decline, foreign direct investment (FDI) inflows to emerging market countries recovered in 2004, rising to an estimated $165.5 billion, an increase of 9 percent over 2003 (Figure 2.45). The increase in FDI flows can be traced largely to strengthened economic growth prospects, increased cross-border merger and acquisitions activity, and several privatizations. FDI expanded strongly in almost all regions in 2004. Latin America experienced the largest increase because of several sizable acquisitions and following official measures to improve the investment climate. In Asia, FDI continued to rise in 2004, particularly in China, India, Indonesia, Malaysia, and Vietnam. FDI flows to Eastern European and Central Asian countries also increased slightly in 2004, mainly because of higher flows to Russia.

The higher level of FDI inflows to emerging market countries is expected to continue in 2005 owing to favorable economic prospects, cross-border acquisitions activity, and further privatization of state-owned companies. Although preliminary estimates for first-quarter 2005 FDI flows are somewhat below the first quarter of 2004, the World Bank projects flows for 2005 as a whole to be above 2004. A number of large announced transactions are in the pipeline, including in the steel sector in India and privatization in Turkey. FDI inflows are expected to concentrate in the oil and gas, telecommunications, and banking sectors. Notwithstanding the growth in inflows, outward FDI from emerging market countries, especially in Asia, has expanded rapidly as firms seek to penetrate new markets as well as to secure needed inputs (Box 2.5).

Balance Sheet Developments in Major Mature Economies

Household Sector

Continued robust gains in real estate values have helped to increase U.S. household net

Figure 2.39. Cumulative Gross Annual Issuance of Bonds, Loans, and Equity
(In billions of U.S. dollars)

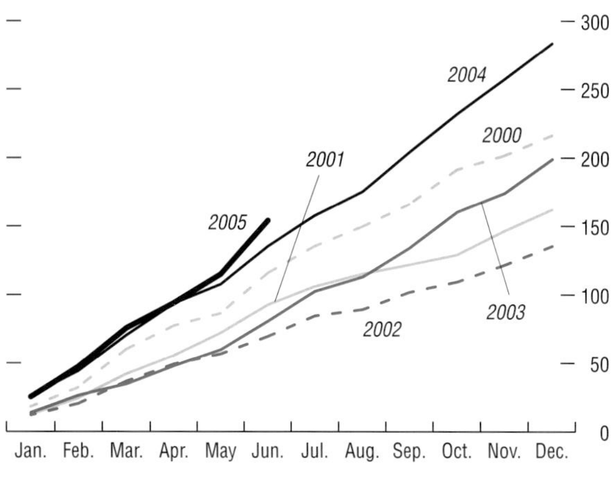

Source: Dealogic.

Figure 2.40. Quarterly Net Issuance
(In billions of U.S. dollars)

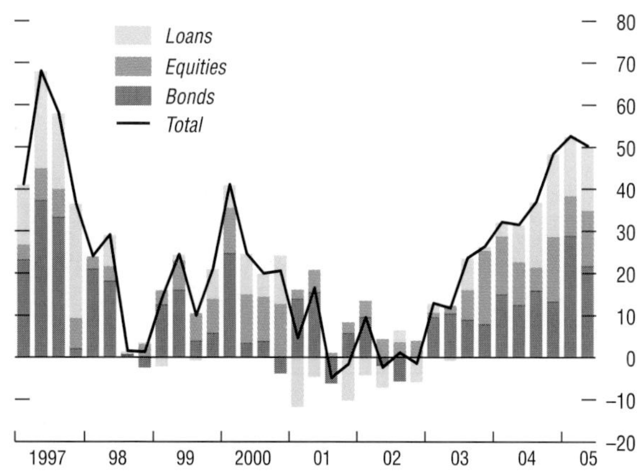

Sources: Dealogic; and IMF staff estimates.

Table 2.3. Emerging Market External Financing

						2004				2005[1]					
	2000	2001	2002	2003	2004	Q1	Q2	Q3	Q4	Q1	Q2	Apr.	May	Jun.	Year-to-date[1]
						(In billions of U.S. dollars)									
Gross issuance by asset	**216.4**	**162.1**	**135.6**	**198.7**	**283.4**	**70.6**	**64.7**	**68.8**	**79.5**	**75.9**	**78.1**	**18.1**	**20.9**	**39.1**	**154.0**
Bonds	80.5	89.0	61.6	98.8	132.8	40.0	30.4	33.0	29.3	42.8	36.0	8.1	8.8	19.2	78.9
Equities	41.8	11.2	16.4	27.7	44.9	13.8	10.3	5.6	15.4	10.5	15.2	1.7	4.1	9.5	25.7
Loans	94.2	61.9	57.6	72.2	105.7	16.8	24.0	30.1	34.8	22.5	26.9	8.4	8.1	10.4	49.4
Gross issuance by region	**216.4**	**162.1**	**135.6**	**198.7**	**283.4**	**70.6**	**64.7**	**68.8**	**79.5**	**75.9**	**78.1**	**18.1**	**20.9**	**39.1**	**154.0**
Asia	85.9	67.5	53.9	87.5	123.9	33.8	29.6	25.5	35.0	25.7	31.5	6.5	6.3	18.6	57.1
Latin America	69.1	53.9	33.4	42.8	53.6	14.4	9.7	16.2	13.3	17.4	11.4	3.1	4.5	3.8	28.7
Europe, Middle East, and Africa	61.4	40.8	48.3	68.5	105.9	22.4	25.3	27.0	31.2	32.8	35.3	8.6	10.1	16.6	68.1
Amortization by asset	**114.3**	**148.0**	**129.3**	**124.2**	**134.5**	**38.4**	**33.2**	**31.9**	**31.0**	**22.3**	**25.9**	**9.2**	**8.6**	**8.1**	**48.1**
Bonds	52.2	60.0	59.8	61.8	76.0	25.0	17.9	17.1	16.0	13.9	14.3	6.0	4.8	3.5	28.2
Loans	62.1	88.0	69.5	62.4	58.5	13.5	15.3	14.7	15.0	8.3	11.6	3.2	3.8	4.6	19.9
Amortization by region	**114.3**	**148.0**	**129.3**	**124.2**	**134.5**	**38.4**	**33.2**	**31.9**	**31.0**	**22.3**	**25.9**	**9.2**	**8.6**	**8.1**	**48.1**
Asia	57.1	66.5	56.2	49.4	53.2	16.1	13.2	11.9	11.9	8.9	6.2	2.3	1.4	2.6	15.1
Latin America	32.3	45.9	41.2	40.8	47.7	12.7	13.4	10.6	11.0	7.7	10.3	4.5	2.9	2.8	18.0
Europe, Middle East, and Africa	24.9	35.5	31.9	33.9	33.6	9.6	6.6	9.4	8.0	5.6	9.4	2.4	4.3	2.7	15.0
Net issuance by asset	**102.2**	**14.2**	**6.4**	**74.5**	**148.9**	**32.1**	**31.5**	**36.9**	**48.5**	**53.6**	**52.3**	**9.0**	**12.3**	**31.0**	**105.9**
Bonds	28.3	29.1	1.8	37.0	56.8	15.1	12.5	15.9	13.3	28.9	21.8	2.1	4.0	15.7	50.6
Equities	41.8	11.2	16.4	27.7	44.9	13.8	10.3	5.6	15.4	10.5	15.2	1.7	4.1	9.5	25.7
Loans	32.1	–26.1	–11.8	9.8	47.2	3.3	8.7	15.4	19.8	14.2	15.3	5.2	4.2	5.8	29.5
Net issuance by region	**102.2**	**14.2**	**6.4**	**74.5**	**148.9**	**32.1**	**31.5**	**36.9**	**48.5**	**53.6**	**52.3**	**9.0**	**12.3**	**31.0**	**105.9**
Asia	28.8	0.9	–2.3	38.0	70.8	17.7	16.4	13.6	23.1	16.8	25.3	4.2	5.0	16.0	42.0
Latin America	36.9	7.9	–7.8	1.9	5.9	1.7	–3.6	5.6	2.2	9.7	1.1	–1.4	1.5	1.0	10.8
Europe, Middle East, and Africa	36.5	5.3	16.4	34.6	72.3	12.7	18.7	17.6	23.2	27.2	25.9	6.1	5.8	13.9	53.1
Secondary markets															
Bonds															
EMBI Global (spread in basis points)	735	728	725	403	347	414	482	409	347	373	297	384	364	297	284
Merrill Lynch High-Yield (spread in basis points)	890	795	871	418	310	438	404	384	310	352	385	419	413	385	339
Merrill Lynch High-Grade (spread in basis points)	200	162	184	93	83	94	97	91	83	92	95	102	97	95	89
U.S. 10-year treasury yield (yield in percent)	5.12	5.05	3.82	4.25	4.22	3.84	4.58	4.12	4.22	4.48	3.92	4.20	3.98	3.92	4.22
						(In percent)									
Equity															
DOW	–6.2	–7.1	–16.8	25.0	3.1	–0.9	0.8	–3.4	–1.9	–2.6	–2.2	–3.0	2.7	–1.8	–1.2
NASDAQ	–39.3	–21.1	–31.5	50.5	8.6	–0.5	2.7	–7.4	1.9	–8.1	2.9	–3.9	7.6	–0.5	0.2
MSCI Emerging Markets	–31.8	–4.9	–8.0	51.2	22.4	8.9	–10.3	7.4	–0.2	1.2	3.0	–3.0	3.0	3.1	10.0
Asia	–42.5	4.2	–6.2	46.1	12.2	7.6	–12.2	4.2	–0.5	2.1	2.8	–3.0	3.5	2.4	10.3
Latin America	–18.4	–4.3	–24.8	66.7	34.8	6.2	–9.2	16.6	–1.1	1.8	7.1	–3.8	6.4	4.6	14.7
Europe, Middle East, and Africa	–22.3	–20.9	4.7	51.9	35.8	13.2	–7.4	7.8	1.0	–1.0	0.5	–2.6	–0.4	3.5	6.0

Sources: Bloomberg L.P.; Dealogic; JPMorgan Chase & Co.; Merrill Lynch; Morgan Stanley Capital International; and IMF staff estimates.
[1]Issuance data as of June 30, 2005, close-of-business London; secondary market data as of July 22, 2005, close-of-business New York.

worth, which rose by 8.2 percent (year-on-year) in the 12 months through March 2005, and by 2.0 percent relative to disposable income. Despite monetary tightening, persistent low mortgage rates have supported ongoing increases in house prices. The value of household real estate wealth increased by 14.9 percent in the four quarters ending on March 31, 2005, compared with a 10.9 percent rise the previous year. Households' financial net worth grew at a slower pace (4.0 percent) than total net worth during the year ending in March 2005, because of a decline in the already low personal savings rate (from an average of 1.3 percent in 2004 to 0.9 percent in the first quarter of 2005) and muted gains from equity price appreciation in household portfolios. Indeed, with the ownership of U.S. financial assets highly skewed, most of the gains from rising net worth accrued to those in the wealthiest 10 percent of households.[15] By contrast, households that belong simultaneously to the middle-income quintiles and the middle age cohorts typically own a relatively small share of total household assets, and thus have relatively low levels of net worth to buffer them against severe shocks. Similarly, such middle-income/middle age households have also sufficiently high income so as to make them ineligible for support from public-sector safety nets. Therefore these households appear to be the most vulnerable to adverse financial shocks.[16]

Household financial liabilities grew by 11.1 percent and mortgage debt rose by 13.0 percent during the past year, as home buyers borrowed more in absolute terms to purchase higher priced houses and, to a lesser extent, due to consumer debt. Aggregate household leverage (the ratio of liabilities to assets) rose to 18.2 percent, from its recent low of 17.8 percent in 2003, but housing leverage—the ratio of mortgage debt to housing value—has been stable at approximately 43.6 percent,

[15]Kennickell (2003).

[16]In the United States, the middle-income quintiles represent approximately 14 percent of U.S. household net worth, compared with their counterparts in Japan, for example, who represent as much as 32 percent of Japanese household net worth. Viewed by age groups, household net worth exhibits a "hump-shaped" pattern consistent with life-cycle saving behavior, where peak saving occurs in the 55–64 age group. In addition, more than half of U.S. household net worth is owned by the 50 years or over cohorts. See April 2005 GFSR for a detailed analysis of household balance sheets, a comparative analysis of developments across countries, and implications for financial stability.

Figure 2.41. Cumulative Gross Annual Issuance of Bonds[1]

(In billions of U.S. dollars)

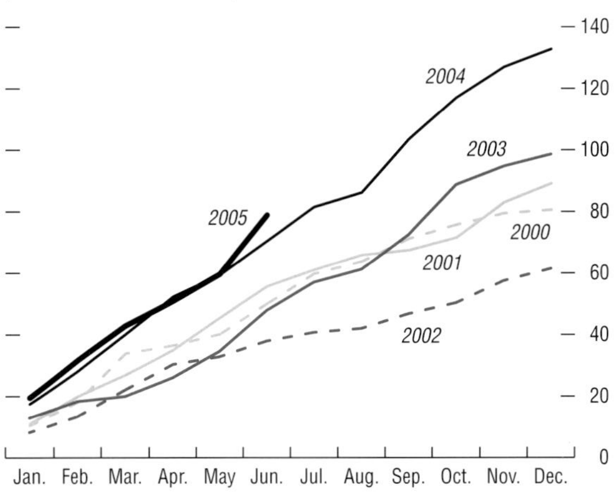

Source: Dealogic.
[1]Bonds adjusted for Brady exchanges.

Figure 2.42. Emerging Market Bond Issuance by Currency

(Percentage of total)

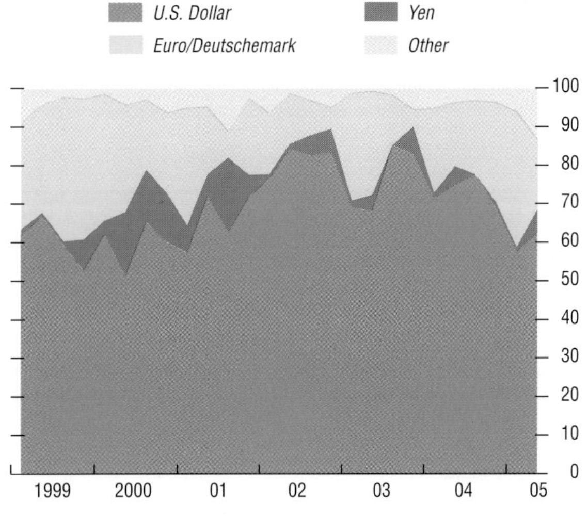

Source: Dealogic.

Figure 2.43. Equity Placements
(In billions of U.S. dollars)

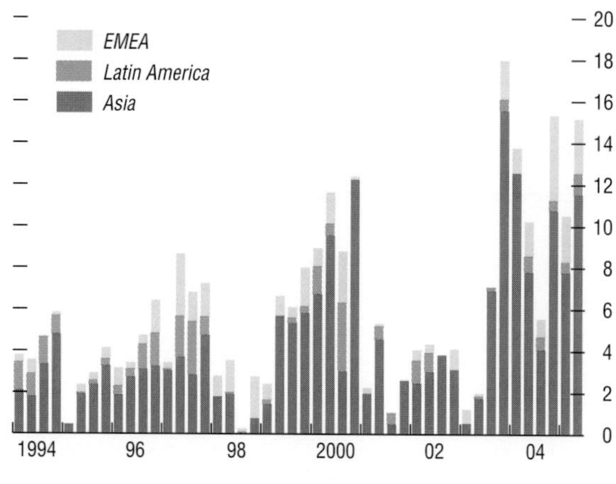

Source: Dealogic.

Figure 2.44. Syndicated Loan Commitments
(In billions of U.S. dollars)

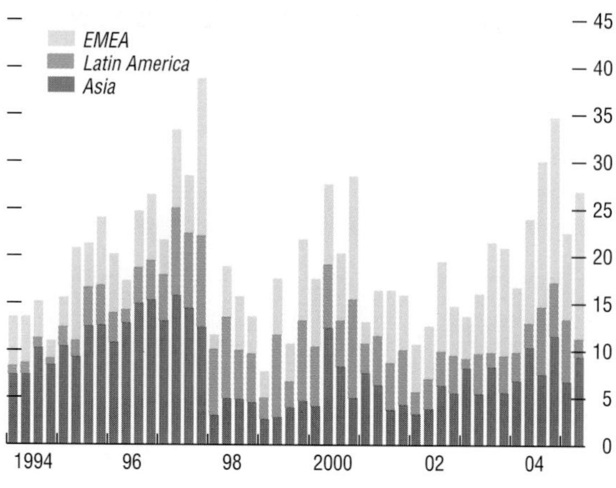

Source: Dealogic.

reflecting rising home values. Nevertheless, the rise in mortgage debt at a time of high home values may be a cause for concern. Moreover, household debt service payments as a percentage of disposable income has risen steadily since the mid-1990s and, in the first quarter of 2005, it reached 13.4 percent, exceeding its recent historical high of 13.36 percent in the first quarter of 2003.[17] Of greater concern are the debt and leverage levels of middle- and lower-income groups, which may have benefited much from low mortgage rates and more sophisticated mortgage products, but are particularly vulnerable to interest rate and economic shocks.

In Japan, household net worth has remained stable as a share of total assets since 2000, as the decline in real estate values has been largely offset by the rise in the value of household financial asset holdings (Table 8 in the Statistical Appendix).[18] Following an improvement in 2003, Japanese household financial net worth has not changed significantly during the last fiscal year beginning in April 2004. The share of total financial assets in equity rose to 8.6 percent at the end of March 2005 from 8.4 percent a year ago. The share of currency and deposits has remained unchanged, at approximately 55 percent during this period. Meanwhile, securities investment trusts as a share of household assets have grown steadily since its trough in 1997 (1.9 percent of household assets). The recent increase was primarily because of a continuing flow of retail funds into foreign sovereign bond products sold mainly through banks. As of March 2005, securities investment

[17]These data and a more advanced financial obligations ratio can be found at the Federal Reserve Board website: *http://www.federalreserve.gov/releases/housedebt/default.htm.*

[18]Data on nonfinancial assets are available only through FY2003. However, real estate analysts and other market participants agree that the trend in real estate valuations has continued to decline, with perhaps some large cities, such as the Tokyo area, showing some recent signs of stabilizing.

trusts still comprise a relatively small portion (2.7 percent) of household financial assets, which reflects households' general aversion to owning equities, following the steady decline of equity prices since the early 1990s. Financial liabilities, mainly home mortgages, have not changed during this period, representing about 77 percent of GDP.

Despite increased indebtedness, household net worth in the euro area has remained generally stable. Household debt in the euro area reached new highs at the end of 2004, rising to 50 percent of GDP from 47 percent a year ago. In an environment of low interest rates and rising home prices, housing loans remain the fastest rising component of household credit, growing at a 10 percent annual rate through the first quarter of 2005. Mortgage loans with a medium- or long-term maturity still represent the bulk of new lending. Growth in consumer credit has been less dynamic than mortgage lending, but is now gaining momentum. Consumer credit growth reached 6.7 percent in the 12 months through March 2005, up from 2.8 percent in late 2003. However, the burden of higher indebtedness has been largely offset by lower interest rates, and the debt service ratio has remained remarkably stable at about 12 percent over the last five years. Financial markets have provided support to household balance sheets, thereby contributing to sustaining net worth. However, over the medium term, the recent increase in the use of variable rate mortgages, and rising loan-to-value ratios, are potential sources of vulnerability for household balance sheets, especially if income growth weakens.[19]

[19]However, mortgage products and customs (the popularity of variable versus fixed-rate loans, the maturity of mortgage loans, and the conditions attached to early repayment) differ significantly from one country to another within the euro area. Therefore, the risks associated with a possible decline in house prices, or a rise in interest rates, would have different effects on borrowers and lenders in various countries (see Chapter III of the April 2005 GFSR for a comparative analysis of mortgage markets).

Figure 2.45. FDI Inflows into Emerging Markets
(In millions of U.S. dollars)

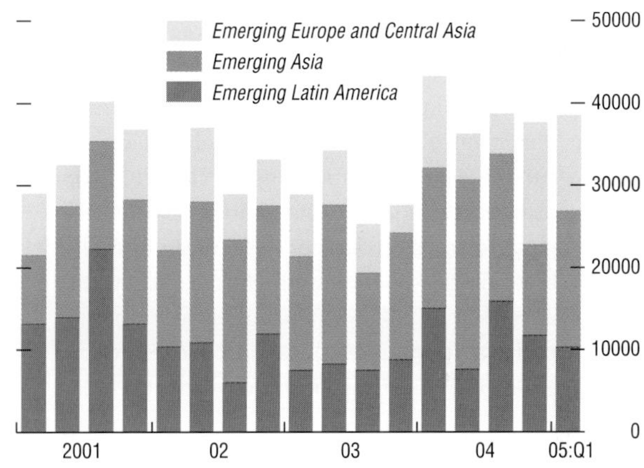

Source: World Bank.

Box 2.3. Foreign Investment in Local Currency Instruments: A Cyclical or Fundamental Phenomenon?

The level of foreign investment in emerging market local currency bonds has risen dramatically in recent years. In the more developed and open markets, such as Mexico, Poland, and Turkey, the share of local currency government bonds held by nonresidents has increased rapidly and, in some cases, more than doubled in the last two years (see first figure, below). In surveys of investors carried out by the EMTA, the volume of trade in secondary markets in local currency bonds, as a percent of total trade volume, has risen from 25 percent in 1997 to 45 percent in 2004 (see second figure, right).

Is this rapid rise in local currency investments a cyclical or a fundamental phenomenon? The trend undoubtedly has a strong cyclical component. Abundant global liquidity has fostered a quest for high-yielding assets such as emerging market local currency bonds as spreads on more conventional asset classes (including hard currency emerging market bonds) have compressed. However, there are also some fundamental changes in financial markets that suggest local currency bonds are emerging as an important asset for foreign investors. This box focuses on the following changes:

- innovations that have enhanced foreign investor access to, and knowledge of, local currency bond markets;
- a wider, more stable foreign investor base; and
- the development of local currency bond markets by emerging market governments.

Emerging Market Debt Trading: Market Share by Instrument
(In percent)

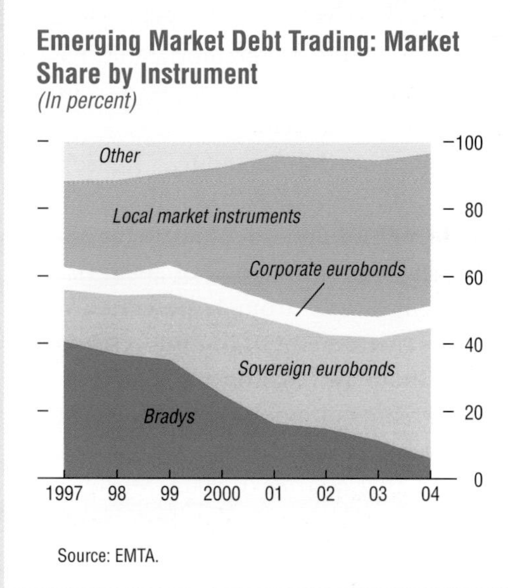

Source: EMTA.

Share of Nonresident Holdings of Government Local Currency Bonds
(In percent)

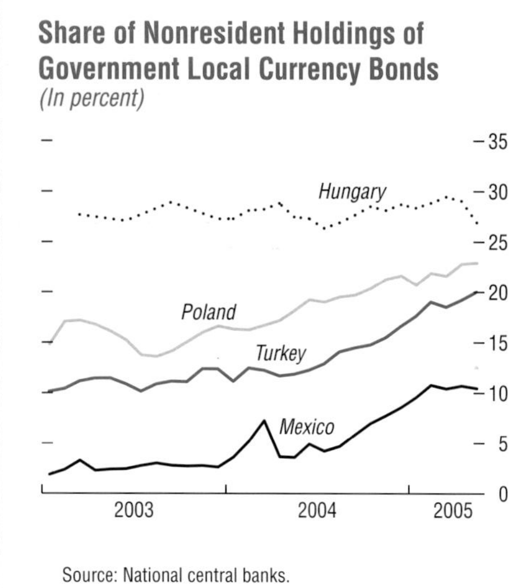

Source: National central banks.

Innovations in Investor Access to Local Currency Bond Markets

The key innovations facilitating market access to local currency bond markets are as follows:

- The development of indices give active managers a benchmark against which to track performance. Such indices are essential market infrastructure. In June, JPMorgan Chase & Co. launched a local emerging market index, the "Government Bond Index—Emerging Markets" (GBI-EM), which is a local market equivalent of its widely used EMBI family of indices that track emerging market hard currency bonds. The index tracks 19 local-currency-denominated government bond markets worldwide in major

GBI-EM Index Return Analysis
(In U.S. dollars; unhedged)

	GBI-EM						
Total Returns	Composite	Asia	Europe	Middle East/ Africa	Latin America	EMBIG Diversified	U.S. Treasuries
2002	19.1	17.0	34.9	19.9	0.2	13.7	12.2
2003	18.8	11.8	8.3	48.5	8.8	22.2	2.4
2004	12.3	0.7	32.4	30.2	11.6	11.6	3.8
2005 (year-to-date)	–0.9	4.1	–5.6	–11.9	6.3	2.9	2.7
Cumulative	57.4	37.0	82.6	104.1	29.2	59.5	22.5
Annual return	14.2	9.7	19.3	23.2	7.8	14.7	6.1
Annual volatility	7.4	4.4	13.7	20.7	9.9	8.2	5.9
Sharpe ratio	1.7	1.8	1.3	1.0	0.6	1.6	0.8

Source: JPMorgan Chase & Co.
Note: GBI-EM (Government Bond Index-Emerging Markets) is JPMorgan Chase & Co.'s local emerging market index.

emerging markets.[1] The creation of the index was a response to the increasing appetite for emerging market local currency debt as investors sought to diversify their portfolios. The index was calculated retroactively to December 31, 2001, and shows that investors would have achieved striking returns in emerging market local currency bonds in recent years, continuing into 2005 in Latin America and Asia (see table).

- In Asia, the opening up of local currency bond markets has been facilitated by the public sector under the Asia Bond Fund 2 (ABF2), which is a family of funds established by a group of 11 central banks and monetary authorities in the region (EMEAP), for the purpose of investing in local currency bond markets.[2] ABF2 consists of nine separate funds: a Pan-Asian Bond Index Fund (PAIF) investing in sovereign and quasi-sovereign local currency bonds of eight EMEAP economies,[3] and eight single market funds investing in sovereign and quasi-sovereign local currency bonds of the respective EMEAP markets. Management of the funds will be undertaken by designated private managers using indices created by the International Index Company (formerly known as iBoxx). EMEAP have invested $2 billion to launch the nine funds that will be open to subscription by other investors. The Hong Kong SAR fund was first, launched, on June 21, 2005, the PAIF fund was launched in Hong Kong SAR on July 7, 2005, and the Malaysia Fund was launched on July 18, 2005. The remaining funds are expected to be launched by October 2005.[4]

In addition to offering a low-cost option for investors to take local currency bond risk in

[1]The economies in the index are Brazil, Chile, China, Colombia, the Czech Republic, Hong Kong SAR, Hungary, India, Indonesia, Israel, Korea, Malaysia, Mexico, Poland, Russia, Singapore, South Africa, Thailand, and Turkey.

[2]The group is called the Executives' Meeting of East Asia and Pacific Central Banks (EMEAP) and includes the Reserve Bank of Australia, People's Bank of China, Hong Kong Monetary Authority, Bank Indonesia, Bank of Japan, Bank of Korea, Bank Negara Malaysia, Reserve Bank of New Zealand, Bangko Sentral ng Pilipinas, Monetary Authority of Singapore, and Bank of Thailand. ABF2 follows the establishment of the Asia Bond Fund 1, a fund established to invest in Asian sovereign and quasi-sovereign dollar-denominated debt. Additional information can be found on the EMEAP webpage: *http://www.emeap.org.*

[3]The eight EMEAP economies are China, Hong Kong SAR, Indonesia, Korea, Malaysia, the Philippines, Singapore, and Thailand.

[4]In the first week after its opening, the Hong Kong SAR fund received enough private investment to increase its value by 33 percent, reducing the EMEAP central banks' collective share to 75 percent of the fund's assets.

Box 2.3 *(concluded)*

the region, the ABF2 has spurred the development of competing local currency bond indices; it has also led to improvements in market infrastructure and the regulatory environment in relevant markets. For example, the ABF2 has spurred the development of regulations for exchange-traded funds in China and Malaysia. It has also encouraged countries to increase foreign investor access to local bond markets, accelerate tax reforms to eliminate withholding taxes on interest income from investments in local securities, and liberalize foreign exchange administration rules.[5]

- Two emerging market countries, Colombia and Uruguay, have issued local currency bonds in the international market in the last year, facilitating investor access to local currency exposure.[6]

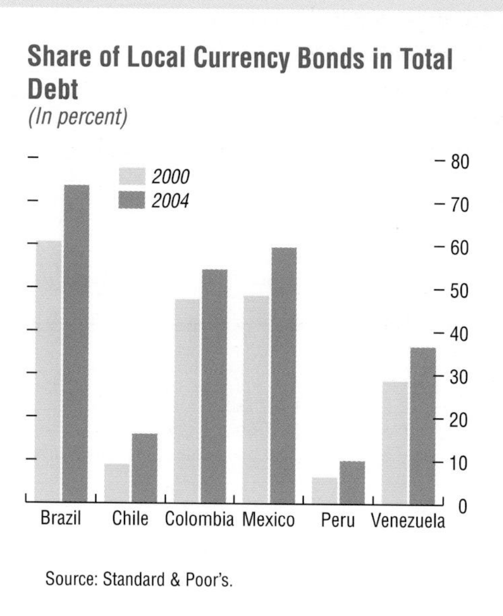

Foreign Investor Base for Local Currency Bonds

The investor base for local currency emerging market bonds has expanded from a variety of sources (see figure):

- Evidence suggests that institutional investors have moved as much as 10 percent of their emerging market exposure into emerging market local currency instruments, compared with minimal exposure three years ago. These investors, such as large pension funds and insurance companies, tend to make long-term allocations, thus they may constitute a relatively stable part of an investor base. Dedicated emerging market bond funds have also increased their exposure to local currency instruments.
- Global bond funds (those that include bonds from a broad range of countries, both mature and emerging) are also including some emerging market local currency bonds in their portfolios. This trend has been accelerated since the incorporation of bonds from eight investment-grade emerging market countries in the Lehman Global Aggregate Index, a commonly used benchmark for global bond funds.[7]

Development of Local Currency Bond Markets

The development of local currency bond markets by emerging market governments has resulted in a wider variety of instruments and greater liquidity in local bond markets, which make local currency bond markets more attractive for international investors. Over the past year, a number of countries—most prominently Brazil, Chile, Mexico, Peru, and Turkey—have extended the maturity of their domestic debt profiles, partly to cater to the desires of investors for longer duration. In some cases, foreign investors have taken up a majority of the bond issues at particular maturities (e.g., in Mexico, where some of the issues at the long end of the curve have been taken up almost entirely by foreign investors). Sovereigns have also shifted the

[5]An evaluation of the effects of ABF2 on the development of local bond markets can be found in the latest *BIS Quarterly Review* (June 2005); available via the internet at *http://www.bis.org/publ/quarterly.htm.*

[6]For a fuller account, see IMF (2005a, Box 2.6).

[7]Since 2004, Chile, the Czech Republic, Hungary, Mexico, Poland, the Slovak Republic, Slovenia, and South Africa have been added.

composition of their debt toward local currency denomination, reducing the vulnerability of their debt stocks to exchange rate risk and increasing the liquidity of local currency markets.[8] This has been a factor in increasing credit ratings and making local currency debt more attractive.[9] As a result, the proportion of external debt in total debt has fallen in a number of countries, while the proportion of local currency debt has increased (see third figure).

[8]Increased reliance on domestic currency borrowing by sovereigns helps reduce currency mismatches. However, domestic bonds in many emerging markets tend to have shorter maturities than the external bonds that they are replacing, raising refinancing risk. In addition, the development of the local institutional investor base is important to balance foreign participation so that local markets are less prone to reversals in investor sentiment.

[9]The two highest-rated sovereigns in Latin America, Chile and Mexico, have made the most progress in the region in replacing foreign-currency-denominated debt with local currency debt over the last 10 years. In addition, recent upgrades or outlook revisions for a number of sovereigns by Standard and Poor's, including Chile (January 2004), Peru (June 2004), Brazil (September 2004), and Mexico (January 2005) were all influenced to some degree by the increasing share of local currency debt in their total debt.

In the United Kingdom, demand for housing loans began to slow in the second half of 2004, as lending rates rose. While the annual growth rate of consumer debt remained above 13 percent, growth in mortgage borrowing slowed to 11.5 percent in the 12 months through May. Demand for residential real estate has declined significantly, as mortgage approvals in May 2005 were down 24 percent from May 2004. A decline in mortgage equity withdrawals may signal an increased reluctance of households to borrow for consumption and, therefore, could be followed by a more pronounced slowdown in consumer borrowing in the coming months. At the end of 2004, household debt represented 102 percent of GDP, and about 150 percent of annual household income, pointing to some potential vulnerability in household balance sheets.

Corporate Balance Sheets

U.S. corporations experienced a prolonged period of relatively high productivity and profit growth, with strengthening balance sheets since 2000, but the growth in their cash flow has since slowed. Corporate cash flow for nonfarm nonfinancial companies slowed to 2.2 percent (year-on-year) in the first quarter of 2005, compared with an annual average of 8.7 percent during the 2000–03 period. Owing to corporates' strong earnings and relatively muted growth in capital expenditures, there was little need for external financing, and the cash positions of corporate balance sheets grew (e.g., holdings of U.S. treasury securities grew from an average of $18.1 billion in 1999–2001 to $34.9 billion in the first quarter of 2005). These relatively large cash holdings have accelerated corporate share buybacks (e.g., equity buybacks reached an annual rate of $226 billion in the first quarter of 2005 compared with $157 billion during 2004), increased announced (and anticipated) dividend growth rates, and spurred merger and acquisitions activity. These trends, if sustained, could raise corporate leverage and eventually weaken credit quality to some degree.

Japanese corporations have continued to strengthen their balance sheets. Since the end of March 2004, the ratio of capital to assets in the Japanese corporate sector has remained high, at approximately 30 percent, and on par with its historically high level reached in 1990

Box 2.4. Collective Action Clauses

The use of collective action clauses (CACs) in international sovereign bonds issued under New York law has become standard market practice. In the first two quarters of 2005, with one exception, all sovereign bond issues under New York law by emerging market countries included CACs. To date, there has been no observable impact on the pricing of bonds issued under New York law that included CACs.

Since March 2005, two more countries, Argentina and the Dominican Republic, included CACs in their bonds issued following their respective debt exchanges. This contributed to an increase in the stock of outstanding sovereign issues by emerging market countries that include CACs to approximately 53 percent in value terms as of June 30, 2005.

Ten emerging market countries—Brazil, Colombia, El Salvador, Indonesia, Lebanon,[1] Mexico, the Philippines, Turkey, Uruguay, and Venezuela—continued with their established practice of including CACs in their bonds issued under New York law. Jamaica was the only country that did not include CACs in its New York law bond. Italy, the only mature market country to issue under New York law, continued to include CACs in its bonds in that jurisdiction.

The bonds issued by Argentina and the Dominican Republic following their respective debt exchanges included an aggregating voting provision, in addition to majority restructuring and majority enforcement provisions. The aggregation provision provides the option to amend key terms on the basis of aggregate voting across affected bonds in cases where the amendment affects two or more series of bonds. This practice in the design of restructured bonds was initially set by Uruguay, which has continued to include such provisions in its recent issues.

As is customary, all bonds issued under English and Japanese law included CACs. Austria, the Czech Republic, Hungary, Poland, Sweden, and Tunisia issued under English law. Hungary, Poland, and Thailand issued under Japanese law.

There were no new issues under German law.

[1]The Lebanon bonds include only majority restructuring provisions.

Emerging Market Sovereign Bonds Outstanding Issuance by Governing Law

	Number of Issues		Value of Issues	
	(In billions of U.S. dollars)	*(In percent)*	*(In billions of U.S. dollars)*	*(In percent)*
New York	435	62	264	63
English	182	26	120	29
German	45	6	20	5
Japan	41	6	12	3
Total	703	100	416	100
Of which:				
with CACs	338	48	220	53

Sources: Dealogic; and IMF staff estimates (as of June 30, 2005).

Emerging Market Sovereign Bond Issuance by Jurisdiction[1]

	2003				2004				2005[2]	
	Q1	Q2[3]	Q3	Q4	Q1	Q2	Q3	Q4	Q1	Q2[4]
With CACs[5]										
Number of issues	9	31	10	5	25	19	19	15	18	39
Of which: New York law	1	22	5	4	14	12	12	13	11	23
Value of issues *(in billions of U.S. dollars)*	5.6	18.0	6.4	4.3	18.5	15.9	10.7	9.1	22.3	35.1
Of which: New York law	1.0	12.8	3.6	4.0	10.6	9.5	6.5	7.7	11.1	20.2
Without CACs[6]										
Number of issues *(in billions of U.S. dollars)*	14	4	7	7	2	1	1	4	0	1
Value of issues	8.1	2.5	3.5	4.2	1.5	0.1	0.2	2.7	—	0.3

Source: Dealogic.
[1]Number of issuance is in number. Volume of issuance is in billions of U.S. dollars.
[2]Data as of June 30, 2005.
[3]Includes issues of restructured bonds by Uruguay.
[4]Includes settlements of restructured bonds by Argentina and the Dominican Republic.
[5]English and Japanese laws, and New York law where relevant.
[6]German and New York laws.

Box 2.5. Foreign Direct Investment to Emerging Market Countries: An Asian Perspective

The IMF and the World Bank Group staff have been working to develop forward-looking qualitative assessments of prospective FDI flows to and from emerging market countries.[1] To capture FDI prospects and overseas business strategies, the IMF and World Bank staff have been building an informal contact network with senior executives from private sector companies and financial institutions. The results of this ongoing joint work will be reported regularly in future issues of the GFSR. In this box, we focus on developments in Asia and discuss recent contacts with selected companies active in various sectors and financial institutions in India, Japan, Malaysia, and Singapore. Other regions and selected cross-cutting FDI issues will be discussed in future issues of the GFSR.

The overall level of FDI into Asian emerging markets seems likely to continue growing. A broad interest in expanding FDI and overseas businesses was reported by both companies and financial institutions throughout the region. The main driver is the search for new markets in large, fast-growing countries and regions. China remains the most important planned destination, but interest in Indonesia and especially India is increasing rapidly.

There are some tentative signs of a reallocation of FDI inflows within Asia. While China remains the predominant location for FDI inflows, there are signs of a leveling off. Indeed, some investors are reassessing their investment plans in China, and the authorities are slowing down approvals in several overheated sectors. Within Southeast Asia, some reallocation of FDI inflows seems to be under way (with a decline of interest in large new investments) into Malaysia and Singapore owing to higher local costs and more modest growth prospects, and an increase into Indonesia and, to a lesser extent, Vietnam. Interest by foreign investors in India is continuing to grow substantially, yet inward FDI flows are seen by investors as remaining well below potential.

Outward FDI from Asian emerging market countries is expanding rapidly. FDI flows from China, India, Korea, Malaysia, Singapore, and Thailand are expanding rapidly and go beyond the well-publicized recent proposed large investments by Korea's POSCO and China's CNOOC.[2] Outward FDI is driven largely by the desire to penetrate new markets, while firms engaged in processing raw materials are aiming to secure upstream equity overseas. FDI has stayed largely within Asia except for those companies needing assured access to raw materials.

FDI flows from emerging market Asian companies are expected to continue expanding in the future. The slowing of domestic growth in some of the more mature Asian markets, coupled with the greater opportunities both within and outside the region is expected to fuel this growth. In the large economies of China and India, local companies will continue to want to secure natural resources—often from the developing world—to fuel their own growth. In addition, many firms in emerging Asia see a number of competitive advantages to investing elsewhere in the region, including geographic proximity, cultural affinity, and the ability to operate in smaller niche markets.

A trend toward greater reliance on local financing for FDI and overseas businesses was reported. Parent companies stated that they allow their subsidiaries to retain local profits for reinvestment. For funding the nonequity component of major new investments, companies look first to local banks, and in some cases—such as India and Malaysia—reliance is placed on local bond markets as well. However, there are exceptions. Most Japanese firms report that for large investments the parent company provides financing to overseas businesses and subsidiaries.

[1]The staff from the IMF's International Capital Markets Department, and from the Foreign Investment Advisory Service, International Finance Corporation, and the World Bank are participating and have jointly prepared this box. This work builds on the 2003 report: *Foreign Direct Investment in Emerging Market Countries Report of the Working Group of the Capital Markets Consultative Group* (CMCG); it is available via the Internet at *http://www.imf.org/external/np/cmcg/2003/eng/091803.HTM.*

[2]CNOOC withdrew its offer for Unocal in early August.

Figure 2.46. Japan: Capital-to-Asset Ratio of Corporate Sector
(In percent)

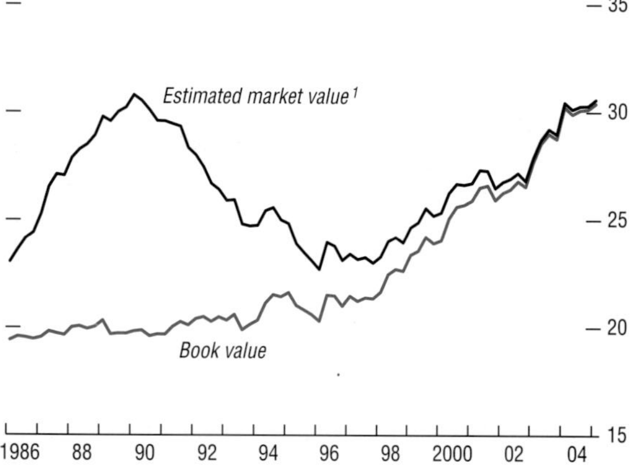

Sources: Ministry of Finance, *Financial Statements Statistics of Corporations by Industry*; and IMF staff estimates.
[1]For capital and assets, equity and real estate are marked to the market.

Figure 2.47. Japan: Corporate Debt and Cash Flow Relative to GDP
(March 1984 = 100)

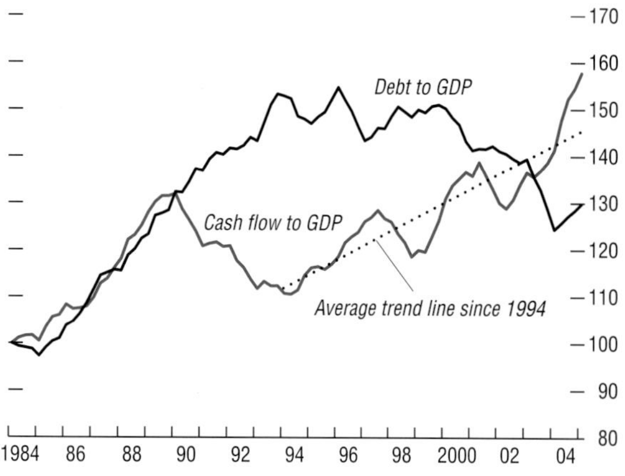

Sources: Ministry of Finance, *Financial Statements Statistics of Corporations by Industry*; and IMF staff estimates.

(Figure 2.46).[20] Corporate balance sheets have strengthened since the mid-1990s because of accumulated earning from the recovery in economic activity, the long but steady corporate restructuring process, and the current very low financing cost environment.

Fixed investment in the Japanese corporate sector has turned up, particularly since last year. This upturn has been supported by a rise in cash flow relative to GDP since early 2004, and, notably, external financing appears to have also risen, as indicated by the recovery in the debt-to-GDP ratio during the same period (Figure 2.47). The recent upturn in external financing has mainly been long-term borrowing, which usually finances private fixed investment.[21]

Although cash flow and profits relative to sales have been strong in the corporate sector as a whole, there appears to be some disparity in industry sentiment concerning business conditions between manufacturers and nonmanufacturers. For example, judgments about business conditions have been generally improving for most industries in recent years, but the gap between manufacturing and nonmanufacturing sectors has widened since 2002, and it has remained persistent during that period (Figure 2.48). Nonmanufacturing industries—which account for about 70 percent of all industry sales, including the so-called "bubble sectors" such as construction,

[20]Prior to the late 1990s, Japanese corporations reported equity and real estate assets at book value. If these assets were marked to market, corporate capital to asset ratios would have reached approximately 30 percent in 1990. Since that time, differences between book and mark-to-market valuations have narrowed, and have disappeared since 2001. See September 2004 GFSR for a more detailed explanation.

[21]According to the survey by the Ministry of Finance, "Financial Statements Statistics of Corporations by Industry," the year-to-year change in nominal fixed investment by all industries grew at double-digit rates for the first three quarters of 2004, and continued to grow at 3.5 percent in the fourth quarter of 2004 and 7.4 percent in the first quarter of 2005, respectively.

real estate, and large retailers—continue to restructure, with relatively large amounts of debt on their balance sheets.

Earnings of nonfinancial corporations in the euro area improved in 2004, driven more by cost cutting than by revenue growth. Corporate demand for external financing has remained low, reflecting limited perceived investment opportunities and relatively liquid balance sheets. In contrast with previous periods, the growth of bank loans to the corporate sector, at 6.0 percent in the year through March 2005, has been mostly fueled by medium- and long-term borrowing. However, firms have been shifting from paying down existing higher-cost debt to shortening its maturity and increasing the share of variable rates with lower-cost and shorter maturity debt. This results in lower debt servicing costs in the short term, but increases vulnerability to rising interest rates. About 60 percent of outstanding corporate loans reset within a year.

In the United Kingdom, corporate loan demand remained soft, picking up only slightly toward the end of 2004. Debt servicing costs rose, however, by about 12 percent over the year, as interest rates on corporate debt rose moderately. The corporate sector has been running a financial surplus for more than two years, accumulating record levels of liquidity. However, as in the euro area, corporations are now devoting a growing share of their financial surplus to increased share buybacks or M&A activity, despite historically high levels of debt (Figure 2.49).[22]

Bank Balance Sheets

Since the mid-1990s, U.S. commercial banks have continued to produce elevated returns on assets (ROA) and equity (ROE).

[22]For example, the number of domestic acquisitions by U.K. firms in 2004 rose by 32 percent (to 741 from 558) compared with the previous year, and the value of these acquisitions rose by 68 percent. See U.K. Office of National Statistics (2005).

Figure 2.48. Japan: Business Conditions
(In percent, "favorable" - "unfavorable")

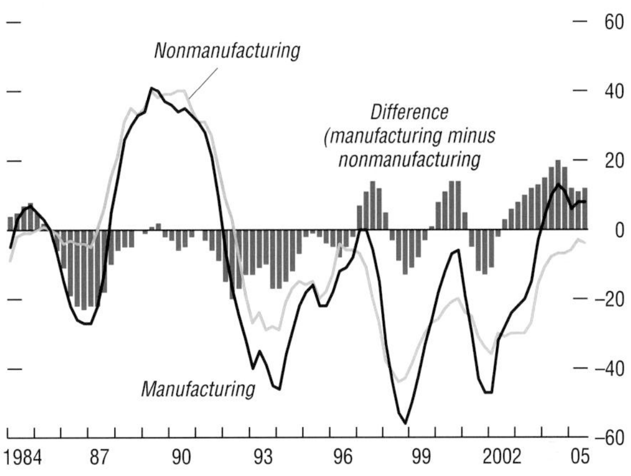

Source: Bank of Japan, *TANKAN: Short-Term Economic Survey of Enterprises in Japan.*

Figure 2.49. Euro Area and United Kingdom: Ratio of Nonfinancial Corporate Debt to GDP
(In percent)

Sources: ECB, *Monthly Bulletin*; and United Kingdom, Office for National Statistics.

In the first quarter of 2005, ROA and ROE were 1.35 and 13.1 percent, respectively, which are approximately in line with their 2002–04 averages (1.32 and 14.1 percent, respectively). The flattening yield curve during 2004 has narrowed net interest margins and partly limited the growth in interest income. Moreover, strong cash flow of U.S. corporates reduced financing needs, which led to modest growth in commercial and industrial loan revenues. Gains in noninterest income moderated to 2.6 percent from 8.9 percent in 2003. Among the 100 largest banks, noninterest income from fiduciary and securitization activities rose, but income from investment banking was approximately flat relative to 2003. Bank earnings were also helped by reduced provisioning, as cyclical improvements in economic conditions during 2004, and the continued trend of strengthening corporate balance sheets contributed to a decline in provisions for loan losses from approximately 12 percent in 2001 to 5 percent of total revenue, its lowest level since the mid-1990s.

Bank balance sheets expanded at an increased pace in 2004, as asset growth benefited from robust real estate (15.4 percent) and consumer lending (10.1 percent). Low mortgage rates in 2004 and robust growth in the housing sector led to strong gains (15.8 percent) in residential mortgage lending. Much of the acceleration in residential mortgage lending resulted from growth in revolving home equity loans, which grew by 40 percent. After a prolonged period of tepid growth, commercial lending has also showed signs of increasing, growing at a moderate 4.4 percent rate in 2004. Although bank holdings of securities also grew rapidly (10.6 percent), they constitute a relatively small share of bank assets (22.3 percent). Bank equity capital also rose rapidly (by 23 percent), although much of this increase was attributable to several large mergers that boosted the value of goodwill (i.e., the excess of the cost of the acquired entity over the net of assumed assets and liabilities).[23] Credit quality also continued to improve as indicated by the rise in the ratio of reserves to delinquent loans to 85 percent, which is at the top end of the levels reported during the last decade (approximately 80–85 percent), even as the ratio of reserves to loans fell steadily by about one percentage point to its lowest level since the early 1990s (1.5 percent in 2004).

Among Japanese banks, the recent economic recovery and efforts to dispose of nonperforming loans (NPLs) have helped improve bank balance sheets further. The ratio of NPLs to total loans in all banks decreased to 4.0 percent at the end of March 2005, from its peak of 8.4 percent at the end of March 2002, and from 5.8 percent at the end of March 2004. This also reflects improvements in the corporate sector's balance sheets. Regional banks, however, have been slow to resolve the NPL problem, relative to major banks, particularly since the end of March 2002. The NPL ratio of regional banks was 5.5 percent at the end of March 2005; it has been reduced only moderately (by 2.5 percentage points) in this three-year period. In contrast, major banks reduced the NPL ratio drastically from 8.4 percent to 2.9 percent during the same period, and all of the major banks have met the government's target of halving NPL ratios.[24]

In addition to reducing the NPL ratios, Japanese banks have also reduced their stock holdings in recent years. Traditionally, Japanese banks, particularly the major banks, hold a significant amount of corporate stock on their asset side (i.e., stock market risk), largely for relationship purposes, which requires corresponding economic capital

[23]See Federal Reserve (2005).

[24]The government's target was to halve major banks' "aggregate" NPL ratio to approximately 4 percent by the end of March 2005.

to satisfy banking regulations. To improve their balance sheets, major banks have reduced their stock holdings to approximately 61 percent of Tier I capital at the end of March 2005, from 71 percent a year earlier from 99 percent at the end of March 2003, and from 133 percent at the end of March 2002.

Despite stronger balance sheets, Japanese banks have not improved their weak profitability. Most banks recorded net profits in fiscal year 2004, but some of them, including a couple of major banks, continue to suffer losses. To be sure, Japanese banks have increasingly focused on the relatively more profitable retail banking business, including housing loans, and fee income business, such as over-the-counter sales of investment trusts and annuity insurance. These fee-oriented businesses have been growing significantly in recent years.[25]

In the euro area, bank profitability improved significantly in 2004, in many countries surpassing records set in 2000. For the major banks, return on equity reached an average of 11 percent in 2004 (Figure 2.50), supported by a combination of factors:

- Loan loss provisions continued to decline, and represented an average of 0.12 percent of assets at the end of 2004. In some countries they were close to all-time lows. Accordingly, the scope for further declines in provisions appears limited. However, we believe provisions and possibly loan losses have reached cyclical lows, and may be expected to rise cyclically going forward.
- Bank revenue continued to benefit from the growth in household activity and, more recently, corporate borrowing. While only

[25]For example, the Bank of Japan estimates that noninterest income of major banks has grown steadily to approximately 37 percent of total income in fiscal year 2004, compared with 33 percent in 2003, 28 percent in 2002, and 25 percent in 2001. However, the major banks continue to depend significantly on the traditional lending business, compared with U.S. counterparts.

Figure 2.50. Selected Countries: Return on Equity[1]
(In percent)

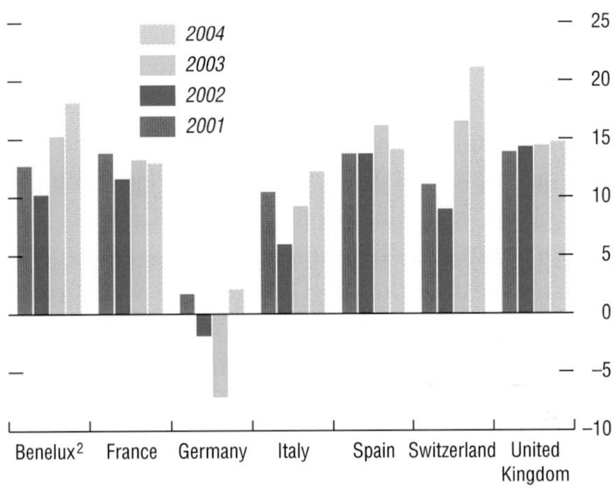

Source: ©2003 Bureau van Dijk Electronic Publishing-Bankscope.
[1]Return on average equity of five largest commercial banks.
[2]Composed of Belgium, Luxembourg, and the Netherlands.

about one-third of the current stock of mortgages is variable, the share of such mortgages has been increasing rapidly. At the same time, competition among lenders has narrowed lending margins and loan-to-value ratios have edged higher, reaching 100 percent or more in some countries. Bank income may be better protected against interest rate increases with adjustable rate loans, but banks face potential uncertainties with regard to collateral value and households' ability to service mortgage debt.

- Noninterest income, fees, and commissions also contributed to income growth. Some banks have moved to buffer volatile trading revenues with higher fees and commissions. A number of European banks have also developed prime brokerage activities.

Similar trends have been evident among banks in the United Kingdom. Mortgage loans have remained among the major sources of bank revenue. Lending to nonfinancial corporates has been more dynamic in the United Kingdom than in the euro area, growing 9.9 percent annually through the first quarter of 2005. However, among corporates, real estate companies now account for more than 50 percent of new lending and more than one-third of outstanding bank loans. In contrast, bank lending to the manufacturing sector was down 3.7 percent (year-on-year) in March 2005.

The situation of German banks improved during 2004, but it remains less favorable than that of other European banks. Operating profits and net income of private banks rose significantly, as did returns on equity. Increased opportunities for securitization, particularly as the True Sale cash securitization platform has now become operational, may prove helpful as banks continue to strengthen their balance sheets and improve profitability. Similarly, the introduction of real estate investment trusts (REITs) in Germany may help banks (and insurers) manage more actively their real estate exposure. In preparation for the removal of public guarantees, a reorganization of German landesbanks and savings banks appears to be under way.[26] However, German banks still need to improve their revenue base (as do banks elsewhere in Europe). Among European banks, those in the United Kingdom and Switzerland are the most profitable, with ROEs ranging from 14 percent to 25 percent in 2004.

Issuing activity in the covered bond market rose slightly in 2004, to an estimated volume of 211 billion euros across Europe. In several countries—including Belgium, Germany, and Italy—new or revised country-specific covered bond legislative frameworks were developed. As loan growth improves, one can anticipate greater volume in the covered bond and securitization markets.

Market and Credit Risk Indicators for the Mature Market Financial System

This issue of the GFSR continues to refine our use of market risk indicators (MRIs) and credit risk indicators (CRIs) to review mature market financial systems. In the April 2005 issue, the MRI Index methodology was adapted to capture institution-specific risks. Also, a new CRI Index was introduced, that measured the default probabilities associated with first-to-default baskets of credit default swaps (CDSs) on financial institutions. In addition, much focus has been placed on the differentiation of these indices by type of financial institution. In this regard, three main groups were identified; large complex financial institutions

[26]One example is the increasing vertical integration between the landesbank and the savings banks in Hesse Thuring, which has led to the adoption of a common risk management system and a mechanism for mutual support. Another innovative approach to reorganization is the cross-border alliance between Nord-Landesbank and the Norwegian bank, DnB NOR.

(LCFIs), commercial banks, and life insurance companies.[27]

In this issue, the CRI Index is modified to reflect the probability of multiple defaults. This approach may be superior to a focus on the likelihood of a single default, because understanding the potential for systemwide or multiple defaults (particularly of key institutions) is arguably more relevant from a financial stability policy perspective. Of course, the failure or severe distress of a single institution that plays a dominant role in the functioning of a market can also have systemic implications.

Also, in order to make the CRI more consistent between LCFIs and commercial banks, we made some adjustments to the list of commercial banks used in the CRI.

Market Risk Indicators

The following MRIs attempt to highlight the risks related to a set of particular institutions, and are based on the value at risk (VaR) of a portfolio of equities issued by these institutions.[28] In order to isolate the

[27]The definition of LCFIs is the same as that suggested in Hawkesby, Marsh, and Stevens (2005) and comprises ABN Amro, Bank of America, Barclays, BNP Paribas, Citigroup, Credit Suisse Group, Deutsche Bank, Goldman Sachs, HSBC Holdings, JP Morgan Chase & Co., Lehman Brothers, Merrill Lynch, Morgan Stanley, Société Générale, and UBS. The commercial banks captured in the MRI are Australia and New Zealand Banking Group, Banca Intesa, Banco Bilbao Vizcaya Argentaria, Bank of East Asia, Bank of Nova Scotia, CIBC, Commerzbank, Fortis Bank, HVB Group, ING Bank, KBC Bank, Misubishi Tokyo Financial, Mizuho Financial, National Australia Bank, Nordea, Royal Bank of Canada, Royal Bank of Scotland, SanPaolo IMI, Santander Hispano Group, Skandinaviska Enskilda Banken, Sumitomo Mitsui Financial, Svenska Handelsbanken, Toronto Dominion, UFJ Holdings, UniCredito, Wachovia, and Westpac Banking Corp. The CRI focuses on a smaller group of such banks for which CDS quotations are available.

[28]More specifically, our VaR measures the market capitalization–weighted potential loss over a 10-day period at the 95 percent confidence level. The variances and correlations used in the computations are, at each point in time, daily estimates over a 75-day rolling period, and are obtained using an exponential smoothing technique that gives more weight to the most recent observations.

Figure 2.51. VaR With and Without Market Effects (VaR-Beta) for the Full Portfolio of Financial Institutions
(In percent)

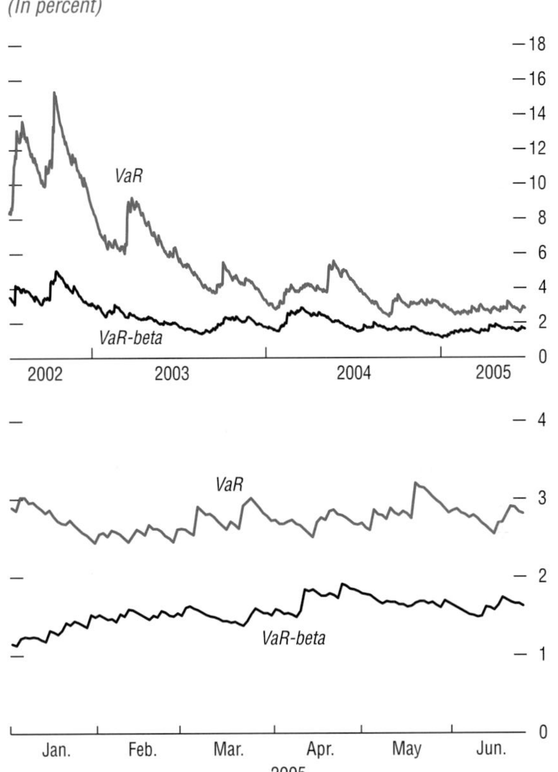

Sources: Bloomberg L.P.; and IMF staff estimates.

Figure 2.52. VaR-Betas for LCFIs Versus Commercial Banks
(In percent)

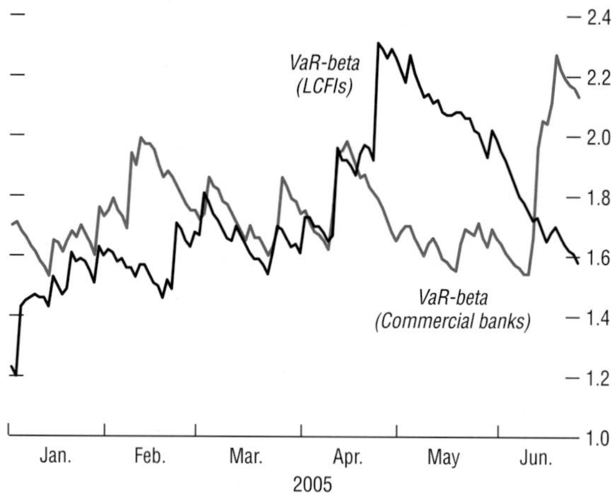

Sources: Bloomberg L.P.; and IMF staff estimates.
Note: LCFIs are large complex financial institutions.

Figure 2.53. Market Implied Correlation on CDX 5-Year Investment-Grade Tranches
(In percent)

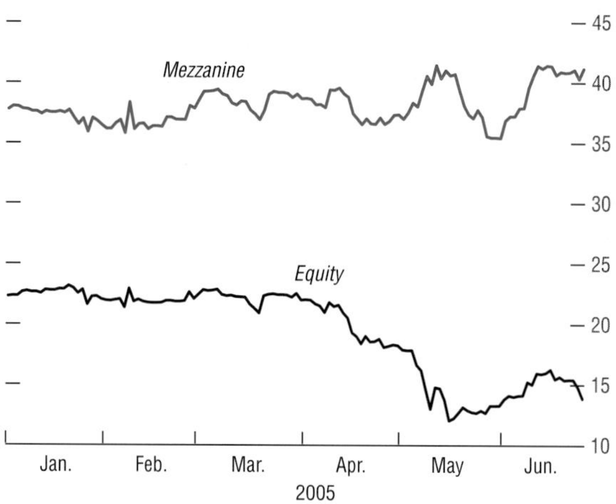

Source: JPMorgan Chase & Co.

risks to the specific institutions in question, a methodology suggested by Hawkesby, Marsh, and Stevens (2005) is used to filter their equity price changes to remove the effects of global and domestic equity market volatility (VaR-beta). During the first quarter of 2005, both VaR measures for the portfolio of financial institutions continued to fluctuate in fairly narrow bands (Figure 2.51), suggesting that there have not been any significant changes to the aggregate risk profile of these financial institutions.

The VaR-betas in Figure 2.52 isolate the VaR-betas of the LCFI and commercial bank groups. They show that there was a surge in the risk profile of the LCFI portfolio at the end of April, as its VaR-beta rose sharply. However, it gradually returned to pre-April levels by the end of June. The jump in the VaR-beta of the LCFIs corresponds to market reports that a number of the credit derivative dealers among the LCFIs experienced relatively material losses from engaging in complex arbitrage trades with single-tranche collateralized debt obligations (as had some of their counterparties). These losses stemmed from a reassessment of idiosyncratic risks in the markets for these instruments.

More specifically, there was a structural shift in the trends among the implied correlations and prices for CDO tranches on which market participants based their trading strategies (Figure 2.53).[29] Many insurance compa-

[29]The correlations referred to here are the correlations between the reference credits that underlie the CDO. As explained in Box 2.6, decreases in this correlation measure are associated with increases in equity tranche risk, and therefore spread widening (and price decreases). The specific details of this trade are discussed in Box 2.1, but the following will highlight the structural elements of the CDO market that underpin this transaction, and discusses structural changes that affected market dynamics. These changes in the correlation structure are an example of the risks and vulnerabilities associated with specialized capital arbitrage strategies driven largely by quantitative valuation models.

nies purchase the lower-risk senior and mezzanine tranches of CDOs for diversification and yield pickup, and generally employ a buy-and-hold strategy. Also, commercial banks and pension funds that participate in the CDO market tend to focus on the senior and super-senior tranches. By contrast, hedge funds and bank proprietary trading desks often purchase the higher-risk equity tranches, and employ trading and hedging strategies that depend on relatively stable price differentials (and correlations) between the different CDO tranches.[30]

In late April 2005, however, the implied correlations between equity and mezzanine tranches began to depart from their perceived historical patterns, in part because of selective spread widening attributable to increased idiosyncratic risks, such as arose in the auto sector (see earlier discussion on the downgrading of GM and Ford). Instead of declining, prices on mezzanine CDO tranches rose in late May and early June largely because of short-covering activity. A surprising source of liquidity and price support for the CDO equity market was other hedge funds, which had capital to employ and subsequently purchased the equity CDO tranches when prices dropped to attractive levels. Their actions helped prices to recover and limited losses during late May and early June, and this pattern is clearly evident in Figure 2.52, as the LCFI VaR-betas returned to pre-April levels.

There was a mid-June surge in the commercial bank VaR-beta following the aforementioned uncertainty over the direction of ECB interest rate policy (see Figure 2.52).

The VaR-betas for a portfolio of European life insurance companies, based on the prices of their outstanding equity securities, continued to fluctuate in a fairly tight range, suggesting that there have not been any significant changes to the aggregate risk profile of these insurance companies (Figure 2.54).[31] However, the VaR-betas of the U.S. insurers surged higher between late March and early April, largely as a result of the acknowledgment by the American International Group (AIG) of financial statement inaccuracies, and because of their much larger fixed-income and credit risk exposure compared with their European peers.[32] AIG's credit ratings have since been downgraded from "AAA" to "AA" by all the major rating agencies, with S&P and Fitch indicating that the firm's rating outlook remains negative. The VaR-betas of the U.S. insurers also spiked up on May 4 as the share price of MetLife surged on better-than-expected quarterly earnings.

It is noteworthy that the increase in this MRI was caused by rising share prices. One of the characteristics of these parametric VaR risk measures is that the risk metric increases with the volatility of the underlying assets, regardless of whether the volatility is associated with price increases or decreases. We will address this and other shortcomings as we continue to develop our risk indicators. However, as it stands now, our MRI analysis for this period highlights the increased volatility related to the auto sector downgrades, but does not point to any particular or sustained financial stability concerns at this time.

[30]As noted in Box 2.1, a popular transaction was to partially finance long positions in equity CDO tranches with short positions in mezzanine tranches, so that any price decline in the equity tranche would be offset so long as the correlation and relative price structure among CDO tranches remained stable. Similarly, many hedge funds partially hedged their equity CDO positions with positions in the underlying credit derivative indices and/or single-name CDSs, which was meant to protect against CDS spread widening, but not against shifts in correlations.

[31]The life insurance companies captured in the MRI were Aegon, AIG, Allianz Group, AXA, Friends Provident, Gruppo Generali, Hartford Financial Services Group, MetLife, Prudential Financial, Prudential PLC, Sampo, Skandia, and Swiss Life.

[32]Figure 2.54 also charts the VaR-betas for the portfolio of U.S. life insurers excluding AIG ("U.S. ex-AIG") to highlight the specific impact of AIG.

Figure 2.54. VaR-Betas for Portfolios of Life Insurance Companies
(In percent)

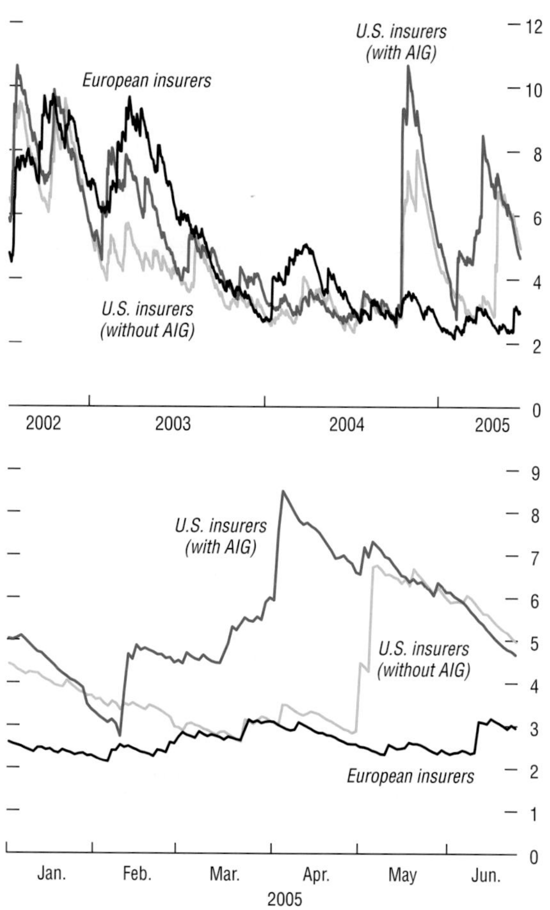

Sources: Bloomberg L.P.; and IMF staff estimates.

Credit Risk Indicators

The following CRIs attempt to measure the risk associated with the world's largest financial institutions, as implied by the market's pricing of credit default swaps. To capture potentially correlated defaults, the CRIs are based on a basket of CDSs referenced to the institutions in question. Since, from a systemic risk perspective, it is the potential for systemwide or multiple defaults that may be most relevant for financial stability considerations, the probability of more than one default in the basket will be the specific CRI metric evaluated.[33] In calculating the CRI, two important assumptions are made. First, risk-neutral default probabilities are imputed from five-year CDS quotes, assuming a 45 percent loss-given-default (LGD) rate. Second, the methodology is based on a "structural" model that requires inter-obligor equity correlations as an input. The impact of correlation assumptions on the CRI is discussed in Box 2.6.[34]

For both the LCFIs and commercial banks the probability of multiple defaults rose steadily from mid-March and surged higher in mid-May, as the market digested the auto company downgrades and the related volatility in the structured credit market (Figure 2.55).[35]

[33]In future issues of the GFSR, we will focus on the probability distributions of loss amounts, rather than on probabilities. This would recognize a size effect, in that the default of one large financial institution could be systemically more important than the simultaneous default of two smaller institutions.

[34]All of these assumptions will be reviewed in future issues of the GFSR. For example, rather than using risk-neutral probabilities, consideration will be given to using empirically based probabilities. Hull, Predescu, and White (2005) compare the two measures, and Vassalou and Xing (2004) show how default probabilities can be derived from equity prices. The equity correlations used in this issue are roughly based upon those estimated by Hawkesby, Marsh, and Stevens (2005), but we will base the correlations on our estimates in the forthcoming GFSR issues.

[35]The LCFIs referenced by the CDSs are the same institutions used in the MRIs, but a smaller sample of reference commercial bank obligors was selected for the CRIs. For purposes of comparing basket default

The increased LCFI default probability may have been exacerbated by the potential for losses on the aforementioned CDO equity tranche arbitrage trades.

Unfortunately, it is not possible to filter from this CRI the impact of general market factors as done for the MRIs. However, general credit risk levels, as measured by the par spread on the five-year CDX investment-grade index, moved roughly in unison with the multiple default probabilities among financial institutions (Figure 2.56).

CDS price data for individual insurance companies remains very limited, but as more data become available, we will expand our CRIs for the insurance sector. We hope this will produce some interesting financial stability analyses, as the pricing of CDSs referenced to insurance companies may reflect less or no perceived government support in the event of failures (compared with commercial banks and LCFIs). Also, many insurers are currently adjusting their investment portfolios and increasing their exposure to credit instruments.

Summary

Aside from some transitory volatility in the structured finance market related to the GM and Ford downgrades, neither the MRIs nor CRIs point to any particular fundamental financial stability concerns. However, the volatility and related price movements from the April–May CDO activity merits careful attention. Although the market is still relatively small, this particular episode did highlight generally the concentration of participants and the related potential liquidity concerns.

Figure 2.55. Probability of More Than One Default Among the Portfolios of Financial Institutions
(In percent)

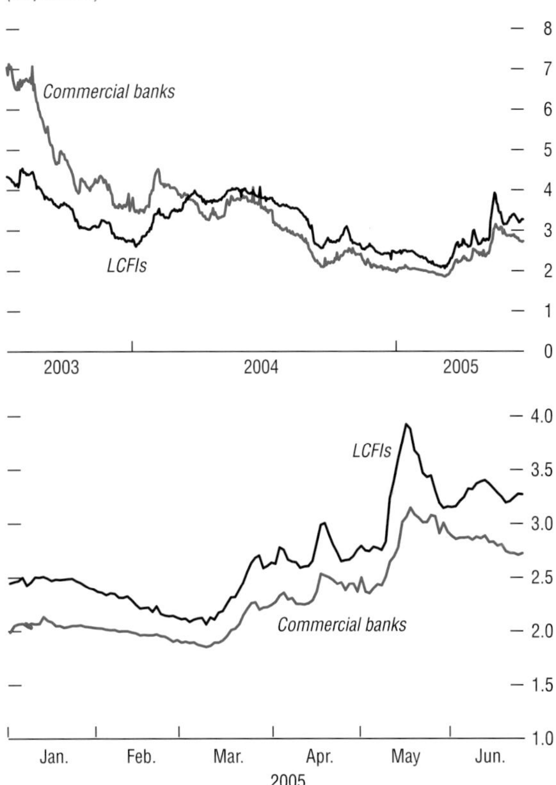

Sources: Bloomberg L.P.; and IMF staff estimates.
Note: LCFIs are large complex financial institutions.

---

probabilities, the number of banks in the commercial bank basket was set equal to the number selected for the LCFI basket. Hence, the following commercial banks were selected for the CRIs: Fortis Bank, Crédit Agricole, HVB Group, Commerzbank, Unicredito, SanPaolo IMI, Mizuho Financial, UFJ Holdings, Sumitomo Mitsui Financial, ING Bank, Skandinaviska Enskilda Banken, Royal Bank of Scotland, HBOS, Wachovia, and Santander Hispano Group.

Figure 2.56. Spread Levels on 5-Year CDX Investment-Grade Index
(In percent)

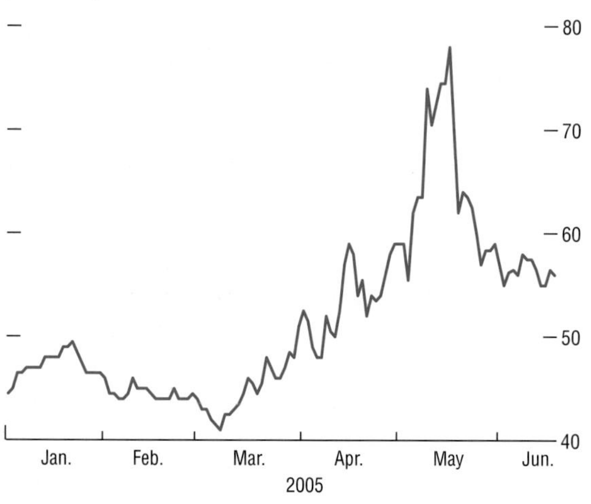

Source: JPMorgan Chase & Co.

More specifically, one concern is with respect to the "model risk" discussed in Fender and Kiff (2004), with most practitioner pricing and risk measurement models making fairly simplistic assumptions about the probability distributions of defaults. In addition, key inputs such as individual obligor default probabilities and correlations are open to debate. The Bank of England (2005) also points to delays in model recalibration, following the kind of input gaps seen in April–May, as potential destabilizers. They report that recalibration can take days or even weeks, during which time hedge positions may be ineffective.

Another concern is with respect to potential contagion, particularly liquidity-related issues surrounding hedge fund involvement in these activities. In the first instance, as participants (primarily hedge funds and dealer proprietary trading desks) attempt to adjust their hedges, often by purchasing protection on the underlying indices or CDS contracts, spreads widen out (or even overshoot fundamentals) in the particular indices or contracts. As spreads widen and liquidity dries up, participants may look for other asset classes, and possibly more liquid and relatively well-performing assets for liquidity (e.g., emerging market bonds) and thereby widen spreads in other areas. Moreover, as the losses associated with these trades become apparent to hedge fund investors, or are not reversed in subsequent months, redemption pressures may manifest themselves in further market volatility, as hedge funds are forced to liquidate positions. This did not materialize in the April–June period. However, the situation should be monitored with respect to potential September 2005 redemptions.[36]

[36]According to a recent Fitch Ratings report, hedge funds generally add liquidity to credit markets, but that the high-yield corporate sector (which may include emerging market bonds) could be vulnerable to a forced deleveraging of one or more large credit-oriented funds (Merritt and others, 2005).

Box 2.6. Impact of Correlation Assumptions on Multiple Default Probabilities and CDO Tranche-Specific Default Risk

The credit risk indicator (CRI) multiple default probability metric is based on a basket that consists of 15 equal-sized credit default positions. The probability of multiple defaults is a function of the individual reference obligor default probabilities and their potential correlation. Codependence in the CRIs is based on a Gaussian copula model that assumes that a single common factor (m) drives the correlation of defaults in the basket. The normalized asset values (x_i) are produced by the following formula:

$$x_i = \sqrt{a_i}\, m + \sqrt{1-a_i}\, z_i,$$

where x_i, m, and z_i are mean-zero, unit-variance normally distributed random variables, and a_i is the correlation of x_i with m. All of the m and z variables are assumed to be independently distributed, and m is constrained to be between zero and one. Default is assumed to occur when x_i is less than the negative of the distance to default which, in the context of the Gaussian copula model is equal to $N^{-1}\{q_i(t)\}$ where $N^{-1}\{\}$ is the inverse of the standard cumulative normal distribution and $q_i(t)$ is the risk-neutral probability of obligor i defaulting before t.[1]

We will use a simplified example to show what this means for our CRIs. It assumes that all 15 obligors have the same one-year risk-neutral default probability (i.e., $q = q_1 = q_2 = \ldots = q_{15} = 1$ percent) and all have the same correlations with each other ($a = a_1 = a_2 = \ldots = a_{15}$). The figure shows the default probability distributions for three scenarios that differ only by the inter-obligor asset correlations (a = 0, 50, and 100 percent). In broad terms, with these assumptions, the chart shows that the higher the correlation, the fatter the tail of the distribution. For example, the probability of there being more than 10 defaults is zero when the correlation is zero, 0.02 percent when it is 50 percent, and 1.00 percent when the obligors' assets are perfectly correlated. (In the last scenario, either none or all default.)

Hence, for our CRI metric, and for the trading and hedging of portfolios credit risk exposure, the correlation assumption is quite important. The assumption used in this issue, based on recent equity price correlations, was that the inter-LCFI correlations were a uniform 50 percent, and for the commercial banks 30 percent. The 50 percent inter-obligor correlation, in particular, may seem rather high, but both correlation assumptions are roughly con-

[1]For more detailed information on the implementation of the Gaussian copula model used here, see Gibson (2004).

Impact of Correlation Assumptions on Tranche Loss Probabilities[1]
(In percent)

	Correlation Assumption		
Tranche[2]	0%	50%	100%
Equity	13.03	5.75	1.00
Mezzanine	0.96	3.07	1.00
Senior	—	—	1.00

Source: IMF staff estimates.
[1]Calculations are based on a basket of 15 equally sized reference assets all with 1 percent probability of default.
[2]The equity tranche absorbs the first loss, while the senior tranche absorbs the last loss.

Probability of Multiple Defaults by Inter-obligor Asset Correlations
(In percent)

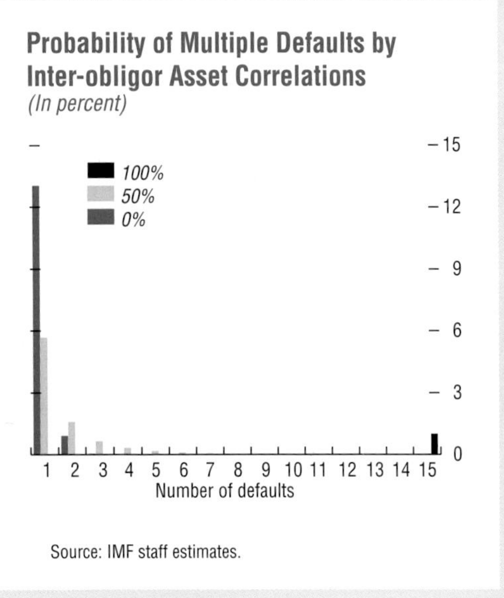

Source: IMF staff estimates.

Box 2.6 *(concluded)*

sistent with the findings reported in Hawkesby, Marsh, and Stevens (2005).

The correlation assumption is also important to the valuation and risk analysis of CDO and CDS index tranches. Essentially, such tranched products are derivatives on different parts of the loss distribution. For example, in the context of the 15 obligor CRI basket, an equity tranche might absorb the first loss, a senior tranche might absorb the fifteenth loss, and a mezzanine tranche might absorb the rest (the second to fourteenth). The table shows what the loss probabilities would be for the three tranches under the three aforementioned correlation assumptions. It is apparent that low correlations (i.e., more idiosyncratic risk) increase equity tranche default risk, and that high correlations increase senior tranche risk.[2]

[2]It is believed that the main participants in the market for equity and mezzanine tranches are the hedge funds and dealers, whereas the insurers and pension funds are more focused on the mezzanine and senior tranches. Banks are also buyers of senior and supersenior tranches.

In future issues of the GFSR, these MRIs and CRIs will continue to evolve, in terms of the measures themselves and their inputs. The question of threshold levels will also be addressed, since the ultimate purpose of these indicators is to serve as potential early warning signals of possible stresses on mature market financial institutions and markets more broadly.

Banking Sector Developments in Emerging Market Countries

Banking systems in emerging markets have generally maintained their trend improvement, although in several countries rapid credit growth is contributing to higher risk exposures (Table 2.4).[37] In Asia, the recovery in the financial positions of banks has largely continued, although not uniformly. In Latin America, while banks in previously distressed systems are showing stronger results, the recovery is not yet well entrenched and hinges on implementation of fundamental banking reforms. In emerging Europe, the drive for market share by foreign banks is fueling rapid credit growth in a number of countries, underscoring the need for closer supervisory oversight. In the Middle East, Central Asia, and Africa, longstanding structural weaknesses in some countries are being exacerbated by political uncertainties.

Asia

Performance indicators for the banking systems in the region are on an upward trend. An environment of low interest rates and growth in household credit have contributed to better bank earnings. Banks in countries with an overhang of nonperforming loans have to varying degrees increased provisioning and write-offs to strengthen their balance sheets, even in countries with weak economies. However, significant vulnerabilities persist in the banking systems in a number of countries faced with high levels of distressed assets, underprovisioned bad loans, and significant exposure to interest rate increases. The main risks in the region are rapid growth of household lending and market risk. Following the Asian financial crisis, banks in the region adopted a more cautious attitude toward corporate lending and shifted toward greater retail lending, residen-

[37]Classifications and definitions of various financial soundness indicators are not uniform across countries.

Table 2.4. Emerging Market Countries: Selected Bank Financial Soundness Indicators
(In percent)

	Return on Assets			Nonperforming Loans to Total Loans[1]			Regulatory Capital to Risk-Weighted Assets		
	2002	2003	2004[2]	2002	2003	2004[2]	2002	2003	2004[2]
Emerging Asia									
Mean	0.8	0.9	1.3	15.5	13.1	10.8	13.8	14.3	14.3
Median	0.8	1.1	1.2	15.8	13.4	11.9	13.2	13.8	13.8
Standard deviation	0.4	0.5	0.5	10.0	8.5	7.5	3.7	3.9	3.6
Emerging Europe									
Mean	0.9	1.5	1.5	9.8	8.7	7.6	19.1	18.7	17.5
Median	1.2	1.4	1.4	8.2	6.2	5.0	18.0	15.7	16.6
Standard deviation	2.5	1.1	1.1	6.7	8.0	7.8	6.6	7.0	6.5
Latin America									
Mean	−1.3	1.3	1.6	12.0	9.6	6.6	13.7	14.7	16.1
Median	1.1	1.3	1.6	9.0	7.8	5.2	14.4	14.2	14.5
Standard deviation	9.3	2.0	1.4	9.9	7.9	4.8	5.2	2.7	4.3
Middle East									
Mean	1.2	1.2	1.5	14.7	14.3	13.4	15.2	14.9	14.6
Median	0.8	1.2	1.3	16.1	14.0	11.3	15.7	14.8	14.2
Standard deviation	0.8	0.9	0.8	4.5	6.5	8.1	4.4	5.3	4.7
Sub-Saharan Africa									
Mean	2.1	3.1	3.1	16.9	14.6	13.3	17.7	16.6	16.9
Median	1.3	2.9	3.1	18.5	13.8	14.2	17.3	17.2	17.2
Standard deviation	2.1	1.7	1.5	7.4	7.8	6.3	4.2	4.2	3.6

Sources: National authorities; and IMF staff estimates.
[1]Refers to gross nonperforming loans.
[2]Latest available figures in 2004.

tial mortgage loans, credit cards, and other consumer lending. For most Asian countries, mortgage loans account for about 55–65 percent of household lending. While household loans have helped resuscitate banks' rates of return, the rapid growth, lack of bank experience in lending to this sector, and widespread gaps in information on borrowers' creditworthiness have raised concerns that risks are growing in some countries.

The authorities in the region are responding to the hard lessons of the past and have introduced various measures, including minimum eligibility criteria on credit card applications and tightening other regulations on debt limits. Many countries have also taken steps to accelerate the development of both public and private credit information bureaus. Gaps, however, remain with respect to bankruptcy laws and creditor protection.

A number of Asian banking systems have a significant exposure to higher interest rates arising from large government securities holdings and other long-dated assets. These risks are mitigated for some of these countries, where strong capital inflows and upside pressures on exchange rates limit the risk of higher interest rates or where securities held are predominantly with floating rates.

Regulators in the region are at varying stages in implementing plans regarding Basel II. The more sophisticated financial systems in the region seem most prepared to apply the advanced Basel II approaches in accordance with the Basel Committee timetable. Most other countries in the region will likely implement Basel II in a phased manner, moving first to the less complex standardized approach, typically in 2007–08.

Emerging Europe

Solid economic growth in most of emerging Europe has contributed to increased bank profits and falling NPLs. While macropolicies have, for the most part, been supportive of financial sector stability, credit growth in many countries in the region has continued to be very rapid. Although the credit-to-GDP ratios in these countries are below industrial country norms, so that the growth often reflects financial deepening, overly rapid growth on a sustained basis could ultimately lead to credit quality problems.

In some countries in the region, the trend toward increased foreign currency lending is continuing, especially for unhedged consumer loans and mortgage loans. This reflects relatively high interest rates on domestic currency loans and the ready availability of foreign currency funding from the parent institutions of foreign-owned banks in some cases. A few countries have considered supervisory actions to ensure that banks are adequately assessing and pricing the inherent risks of foreign currency lending and are provisioning appropriately. The emphasis, however, generally has been on dampening demand by enhancing consumer awareness of the risks, with only limited success.

The structure of the financial system is becoming skewed toward foreign banks, with the expansion of some Western European banking groups in central and southeastern Europe. Currently, close to 70 percent of banking assets in the region are controlled by foreign-based (mostly EU-15) banks.

Emerging European countries have made substantial progress in strengthening supervisory frameworks, especially by implementing EU directives. Significant gaps nevertheless remain in many countries, reflecting the still underdeveloped nature of the nonbank component of many financial systems. Supervision in the region also generally needs to be more risk based and supervisory expertise and staffing need to be strengthened in many cases.

Western Hemisphere

Banking systems continue to benefit from improved economic performance. With the exception of countries emerging from financial crises or affected by political turbulence, overall financial institutions have performed well in recent months, recording in most cases stable, or improving, indicators of bank soundness, such as capital adequacy, asset quality, and profitability. Market indicators also suggest a strengthening of banks' financial position and confidence. These trends are evident in most of the larger economies of Latin America.

Buoyant consumer demand in much of the region is leading to strong growth in lending to the household sector. In the region, this line of business has been developing from a very low base, and growth in consumer credit has been rather strong—in some cases, more than 40 percent in the year to March 2005. Experience in other countries suggest the need for some caution regarding the adequacy of risk assessment processes in systems undergoing such rapid expansion in new forms of lending.

While the countries most affected by major financial crises have seen a rebound in intermediation and bank soundness, the systems in these countries remain vulnerable and restoring both soundness and functionality will take more time. Political factors have also recently complicated the financial landscape in a number of countries in the region and highlighted vulnerabilities in banks that are still bearing the costs of the previous crisis.

The overall positive bank performance in the region is cushioning the effects of tightened prudential requirements as part of the authorities' effort to bring financial sector oversight in line with international standards (including the phased introduction of Basel II requirements).

Middle East and Central Asia

The banking systems of the Middle East and Central Asia region have on the whole strengthened, although it shows considerable differences across countries. In the member countries of the Commonwealth of Independent States (CIS) in Central Asia and the Caucasus, banking sectors remain small and underdeveloped but financial intermediation is deepening, in some cases very rapidly. The banking sector in the Maghreb countries are more developed overall but, in several cases, are weighed down by state-owned institutions that play quasi-fiscal roles, suffer from weak asset quality, and retain large market shares. In the petroleum-exporting countries of the Gulf Cooperation Council (GCC), high oil prices have supported strong economic activity and asset prices, although the extent to which booming stock and real estate markets are being fueled by bank credit is not clear. Financial soundness indicators are also fairly robust across the region, in most cases pointing to constant or improving asset quality and capitalization. Profitability is particularly strong in the GCC countries, where banks hold relatively large proportions of noninterest-bearing deposits because of the cultural preferences of many customers. In some GCC countries, noninterest income (e.g., from brokerage fees) has also been strong. Islamic banking has also played a significant role in several GCC countries.

Rapid and accelerating credit growth requires careful monitoring in a number of countries in the region. The expansion of private sector credit has been most bullish in the CIS area, followed by the GCC countries. In many cases, this is concentrated in consumer lending or other areas where banks are relatively inexperienced; in many countries, consumer loans are secured on the basis of salaries; this practice mitigates risks. Although in most instances banks' direct exposures to the stock and real estate markets remain limited, growing loan volumes could stretch risk management capacities. Supervisors in the region need to be alert to any dilution of credit quality.

Africa

The performance of the banking systems in sub-Saharan Africa is improving in the context of a favorable macroeconomic environment and, in particular, loan quality seems to be improving in many countries. However, data deficiencies continue to impede an accurate assessment of developments in the financial systems in the region. Moreover, the macroenvironment is susceptible to large external shocks, emanating from lingering conflicts in the region, uncertainties in donor flows, dependence of many countries on agriculture and/or minerals, and related vulnerability to droughts and commodity price shocks. Banks also have large exposures to governments. While large holdings of government securities make banks appear liquid, in reality liquidity is hampered by the absence of secondary markets for the government securities and the shallow money markets.

At a structural level, the contribution of the banking system to economic development remains limited. Banks often have large surplus liquidity, but financial intermediation and access to financial services is low because of structural impediments. Lending to the private sector is constrained by a range of factors including a poor credit culture, weaknesses in enforcement of creditor rights, lack of suitable collateral, the absence of a sufficiently diversified range of products, and deficiencies in the credit information systems. Although there has been progress in reforming the banking systems in sub-Saharan Africa, the remaining agenda is substantial. Policy priorities include (1) improvements in the judicial and other mechanisms for enforcing contracts; (2) sustaining reforms in the legal, regulatory, and supervisory framework for banks; and (3) developing exit strategies for weak banks and timely responses to bank restructuring.

Rapid Credit Growth

As noted in the preceding regional reviews, a number of countries around the world are experiencing rapid growth in credit to the

Table 2.5. Countries with High Credit Growth in 2004 by Region: Financial Soundness Indicators[1]
(In percent)

	Growth in Credit to Private Sector[2,3]			Three-Year Average Credit Growth	Private Sector Credit to GDP[3]			Three-Year Average Credit to GDP	Regulatory Capital to Risk-Weighted Assets[3]			Nonperforming Loans to Gross Loans[3]			Return on Assets[3]		
	2002	2003	2004		2002	2003	2004		2002	2003	2004[4]	2002	2003	2004[4]	2002	2003	2004[4]
Emerging Asia	7.3	7.0	11.8	8.7	77.5	78.1	77.1	77.6	13.8	14.3	14.3	15.5	13.1	10.8	0.8	0.9	1.3
India	21.5	9.7	30.0	20.4	33.5	32.9	38.3	34.9	11.9	12.9	13.4	10.4	8.8	6.6	0.8	1.0	1.2
Indonesia	17.9	21.1	26.2	21.7	18.9	20.9	23.4	21.0	20.1	22.3	20.9	22.1	17.9	13.4	1.4	1.6	2.5
Bangladesh	16.7	9.3	17.0	14.3	27.2	26.8	28.2	27.4	7.5	8.4	8.7	28.0	22.1	17.6	0.5	0.5	0.7
China*	17.2	20.8	11.2	16.4	135.8	147.1	140.5	141.1	3.8	4.3	3.9	26.0	20.4	15.6	0.1	. . .	. . .
Emerging Europe[5]	24.5	30.4	28.0	27.7	32.1	34.7	38.1	34.9	19.1	18.7	17.5	9.8	8.7	7.6	0.9	1.5	1.5
Belarus	68.8	81.2	60.7	70.2	9.1	11.7	14.0	11.6	24.2	26.0	25.2	10.8	6.2	4.6	1.0	1.5	1.4
Turkey	10.2	44.6	52.8	35.8	13.9	15.5	20.0	16.5	25.1	30.9	28.8	17.6	11.5	6.0	1.1	2.3	2.5
Latvia	36.9	45.3	50.0	44.1	26.5	34.6	45.4	35.5	13.1	11.7	11.7	2.0	1.4	1.1	1.5	1.4	1.7
Bulgaria	42.4	48.8	49.1	46.8	19.6	27.4	36.7	27.9	25.2	22.4	16.6	8.6	7.3	7.1	2.1	2.4	2.1
Russia	36.0	46.6	46.7	43.1	18.7	22.4	26.0	22.4	19.1	19.1	17.0	5.6	5.0	3.8	2.6	2.6	2.9
Western Europe	5.5	7.3	9.0	7.3	133.7	137.2	141.1	137.3	12.0	12.9	12.8	2.5	2.3	2.1	0.7	0.8	1.0
Ireland	8.7	13.7	24.1	15.5	136.9	147.8	169.4	151.4	12.3	13.9	12.6	1.0	0.9	0.8	1.0	0.9	. . .
Spain	11.6	15.2	18.0	14.9	113.7	122.9	135.2	124.0	12.5	12.5	11.6	1.1	1.0	0.8	0.9	0.9	1.0
Greece	14.7	16.2	17.2	16.0	68.7	73.6	80.2	74.2	10.5	12.0	11.9	7.3	7.0	7.1	0.5	0.6	0.8
United Kingdom	8.2	9.8	11.3	9.7	141.7	147.5	155.8	148.4	12.2	12.4	12.3	2.6	2.5	2.2	0.9	0.6	0.8
Finland	7.6	12.4	10.7	10.2	60.0	66.0	70.0	65.3	11.7	18.9	19.1	0.5	0.4	0.4	0.5	0.7	1.0
Latin America	8.2	5.0	14.0	9.1	33.8	31.5	31.0	32.1	13.7	14.7	16.1	12.0	9.6	6.6	–1.3	1.3	1.6
Venezuela	0.9	10.5	98.8	36.7	9.6	8.5	11.3	9.8	15.9	14.3	12.5	9.2	7.7	2.8	5.3	6.2	5.9
Ecuador*	–12.1	4.8	22.9	5.2	21.2	19.8	22.2	21.1	10.3	10.2	9.9	8.4	7.9	6.4	1.5	1.5	1.6
Argentina*	–26.1	–13.2	22.9	–4.3	15.1	10.6	10.3	12.0	13.9	11.7	11.2	38.6	33.6	18.6	–8.9	–2.9	–0.5
Paraguay	0.3	–25.4	15.4	–3.2	21.2	13.0	13.9	16.0	17.9	20.9	20.5	19.7	20.6	10.8	1.0	0.4	1.7
Chile	9.9	5.4	14.7	10.0	62.9	61.7	61.8	62.1	14.0	14.1	13.6	1.8	1.6	1.2	1.1	1.3	1.2
Middle East and Central Asia	16.8	19.2	26.3	20.8	35.1	36.0	37.6	36.2	18.7	18.7	17.5	14.7	14.7	13.5	1.5	1.5	1.7
of which:																	
Central Asia	26.9	38.5	48.6	38.0	10.3	13.4	16.9	13.5	. . .	. . .	. . .	. . .	. . .	. . .	. . .	. . .	. . .
Kyrgyz Republic	11.4	27.9	67.4	35.6	4.1	4.8	7.2	5.4	36.4	35.3	27.7	13.3	11.2	8.0	1.1	1.3	2.0
Azerbaijan	25.2	41.6	61.8	42.9	5.5	6.7	9.1	7.1	. . .	14.7	20.9	. . .	15.1	9.5	1.5	1.8	1.9
Kazakhstan	35.5	44.6	53.8	44.6	18.5	21.9	28.0	22.8	17.2	16.9	15.9	18.3	25.9	29.9	2.0	2.0	1.4
Armenia	1.8	3.9	40.7	15.5	6.9	6.0	7.2	6.7	30.5	33.8	32.3	12.5	9.9	7.2	3.9	2.7	3.2
Saudi Arabia	10.0	11.0	37.4	19.5	29.1	28.4	33.7	30.4	18.7	19.4	18.0	9.2	5.4	3.1	2.3	2.3	2.5
Sub-Saharan Africa**	26.8	38.6	22.1	29.2	14.1	15.2	14.7	14.7	17.7	16.6	16.9	16.9	14.6	13.3	2.1	3.1	3.1
Zimbabwe	189.9	621.5	135.3	315.6	17.3	38.4	20.4	25.4	30.6	16.2	. . .	4.2	4.7	. . .	4.0	6.7	. . .
Angola	221.5	135.6	59.5	138.9	4.8	5.2	5.3	5.1	20.1	18.1	20.5	10.4	9.0	13.3	0.7	4.7	3.6
Zambia	6.2	40.5	51.9	32.8	5.9	6.6	7.9	6.8	28.0	23.7	22.2	11.4	5.3	7.6	—	3.8	2.1
Sudan*	76.4	56.7	50.6	61.3	4.4	6.0	7.7	6.0	9.0	9.9	10.8	12.7	11.4	10.2	1.1	1.5	3.5
Sierra Leone	53.3	80.8	45.9	60.0	2.6	3.9	4.6	3.7	48.4	39.8	37.1	17.1	9.9	14.3	10.4	10.7	8.4

Sources: IMF, *International Financial Statistics* and *World Economic Outlook.*
[1]The table reports the top five countries with highest nominal credit growth in 2004 from each region.
[2]Nominal growth.
[3]Simple average for the regional averages.
[4]Latest available in 2004.
[5]Credit in Emerging Europe is growing rapidly also in Estonia, Lithuania, Romania, and Ukraine.
*Not risk-weighed capital ratio. For China, the indicators refer to state-owned commercial banks.
**The credit growth figures for Zimbabwe and Angola reflect high inflation.

private sector (Table 2.5).[38] Many countries in emerging Europe and Central Asia experienced credit growth of around 50 percent—Azerbaijan, Belarus, Bulgaria, Kazakhstan, Kyrgyz Republic, Latvia, Russia, and Turkey. In the Western Hemisphere, credit growth was especially strong in Ecuador and Venezuela,

[38]Table 2.1 presents countries with the highest growth rates in private sector credit in 2004 in each region.

and robust credit expansion was observed in 2004 in India and Indonesia. In Africa, credit expanded by about 50 percent in several countries.

The fast expansion in credit is taking place against the backdrop of relatively shallow financial markets in some regions. In Central Asia, average credit to GDP almost doubled over the last three years, but remains relatively low at about 17 percent. In many countries in emerging Europe, the level of financial deepening is also still quite low, especially relative to EU levels. The rate of growth of credit in some African countries has been high, but the change relative to GDP has not been very large because the base is low.

In a number of countries in emerging Europe, foreign currency lending to unhedged borrowers remains substantial, and foreign banks have also played a role in rapid growth in domestic credit. Bank of International Settlements data suggest that in some countries this has taken the form of local currency lending by subsidiaries of foreign banks, which accelerated sharply in 2004. Overall, the shift to local currency lending could lessen the risk to emerging market corporate borrowers. However, to the extent that credit expansion is funded by short-term bank borrowing from abroad, it is exposing the banking system to the risk of sudden withdrawal of such funding.

Rapid credit growth may be part of a structural process of re-intermediation, but it may also be caused by temporary factors or overshooting. The eventual reversal of these factors may release inflationary pressures, or reveal a deterioration in credit quality. Concern over rapid credit growth is heightened in cases where it is accompanied by exuberance in real estate markets, and is taking place in the context of macroeconomic imbalances and balance sheet weaknesses. Maintenance of bank soundness may lead supervisors in many of these countries experiencing rapid credit growth to tighten prudential measures even before there is evidence of deteriorating credit quality. Increasing disclosure requirements, implementing more frequent inspections, and periodic stress testing can improve supervisors' ability to evaluate the risks in the financial system. Addressing information-based distortions by providing better information on borrowers' creditworthiness, banks' counterparty exposure, household and corporate indebtedness, trends in asset prices, cross-linkages between financial institutions, and so on, may also influence banks' risk-taking behavior. Banks' willingness to take on additional risk can be constrained by tightening rules on credit concentration and loan classification, by strengthening provisioning and collateral requirements, and by raising or imposing differential capital requirements based on the risk profile of individual banks.

Policies need to be aimed at maintaining credit quality, regardless of the aggregate credit level. Prudential instruments such as strengthening financial sector surveillance, tightening prudential regulations, and increasing transparency and information flows are best suited to achieve this objective. When both macroeconomic and prudential considerations are relevant, the policy response should address both objectives with an appropriate package of macroeconomic and prudential measures.

References

Bank of England, 2005, *Financial Stability Review* (London, June).

Bernanke, Ben S., 2005, "The Global Savings Glut and the U.S. Current Account Deficit," Sandridge Lecture delivered at Virginia Association of Economics, Richmond, Virginia, March 10.

Cassard, Marcel, and Thomas Mayer, 2005, "The Global Real Interest Rate Cycle and Current Account Imbalances," *Global Markets Research* (Deutsche Bank, March 31).

Federal Reserve, 2005, "Profits and Balance Sheet Developments at U.S. Commercial Banks in 2004," *Federal Reserve Bulletin,* Spring, pp. 43–174.

Fender, Ingo, and John Kiff, 2004, "CDO Rating Methodology: Some Thoughts on Model Risk and Its Implications," Bank for International Settlements (BIS) Working Paper No. 163 (Basel, Switzerland: BIS, November).

Gibson, Michael S., 2004, "Understanding the Risk of Synthetic CDOs," Finance and Economics Discussion Paper No. 36 (Washington: Federal Reserve Board, May).

Hawkesby, Christian, Ian Marsh, and Ibrahim Stevens, 2005, "Comovements in the Prices of Securities Issued by Large Complex Financial Institutions," Bank of England Working Paper No. 256 (London).

Hooper, Peter, and Mehmet Beceren, 2005, "Estimated Growth Yield Gap Based on Stable Inflation" and "A Historical Perspective: Are Long-Term Yields Unusually Low" (Deutsche Bank, March 31).

Hull, John, Mirela Predescu, and Alan White, 2005, "Bond Prices, Default Probabilities, and Risk Premiums," *Journal of Credit Risk,* Vol. 1, No. 2, pp. 53–60.

Kennickell, Arthur, 2003, "A Rolling Tide: Changes in the Distribution of Wealth in the U.S.," Federal Reserve Occasional Staff Study (Washington, September).

Loeys, Jan, David Mackie, Paul Meggyesi, and Nikolaos Panigirtzoglou, 2005, "Corporates Are Driving the Global Savings Glut" (JP Morgan, June 24).

International Monetary Fund, 2004, *Global Financial Stability Report,* World Economic and Financial Surveys (Washington, April).

———, 2005a, "Issuing Global Bonds in Local Currencies: Toward the Absolution of Original Sin?" in *Global Financial Stability Report,* World Economic and Financial Surveys (Washington, April).

———, 2005b, *World Economic Outlook,* World Economic and Financial Surveys (Washington, April).

Merritt, Roger W., Ian Linnell, Robert Grossman, and John Schiavetta, 2005, "Hedge Funds: An Emerging Force in the Global Credit Markets," *Fitch Ratings Credit Policy Special Report* (July 18).

U.K. Office of National Statistics, 2005, "First Release: Mergers and Acquisitions Involving U.K. Companies" (London: U.K. Office of National Statistics, May).

Vassalou, Maria, and Yuhang Xing, 2004, "Default Risk in Equity Returns," *The Journal of Finance,* Vol 59, No. 2, pp. 831–68.

PTER III ASPECTS OF GLOBAL ASSET ALLOCATION

The factors that determine changes in asset allocation and, hence, capital flows across national borders and sectors have important implications for the conduct of surveillance of global financial markets. The fast growing importance of institutional investors, mostly in mature markets but increasingly in a number of emerging market economies, has two major consequences that are closely interrelated. On the one hand, these nonbank asset gatherers assume sizable market and credit risks, not the least through modern financial engineering, in the form of swaps, derivatives, and so on. Previous issues of the *Global Financial Stability Report* (GFSR) have examined the driving forces behind that development, potential vulnerabilities, and policies that could mitigate adverse consequences. On the other hand, institutional investors are not only exposed to market and credit risks emanating from financial markets, but their investment decisions increasingly "make markets."

For the purposes of multilateral surveillance, specifically to spot vulnerabilities and potential fault lines at an early stage, it is critical to anticipate and analyze significant trends in the investment pattern of such large institutional investors. While such analysis must be very concrete—and, indeed, Chapter II of the recent issues of the GFSR has increasingly tried to capture the near-term impact of such trends—institutional investors are not a homogenous group. Their investment strategies follow different patterns for a number of reasons: not only are their internal procedures quite diverse, but they also generate capital flows across markets and asset classes. This has important implications for market regulation and related policies, such as the solvency requirement, investment restrictions, consumer protection, and financial stability issues more generally.

This chapter reviews a selection of issues, by no means a comprehensive listing, which directly affect global asset allocation and ultimately the corresponding capital flows. We employ four modules to assess how market discipline, regulation, and financial surveillance procedures may need to adapt to the growing importance and diversity of institutional investors.

Module 1 examines how different institutional investors follow vastly different procedures when allocating assets, reflecting various time horizons, liability structures, and "cultural backgrounds." For example, when it comes to the purchase of emerging market bonds by international investors, it is important to be able to differentiate between an extensive investment process by a strategic investor with a long-term time horizon and a tactical investment by a "cross-over investor" looking for short-term gains. This module aims to provide some insight into the decision-making process of investors. Understanding the basis for investor decisions is useful when analyzing their asset allocation decisions and related capital flows across borders and asset classes. The increasing dominance of strategic asset allocations, driven more by long-term economic fundamentals, is an important development that should make some asset classes, such as emerging market debt, less prone to "boom and bust cycles."

In addition, as Module 2 shows, traditional distinctions between different types of investment funds have begun to blur, and a wider range of investors has gained access to investment vehicles that combine traditional asset classes and financial instruments using complex strategies. Such developments may also pose new challenges for supervisors and regulators, who may have to adjust their traditional focus. It is important for multilateral surveillance to not only monitor the asset allocation by a given institutional investor but also, increasingly, the movements "across families of funds" (not just traditional mutual funds) triggered by the household sector and also by other institutional investors ("fund of fund strategies").

Given the institutional investors' search for uncorrelated asset classes and the need for investors in areas with chronically slow growth for higher returns elsewhere, the issue of "home bias" has become highly relevant, as illustrated in Module 3. The implications for capital flows are self-evident. What is less known, however, is the degree to which, over the past 15 years, deregulation and the spread of modern portfolio management practices have contributed to a substantial decline in home bias among institutional investors throughout mature economies, particularly with regard to equities. The emergence of highly globalized corporations in a number of medium-sized and smaller countries has de facto led to a decoupling of the national equity index from developments in the national economy.

Finally, Module 4 discusses the implications for financial stability of proposals and potential changes in accounting policy. It addresses the powerful influences of accounting and financial reporting standards on market behavior and asset allocation. It asks whether some accounting policies may act to limit the financial stability gains of recent years that stem from the dispersion of financial risks by reducing the diversity of market behavior across different types of institutional investors.

Module 1. Global Asset Allocation

This module sheds some light on how institutional investors decide to allocate their assets and how this decision has the potential to affect financial stability. At the center of this process are large institutional investors, mostly nonbanks, in particular, pension funds, insurance companies, mutual funds, and, increasingly, hedge funds.[1]

This module outlines how different institutional investors follow vastly different procedures when allocating assets, reflecting different time horizons, liability structures, and "cultural backgrounds." Understanding the decision-making process of investors is useful when analyzing the type of capital flows across borders and asset classes. Clearly, both the quantity and the quality of cross-border capital flows are important considerations in assessing financial stability.

Global Asset Allocators

Institutions

This section focuses on the institutions at the center of the international financial system that manage total financial assets exceeding $45 trillion (i.e., 150 percent of OECD countries' GDP). These include institutional investors in all OECD countries—such as pension funds (public and private, occupational, and personal), insurance companies (life and nonlife, and reinsurance), foundations and endowments, and banks and investment banks—and providers of investment vehicles (including mutual funds and hedge funds). The assets under management of these institutions have almost tripled since the early 1990s, with investment companies' assets under management increasing by more than five times from 1990 to 2003 (Table 3.1).

Hedge funds have become an increasingly important investor group, with global assets

[1]The discussion in this module does not include the household sector's direct investment in a particular stock or bond. Indirectly, the household sector is behind much of the holdings of institutional investors and, as such, bears the ultimate financial risk (see IMF, 2005a). However, even in the case of mutual funds, which can also be viewed as an investment vehicle, many investment decisions still rest with the portfolio managers within the broad mandate of the funds rather than with the household sector. In particular, in the case of mutual funds with a global mandate, portfolio managers are expected to allocate funds across countries and to constantly review their exposures.

Table 3.1. Assets Under Management by Institutional Investors

	1990	1995	2000	2001	2002	2003	2004
			(In trillions of U.S. dollars)				
Institutional investors	**13.8**	**23.5**	**39.0**	**39.4**	**36.2**	**46.8**	. . .
Insurance companies	4.9	9.1	10.1	11.5	10.2	13.5	14.5
Pension funds	3.8	6.7	13.5	12.7	11.4	15.0	15.3
Investment companies[1]	2.6	5.5	11.9	11.7	11.3	14.0	16.2
Hedge funds	0.03	0.10	0.41	0.56	0.59	0.80	0.93
Other institutional investors	2.4	2.2	3.1	3.0	2.7	3.4	. . .
			(In percent of GDP)[2]				
Institutional investors	**77.6**	**97.8**	**152.1**	**155.3**	**136.4**	**157.2**	. . .
Insurance companies	27.8	37.8	39.4	45.3	38.4	45.4	44.0
Pension funds	21.2	27.8	52.6	50.1	42.9	50.4	46.4
Investment companies[1]	14.8	22.7	46.3	45.9	42.7	47.2	49.0
Hedge funds	0.1	0.4	1.6	2.2	2.2	2.7	2.8
Other institutional investors	13.6	9.1	12.3	11.7	10.1	11.5	. . .

Sources: International Financial Services, London; OECD; and IMF staff estimates.

Note: The data may reflect some double-counting of assets, such as those owned by defined contribution pension funds and managed by investment companies.

[1]Investment companies include closed-end and managed investment companies, mutual funds, and unit investment trusts.

[2]Total GDP of OECD countries.

under management almost doubling since 2000, to about $1 trillion in 2004. Globally, the assets of institutional investors are generally evenly distributed among the main institutional investor classes (insurance companies, pension funds, and investment companies/mutual funds). This is also the case in the United States, but significant differences exist across other countries (Table 3.2). Insurance companies have a dominant role in Japan, Germany, and the United Kingdom (with pension funds also important in the United Kingdom), while investment companies are key asset gatherers in France and Italy, and pension funds are the main institutional investor class in the Netherlands.

The asset allocation decisions of these institutions have important implications for capital flows and asset prices across asset classes and national borders. Going forward, the size and influence of these institutions can be expected to grow, particularly as some of these institutions are still in their infancy in many countries.[2] Demographic trends and pension reforms will likely reinforce the creation of more and larger asset gatherers. Relatively small changes in the portfolios of such institutions may increasingly affect global financial markets. Unlike financial markets dominated by banks, capital markets tend to transmit changes in risk appetite, credit assessments, or perceived economic fundamentals more broadly, much faster, and more directly. This is particularly relevant for small or narrow asset classes, such as emerging market external bond markets, which total about $265 billion. This is no more than about 0.5 percent of the aforementioned $45 trillion assets under management of institutional investors in mature economies.

Current Asset Allocations

Traditionally, many investors allocated assets primarily between equities and bonds, with some degree of geographical mix, and typically having a fairly strong home bias (Figures 3.1 and 3.2):

- Pension funds have traditionally invested significantly in equities (see IMF, 2004b). Even today, the average share of equities in their

[2]See, for example, European Commission (2005).

Table 3.2. Major Industrial Countries: Assets of Institutional Investors
(In billions of U.S. dollars)

	1990	1995	2000	2001	2002	2003	2004
United States							
Insurance companies	1,884.9	2,803.9	3,997.7	4,084.5	4,264.8	4,832.9	5,310.0
Life insurance	1,351.4	2,063.6	3,135.7	3,224.6	3,335.0	3,772.8	4,132.6
Nonlife insurance	533.5	740.3	862.0	859.9	929.8	1,060.1	1,177.4
Pension funds	2,427.3	4,196.9	6,479.3	5,881.4	5,036.6	5,994.2	6,545.3
Investment companies[1]	1,154.6	2,731.5	6,454.9	6,598.7	6,115.0	7,025.6	7,787.8
Japan							
Insurance companies	1,503.5	2,625.6	2,474.6	2,293.5	2,530.4	2,968.7	2,972.8
Life insurance	1,205.3	2,226.6	2,172.6	2,025.9	2,244.7	2,604.0	2,618.6
Nonlife insurance	298.2	399.0	302.0	267.6	285.7	364.7	354.2
Pension funds	371.4	705.6	748.7	696.6	705.9	928.2	872.1
Investment companies[1]	331.7	411.7	462.6	362.3	366.7	493.4	565.5
United Kingdom							
Insurance companies	472.3	838.0	1,475.7	1,420.1	1,492.5	1,736.2	. . .
Life insurance	387.7	715.9	1,334.2	1,271.4	1,313.4	1,550.3	. . .
Nonlife insurance	84.7	122.1	141.5	148.7	179.1	185.8	. . .
Pension funds	532.5	756.4	1,096.0	989.8	936.7	1,190.9	1,464.0
Investment companies[1]	124.4	238.0	441.0	393.2	384.3	547.3	492.7
Germany[2]							
Insurance companies[3]	400.2	566.8	739.1	741.4	783.3	1,009.4	. . .
Pension funds	150.9	314.5	326.6	324.9	341.4	462.4	. . .
Investment companies[1]	188.9	369.5	773.9	711.4	799.1	1,062.9	1,184.1
France							
Insurance companies and pension funds	. . .	642.2	939.6	894.0	1,053.9	1,356.6	. . .
Investment companies	. . .	703.5	1,128.2	1,106.1	1,285.8	1,769.1	. . .
Italy							
Insurance companies	. . .	107.4	201.4	219.2	297.4	417.1	509.5
Life insurance	. . .	68.7	155.4	172.8	239.3	343.7	426.0
Nonlife insurance	. . .	38.7	46.1	46.4	58.1	73.4	83.5
Pension funds	. . .	39.0	48.8	35.0	50.9	48.7	54.4
Investment companies[1]	. . .	261.1	737.3	685.9	740.8	960.4	980.5
Netherlands							
Insurance companies	83.4	148.8	219.9	224.8	282.6	354.0	421.0
Pension funds	207.9	308.3	391.7	376.8	433.8	590.7	703.8
Investment companies[1]	32.1	53.8	87.0	72.8	71.5	95.0	105.1

Sources: National flow of funds data; Investment Company Institute; and Watson Wyatt.
Note: For some countries, the data may reflect some double-counting of assets, such as those owned by defined contribution pension funds and managed by investment companies.
[1]Investment companies include closed-end and managed investment companies, mutual funds, and unit investment trusts.
[2]For 1990, data refer to 1991.
[3]Life insurance companies.

financial assets has remained close to 50 percent, with a convergence across countries in recent years (Figure 3.3).[3] Bond holdings amounted to about 32 percent of total assets in 2003, and other assets (including real estate and alternative assets classes, such as private equity, commodities, and, increasingly, hedge fund products and strategies) represent a growing share (about 18 percent, of which 3 percent is real estate).

- Insurance companies hold the highest proportion of fixed-income instruments. The average bond and equity shares remained rather stable between 1997 and 2003, at 57

[3]Including countries where equities have traditionally represented a large share of the pension fund portfolio, where equity holdings have declined from 60–80 percent to 50–60 percent today.

percent and 24 percent, respectively (see IMF, 2004a). However, the convergence described above for pension funds is also evident for insurance companies, as the U.S. insurers' large bond holdings are starting to be matched by large European and Japanese life insurers.

- Investment companies (mainly mutual funds but including other investment vehicles such as hedge funds) hold a fairly balanced portfolio of assets, with about 41–43 percent in bonds and 47–48 percent in equities. The split between bonds and equities did not change much between 1997 and 2003. In contrast with pension funds and insurance companies, the asset holdings of investment companies simply reflect the asset allocation decisions by their shareholders, who are mainly retail investors but also include institutional investors, corporations, and public entities.

In recent years, many global investors have shifted their investment strategies, showing greater interest in alternative asset classes. The falling equity market, and the low-inflation, low-yield environment since 2000, have prompted many institutional investors to seek returns from a more diversified range of asset classes. Moreover, a greater focus on asset classes, and their relative performance, correlation, and volatility characteristics, is increasingly influencing investment strategies. Correlation and diversification benefits are now of particular interest, and (particularly in the United States) have fueled interest in emerging markets and alternative asset classes (such as hedge fund products, commodities, and private equity). For example, in many countries, pension funds, a very conservative investor group, are increasingly placing mandates with broader guidelines, including alternative investments.[4]

The degree of home bias has declined, with foreign assets often reflecting a range of invest-

[4]See Greenwich Associates (2005); and UBS Global Asset Management (2005).

Figure 3.1. Asset Allocation of Institutional Investors
(In percent)

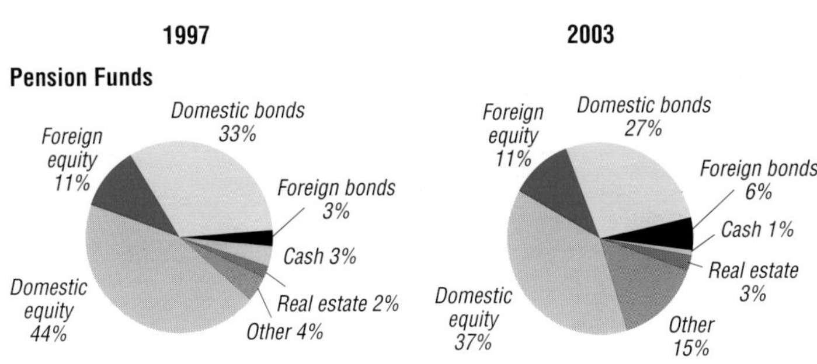

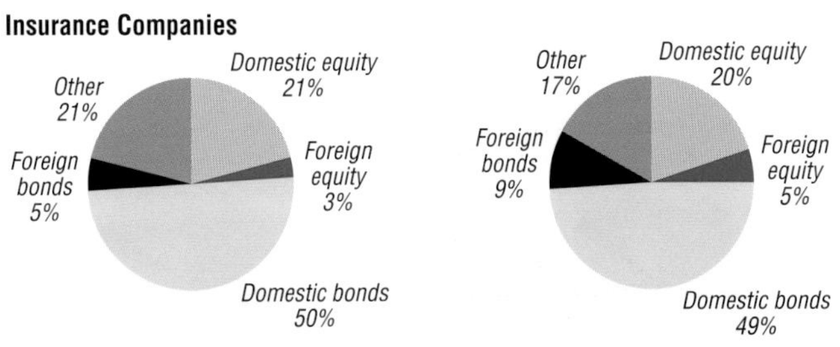

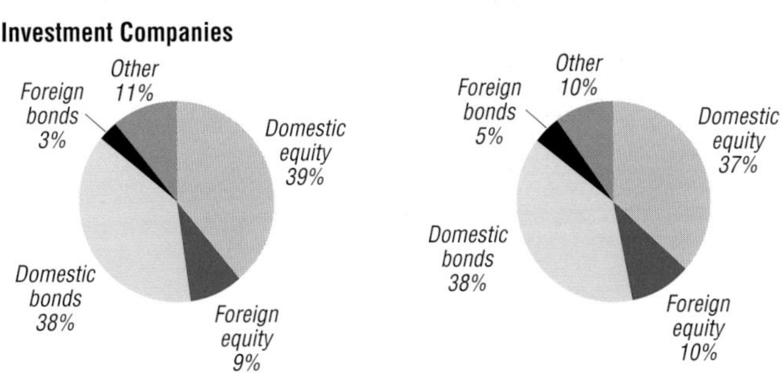

Sources: National flow of funds data; and IMF staff estimates.
Note: Shares computed as market-weighted mean shares of Germany, France, Japan, the United Kingdom, and the United States. "Other" includes commercial loans and credits; financial derivatives; short-term investments; investments in hedge funds, private equity, and commodities; and miscellaneous assets.

Figure 3.2. Global Asset Allocation of Institutional Investors by Country
(In percent)

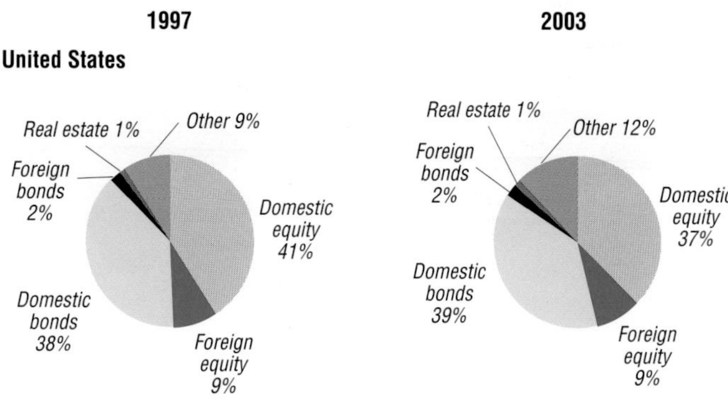

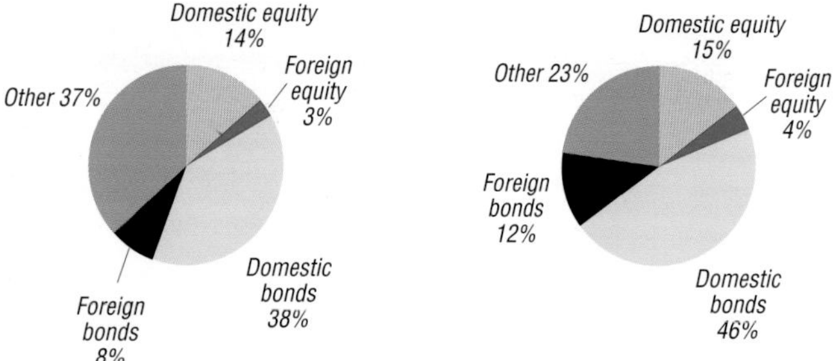

ment objectives (see Module 3 on Home Bias). For all types of institutional investors, the share of foreign assets rose between 1997 and 2003 to an average of about 12 percent (Figure 3.4). Home bias remains somewhat higher for life insurers than for other institutional investors, owing in part to regulatory factors. However, the degree to which geography drives ex ante asset allocation varies across sectors, institutions, and regions. For some sophisticated investors, such as hedge funds, country or regional exposures are increasingly less significant factors in the allocation decision (of course, related national regulatory and tax considerations remain important), but may be implemented at the fund manager level (e.g., as part of global mandates). Nevertheless, many investors still allocate assets and, even more, continue to assess performance against country or regional benchmarks.

Key Influences on Asset Allocation

Historically for many investors, including pension funds, the allocation of their assets often did not reflect their liability structures. For example, pension fund managers frequently measured their investment performance against a market index or peer group benchmark. They also typically assumed that a long-term equity premium above bond yields would provide sufficient "excess returns" to address longevity and inflation risks embedded in their long-term liabilities. However, over time risk managers have begun to better understand the composition of their liability structures, ranging from the long-term promise of a defined benefit pension to the various options and guarantees embedded in a complex insurance product, or the less explicit lifetime objectives of an individual investor. For a number of reasons, including uncertainties regarding the liability side of the balance sheet—such as longevity risk—and a shortage of appropriate assets for investment, purely liability-driven asset-liability management (ALM) may never be a realistic option.

Nevertheless, a greater focus on ALM has gained prominence, not only among senior executives of most institutional investors, but also with regulators and supervisors. In reality, however, many other factors influence investors' behavior and asset allocation.[5]

Accounting and financial reporting standards increasingly influence the investment behavior of institutional investors, potentially making their behavior more procyclical. Together with certain regulatory changes, recent accounting changes may lead insurance companies and pension funds away from managing their portfolios in a manner that is consistent with their liability structures. Indeed, the earnings volatility associated with fair value accounting may not always accurately reflect the economic reality of institutional investors' balance sheets or their risk profiles; this may encourage more procyclical market activity, thereby reducing their traditional role as long-term, stable investors and the associated stabilizing effect on financial markets (see Module 4 on Accounting).

Tax rules can significantly influence the asset allocation strategies of institutional and retail investors. Tax policies designed to encourage long-term savings are often viewed as too complex and/or are too frequently adjusted to encourage investors to pursue long-term savings objectives. This is particularly relevant to the long-term needs of the household and pension fund sectors.[6] In general, a relatively simple and stable tax regime may best encourage households, and their advisers, to develop long-term savings and investment plans. Similarly, in the pension fund industry, tax rules should not penalize firms for building up prudent funding cushions that would be consistent with meeting their long-term liabilities and their rather

Figure 3.2. *(concluded)*

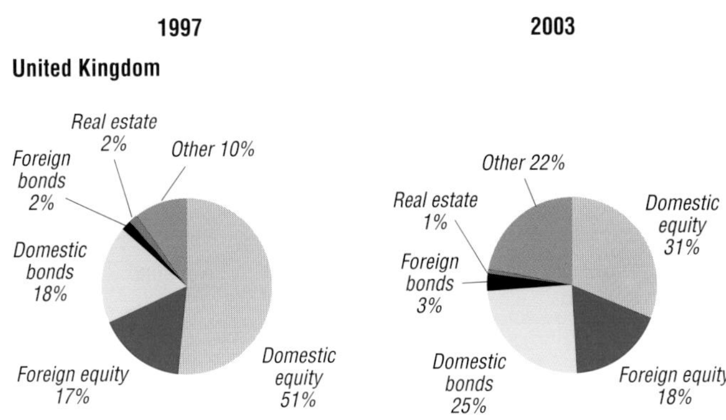

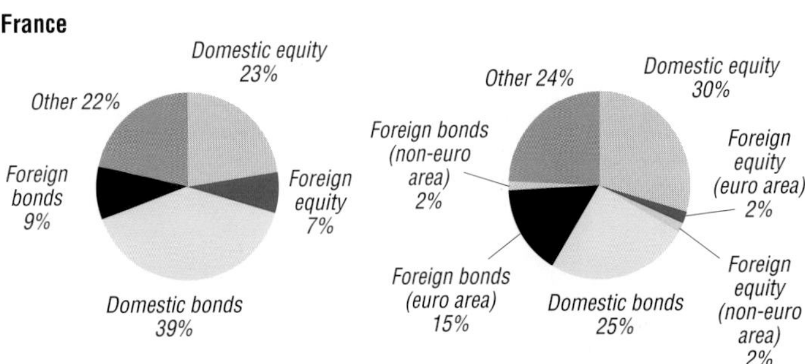

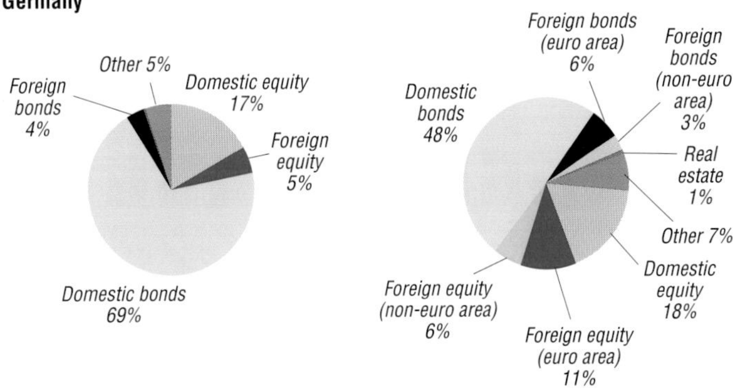

Sources: National flow of funds data; and IMF staff estimates.

Note: "Other" includes commercial loans and credits; financial derivatives; short-term investments; investments in hedge funds, private equity, and commodities; and miscellaneous assets.

[5]See Moore (2004).

[6]See, for example, Committee on Investment of Employee Benefit Assets (CIEBA, 2004); and United Kingdom, Her Majesty's Stationery Office (2004, p. 237).

stable asset allocation strategies. Recent proposals by the U.S. authorities on pension reform and more continuous funding are welcome in this regard.

Finally, rating agencies have a significant impact on asset allocation decisions in some sectors. This was particularly clear during 2000–02, when ratings pressure led some European insurance companies to sell portions of their relatively large equity holdings. In the pension fund industry, the influence of rating agencies has increased more recently, as the unfunded portion of pension obligations is being seen as a form of corporate debt obligations.

When assessing the factors influencing asset allocation, we should never underestimate important constraints, such as the availability of investments, vehicles, instruments, and adequately deep and liquid markets; or instruments tailor-made to meet specific objectives.

Figure 3.3. Equity and Bond Holdings of Pension Funds and Life Insurance Companies
(In percent of total financial assets)

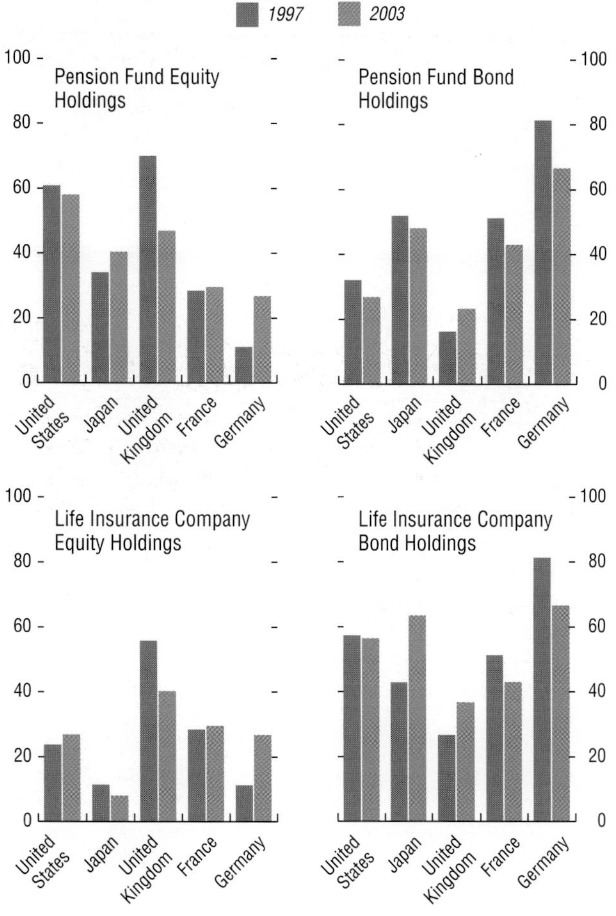

Sources: National flow of funds data; Watson Wyatt; and IMF staff estimates.

The Decision-Making Process

The asset allocation process (i.e., both its design and implementation) is strongly influenced by the institutional arrangements in which it takes place. Market participants have clearly recognized the internal and external factors that have different effects on asset allocation decisions. These include exposure limits set by various guidelines, compensation schemes of portfolio managers, and investment themes that may cause hedging behavior. To appreciate just how these and other factors affect investor groups, we must be clear about how investors differ.

- Bank (including investment bank) proprietary trading units and many hedge funds have short horizons for trading and investment decisions. They are active investors who sometimes employ leveraged investment strategies that capitalize on rapidly changing—sometimes intraday—relative values. However, hedge funds are a diverse investor group that employs a wide range of investment strategies across many asset classes, and under varying time horizons for investment decisions and returns. While many fixed-income or commodity-trading hedge funds may employ relatively shorter horizons, some equity hedge funds may have holding periods on investments as long as five years. But, by and large, hedge funds and trading desks are able and willing to reach quick decisions and to reverse themselves rapidly if and when necessary. Apart from strategic positions, which are often held on behalf of third parties, such as other profit centers of the institution, trading desks and many hedge funds employ elaborate reporting and risk management systems. Automatic triggers, such as stop-loss orders, and other devices may limit the likelihood of engaging in long-term positions.

- Insurance companies typically have very large strategic holdings of financial assets, with a medium- to longer-term time horizon. They review strategic asset allocation on an annual basis, and rarely use external advisors. For most large insurance companies, meetings between portfolio managers, chief investment officers (CIOs), chief risk officers, and actuaries take place every six months or annually at the group and (frequently) country level. Of course, these managers are monitoring performance and, more important, changes in risk exposures, as measured by Value-at-Risk (VaR) on a much more frequent basis, providing senior management with risk reports on a monthly or weekly basis. At the semiannual or annual investment strategy review meetings, these teams seek to optimize the company's asset allocation strategy, taking into account local constraints such as tax and regulatory regimes, market structures, and broader strategic capital allocation goals that are often related to their different lines of business. Of course, top-down decisions at the group level can be quickly implemented to reflect strategic or significant market changes, such as reductions in global equity exposure driven by market and rating

Figure 3.4. Holdings of Foreign Assets by Type of Institutional Investor

(In percent of total financial assets)

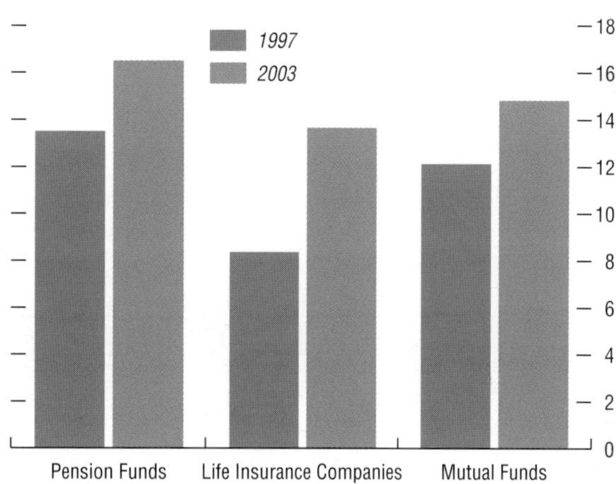

Sources: National flow of funds data; Watson Wyatt; and IMF staff estimates.
Note: Shares computed as market-weighted mean of Germany, France, Japan, the United Kingdom, and the United States.

agency pressures in 2001–02. Insurance companies' increasing exposure to credit in recent years has also implied some convergence in their risk management practices with those of banks, including, in many cases, the hiring of bank risk managers.

- Defined benefit pension funds typically review their asset allocation annually, with a full asset and liability review only every three years, and generally rely more on external advice and expertise. While investment plans may be updated every year to reflect market developments, seldom do such adjustments reflect material reallocations. However, since many pension funds use outside fund managers, such managers generally have authority to alter allocations—based widely on relative judgment—more frequently, often within a predetermined range. Meetings with investment consultants are typically held on a quarterly basis, and tend to reflect a monitoring of established strategies. Key steps in the decision process include (1) an asset/liability study that quantifies the "excess return," relative to targeted contributions or planned benefit increases, required to meet liabilities; (2) defining risk/return objectives, including accounting and other considerations; and (3) selecting an asset allocation strategy consistent with these objectives, for example, degree of active management or role of alternative asset classes.[7] The process relies much more extensively on external consultants, particularly for new or more complex asset classes.
- With defined contribution pension schemes, households—rather than the sponsoring company—direct the asset allocation decision, often influenced by auto-enrollment mechanisms, default options, and plan investment options offered by the employer. Once the funds have been invested, the mutual fund manager makes the tactical investment decision.
- In a similar manner, investment companies develop and market a wide variety of funds, with mandates ranging from global asset allocation, and balanced funds, to equity or fixed-income funds, to more specialized funds dedicated to emerging bond markets, or to leveraged buyout companies. With different mandates also come various investment styles, including "top-down vs. bottom-up," "growth vs. value," or "active vs. passive." Shareholders of these funds effectively decide on how to allocate their assets by buying the funds they view as most suitable for their needs. They then continue to adjust their asset allocation decisions by switching between different funds, either within the same family of funds (offered by one investment company) or to other funds.
- However, within the mandates of the funds, the portfolio managers have the responsibility for selecting securities and, in many cases, sector and country exposures. In the case of fixed-income funds, portfolio managers also select duration and credit quality exposures. Usually, in an investment company offering a family of funds in different asset classes, an investment committee develops a consistent global economic and financial view to guide the investment choices of the portfolio managers.
- The growth of different investment funds in various asset classes over time reflects the global asset allocation preferences of the shareholders and the performance track record of these funds.
- A growing priority for investment companies is to better serve the various investment needs of targeted clients, thereby securing a longer-term relationship. The desire for a longer-term relationship has led many mutual fund companies to offer more planning tools to individuals and, in some cases, to provide a variety of more tailored investment vehicles (see Module 2 on Investment Funds).

[7]See Urwin and others (2001).

- The boards of foundations and endowments generally meet on a quarterly basis to review various policy issues, including the asset allocation strategy. Quarterly, or sometimes monthly, meetings with the chief investment officer are used to keep abreast of portfolio performance and tactical deviations from the longer-term strategic asset allocation. Like pension funds, endowments and foundations frequently rely on consultants for investment advice and portfolio construction and monitoring.
- Private equity funds are quite different from other institutional investors insofar as they usually invest in illiquid assets. Private equity funds become strategic investors in companies that may benefit from a strategic redirection, injection of capital, and often new management. Typically, after five to seven years, private equity funds seek to liquidate and realize profits on these investments through public offerings or trade sales of the company.

Among certain institutional investors, particularly pension funds, and foundations and endowments, investment consultants play a significant role in the asset allocation process. Investment consultants advise institutional investors on the "appropriate" allocations, including the selection of portfolio managers and specific asset classes (e.g., small- or medium-capitalization stocks, private equity, real estate, and credit-spread products), based on their investment objectives, risk appetite, and a variety of models developed by such consultants. Even though the ultimate decision rests with the trustees or the board, and the larger and more sophisticated funds have in-house capabilities to decide, execute, and monitor allocations, consultants are often used by these institutions to perform due diligence and select managers, as well as to carry out analytical work related to risk-adjusted return targets and portfolio construction. However, the incentives of consultants and fund managers are not always aligned with the objectives of investors.[8] Consultants often rely on transaction-based fees that may encourage greater portfolio turnover. Similarly, the performance of external asset managers is often assessed on a monthly basis and against broad equity benchmarks or indices, which may lead to short-term performance bias and greater herding behavior, rather than a stricter ALM focus.[9]

In sum, in addition to institutional investors' different liability structures, other differences, such as in investment time-horizon, in frequency of strategic meetings to review asset allocations, or in whether they rely on outside consultants, result in different investment behaviors by such investors. Most important for financial stability considerations are differences in the frequency and the internal effort required to change asset allocation, and whether the changes can be implemented in gradual adjustments.

Conclusions

As mentioned throughout this issue of the GFSR, the asset allocation of investors—mostly institutional investors—and global financial stability are closely connected. Most capital account crises over the last 10 years can be traced, at least in part, to abrupt changes in asset allocation, often in the form of sharp reversals of capital flows. Short-term considerations on the part of institutional investors have at times contributed to the boom and bust cycles that we have seen in emerging markets and elsewhere. Hence, the GFSR has increasingly focused its financial market surveillance on the different aspects of global asset allocation.

Over time, financial market prices and activity reflect and follow economic fundamentals,

[8]Bank for International Settlements (2003); and OECD (2005).

[9]In the United Kingdom, the Myners Review concluded that broad performance measures, such as peer group benchmarks, often incentivize fund managers to simply copy other funds. See Myners (2001).

but it is well known that, in the short run, market prices may deviate from fundamentals quite significantly. Sometimes driven by short-term considerations, such deviations can at times create various types of market turbulence and/or overshooting.[10] Nonetheless, such investors as hedge funds or trading desks serve a useful purpose, not the least because they often provide liquidity and contrarian views just when markets need them the most, that is, when they tend to overshoot in one direction.

However, as a very general rule, if investors were guided by mostly long-term considerations—that is, more or less economic fundamentals—this alone would reduce somewhat the volatility and "noise" in financial markets, and probably some of their vulnerabilities to short-term developments. In other words, on balance, the financial system would be slightly better off if more investors took a long-term view and adhered to economic fundamentals rather than short-term considerations. Of course, financial markets could still suffer serious problems if the global economy, or some of its major parts, went into recession; there is obviously no way to prevent that, short of bringing fundamentals back on track. Equally, a multitude of different investment strategies on the part of different investors helps to avoid herd behavior and ultimately "contagion."

Based on current trends, global financial markets may very well be on track to be more and more dominated by such investors with a long-term view. As was noted in previous issues of the GFSR, rapidly changing demographics, fundamental policy changes in pension systems toward funded systems, the continuing growth of already large asset gatherers, ceteris paribus, should raise the relative importance of long-term strategic, compared with short-term tactical, investors, so that strategic asset allocations by such long-term investors could ultimately have a greater impact on financial markets over time. In this regard, these institutions' long-term liabilities constitute a structural advantage, allowing them to act as a stabilizing force.

Against this backdrop, it is all the more important that these secular gains in investor behavior strengthening financial stability are not diminished or reversed through the introduction of financial accounting and reporting standards that may force long-term investors to adopt short-term time horizons—hence the importance of Module 4 in this context.

Somewhat separate, but equally important, is the issue of ensuring that "enough assets" exist for institutional investors, so they may address their duration gaps and meet their long-term investment objectives. Certain asset classes or investment vehicles are likely to be increasingly in demand going forward: long-term, index-linked, and annuity-like fixed-income instruments (to better match longer-term liabilities). In today's fixed-income environment, the longer we go along the maturity spectrum, the more the market is dominated by government paper. Under these circumstances, two possible implications would be worth noting. First, because the principal supplier for closing the asset gatherers' duration gap would be the public sector, there would be a likely secular strengthening of demand for such paper, which would raise securities' prices, lower yields, and/or permit higher budget deficits without a rise in bond yields. Such an unintended consequence of asset liability management may, in turn, widen the scope for expansionary fiscal policy. Second, the predominance of government paper in the long maturities would potentially limit the diversity of the balance sheets of pension funds and insurers by overloading them with such paper. Although it would be highly desirable, the private sector has not stepped in to fill the supply shortage of longer-term paper to date. However, this may reflect the

[10]See, for example, Counterparty Risk Management Policy Group II (2005).

current strong liquidity position of the corporate sector worldwide and the relatively low investment returns perceived in many sectors (thereby reducing corporate borrowing needs), as well as the very low cost of short-term credit available to those seeking borrowed funds in recent years.

Module 2. Investment Fund Industry

Investment funds play an important role in the development and functioning of modern financial markets as institutional investors and vehicles channeling savings to capital markets. By broadening access to financial markets and helping investors reach their investment goals, investment funds play a major role in intermediating savings and investment. As such, they may contribute not only to a more efficient allocation of capital and investment but also to financial stability by diversifying investment styles and asset allocations among investor portfolios. This module will analyze the development of investment funds and how they serve the needs of retail and institutional investors. It will highlight some aspects of the transformation that the investment fund industry is experiencing and the tremendous growth potential that many envisage. Finally, it will discuss the challenges that these developments may present.

Development of Investment Funds

Dual Nature of Investment Funds

Investment funds are simultaneously institutional investors and investment vehicles. Their primary purpose is to invest savings using specific investment strategies to allocate assets. However, they are different from other institutional investors. Pension funds or insurance companies invest their own assets, while investment funds invest assets they hold on behalf of their shareholders. Hence, in contrast with other institutional investors, investment funds have no investment-linked liabilities: gains and losses are transferred to the end-investors, their shareholders.

For investors, investment funds are vehicles, or conduits, that either actively or passively channel savings to financial markets. While different categories of investment funds have distinct characteristics and reflect varying degrees of liquidity, transparency, and cost structures, they share common features that, for investors, offer some advantages over direct investment in capital markets. In particular, they pool funds (savings) from various sources and, through economies of scale and scope, provide investors—both retail and other institutional investors—broader access to financial markets through professionally managed portfolios of financial assets. Investment funds cover numerous asset classes and offer a diversified menu of investment styles and risk profiles, including traditional mutual funds, real estate investment funds, hedge funds, and private equity funds. Combining various funds allows investors to build portfolios using "fund of funds" strategies and may be particularly suitable vehicles for investors seeking international diversification.

Investment Funds as a Source of Diversification

Mutual funds are the main investment vehicle for retail investors and households. Mutual funds offer attractive combinations of liquidity and transparency, and a wide range of investment styles. When associated with tax incentives, mutual funds have proved efficient structures to pursue specific investment objectives, such as life insurance, and education and retirement savings. From the $12.9 trillion assets held by U.S. retirement accounts, 24 percent of such funds were invested in mutual funds in 2004, and half of those were held through employer-sponsored accounts, in particular 401(k) accounts. In various European countries, where reforms of retirement schemes have been launched recently, mutual funds are promoted as Pillar 2 and Pillar 3 vehicles. With the ongoing integration of European financial markets, a cross-border, portable "European personal pension

Table 3.3. Assets Under Management of Mutual Funds
(In percent of GDP)

	1998	1999	2000	2001	2002	2003	2004
			(In billions of U.S. dollars)				
United States	5,525.2	6,846.3	6,964.7	6,975.0	6,390.4	7,414.4	8,106.9
Japan	376.5	502.8	432.0	343.9	303.2	349.1	399.5
Europe	2,740.7	3,199.3	3,290.3	3,160.7	3,440.0	4,641.2	5,572.0
Emerging market countries							
Asia	305.3	426.9	384.9	392.0	431.6	535.8	703.3
Latin America	140.7	148.8	180.4	191.5	138.6	218.8	273.7
Europe	2.6	4.1	5.7	7.3	19.2	70.6	88.8
			(In percent of GDP)				
United States	63.2	73.9	70.9	68.9	60.9	67.4	69.1
Japan	9.5	11.2	9.1	8.3	7.6	8.1	8.6
Europe	30.5	35.6	39.5	37.8	37.6	41.9	43.8
Emerging market countries[1]							
Asia	13.2	16.4	13.7	13.8	13.8	15.6	18.0
Latin America	8.6	10.5	11.2	12.4	9.6	14.5	16.0
Europe	0.4	0.8	1.0	1.1	2.1	6.1	6.1

Source: Investment Company Institute.
[1]Asia includes China, Hong Kong SAR, India, Korea, Malaysia, Philippines, Taiwan Province of China, Thailand, and Pakistan; Latin America includes Argentina, Brazil, Chile, Costa Rica, Mexico, Peru, and Venezuela; Emerging Europe includes the Czech Republic, Hungary, Latvia, Poland, Romania, Russia, the Slovak Republic, and Turkey.

account" is being proposed to complement existing domestic and insurance-based pension products.[11] In addition to retail investors, which are the primary investor base, mutual funds are also used by institutional investors, which typically have greater flexibility to tailor fund objectives and risk profiles to meet their particular investment goals, and are frequently held through separately managed accounts.[12]

The mutual fund industry is now a mature industry in the United States, and increasingly so in Europe. However, in Europe, the investment fund industry remains organized largely along domestic lines. European mutual funds are more numerous, but typically smaller in size, on average, than in the United States.[13] Furthermore, while in most countries a few firms dominate their local market, only a handful of asset managers have a market share of more than 1 percent at the European level. As such, significant room for consolidation exists within the industry. The growth potential of the mutual fund industry is possibly most significant in Japan and certain emerging economies (Table 3.3).[14]

Real estate investment funds offer investors a source of diversification, and liquid and transparent vehicles to invest in a variety of real estate assets through companies that often actively manage properties. The U.S. market is the most developed market for real estate investment trusts (REITs), which man-

[11]See European Fund and Asset Management Association (2005).

[12]An interesting development is the recent launch by a large European corporate of a pension-pooling vehicle, set up as a mutual fund and used by the supplementary pension schemes of its subsidiaries and affiliates.

[13]In early 2005, there were an estimated 28,500 mutual funds in Europe (EU-15), with total assets under management of $5,132 billion. In the United States, 8,044 mutual funds represent $8,106 billion of assets under management. For further developments on the situation of the European investment fund industry, see European Commission (2005).

[14]In Japan, households continue to exhibit a strong preference for savings products. However, since 1998, following the deregulation of distribution networks, households have started to invest in mutual funds (mainly foreign sovereign bond products). The share of their financial assets in mutual funds has risen to 2.7 percent at the end of March 2005, from 2.0 percent at the end of 1998.

aged $330 billion assets as of end-2004 in a variety of property sectors. Among the EU-15 countries, assets under management by real estate funds represented around $175 billion in early 2005. In Japan, J-REITs were introduced in 2001, and although they have expanded rapidly, their aggregate size is still relatively small (approximately $13 billion).

Hedge funds and private equity funds are also pooled investment vehicles but offer investors access to alternative investment strategies. Their features distinguish them from other investment funds.[15] Hedge funds and private equity funds routinely impose variable, sometimes multiyear, lock-up periods on investors. As a highly heterogeneous group, hedge funds seek investment opportunities across many asset classes and use innovative and often complex investment techniques. Private equity funds focus on venture capital and buyout financing, mostly among unlisted and start-up companies.

The private equity universe is dominated by U.S. and, to a lesser extent, U.K. funds and investors.[16] Among institutional investors, pension funds, and foundations and endowments have traditionally invested in private equity and are estimated to represent 30 percent of private equity fund capital. European institutional investors have shown increased interest in private equity investment in recent years. Amounts raised in Europe in 2004 were nearly 50 percent higher than the previous year, and are expected to rise by about $50 billion in 2005. To facilitate the broadening investor base, funds of private equity funds have emerged, particularly in Europe.[17]

In Europe, the development of real estate funds, hedge funds, and private equity funds is relatively recent and has lacked a common approach. These funds are not "coordinated funds" (i.e., non-UCITS compliant) and, therefore, do not benefit from the passport that allows mutual funds to be freely sold across borders.[18] Even more than mutual funds, these funds remain fragmented along domestic lines. Significant differences in national structures, tax regimes, and legal backgrounds may have limited the growth of real estate and private equity funds. In various countries, recent changes in the regulatory framework for hedge funds and real estate funds have been implemented, or are being contemplated, in an uncoordinated and heterogeneous way, thereby limiting the ability of these funds to realize greater size and efficiency.[19]

A Changing Industry

Changes in Demand

In mature economies, demographic trends and changing pension arrangements are likely to fuel an increasing demand for retirement solutions from institutional investors (i.e., pension funds, life insurance companies, and the investment fund industry), and also individuals, as they bear more direct responsibility to manage their financial affairs. In developing economies, further development of the invest-

[15]The performance-based fee structure is an important feature of these vehicles.

[16]Out of an estimated $130–$135 billon raised in 2004 by private equity funds (final closes, total commitments), more than 70 percent was raised among U.S. investors. Although growing, amounts raised in Europe represented less than 25 percent of the total, with U.K.-based funds accounting for close to 45 percent of private equity capital raised in Europe. See Private Equity Intelligence Ltd. (2005); and Almeida Capital (2005).

[17]In various countries, specific fund structures give retail investors access to private equity and venture capital vehicles: U.K.-listed Venture Capital Trusts were introduced in 1994; and in France, Fonds Communs de Placement à Risques and Fonds Communs de Placement dans l'Innovation are among the vehicles available to retail investors.

[18]Undertakings for Collective Investment in Transferable Securities (UCITS) are open-ended investment funds that comply with EU regulations, and are freely marketable across the EU.

[19]See recent issues of the GFSR for detailed analysis of recent changes in the regulatory framework of hedge funds. The recently announced new regulatory framework for investment funds in Spain will allow domestic sales of hedge funds. In France, the regulatory framework of real estate funds is being reviewed with the view to offering increased transparency and liquidity. Similar changes are expected in the United Kingdom and in Germany.

Table 3.4. Assets of Exchange-Traded Funds
(In billions of U.S. dollars)

	1993	1994	1995	1996	1997	1998	1999	2000	2001	2002	2003	2004
United States	0.5	0.4	10.1	2.4	6.7	15.6	33.9	65.6	83.0	102.1	151.0	226.2
EU-15	. . .	. . .	. . .	. . .	. . .	. . .	. . .	0.5	5.5	10.4	20.5	34.5
Japan	. . .	. . .	. . .	. . .	. . .	. . .	. . .	. . .	6.8	20.9	28.0	29.8
Total	0.5	0.4	10.1	2.4	6.7	15.6	33.9	66.1	95.3	133.4	199.5	290.5

Sources: Lipper; and Morgan Stanley.

ment fund industry would widen investment options available to domestic and international investors, and more generally contribute to an efficient global allocation of capital.

The growing demand for investment funds is also becoming more diverse and sophisticated. Investors increasingly seek investment products and strategies that maximize the likelihood of meeting specific investment objectives or asset and liability targets, including retirement. Consequently, renewed attention is being given in the investment process to asset allocation and diversification, absolute performance, and the stability of performance. This more sophisticated approach to investment is already significantly embraced by many institutional investors, but is evolving more slowly to include retail investors.

New Investment Products

Exchange-traded funds (ETFs) are rapidly growing cost-effective investment vehicles that offer increased diversification opportunities to a variety of retail and institutional investors. ETFs are investment companies, most often mutual funds or unit investment trusts invested in portfolios of equities and other instruments.[20] Total assets under management with ETFs are estimated to be about $294 billion globally at the end of 2004, with U.S. ETFs accounting for more than 75 percent of the market. In Europe, ETFs developed with the introduction of the euro, giving investors access to euro area "blue chips" and industry sectors through euro area equity indices. In Asia, most ETFs are concentrated in the Japanese market (Table 3.4).[21] Increased diversification possibilities are available with the launch of more equity ETFs tracking sectors, different investment styles and country indices, and with the supply of ETFs expanding to other asset classes, such as fixed-income securities. For institutional investors such as pension funds, bond ETFs may prove efficient vehicles to manage duration gaps and liquidity with reduced costs. New and increasingly complex forms of ETFs are also being developed, from commodity ETFs (e.g., gold) to leveraged, active, and even so-called "intelligent" ETFs (the active ETFs being managed by portfolio managers, and the "intelligent" ETFs adjusting their composition with market developments, according to proprietary investment algorithms).

The distinction between actively and passively managed funds is being increasingly blurred by the development of ETFs, which may have implications for financial stability.[22]

[20]In contrast with "traditional" mutual funds, ETF shares can be purchased and sold among investors intraday, allowing investors to trade a portfolio of underlying securities in a single transaction.

[21]In December 2004, the EMEAP group announced the launch of a second "Asian Bond Fund" initiative (ABF2), a set of nine index bond funds that will invest in sovereign and quasi-sovereign bonds denominated in the local currencies of participating countries: China, Hong Kong SAR, Indonesia, Korea, Malaysia, the Philippines, Singapore, and Thailand. Structured as ETFs, these funds are expected to be accessible to private investors in the coming months.

[22]In the pension fund industry, passively managed portfolio components were estimated to represent around 35 percent in the United States, 30 percent in the United Kingdom, and 10–20 percent in continental Europe (Bank for International Settlements, 2003).

Fears have been expressed that increased use of index funds may reduce market efficiency, especially the price discovery process, facilitate the possible overshooting of markets through investment in procyclical fads or yesterday's winners, and fuel destabilizing price dynamics, particularly because ETFs can be sold short. These concerns are not necessarily misplaced, but they should not detract from the many benefits that ETFs can provide to a variety of investors as tax-efficient and cost-effective investment vehicles. Furthermore, by enabling investors to quickly rebalance portfolios and reallocate across specific sectors, ETFs also serve as a tool for a more active asset management.[23]

Structured investment products have benefited from an environment where the search for yield and capital preservation remain dominant themes. Structured products can be broadly defined as financial products offering specific payout profiles, based on the performance of a basket of reference assets and/or indices (e.g., equities, bonds, currencies or commodities, and, more recently, hedge fund performance). Such products are usually constructed by banks and investment banks, and are often packaged into medium-term notes or investment funds, typically closed-end funds. The vast majority of these products can be described as combinations of two main investment objectives: capital preservation (at the cost of lower returns) and yield (income) enhancement (with higher risk on the capital invested). Structured investment products are now routinely offered to retail investors and, in the current low-yield environment, they have attracted significant demand, particularly in Asia, Australia, and Europe.[24] However, the complexity of the underlying structures and payout profiles is difficult to understand for most investors. In various European countries, concerns about possible mis-selling of such complex products to retail investors in the last few years have led regulators and market participants to focus more on providing investors with adequate information.[25] Increased transparency, particularly in the cost structure of the products, would represent a significant improvement and should be encouraged by product providers and regulators.[26]

The growth of life-cycle funds reflects the increased attention given to asset allocation by the household sector. Life-cycle funds are investment funds, most often funds of mutual funds, offering investors a "prepackaged" asset allocation formula and an automatic rebalancing/reallocation facility.[27] In 401(k) and other individual retirement plans, these features give life-cycle funds an advantage over traditional default options (i.e., money market or "stable value"—typically government bond—funds). The growth of life-cycle funds is closely linked to the development of defined contribution pension plans.[28] Life-cycle funds also offer a solution to the acknowledged lack

[23]See Amenc and others (2004).

[24]In the United States, where a large variety of investment vehicles are available, investors have shown little interest in structured products. Globally, in 2004, issuance of structured products reached $130–$140 billion, according to market research, with European markets representing 59 percent of volume issued, Asia about 32 percent, and the United States a mere 9 percent. Among the EU-15 countries, assets under management with guaranteed/protected funds were estimated to represent 175 billion euros, and were concentrated among a handful of countries (France, Spain, Belgium, and Luxembourg).

[25]The U.K. Financial Services Authority has updated its guidelines for the sale of a range of structured investment products. In Italy, a voluntary "transparency pact" is being implemented to address these issues.

[26]See the report of the Counterparty Risk Management Policy Group II (2005).

[27]Life-cycle funds are typically offered in two different forms. "Target-risk funds" are diversified portfolios built around a predefined risk/return profile and are rebalanced periodically to maintain this profile. "Target-date funds" assume an investor's tolerance for risk declines as the target-date approaches and periodically reallocate the portfolio to reduce risk. See Porter and Garland (2005).

[28]According to Lipper, more than 55 percent of defined contribution (DC) plan sponsors offer life-cycle funds in their 401(k) menu, and 37 percent of DC plan participants use these investment vehicles when they are available.

Table 3.5. United States: Growth and Net Assets of Life-Cycle Funds
(In billions of U.S. dollars)

	1999	2000	2001	2002	2003	2004
Assets under management	57.9	63.3	69.2	68.2	101.4	139.7
Net flows	4.7	5.5	6.7	6.8	21.4	24.2

Sources: Lipper; and Morgan Stanley.

of rebalancing in most individually directed investments, a recognized source of drift and failure to meet investment goals. Life-cycle funds are among the fastest growing vehicles in the U.S. mutual fund industry, and they have also started to develop in other countries (Table 3.5).[29]

On the institutional side, the difficulties encountered by life insurers and defined benefit pension schemes in recent years have highlighted the importance of asset and liability management. The shift in focus, from outperforming a benchmark to minimizing asset and liability mismatches, has prompted the development of new primarily liability-driven investment products by banks and investment providers. Using corporate and government bonds (including index-bonds), and futures and swaps (including inflation swaps), pension funds and life insurers seek to match their projected liabilities. The real novelty lies in the use of lower costs and flexible suites of funds through which the targeted asset allocation is achieved.[30] More broadly, the fund structure allows the extension of this liability-driven investment approach to retail investors.

Challenges from the Growing Complexity of Investment Funds

The innovative products and strategies developed by the asset management industry raise a number of new challenges. For fund providers, the growing variety and complexity of investment products highlights the continuing challenge of providing appropriate investment advice and financial planning. For regulators and authorities responsible for market surveillance and financial stability, the unbundling of investment services, and the blurring of differences between regulated and unregulated investment funds, may call for new approaches in regulation and market surveillance.

Market Surveillance and Regulatory Framework

Regulated investment funds have traditionally not been considered systemically important entities, and have not attracted the attention that unregulated funds (e.g., hedge funds) have. However, as the menu of available funds and strategies grows, traditional distinctions between investment vehicles are becoming increasingly blurred, and as the providers of investment vehicles outsource more investment services, new approaches to market surveillance and possibly regulation may be required.

- Hedge funds and funds of hedge funds have grown rapidly and are becoming mainstream asset management products. Institutional investors seeking uncorrelated asset returns to diversify portfolios are turning to hedge funds and, while direct access remains limited, retail investors are increasingly turning to funds of hedge funds.
- Crossover activities and strategies are being seen among traditional hedge fund and private equity fund providers. Hedge fund managers have also begun to pursue strategies usually considered the core business of traditional asset managers (e.g., long-only equity strategies). More recently, they have also started to offer private equity strategies. Simultaneously, some private equity firms are entering the hedge fund business by establishing proprietary hedge funds, or through fund of funds.
- Faced with increased competition from ETFs and hedge funds, mutual funds are

[29]In France, target-date funds are the default option in the new *Plans d'Epargne Populaire pour la Retraite.*
[30]The funds in the suite cover successive duration buckets.

increasingly relaxing investment constraints. In the retail business, a growing number of investment fund providers offer hedge fund–like strategies (including the use of short sales) wrapped into "traditional" mutual fund vehicles.[31]

The outsourcing of key functions in the provision of investment services raises specific risk management and financial stability issues. Cost benefits, economies of scale, and greater efficiency in the conduct of core business activities are the prime drivers of the trend toward the unbundling of the provision of investment services and outsourcing.

- Investment funds are increasingly viewed as the combination of different building blocks, assembled and packaged to fulfill specific investment objectives. Modeling expertise and access to derivative markets are often provided by outside providers, and banks are frequently asked to provide guarantees to investment funds offering capital preservation or other structured product investment vehicles. Through these links, new dependencies and vulnerabilities may develop among institutional investors, market intermediaries, and providers of investment services that may deserve closer attention from regulators and supervisors.
- From a financial stability perspective, an important issue for regulators and investment companies that unbundled key administrative functions, such as custody and settlement services, valuation of assets, and performance measurement, is the ability of such companies to maintain adequate oversight of third party service providers to contain operational risks associated with the outsourced activities, especially when they are delegated to unregulated service providers. For regulators, concentration risk associated with outsourcing (i.e., a large number of investment firms relying on a limited number of third party providers) is a specific form of operational risk, with possible stability or systemic ramifications.[32] For example, as assets under management by investment funds grow, the failure of a custodian could affect a larger number of investment funds, as well as significant amounts of assets and securities, with rippling effects on other market participants. Similarly, as the complexity of financial products develops, third party providers of data and valuation services have increased responsibilities in the functioning of financial markets.

The emergence of a more complex and a potentially more opaque (or at least multilayered) investment industry may raise new challenges for regulators and public authorities in charge of market monitoring.[33] When considering financial stability issues, it is increasingly important for policymakers and authorities responsible for market oversight and surveillance to be able to identify, track, and understand throughout the production process of investment products (i.e., across asset classes and markets); how various risk components are managed and transferred by investment strategies of both regulated and unregulated entities; and how capital flows are affected by reallocations within and between funds. The traditional supervisory and regulatory focus on investment products and investor protection issues may need to be complemented by a more risk-based/prudential-type monitoring and surveillance approach. Investment products offering similar risk characteristics and implementing similar financial techniques should be subject to

[31]In Europe, the UCITS III directive widens the range of investable assets accessible to mutual funds and increases their ability to use derivatives, and leverage, ultimately allowing regulated funds to implement new, more active and complex investment strategies previously reserved for unregulated vehicles. In various European countries, investment rules for mutual funds are also being relaxed to allow mutual funds to invest in hedge funds and private equity funds.

[32]See IOSCO (2005).

[33]See Financial Services Authority (2005).

Table 3.6. European Mutual Fund Distribution in 2002
(In percent of mutual fund sale by channel)

	France	Germany	Italy	Spain	Switzerland	United Kingdom
Bank networks	70	64	81	93	41	5
Insurance networks	22	18	9	3	9	12
Independent financial advisers	8	15	2	4	50	76
Others	n.a.	3	8	n.a.	n.a.	7

Source: *FERI European Fund Market Yearbook 2003.*

the same monitoring process, irrespective of the formal legal status of the investment vehicle. Such a risk-based approach to market surveillance of investment funds would need to take into consideration a wide set of factors, including the liquidity, volatility, and complexity of the underlying strategies and implied risks. With increasing globalization, more cooperation and exchange of information among supervisors and public authorities, as well as with market participants, may be required to effectively identify potential vulnerabilities.

Providing Advice to Investors

As more responsibilities are being transferred to households to directly manage their financial affairs, and new and more complex investment vehicles are available to address these investment needs, the role of investment funds in the provision of investment advice appears increasingly important.[34] The availability and scope of investment advice are set to expand but face a series of obstacles:

- The advice generally provided to retail investors rarely goes beyond simple counseling on the features of investment products, and seldom includes advice on asset allocation, and asset and liability management. Real and perceived liabilities from fiduciary responsibilities are typically cited by industry participants as constraints on the ability and willingness of advisors to offer financial advice, frequently leading them to offer a standard variety of products and limiting their advice to only very general guidance.
- Technological developments offer an opportunity to provide new channels for advice. A growing number of asset managers and fund distributors offer sophisticated Internet-based asset allocation, and asset and liability management tools. These developments have been met with limited take-up thus far, mainly among the better-educated, younger, and moderately well-off professional cohorts. This may reflect investors' difficulties in formulating their long-term goals, and the complexity and excessive variety of the investment products offered.
- The organization of distribution networks, including distributors' compensation schemes, plays an important role in the provision of investment advice and the range of investment products offered to end-investors. Independent distribution networks offering a range of investment funds from different providers are prevalent only in the United Kingdom and the United States, and, to a lesser extent, in Switzerland (Tables 3.6 and 3.7).[35] In continental Europe, where asset management firms are often subsidiaries of large financial groups, and bank (and to a lesser extent insurance) networks are by far the main channels for

[34]See IMF (2005a).

[35]A feature of the U.S. situation is also the growing role of defined contribution retirement plans as a low-cost distribution channel for mutual funds. See Reid and Rea (2003).

Table 3.7. United States: Mutual Fund Distribution
(In percent of mutual fund assets)

	1980	1990	2000	2003	2004
Discount brokers and fund supermarkets	. . .	. . .	15	17	16
Defined contribution retirement plans	7	7	18	18	19
Direct from mutual fund companies	28	20	13	13	13
Professional financial advisers	65	73	54	52	52

Source: Investment Company Institute.

mutual fund distribution, open architecture (i.e., the opening of distribution networks to outside investment products) is expected to broaden the range of investment products and strategies, and foster competition by introducing new fund providers. In most jurisdictions, investors remain reluctant to adopt fee-based compensation schemes, and mutual fund distribution systems are overwhelmingly commission based. Industry participants recognize that these systems are more prone to conflicts of interest, possibly leading distributors and advisers to favor high margin products rather than "appropriate" products, and encourage high turnover, including by frequently offering "new" products.[36]

Conclusions

Investment funds are likely to grow in size and utilize more complex investment strategies to meet future asset allocation needs of various end-users. As such, they can be expected to play an increasingly important role in shaping financial market dynamics and, therefore, financial stability considerations. This may require that supervisors and other public authorities complement their traditional investor protection approach to investment companies with increased market surveillance. For those regulators and public authorities responsible for financial stability, new challenges will likely arise in monitoring investment funds, and their interactions with other institutional investors and financial market participants, and understanding the increasingly complex strategies embedded in the investment products they develop. Improving transparency to better assess the risk profiles and cost structures of investment funds would also likely contribute to strengthen market discipline.

Module 3. Home Bias

Recent evidence points to a significant increase in acceptance of foreign assets by investors in most mature market economies between 1990 and 2003.[37] Around 1990, the high degree of home bias in mature market portfolios represented an apparently unexploited potential gain in risk-adjusted returns that puzzled academics.[38] Part of the paradox has since dissipated. This reduction in home bias is an aspect of globalization that may have important consequences for financial stability across markets. To better understand these developments and their implications, this module assesses the causes and degree of home bias among institutional investors within major market economies.

The module discusses changes in regulation, financial innovation, asset allocation practices, and other factors that have contributed to the decline in home bias. It exam-

[36]The lack of incentives to distribute lower-margin/low-turnover products may also explain the slow development of ETFs and life-cycle funds in some countries.

[37]See, for example, IMF (2005b, p. 115).

[38]See, for example, Tesar and Werner (1995); and Obstfeld and Rogoff (1996).

ines the role of aversion to currency risk as a source of home bias, focusing on the experience of the euro area. It also examines the potential gains and costs, with regard to both risk-adjusted returns and financial stability, of further reduction in home bias.

Factors driving the reduction in home bias include an increase in investor sophistication and an emphasis on achieving higher risk-adjusted returns. In some markets, notably Japan, financial deregulation has also played a role. Elsewhere, the impact of regulatory change has been more mixed, with changes, such as shifts to asset-liability matching, at times favoring domestic assets. Aversion to currency risk is a continuing source of home bias, as highlighted by the strong and growing preference of euro area investors for euro-denominated bonds, regardless of country of issuance. The gains in risk-adjusted returns from reduction in home bias have been substantial, and further gains are possible, but the degree of the potential future gains may be lower than what financial theory would predict. That is partly attributable to the high degree of diversification already provided by investment in domestically listed firms with significant global operations or exposure to global factors. Reduction in home bias should have a positive effect on financial stability, through diversification and market deepening, although there are some associated risks.

Home Bias and Institutional Investors

What Is Home Bias?

Home bias on the part of an investor is broadly defined as a tendency to select domestic over foreign assets, beyond relative market weights. One useful index is the foreign asset acceptance ratio (FAAR), which measures the extent to which the share of foreign assets in an investor's portfolio diverges from the share of foreign assets that would be held in a "borderless" global portfolio.[39] By this standard, a ratio of 100 percent entails no divergence and therefore no home bias. A lower ratio means greater measured home bias. The term "home bias" itself may introduce some bias in the discussion. Some investors may have good reasons for preferring domestic to foreign assets under certain conditions. Another caution is that the FAAR measure only takes into account portfolio investment, not FDI, and only considers the market in which a firm is listed, even if the firm is global in scope. Accordingly, the FAAR may understate the overall degree of actual diversification of investors in highly internationalized markets, particularly smaller markets where a few global firms may dominate the market index.

Data needed to measure home bias are often inadequate, although there have been substantial improvements in recent years. Many statistical authorities have only recently begun to track international investment positions in enough detail to provide useful measures. Consequently, time-series data often extend back only a few years. Even in cases where aggregate information on foreign asset holdings for a particular country is available, the data on foreign asset holdings by important investor classes (e.g., pension funds) are often limited. While breakdowns of foreign assets between bonds and equities are the general rule, further detail is not usually available—for example, distinctions between foreign sovereign and foreign corporate bonds.

[39]This is measured as [(foreign assets held by domestic residents)/(domestic market capitalization + foreign assets held by domestic residents – domestic assets held by foreign residents)]/[(world market capitalization – domestic market capitalization)/(world market capitalization)]. This measure is also used, for example, in Bertaut and Griever (2004). Optimal portfolio allocation under the international capital asset pricing model entails an FAAR of 100 percent.

Home Bias Indicators in the Aggregate and by Type of Investor

Since 1990, there has been a steady increase in the share of foreign assets in domestic portfolios within major market economies (Figure 3.5). The increase has been most pronounced for equities, where the aggregate FAAR rose from 8 percent to 30 percent between 1990 and 2003.[40] Acceptance of foreign bonds has also risen, but at a slower pace. All six countries covered in this study saw significant declines in home bias between 1991 and 2003. The two countries most inclined to hold foreign assets in 1991, the United Kingdom and the Netherlands, also had the highest foreign asset ratios in 2003. France shifted from being relatively averse to holding foreign assets in 1991 to relatively accepting in 2003. Home bias in the United States also fell from 1991 to 1997, but has stayed roughly unchanged since that time. Acceptance of foreign equities in the United States has continued to rise, but U.S. interest in foreign bonds has declined since 1997.

Holdings of foreign bonds increased sharply between 1997 and 2003 in the three countries studied that adopted the euro in 1999—France, Germany, and the Netherlands. This development points to a currency effect that may be a significant and continuing driver of home bias among institutional investors in bond markets. (For countries in the euro area, foreign assets are defined, for purposes of this module, as including euro-denominated assets supplied by other euro area countries. However, when data are available, a distinction is made between euro area and non–euro area foreign assets of the countries in the euro area.)

Mutual fund foreign asset holding ratios are higher than those of some other investors, but they rose only slightly between 1994 and 2003

[40]Aggregate cross-country measures are market-weighted averages across six countries—the United States, Japan, the United Kingdom, Germany, France, and the Netherlands.

Figure 3.5. Foreign Asset Acceptance Ratios for Portfolio Assets[1]
(In percent)

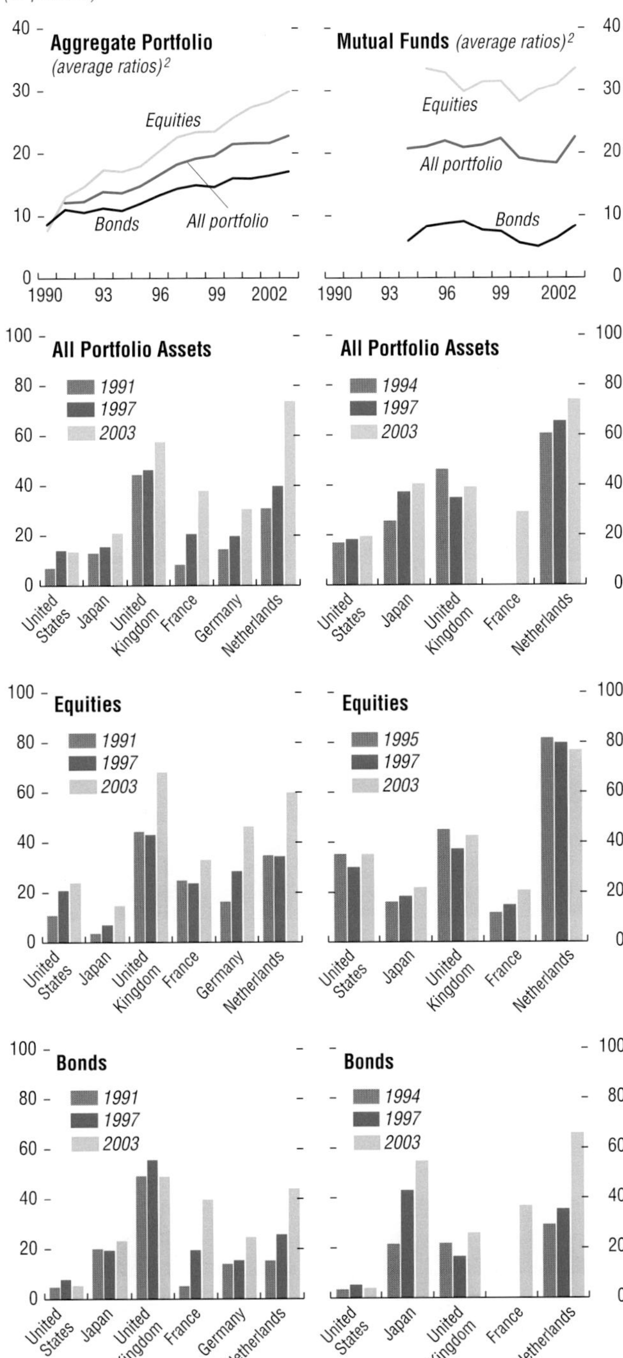

Sources: National flow of funds data; IMF, *Coordinated Porfolio Investment Survey* and *International Financial Statistics*; and IMF staff estimates.

[1]A foreign asset acceptance ratio of 100 percent corresponds to zero home bias. The lower the ratio, the greater the degree of home bias.

[2]Market-weighted averages of foreign asset acceptance ratios for the United States, Japan, the United Kingdom, France, Germany, and the Netherlands.

Figure 3.6. Foreign Asset Acceptance Ratios[1]
(In percent)

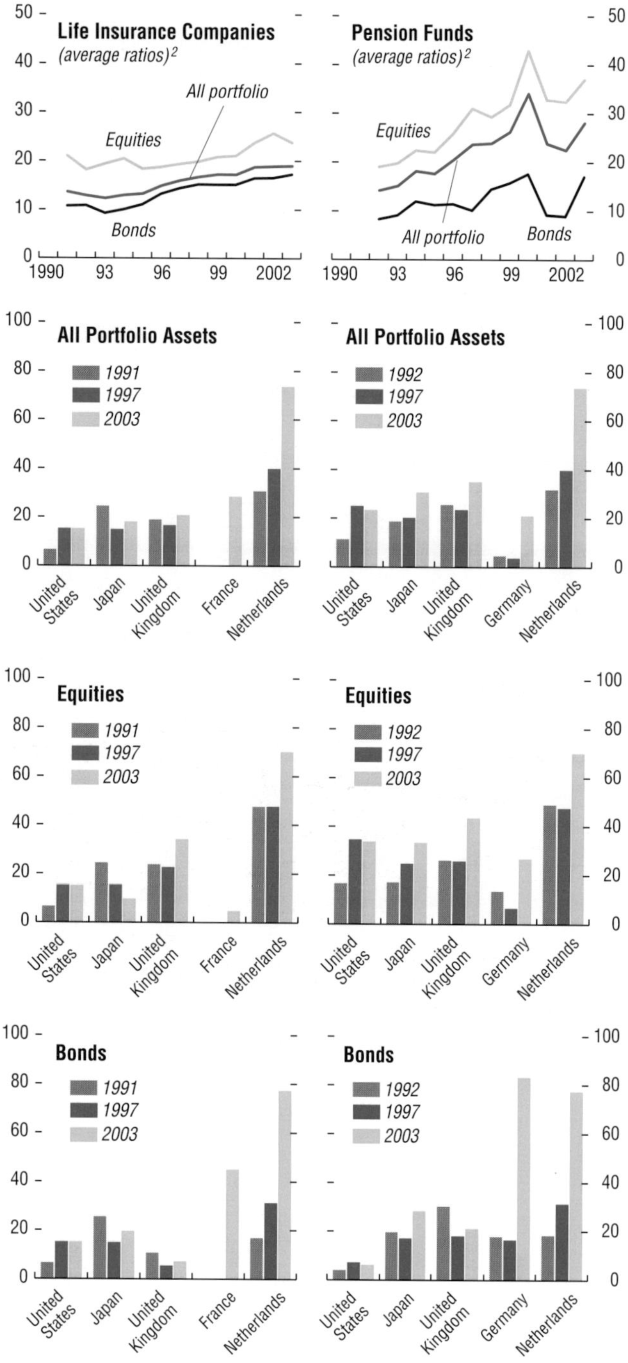

Sources: National flow of funds data; IMF, *Coordinated Porfolio Investment Survey* and *International Financial Statistics*; Watson Wyatt; and IMF staff estimates.

[1]A foreign asset acceptance ratio of 100 percent corresponds to zero home bias. The lower the ratio, the greater the degree of home bias.

[2]Market-weighted averages of foreign asset acceptance ratios for the United States, Japan, the United Kingdom, France, Germany, and the Netherlands.

(Figure 3.5), from 21 percent to 23 percent.[41] More than most investors, owners of mutual funds have demonstrated a relatively greater willingness to hold foreign equities than foreign bonds. There have been steady increases in mutual fund holdings of foreign assets in the United States, the Netherlands, and, especially, Japan. Japan is an important exception to the mutual fund owners' tendency to focus on increasing foreign equities rather than foreign bonds. The share of foreign bonds among mutual funds in the Netherlands also increased sharply, with most of the increase accounted for by euro-denominated bonds.

Life insurers' foreign asset acceptance ratio increased from 13 percent in 1991 to 18 percent in 2003 (Figure 3.6), but remained somewhat lower than that of other classes of institutional investors. Because life insurers' portfolios are concentrated more heavily in bonds than those of other institutional investors (see Module 1 on the Global Asset Allocation Process), the overall FAAR closely tracks that for bonds alone. Life insurers in the United States, the United Kingdom, and the Netherlands increased their holdings of foreign assets between 1991 and 2003, while insurers in Japan reduced foreign holdings from 1991 to 1997, then raised them in 2003.

Private pension funds' foreign asset acceptance ratios increased more rapidly, and to a higher level, than those of the other major institutional investors examined in this section. Between 1992 and 2003, the average pension fund FAAR rose from 14 percent to 28 percent (Figure 3.6). Pension funds in the United States, Japan, the United Kingdom, the Netherlands, and Germany all had large increases in holdings of foreign assets between 1991 and 2003. In the United States and the United Kingdom, the increase was

[41]Cross-country comparisons of trends among mutual funds or other single investor classes should be regarded as more tentative than cross-country comparisons of aggregate investor trends, because of gaps in the institutional investor data.

concentrated in equities. In the two euro area countries, Germany and the Netherlands, there were increases in both foreign equity and foreign bond ratios, but the increases in foreign bonds were especially pronounced. Japanese pension funds raised holdings of foreign bonds and foreign equities in roughly equal proportions.

Structural Factors That Contribute to Home Bias

Regulatory Factors

Home bias in asset allocations may arise from a variety of sources. At times, regulators have indicated ceilings on holdings of certain types of foreign assets, as was informally the case for insurance companies and pension funds in Japan until 1998.[42] There have also been reporting requirements or other restrictions that have raised the cost of acquiring foreign assets for all classes of investors, as was once the case in Japan and in the United Kingdom.

At present, authorities in the six countries covered in this module report no restrictions on outward portfolio investment for institutional investors, with some exceptions related to insurance companies. German insurers are bound by limitations on the concentration of insurance company assets by country and issuer, and by some percentage limits on holding of foreigh equity. France limits the concentration of insurance company equity holdings by country and issuer and, in the United States, some state regulators impose percentage limits on insurance company holdings of foreign assets.

Differential regulatory treatment of domestic and foreign currency assets may also affect institutional investors' willingness to hold foreign assets. For insurers (and banks) that operate under risk-based capital regulatory regimes, the risk weighting attached to a foreign asset may be higher than the weighting for a similar domestic asset. That is the case in Japan and the United States for foreign bonds relative to domestic bonds, a factor that could serve as a disincentive to hold foreign bonds.

An additional potential regulatory source of home bias stems from accounting standards. Hedge accounting standards, such as those now in use in the United Kingdom, the United States, and, to some extent, Japan, encourage the selection of assets with durations and currency denominations closely matching those of long-term liabilities—examples of such liabilities include death benefits or expected pension payments. Such standards have not been as binding in continental Europe, but may become more so as European institutional investors implement the International Financial Reporting Standards (IFRS).

Other regulatory changes may also affect the share of foreign assets in domestic portfolios. In Japan, a change to allow the sale of mutual funds by banks has been an important factor in the growth of funds that specialize in foreign bonds. The imposition of limits on bank deposit guarantees also played a role in increasing the relative attractiveness of foreign assets to Japanese investors, according to a number of market participants.

Institutional Practices

Industry practices, including benchmarking and compensation, also may contribute to home bias. For mutual funds and defined contribution pension funds in particular, an asset manager's performance is often measured relative to a benchmark. Traditionally such benchmarks have been geared to domestic market indices, such as the S&P 500 in the United States. More recently, a growing proportion of funds and fund managers have adopted global benchmarks, indicating that benchmarking may be evolving from a source of home bias to a source of international

[42]The widely understood limit for foreign asset holdings was 30 percent.

diversification. Some managers, not only of mutual funds but also of hedge funds and university endowments, have reported that they increasingly allocate assets with less focus on geographic mix than on other characteristics of the targeted asset class.

Transaction Costs, Market Risks, and Other Factors

Globalization and deregulation have steadily reduced the average costs of international trading of portfolio assets, to the extent that most asset managers report that costs are no longer major obstacles to investment in foreign assets. Nevertheless, the transaction costs of international asset trades are often higher than the costs of domestic asset trades. There may be extra costs associated with registering in, or otherwise gaining access to, a foreign market. In addition, foreign currency transactions typically require payment of a commission. Such costs raise the required return threshold of a foreign portfolio investment.

Information costs and asymmetries have also declined, particularly with advances in global communications and with the rapid increase in the availability of market information. However, market participants report that relative scarcity of information about some foreign markets may still be an important obstacle to certain investments, particularly where language differences are great, geographical separation is considerable, or disclosure standards differ substantially from home markets. Some asset managers cite the example of investment in smaller firms in emerging markets as an area where information limitations may lead to underweighting a market, or to herding behavior in which most foreign investors concentrate on the same few firms. Some impediments to inward foreign investment may be more than informational. Where legal systems and other market institutions are less conducive to entrepreneurial activity (e.g., emerging markets with limited property rights or weak corporate governance), inward investment may be lower.

Aversion to currency risk continues to be an important source of home bias, particularly with regard to bond investments, according to a number of market participants. For example, asset managers in Japan have cited a decline in recent and expected yen volatility as one important factor in the continuing decline in Japanese home bias. While currency risk can generally be hedged, the availability of longer-term hedges may be limited. Moreover, covered interest parity implies that the cost of a full duration-matched hedge on a foreign fixed-income investment would offset the expected gain from the investment.

The experience of countries that adopted the common euro currency in 1999 gives credence to the importance of currency risk in bond investment. Investors in France, Germany, and the Netherlands all boosted the share of foreign bonds in domestic portfolios between 1997 and 2003 (Table 3.8), with most of the increased allocation going to bonds issued by other euro area countries.[43] Indeed, French investors reduced holdings of bonds from non–euro area issuers over this period while dramatically raising their holdings of bonds issued by the other 11 euro area countries. Investors in the Netherlands did raise the share of non–euro area bonds in their bond portfolios, but not by as much as they increased the share of euro area foreign bonds. The more limited data on Germany also point to an increasing share of euro area bonds. The fact that foreign euro area bonds became more attractive in each country as the currency union went into effect suggests that investors in each of the three countries had a relative preference for own-currency bonds and, presumably, an aversion to currency risk.

[43]The tendency to switch into euro area bonds, rather than other foreign bonds, was particularly pronounced among life insurers, typically the most conservative of major institutional investors.

Table 3.8. Share of Foreign Bonds from Inside and Outside Euro Area
(As a percentage of total domestic bond market capitalization)

	1997	2001	2003
Inside euro area[1]			
France	8.4	29.3	34.1
Germany	. . .	13.7	15.0
Netherlands	17.5	24.7	28.3
Average[2]	. . .	20.3	23.3
Outside euro area			
France	10.2	5.2	3.5
Germany	. . .	7.5	7.6
Netherlands	7.8	12.4	14.7
Average[2]	. . .	7.5	7.3

Sources: National flow of funds data; IMF, *Coordinated Portfolio Investment Survey*; and IMF staff estimates.
[1]Euro area excluding domestic market bond share.
[2]Market-weighted average of the three countries.

Cyclical factors may also influence measured home bias, in some cases working to reduce it. One example is the "search for yield" on the part of fixed-income investors in low-interest-rate countries. Investors, such as retired households, with a need for a steady flow of interest income may be impelled to venture abroad in search of yield when domestic interest rates fall too far. This appears to be occurring in Japan, where the popularity of foreign bond funds that are structured to provide a steady flow of yen income has risen rapidly.

Potential Benefits and Costs of Reduction in Home Bias

The gain to an investor from international diversification arises from the fact that foreign assets provide a natural hedge that the investor can exploit to reduce portfolio volatility while maintaining expected returns. Alternatively, the investor can achieve higher returns with the same ex ante volatility by taking advantage of diversification opportunities. In theory, increasing exposure to foreign assets when one's foreign asset allocation ratio is below 100 percent is always desirable.[44] The greater the cross-border difference between asset characteristics, the greater are the potential gains of diversification. A good example is the potential gains available to both countries from financial diversification between a demographically older mature economy and a more rapidly growing emerging economy. For some investors, diversification across asset classes (e.g., into commodities or real estate), even if it is not aimed primarily at increasing foreign asset holdings, may also have the effect of reducing home bias while raising risk-adjusted returns.

In practice, however, it is possible that expected returns on foreign assets are not high enough, and the volatility and correlation with domestic assets are not low enough, to justify increasing foreign asset holdings. It is even possible that an investor with an FAAR well below 100 percent would gain from reducing exposure to foreign assets. Box 3.1 illustrates one approach to estimating the potential gains available to investors in each of four countries—the United States, Japan, the United Kingdom, and Germany—from adjusting portfolios. The calculation, which is illustrative only, and includes too few classes of assets for precise measurement, suggests that Japanese investors still have much to gain from further diversification, while investors in the United Kingdom and Germany have already attained most of the potential benefits of diversification. The potential gain for U.S. investors is surprisingly small, given the extent of home bias still present in U.S. portfolios.

One crucial consideration not included in risk-adjusted return calculations is an investor's institutional liability structure, which is important for life insurers and defined benefit pension providers. While such investors still prefer higher returns to lower returns, they also wish

[44]Under the international capital asset pricing model, this is because the prices of different assets reflect expected returns and correlations (a condition not always met in practice).

Box 3.1. A Sample Calculation of Potential Gains from International Diversification

To provide a basis for assessing the costs of home bias, a standard portfolio optimization model is used to estimate the "best" available combinations of risk and return available to each of the four countries—the United States, Germany, the United Kingdom, and Japan.[1] Using an iterative optimization algorithm, the model estimates the potential gains in risk-adjusted returns available from portfolio adjustment, with the relevant asset class characteristics estimated from historical returns, volatilities, and correlations, converted into the domestic currency. For most assets, 25-year annual time series are used to calculate expected returns, volatilities, and correlations. Bond returns are calculated as annual ex post own-currency returns on a one-year bond. For Japan, Germany, and the United Kingdom, returns based on own currency—yen, DM/euro, pound—from U.S. equity and bond markets are used for the foreign bond and equity markets. For the United States, an optimally weighted average of the other three markets is used to calculate equity returns; fixed-income returns are calculated from German data.

[1]For ease of computation, the model makes several simplifying assumptions, including consideration of a restricted set of assets for each country and the exclusion of emerging market assets. Inclusion of a wider range of assets, particularly assets that are not strongly correlated with domestic markets, could show greater gains to diversification.

Actual portfolios for each country are calculated in the aggregate. The first four rows of the table show the average shares of residents' portfolios presently devoted to domestic equities, foreign equities, domestic bonds, and foreign bonds. Rows 5–8 show the expected return of the current portfolio and the standard deviation, in percent, together with the potential gain in returns from a portfolio adjustment (maintaining the same volatility). The bottom row describes the indicated portfolio adjustment to achieve the potential gain.

Because this calculation is abstracted from important portfolio features, including variation within the foreign portfolio mix, taxes, and dividends, the results must be interpreted with caution, and should be regarded as only suggestive. Nevertheless, the qualitative results are of interest. Of the four countries, Japan is shown to have the most to gain from further reduction in home bias, despite its recent rapid accumulation of foreign assets. By holding more foreign bonds and foreign equities, Japanese investors could raise expected average returns by almost 1 percent. In contrast, the United States stands to gain only a limited amount in expected returns, even though its FAAR is relatively low. Germany, which is already well diversified internationally, is on its risk-return frontier; it cannot raise expected return without increasing volatility. Based on historical returns, investors in the United Kingdom would potentially benefit from a small shift into their own equity market.

Potential Gains from Portfolio Adjustment
(In percent)

Current Allocation	United States	Germany	Japan	United Kingdom
Domestic equity	39	15	20	34
Foreign equity	6	12	3	16
Domestic bond	53	56	61	27
Foreign bond	2	17	16	22
Expected return	5.8	4.3	1.9	7.6
Standard deviation	7.0	7.4	5.3	9.8
Potential gain in return	0.3	0.0	1.0	0.1
Indicated portfolio adjustment	Higher share of foreign bonds, *lower* foreign equity share, more foreign assets overall.	No change; portfolio is already optimized for given risk level.	Higher shares of both foreign bonds and foreign equities.	Small *reductions* in foreign bonds and foreign equities.

Sources: National flow of funds; Bloomberg; and IMF staff estimates.

to hold assets that are duration- and currency-matched to their (usually long-term) liabilities.[45] Liability matching considerations are therefore a "legitimate" source of home bias, but it is not necessarily the case that currency-matched assets are always the most appropriate, particularly for pensions. Since pension beneficiaries are ultimately concerned with future consumption rather than nominal income, they may be better off with a portion of their benefits pledged in real terms. In this case, foreign currency assets may be better suited than domestic assets for providing the requisite inflation hedge.

Additional Sources of Foreign Exposure

Some of the diversification benefits of foreign portfolio investment may also be achieved through investment in global companies. Domestically listed firms that supply goods or services in foreign markets, or that compete with foreign firms in domestic markets, are exposed to foreign cyclical conditions. In the case of some emerging markets, investment in global firms (e.g., energy, financial, or consumer products companies) may be the most efficient means of gaining diversified exposure. For a retail investor, such an investment may even be superior to buying the shares of an unfamiliar foreign company. Investment in a global company, or in a firm with significant business interests in a few foreign markets, gives local investors exposure to foreign economic performance through professional management, substituting the firm's own foreign direct investment for an investor's purchase of foreign shares or bonds.

The case of Germany illustrates the possible gains available from such alternative channels of diversification. In the previous section, German investors are shown as having realized the full potential gains of diversification, despite having 71 percent of their portfolio assets concentrated in the domestic market. To a degree, this is a consequence of the high correlation between the German equity market and foreign markets, reflecting the large share of global firms contained in the German DAX index.[46] Smaller countries with highly internationalized financial sectors, such as the Netherlands, Switzerland, or Singapore, may have a similar or even greater degree of "built-in" diversification.

The United States provides a different type of example. Domestic assets make up 92 percent of U.S. portfolios, and even the FAAR for the United States, which accounts for the size of the U.S. market, is the lowest of the six countries in the analysis, at 13.4 percent in 2003. Yet the potential gains to portfolio diversification for U.S. investors appear to be quite limited, according to the analysis of the previous section. A possible explanation is that, even though the foreign exposure available through the S&P 500 may be lower than what is available from domestic indices to domestic investors elsewhere, it is large enough so that much of the potential gain from exposure to foreign markets for U.S. investors has already been achieved through the direct foreign investments of U.S.-listed firms.

Other possible substitutes for foreign portfolio investment may include currency derivatives or structured products linked to foreign exchange rates. For some investors, domestic instruments that provide yields linked to the domestic currency return on foreign bonds offer useful diversification opportunities. However, a general increase in demand from a large domestic investor class (e.g., life insurers) for returns linked to foreign fixed-income instruments would still tend to result in net outward foreign portfolio investment, as the number of domestic counterparties willing to

[45]The liability matching requirement can be incorporated in the risk-adjusted return calculation by taking account of the expected correlation between assets and liabilities.

[46]For example, the correlation coefficient for returns from the DAX and German-currency-denominated returns from the S&P 500 for 1981–2004 is 0.79.

supply such instruments without themselves hedging overseas would likely be limited.

Conclusions

Changing institutional incentives, including elimination of restrictions on foreign portfolio investments, the adoption of global benchmarks, and greater emphasis on the importance of risk-adjusted returns, have led to a persistent decline in home bias over the past 15 years. While almost all countries have registered some decline in home bias, certain classes of investors—for example, owners of Japanese mutual funds, and British and continental European pension funds—have increased foreign asset allocation much more rapidly. In general, the pace of foreign asset acquisition appears to have depended on the possible gains available in risk-adjusted returns, and, in the case of euro area countries, on the redenomination of some foreign assets into domestic currency.

The trend in further reduction in home bias is expected to continue, particularly in markets where the potential gains are perceived as large, such as Japan. But there are some grounds for caution. Cross-border integration of asset markets also increases the likelihood that some asset price shocks will travel across borders. Should the domestic consequences of such a shock be severe, there may be pressure for some asset managers to reduce foreign asset holdings. Similarly, an increase in currency volatility could end the decline in home bias and diminish cross-border flows.

Continued reduction in home bias would benefit high-savings countries with aging populations, while encouraging countries with less-developed markets to upgrade their financial infrastructure. That could eventually make some developing countries more resistant to the destabilizing effects of short-term "hot money" flows. Higher exposure to foreign assets offers the prospect of raising returns on investment while reducing volatility, thereby supporting financial stability. Authorities therefore have incentives to consider regulatory and other policy changes that may reduce home bias. However, the increase in cross-border capital flows associated with a continued reduction in home bias may increase the degree of correlation among asset markets, presenting new challenges for policymakers. In light of the anticipated increased demand for internationally diversified assets and portfolios, smaller and developing countries should continue to improve their local markets, as investors will likely favor markets with stronger infrastructures.

The financial internationalization entailed by reduction in home bias also poses challenges at the multilateral level. Efforts that promote transparency, such as the IMF-World Bank Standards and Codes Initiative, are likely to help reduce the danger of contagion between financial markets as a result of partial or erroneous information. Financial integration also raises the premium on strong multilateral surveillance from the IMF and other international organizations, both as an information source in its own right and as a means of improving public and corporate governance.

Module 4. Financial Stability Considerations Related to Trends in Accounting Standards

Our series on risk transfer in the previous issues of the GFSR highlighted how accounting standards (and regulations) may significantly influence investment and risk management behavior, as well as asset allocation among key institutional investors, such as pension funds and insurance companies. As part of this chapter's theme of global asset allocation, this module steps back from detailed issues associated with recent or proposed accounting reforms to ask how accounting standards, particularly as applied to pension funds and insurers, may influence financial stability. Without a doubt, these are complicated issues, and the major standards setters (the U.S. Financial Accounting Standards Board and the International Accounting Standards Board) are working to improve accounting principles in order to enhance the comparability and transparency of accounts, which deserves strong support. Indeed, many of the recently considered and proposed accounting standards are aimed at moving toward a broadly applicable best practice for measurement, and away from long-standing measurement methods that arguably contributed to or masked some of the recent problems experienced by pension funds and insurance companies. However, there has been very little commentary or analysis that broadly assesses the impact of these proposals on the larger issue of financial stability. This module presents a balanced review of the relevant policy issues, and raises questions related to financial stability that policymakers may consider as accounting standards are being reviewed.

Risk Transfer

In recent years, financial stability is generally viewed by authorities as having improved, in large part through more proactive risk management activities by banks and the related transfer and dispersion of risks from banks to diverse nonbanking institutions, which often have longer-term liability structures, and therefore may be more appropriate holders of such risks. As a result, systemically important banks are broadly recognized today as more financially stable and resilient. Banks are also currently viewed as leaders with regard to risk management practices, encouraged in part by regulatory and supervisory developments (e.g., risk-based capital requirements). This has encouraged the spread of various risk management practices from banks to nonbanking institutions.

The risk management techniques increasingly being adopted in other sectors are often designed to control exposures to credit and market risks in an environment where asset prices and liquidity may change rapidly. While relevant to certain parts of their business and activities, such short-term risk tools may not be as relevant to all parts of the activities of insurers and pension funds as they are for commercial and investment banks. As such, this module asks whether certain risk management and related financial reporting standards typically applied to such banks are equally appropriate for all nonbanking sectors, particularly pension funds and insurers.[47] Clearly, numerous cross-sector benefits have emerged. However, the possible impact on financial stability may remain open, unless policymakers and standard setters consider fully the potential influence of such standards on the investment and risk management behavior of nonbanks.

Accounting Affects Behavior

There is widespread agreement that accounting, financial reporting, and other issues of measurement influence the behavior of market participants (i.e., managers, creditors, shareholders, and other stakeholders). In addition, researchers have analyzed and assessed different channels by which accounting standards influence a firm's management and various stakeholders' behavior.[48]

It is also important to acknowledge a few practical considerations relevant to this discussion. First, markets may sometimes be imperfect, at least in the short run, and thus may

[47]Some bank regulations and risk management practices are considered to have undesirable operational characteristics. For example, Clerc, Drumetz, and Jaudoin (2002) discuss how bank capital requirements, regulations, and risk management models have procyclical properties that must be moderated by proactive bank supervision.

[48]For example, Plantin, Sapra, and Shin (2005) develop a model to demonstrate that accounting changes influence the actions of market participants. Hill and others (2005) and the Geneva Association (2004) highlight how changes in accounting standards could affect risk management practices in insurance companies.

not always reflect fundamental values or operate in a frictionless manner. As such, markets are frequently influenced by outside factors, such as accounting standards, that can contribute to procyclical behavior caused by a feedback mechanism from short-term price movements. In part, such market behavior may relate to the fact that many markets do not exhibit the depth and liquidity assumed in "perfect" markets, and therefore only in the longer term do markets "correctly" reflect fundamental values. Finally, and most important, many assets classes, and even more so balance sheet liabilities, lack a reasonably transparent and observable market price. Of course, this is an important impediment to any standards setter given the task of measuring financial performance. This is particularly true for many of the long-term liabilities (and related embedded options) on the balance sheets of pensions and insurers. Indeed, the inability to reliably measure and report liability values may represent the greatest source of "accounting volatility" as standards setters seek to develop measurement and valuation approaches.[49]

As discussed in the first module of this chapter, pension funds and life insurance companies are each a very important and significant investor class, with pension funds the largest investor group in many countries. The liability structures of pension funds and insurance companies have historically allowed them to play a supportive role in financial stability by maintaining a longer-term investment horizon and an asset allocation strategy rarely influenced by short-term market fluctuations. Indeed, from a financial stability perspective, the "acyclical" investment behavior of pension funds and (to a lesser extent) insurance companies has represented a relatively stable and steady source of investment capital.[50]

The desire by the standards setters to increase the "accuracy" of financial reports has promoted the broader use of mark-to-market valuations for all companies, including their pension funds. However, fair value approaches require the existence of active and liquid markets, or some reasonable proxy, that can readily provide observed "value-in-exchange" prices. Moreover, to be implemented effectively, fair value approaches should require the same for liabilities. By comparison, "value-in-use" prices, which are meant to reflect the asset value to that particular business or purpose, are derived from projected future cash flows or the hedging value of a firm's assets and liabilities. As such, both approaches present measurement challenges.

An important consideration is whether fair value accounting may shorten the decision horizons of market participants, both users and preparers of accounts. Recent studies, and discussions with company executives and investors, suggest that shifting to fair value accounting, with frequent adjustments to earnings, may reinforce incentives to engage in short-term, procyclical activities.[51] Furthermore, many corporate officers have noted the rising tension between company sponsors and their defined benefit pension funds, as spon-

[49]The measurement difficulties may represent the greatest obstacle to fair or market value principles, particularly longer-term assets and (even more so) liabilities. As such, in discussions with the standards setters, it was discussed that full fair value accounting standards (including reporting all value changes in the earnings statement) may be best applied to those assets and liabilities with a shorter remaining life (e.g., 5 or 10 years), in order to reflect the more pending and measurable financial requirements.

[50]A recent example of this acyclical behavior was evident in the structured credit markets of April and May. Market participants widely commented on how insurers (especially) and pension funds during this volatile period did not sell into downward price swings, and frequently referred to their "non–mark-to-market behavior," compared with the trading or "mark-to-market" behavior of hedge funds or investment banks.

[51]Burkhardt and Strausz (2004) present a model outlining how fair value accounting may provide incentives for increased procyclical behavior. They also show that there may be incentives for an intermediary to sell its higher quality assets, leaving lower quality assets on its books.

sors seek to manage down the potential earnings volatility from their pension funds. As such, pursuant to a full implementation of fair value accounting (i.e., whereby all valuation changes are reported through the earnings statement) companies with large pension funds may have greater incentives to procyclically sell assets during market downturns to limit valuation effects, and thereby exacerbate market swings. In other words, when the decision horizon is shortened, the recent experience or anticipation of price movements will affect a firm's decisions, which in turn may inject further volatility into markets and prices. Indeed, this may be more likely for longer duration assets and more illiquid asset classes and markets (e.g., structured credit, or smaller domestic or developing markets), which has particular relevance for pensions and insurers.[52]

To be clear, pension funds and hedge funds are not expected to pursue similar trading strategies because of accounting policy, nor does volatility alone equal financial instability. However, extreme volatility or liquidity "black holes" can create disorderly markets and lead to financial instability.[53] As such, this module asks whether the financial stability gains in recent periods, due in large part to the dispersion of risks and the diversity of investor behavior in a variety of markets, may be reduced, and procyclical behavior increased, by such accounting or financial reporting policies.

Fair value accounting is certainly a useful measure and representation of financial activities under many circumstances, and is appropriate and desirable for a variety of uses. For example, management and regulatory accounting should include all relevant and reliable market valuations for risk management and other purposes, and would clearly benefit from market or fair value measures. Fair value measures can also serve as an instrument of discipline for financial intermediaries, where senior executives in the past may have been slow to face the reality of persistently lower asset prices or inappropriate risk management systems. Valuation of assets and liabilities closer to market values would also make more explicit the amount of intertemporal risk sharing provided by life insurers. Risk sharing over time is a result of mismatches between an insurer's assets and liabilities, and is therefore linked to one of the key concerns expressed about fair value accounting: namely, the fact that reported earnings would likely become more volatile as values of assets and liabilities behave differently. To the extent that the higher earnings volatility stems from an asset and liability mismatch, it is in large part a real risk and is the result of risk sharing over time provided by the insurer. Fair value accounting will likely make this intertemporal risk sharing more explicit and apparent, and would reveal its costs more clearly. This type of risk sharing would therefore likely be priced by the market more appropriately.[54]

Financial reports are used differently by different parties, and an accounting framework that mandates a single approach for valuing assets and liabilities may not reflect the economic fundamentals or reality for all stakeholders, including regulators. These differing requirements may depend on whether the user is assessing the credit quality (e.g., estimating the probability of default) or the long-

[52]Plantin, Sapra, and Shin (2005) demonstrate that, influenced by accounting treatment, managers may sell assets following price swings or market shocks that they would otherwise have retained, particularly longer-duration assets. Moreover, they also highlight conditions under which such actions may amplify the effects of market shocks. See also Hann, Heflin, and Subramanyam (2004).

[53]Liquidity black holes are extreme situations where selling activity increases the incentives or pressures for other market participants to sell into declining markets (i.e., a one-sided market develops), and the process becomes self-reinforcing. See Morris and Shin (2004); and Plantin, Sapra, and Shin (2005) for a more detailed analysis.

[54]See Häusler (2003).

run value (e.g., equity price) of a firm.[55] For example, certain public bodies, such as the U.S. Pension Benefit Guaranty Corporation or the U.K. Pension Protection Fund, may require current market valuations (including liquidation or run-off values) in forming their regulatory or prudential assessments. By comparison, equity investors may focus more on the value of assets in the business, including as held against certain pension or insurance liabilities, as they evaluate the longer-term performance of a firm.[56] In this latter case, separating the short-term or transitory effects from the more permanent changes in value may be very difficult in a full fair value system. In such a situation, fair value accounting principles may induce a much greater focus on short-term (e.g., quarterly) earnings management, and thus produce more active rebalancing or trading of the investment portfolios of pension funds and insurers in the financial markets.

Efforts by Accounting Standards Setters

Standards setters, such as the FASB and the IASB, are currently considering a variety of accounting and reporting standards with the goal of reflecting economic reality, maintaining or enhancing comparability and use, and improving the transparency of the financial affairs of the business. They are guided by principles such as relevance and reliability, and utilize tools such as measurement, disclosure, and presentation to accurately reflect a company's underlying fundamentals. Policymakers and regulators have also sought to ensure that changes in international accounting standards work to enhance transparency and improve the understanding and comparability of accounts, and thereby promote efficient cross-border investment and company access to capital.[57] These are clearly appropriate and necessary goals and conditions for the functioning of financial markets.

The current "mixed attributes" model of accounting and financial reporting has attempted to recognize different investment periods, where some assets are valued at market prices and others are carried at historical cost (e.g., "hold-to-maturity" versus "assets available for sale," and trading assets). The banking industry illustrates requirements for using different reporting frameworks even within a single institution—a practice that can be accommodated with the "mixed attributes" model. Bank earnings often stem from a variety of activities. Trading activities by banks are driven largely by the buying and selling of securities, where assessments of rapidly changing relative values are critical. Fair value accounting seems an appropriate framework in this case, since it mirrors the information and decision process of the business activity. By comparison, banks often hold loans to maturity. Under these circumstances, historical or amortized cost accounting may be appropriate where the value of the loan

[55]Hann, Heflin, and Subramanyam (2004) discuss the different information requirements of creditors compared with equity investors. They present evidence that, under certain market conditions, the increased earnings volatility in fair value reporting may make it more difficult for investors to separate transitory from permanent changes in a company's earnings potential.

[56]The importance of financial reporting and the disclosure of relevant information for financial stability is emphasized in Michael (2004). Allen and Gale (1998) discuss some of the literature on the impact of stakeholder perceptions of bank asset valuations, and develop a model of bank runs induced by changes in perceived bank asset values. Bank industry groups have long called for an accounting and financial reporting framework that allows for a variety of valuation methodologies for measuring balance sheets and reporting performance (e.g., Joint Working Group of Banking Associations, 1999).

[57]Bies (2004) and Large (2004) are two recent examples of central bank policymakers recognizing the important influence accounting has on investors, creditors, and other market participants, and offering potential guidelines for accounting standards to promote efficient capital allocation and sound banking standards. In addition, the desire to improve transparency and promote comparability recently led the Securities and Exchange Commission (SEC) staff to recommend continued efforts to facilitate the implementation of fair value accounting (see SEC, 2005).

depends more on credit quality and the cost of servicing the loan.[58]

Despite the efforts of standards setters to improve accounting and financial reporting standards, financial officers and other market participants frequently highlight how new or proposed standards may influence their decision making. Some accounting conventions (e.g., hedge accounting) may cause listed companies to forgo economically beneficial decisions to avoid increased earnings volatility and potentially adverse investor reactions, even if the increased reported volatility does not reflect the firm's underlying business or risk profile.[59] The standards setters are aware and sensitive to these issues and concerns. Indeed, at present, a potentially very important joint FASB and IASB project is under way, called "Financial Performance Reporting by Business Enterprises." In short, the project seeks to preserve the measurement benefits of using market or fair values wherever possible, while addressing concerns about transitory or nonrecurring volatilities through a variety of presentation frameworks. For example, one possibility is that short-term, transitory value effects may be reported "below the line," and as such be included in a "comprehensive income" figure for the period, but more easily separated for an analysis of longer-term value effects on a firm and (possibly) certain widely used earnings figures (i.e., net income, earnings per share, etc.). While this may represent an attractive way forward, it does not reconcile the difficulty of objectively measuring all balance sheet items, particularly liabilities, which may eliminate any reasonable concerns with fair value standards.

Preserving Financial Stability Gains

An important financial stability consideration is the depth of markets and the related diversity of investors, targeting a healthy mix of investors with a variety of investment behaviors, often related to liability and liquidity structures. However, as discussed above, different accounting and financial reporting standards that have historically facilitated such diversity are being reviewed. An important question is whether, in light of evolving accounting standards for pension funds and insurers, we may reduce the diversity of investment behavior, particularly as it relates to their long-term, stable investment behavior. In other words, would full implementation of fair value accounting lead to more procyclical market behavior among these large and important investors?

Our market surveillance produces an uncertain answer to these questions, at least in the near term. On the one hand, risk managers of insurance companies and pension funds repeatedly describe such accounting changes as increasing their need to more actively trade their investment portfolio to avoid accounting volatility. However, particularly for pension funds, such increased market activity would represent a significant change from their historical behavior. Indeed, their traditionally patient investment behavior, stemming in part from their longer-term liability structure, has enhanced financial stability. As such, if accounting changes cause these large and important investors to become more proactive and short-term focused, financial stability may also suffer.

There is strong support among company treasurers, financial officers, and regulators for designing financial accounting and reporting frameworks for shareholders and other stakeholders (i.e., external reports) that reflect the economic reality of an enterprise as a going concern in a full and transparent manner. Moreover, much of the "accounting volatility" that industry participants highlight,

[58]This banking example was adapted from Bies (2004).
[59]See Weinberg (2003).

particularly as it concerns the potential influence on pension funds and insurers, would either not exist or, alternatively, would correctly reflect asset-liability mismatches, if liabilities could be reliably measured and reported in the accounts. However, liability measures are broadly viewed as more problematic than asset values, so standards setters continue to struggle with a variety of "mixed" measurement frameworks. Therefore, in an imperfect world, policymakers need to consider whether proposed accounting reforms may not diminish the diversity of investment behavior and the long-term orientation of important institutional investors, which has typically enhanced financial stability.

Standards setters are currently considering a variety of accounting and reporting standards with the goal of better reflecting economic reality, maintaining or enhancing comparability and use, and improving the transparency of the financial affairs of the business. These are very desirable and appropriate goals, and important progress and improvements have been made in recent years related to these efforts. However, as standards setters and other policymakers reassess accounting and reporting standards, they should consider the broader financial stability issues, and the benefits from risk dispersion and investor diversity. As in other areas, we need to consider the consistency of various policies with the intended goals, as well as trying to understand the consequent flows of risk and behavioral effects related to such policies and standards.

References

Allen, Franklin, and Douglas Gale, 1998, "Optimal Financial Crises," *The Journal of Finance,* Vol. 53, No. 4 (August), pp. 1245–84.

Almeida Capital, 2005, *Fundraising Review 2004: A Preview for 2005* (London: Almeida Capital Limited, April). Available via the Internet: *http://www.altassets.com/2005review.php.*

Amenc, Noël, Jean-René Giraud, Philippe Malaise, and Lionel Martellini, 2004, *Be Active with Your Bond Trackers* (EDHEC Risk and Asset Management Research Centre, October).

Bank for International Settlements (BIS), Committee on the Global Financial System (CGFS), 2003, *Incentive Structures in Institutional Asset Management and Their Implications for Financial Markets* (Basel: BIS, March). Available via the Internet: *http://www.bis.org/publ/cgfs21.pdf.*

Bertaut, Carol C., and William Griever, 2004, "Recent Developments in Cross-Border Investments in Securities," *Federal Reserve Bulletin* (Winter), pp. 19–31.

Bies, Susan Schmidt, 2004, "Challenges Facing the Accounting Profession Today," speech delivered to the Cincinnati Chapter of the Ohio Society of Certified Public Accountants, September.

Burkhardt, Katrin, and Roland Strausz, 2004, "The Effect of Fair vs. Book Value Accounting on the Behavior of Banks" (unpublished; Berlin: Free University of Berlin).

Clerc, Laurent, Françoise Drumetz, and Olivier Jaudoin, 2002, "To What Extent Are Prudential and Accounting Arrangement Pro- or Counter-Cyclical with Respect to Overall Financial Conditions?" in *Bank for International Settlements Papers No. 1* (Basel: BIS, March), pp. 197–210.

Committee on Investment of Employee Benefit Assets (CIEBA), 2004, *The U.S. Pension Crisis—Evaluation and Analysis of Emerging Defined Benefit Pension Issues,* (Bethesda, Maryland: Association for Financial Professionals, March).

Counterparty Risk Management Policy Group II, 2005, *Toward Greater Financial Stability: A Private Sector Perspective* (July). Available via the Internet: *http://www.crmpolicygroup.org/docs/CRMPG-II.pdf.*

European Commission, 2005, *Green Paper on the Enhancement of the EU Framework for Investment Funds* (Brussels, July). Available via the Internet: *http://europa.eu.int/comm/internal_market/securities/docs/ucits/greenpaper_en.pdf.*

European Fund and Asset Management Association, 2005, *The European Personal Pension Account* (Brussels, May). Available via the Internet: *http://www.efama.org/30 Documents/80Pensions/1025Regulation/EFAMA%20Documents/eppareport/documentfile.*

Financial Services Authority, 2005, "Wider-Range Retail Investment Products," Discussion Paper No. 05/3 (London, June). Available via the

Internet: *http://www.fsa.gov.uk/pubs/discussion/dp05_03.pdf.*

Geneva Association, 2004, "Impact of a Fair Value Financial Reporting System on Insurance Companies: A Survey," *The Geneva Papers on Risk and Insurance Issues and Practice* (Geneva: International Association for the Study of Insurance Economics).

Greenwich Associates, 2005, "For U.S. Funds, Asset Allocation Strategies Feature International Equities and Alternative Investments" (March 11).

Hann, Rebecca, Frank Heflin, and K.R. Subramanyam, 2004, "Fair-Value Based Pension Accounting" (unpublished; Los Angeles: Leventhal School of Accounting, University of Southern California).

Häusler, Gerd, 2003, "The Insurance Industry, Fair Value Accounting and Systemic Financial Stability," speech delivered to the 30th General Assembly of the Geneva Association, London, June 13.

Hill, Andrew, Alexander Dieter Hofmann, Francesco Nagari, and Erica Nicholson, 2005, "The Implications of IFRS for General Insurers," IFRS Global Reporting Revolution (Pricewaterhouse Coopers, June).

International Monetary Fund, 2004a, "Risk Transfer and the Insurance Industry," *Global Financial Stability Report,* World Economic and Financial Surveys (Washington, April).

———, 2004b, "Risk Management and the Pension Fund Industry," *Global Financial Stability Report,* World Economic and Financial Surveys (Washington, September).

———, 2005a, *Global Financial Stability Report,* World Economic and Financial Surveys (Washington, April).

———, 2005b, "Globalization and External Imbalances," *World Economic Outlook,* World Economic and Financial Surveys (Washington, April).

International Organization of Securities Commissions (IOSCO), 2005, *Principles on Outsourcing of Financial Services for Market Intermediaries* (Madrid, February). Available via the Internet: *http://www.iosco.org/library/pubdocs/pdf/IOSCOPD187.pdf.*

Joint Working Group of Banking Associations, 1999, "Accounting for Financial Instruments for Banks" (October). Available via the Internet: *http://www.aba.com /aba/pdf /GR_tax_va4.PDF.*

Large, Andrew, 2004, "Financial Instrument Accounting," speech delivered to the 13th Central Banking Conference, London, November 22.

Michael, Ian, 2004, "Accounting and Financial Stability," *Financial Stability Review* (London: Bank of England, June).

Moore, James F., 2004, *Changing Paradigms in Asset Allocation for Pension Plans* (Newport Beach, California: PIMCO, May).

Morris, Stephen, and Hyun Song Shin, 2004, "Liquidity Black Holes," *Review of Finance,* Vol. 8, No. 1, pp. 1–18.

Myners, Paul, 2001, "Institutional Investment in the United Kingdom: A Review" (London: Her Majesty's Treasury, March). Available via the Internet: *http://www.hm-treasury.gov.uk/media/2F9/02/31.pdf.*

Obstfeld, Maurice, and Kenneth Rogoff, 1996, *Foundations of International Macroeconomics* (Cambridge, Massachusetts: MIT Press).

Organization for Economic Cooperation and Development (OECD), 2005, "White Paper on Governance of Collective Investment Schemes (CIS)," *Financial Market Trends,* No. 88 (March).

Plantin, Guillaume, Haresh Sapra, and Hyun Song Shin, 2005, "Marking-to-Market: Panacea or Pandora's Box" (London: London School of Economics, March).

Porter, Michael, and Lucas Garland, 2005, "Life Cycle Funds: Fit for Life," *Lipper Insight Reports* (March).

Private Equity Intelligence Ltd., 2005, *The 2005 Global Fund Raising Review* (London).

Reid, Brian, K., and John, D. Rea, 2003, "Mutual Fund Distribution Channels and Distribution Costs," *Perspective,* Vol. 9, No. 3 (Investment Company Institute, July).

Tesar, Linda L., and Ingrid Werner, 1995, "Home Bias and High Turnover," *Journal of International Money and Finance,* Vol. 14., No. 4, pp. 467–92.

UBS Global Asset Management, 2005, "Pension Fund Indicators 2005: A Long-Term Perspective on Pension Fund Investment" (London, May).

United Kingdom, Her Majesty's Stationery Office, 2004, "Pensions: Challenges and Choices, The First Report of the Pensions Commission" (London). Available via the Internet: *http://www.pensionscommission.org.uk/publications/2004/annrep/index.asp.*

United States Securities and Exchange Commission (SEC), 2005, "Report and Recommendations Pursuant to Section 401(c) of the Sarbanes-Oxley Act of 2002 on Arrangements with Off-Balance Sheet Implications, Special Purpose Entities, and Transparency of Filings by Issuers" (Washington, June 15). Available via the Internet: *http://www.sec.gov/news/studies/soxoffbalancerpt.pdf.*

Urwin, R.C., S.J. Breban, T.M. Hodgson, and A. Hunt, 2001, "Risk Budgeting in Pension Investment," *British Actuarial Journal,* Vol. 2, No. 3, pp. 319–64.

Weinberg, John A., 2003, "Accounting for Corporate Behavior," *Economic Quarterly,* Vol. 89, No. 3 (Richmond: Federal Reserve Bank of Richmond).

CHAPTER IV

DEVELOPMENT OF CORPORATE BOND MARKETS IN EMERGING MARKET COUNTRIES

The macroeconomic and financial dislocations experienced following the crises in emerging markets (EMs) in the late 1990s have led to increased efforts in these countries to develop local bond markets as an alternative source of debt financing for corporates. A well-functioning bond market can strengthen corporate and bank restructuring and thus accelerate the resolution of a crisis. At the same time, local bond issues facilitate the reduction of currency and maturity mismatches on their balance sheets and thus reduce the vulnerability of the corporate sector. Recent work by the IMF on the use of the balance sheet approach to detect vulnerabilities in EMs has highlighted the importance of corporate sector vulnerabilities and their linkages to other sectors and markets. In this context, the April 2005 *Global Financial Stability Report* (GFSR) demonstrated the importance of having alternative sources of funding for the corporate sector, both to finance growth and to strengthen balance sheets. In this chapter, we continue this line of work and focus on ways to further develop corporate bond markets in EMs.

Well-functioning local corporate bond markets provide institutional investors with an instrument that satisfies their demand for fixed-income assets, especially of long maturities, as well as for yield pickup over government bonds. Thus, corporate bonds also help strengthen balance sheets of pension funds and life insurance companies. In many countries, assets under management of institutional investors have been growing faster than the supply of local instruments in which to invest. In addition to allowing institutional investors to invest internationally, a deep and liquid corporate bond market may help prevent the development of asset price bubbles and reduce this source of financial instability.

This chapter provides an overview of the factors and reform measures that contribute to and promote effective corporate bond markets. It highlights lessons from the experiences of mature markets (MMs), as well as from a small group of EMs that either have large corporate bond markets or have seen them grow rapidly in recent years.[1] Many EMs have achieved a degree of macroeconomic stability—through fiscal consolidation and enhanced monetary policy credibility—and have made progress in the areas of banking supervision as well as in transparency and corporate governance. Some of these countries have been seeking to develop their corporate bond markets, but so far only the best corporates have been able to access these markets. Moreover, after a period of rapid growth in local corporate bond markets, issuance has slowed in the last two years, raising concerns that the initial growth was a purely cyclical phenomenon. In this chapter, we argue that a further broadening and deepening of these markets requires the removal of constraints mainly on the supply side, as well as improvements in market microstructure. Also, the lessons identified in this chapter could be relevant for other EMs that want to jump-start corporate bond markets.

Domestic corporate bonds may not, however, be a suitable instrument for all enterprises. Collateralized loan financing may be more accessible and appropriate for corporates that lack adequate credit information (IOSCO, 2004). In particular, small and medium-sized enterprises in many EMs are

[1]The chapter also draws some lessons from a few cases where clear constraints have prevented the emergence of corporate bond markets.

not able to access bond markets because of the inflexible structure of bond contracts, the high costs associated with issuance, and the need for large issuance size. At the other extreme, large corporates could find it more efficient to issue bonds in international or regional markets, although this may expose them to currency risks.

Moreover, despite the benefits associated with the provision of an alternative source of funding for corporates and a suitable instrument for local institutional investors, a rapid development of local corporate bond markets could be potentially risky. The development of these markets without minimum institutional support to deal with asymmetric information problems and other capital market imperfections—such as effective bankruptcy laws and transparency—could cause market turmoil and slow the development of such markets over the medium term.

Following a brief description of recent trends in global corporate bond markets, the next section focuses on demand and supply factors behind the development of corporate bond markets, as well as on the role played by financial intermediaries. Aspects of the microstructure of primary and secondary markets are discussed in the following section, after which a concluding section discusses the main challenges for and policy issues related to the development of these markets and their relation to financial stability.

Recent Trends in Local Corporate Bond Markets

This section looks at trends in corporate bond market development in emerging markets, focusing on some of the largest EMs over the past 10 years, with the pattern of development in the mature markets as background.[2]

The government and financial institutions remain the main issuers of local currency bonds, but corporate issuers are becoming important. As of end-2004, in mature markets, outstanding securities issued by the government, financial institutions, and corporates accounted for 66, 57, and 16 percent of GDP, respectively. In EMs, these figures were 25, 8, and 5 percent of GDP, respectively (Table 4.1). The existence of a well-developed government bond market has been important in the development of the corporate bond markets,[3] and cross-country analysis suggests that countries with larger outstanding government debt securities tend to have larger corporate bond markets (Figure 4.1).[4] Also, while bank lending remains the main source of corporate finance in most mature and emerging markets (excluding retained earnings), corporate bond financing is increasing in relative terms.[5]

The size of local corporate bond markets, as a percent of GDP, varies widely across countries. Among MMs, the United States has the largest (deepest) corporate bond market accounting for about 22 percent of GDP, followed by Japan at 16 percent of GDP, and the euro area countries at 10 percent of GDP. For most of the emerging markets countries, corporate bond markets remain small. However, the corporate bond markets in Malaysia and Korea are among the largest in the world in terms of GDP: 38 and 21 percent, respectively. Corporate bond markets in Thailand have been growing fast and reached about 12 percent of GDP by end-2004. In Latin America, Chile stands out; the outstanding volume of its corporate bonds amounts to 11 percent of GDP.

[2]In this chapter, local bonds are defined as bonds issued under local law.

[3]For further details, see Mathieson and others (2004); and Eichengreen and Luengnaruemitchai (2004).

[4]Japan's exceptionally high ratio of government bonds to GDP is a result of the strong longer-term financing needs for the past fiscal stimulus policies in the 1990s, when the government sector's balance sheet deteriorated rapidly. In addition to the absolute amount of government bonds, the well-balanced maturity of government bonds outstanding is important for the corporate bond market in terms of forming a stable benchmark of yield curves.

[5]See IMF (2005) for the main trends in corporate finance in emerging markets.

Table 4.1. Outstanding Domestic Debt Securities, Stock Market Capitalization, and Bank Credit, 2004

	Total Outstanding	Government Securities	Financial Institutions	Corporate Issuers	Stock Market Capitalization	Bank Credit
			(In billions of U.S. dollars)			
Emerging markets	**2,668.4**	**1,772.0**	**585.5**	**320.3**	**4,286.4**	**4,568.6**
Africa	**104.6**	**78.3**	**12.1**	**14.2**	**455.5**	**177.4**
South Africa	104.6	78.3	12.1	14.2	455.5	177.4
Asia	**1,508.9**	**791.2**	**472.7**	**244.9**	**2,622.8**	**3,668.7**
China	483.3	287.4	183.7	12.2	639.8	2,318.0
Hong Kong SAR	46.5	15.8	24.9	5.8	861.5	244.8
India	239.2	235.0	1.4	2.8	387.9	253.4
Korea	568.4	171.6	237.5	159.2	428.6	605.8
Malaysia	106.6	45.2	16.4	45.0	190.0	123.3
Thailand	64.9	36.2	8.8	19.9	115.1	123.3
Europe	**403.9**	**391.2**	**7.2**	**14.8**	**496.9**	**353.9**
Czech Republic	65.6	57.7	3.6	4.3	30.9	34.5
Hungary	52.5	47.7	3.6	1.2	28.7	45.7
Poland	95.9	95.9	—	0.0	71.1	67.1
Russia	20.1	20.1	—	9.3	268.0	143.1
Turkey	169.8	169.8	—	0.0	98.3	63.6
Latin America	**651.0**	**511.3**	**93.5**	**46.4**	**711.1**	**368.6**
Argentina	23.4	8.7	5.2	9.6	46.4	15.7
Brazil	371.6	295.9	71.7	4.0	330.3	166.6
Chile	41.8	20.0	10.4	11.5	117.1	57.9
Colombia	30.2	29.6	—	0.6	25.2	18.7
Mexico	176.9	153.1	5.3	18.5	171.9	97.2
Peru	7.1	4.0	0.9	2.2	20.1	12.5
Mature markets	**37,623.5**	**17,858.1**	**15,371.0**	**4,394.1**	**24,533.2**	**20,600.4**
Euro area[1]	9,570.2	5,495.0	3,051.6	1,023.4	5,595.2	10,652.3
Japan	8,866.7	6,836.7	1,240.6	789.4	3,805.8	4,577.9
United States	19,186.6	5,526.4	11,078.8	2,581.3	15,132.2	5,370.3
			(In percent of GDP)			
Emerging markets	**38.1**	**25.3**	**8.4**	**4.6**	**61.2**	**65.2**
Africa	**42.8**	**32.1**	**5.0**	**5.8**	**186.5**	**72.6**
South Africa	42.8	32.1	5.0	5.8	186.5	72.6
Asia	**42.6**	**22.3**	**13.4**	**6.9**	**74.1**	**103.6**
China	29.3	17.4	11.1	0.7	38.8	140.5
Hong Kong SAR	28.2	9.6	15.1	3.5	522.5	148.5
India	34.8	34.2	0.2	0.4	56.4	36.9
Korea	75.5	22.8	31.5	21.1	56.9	80.4
Malaysia	90.5	38.4	13.9	38.2	161.3	104.7
Thailand	38.6	21.5	5.2	11.8	68.4	73.2
Europe	**27.7**	**26.9**	**0.5**	**1.0**	**34.1**	**24.3**
Czech Republic	53.3	46.9	2.9	3.5	25.1	28.1
Hungary	45.9	41.7	3.1	1.0	25.1	39.9
Poland	32.5	32.5	—	0.0	24.1	22.7
Russia	3.3	3.3	—	1.5	44.3	23.7
Turkey	53.3	53.3	—	0.0	30.9	20.0
Latin America	**36.8**	**28.9**	**5.3**	**2.6**	**40.2**	**20.9**
Argentina	15.5	5.8	3.4	6.4	30.7	10.4
Brazil	56.2	44.7	10.8	0.6	50.0	25.2
Chile	41.0	19.6	10.2	11.3	114.8	56.8
Colombia	29.1	28.5	—	0.6	24.3	18.0
Mexico	26.1	22.6	0.8	2.7	25.4	14.3
Peru	10.0	5.6	1.3	3.1	28.3	17.6
Mature markets	**140.2**	**66.5**	**57.3**	**16.4**	**91.4**	**76.8**
Euro area[1]	93.3	53.6	29.8	10.0	54.6	103.9
Japan	182.9	141.0	25.6	16.3	78.5	94.4
United States	163.5	47.1	94.4	22.0	129.0	45.8

Sources: Bank for International Settlements (BIS); Bloomberg; Standard and Poor's; and IMF staff estimates.

[1]Euro area includes Austria, Belgium, Finland, France, Germany, Greece, Ireland, Italy, the Netherlands, Portugal, and Spain, excluding Luxembourg.

Figure 4.1. Size and Composition of Local Bond Markets Outstanding, 2004
(In percent of GDP)

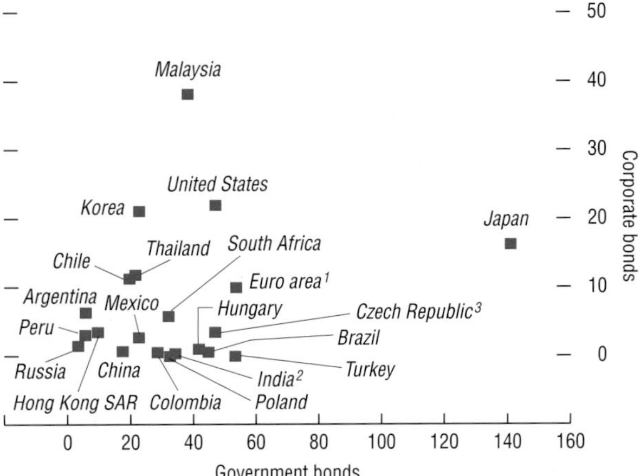

Sources: Bank for International Settlements (BIS); and IMF staff estimates.
[1]Euro area includes Austria, Belgium, Finland, France, Germany, Greece, Ireland, Italy, Netherlands, Portugal, and Spain, excluding Luxembourg.
[2]Indian corporate sector issues only cover commercial paper, as reported by the BIS. Under the more inclusive definition provided by JPMorgan & Chase Co., the outstanding volume of corporate securities would reach 5.4 percent of GDP.
[3]The outstanding volume of government bonds for the Czech Republic includes issuance by the overall public sector, as reported by the BIS. This contrasts with the narrower definition of general government used to compute public debt under the IMF's *Government Finance Statistics* methodology.

Global bond issuance expanded sharply in the 1990s. During 1999–2003, average annual corporate bond issuance in the United States was about $900 billion compared with $280 billion in 1994. In the euro area, it was about $550 billion, quadruple the 1994 level. (In Japan, it was government debt issuance that almost doubled, from $250 billion to about $450 billion.)[6] Several EMs also experienced strong growth in corporate bond issuance since the mid-1990s. Cyclical factors, as well as diversification away from banks and the need for alternative sources of funding to reduce currency and maturity mismatches, have been important drivers of the growth in local corporate bond markets. While in Asia most of the growth took place in domestic bond markets, in Latin America corporates mainly accessed international bond markets until the emerging market crisis of 1998; since then, corporates have increased issuing in domestic bond markets.

Corporate bond markets in most mature markets were almost nonexistent in the early 1980s, except in the United States, where historically the local bond market has been an important source of funding for the corporate sector. The traditional importance of bank lending in financing large and medium-sized corporates in most MMs began to erode in the second half of the 1990s both in the euro area and, to a lesser extent, in Japan. In the United States, the economic boom of the 1990s led to a strong increase in corporate debt issues. Although private sector issues declined in 1999–2000, following the Long-Term Capital Management and Russian debt crises, issuance picked up again after 2000. In Japan, the corporate bond market was heavily regulated until 1985. The relaxation of market eligibility standards, the establishment of rating agencies, and the start of bond futures trading followed by the liberalization of financial transactions (the "Big-Bang" reforms in the

[6]See Pagano and von Thadden (2004).

Table 4.2. Corporate Issuers: Outstanding Domestic Debt Securities
(In percent of GDP)

	1989	1990	1991	1992	1993	1994	1995	1996	1997	1998	1999	2000	2001	2002	2003	2004	Average 1989–94	Average 1995–99	Average 2000–04
Emerging markets	**4.2**	**3.9**	**4.5**	**3.9**	**3.9**	**4.2**	**5.1**	**3.9**	**2.8**	**4.6**	**5.3**	**4.9**	**5.3**	**6.0**	**5.9**	**5.2**	**4.1**	**4.4**	**5.5**
Africa	**12.8**	**11.5**	**10.6**	**9.2**	**8.7**	**8.4**	**7.6**	**6.5**	**6.3**	**6.0**	**5.6**	**5.3**	**4.6**	**7.0**	**6.6**	**6.7**	**10.2**	**6.4**	**6.0**
South Africa	12.8	11.5	10.6	9.2	8.7	8.4	7.6	6.5	6.3	6.0	5.6	5.3	4.6	7.0	6.6	6.7	10.2	6.4	6.0
Asia	**4.8**	**5.7**	**6.6**	**5.1**	**5.0**	**5.9**	**7.5**	**6.6**	**4.3**	**7.7**	**8.1**	**7.8**	**8.3**	**8.9**	**8.4**	**7.1**	**5.5**	**6.8**	**8.1**
China	0.7	1.0	1.5	1.2	0.9	0.7	0.6	0.5	0.7	0.9	0.9	1.0	1.0	1.0	0.9	0.7	1.0	0.7	0.9
Hong Kong SAR	. . .	0.1	0.8	0.9	0.9	1.4	2.1	1.9	2.1	2.0	3.7	3.6	4.2	4.4	4.1	3.5	0.8	2.3	4.0
India	. . .	—	0.0	0.1	0.4	0.2	—	0.0	0.3	0.3	0.4	0.4	0.4	0.4	0.3	0.4	0.1	0.2	0.4
Korea	12.3	14.5	15.3	15.8	15.7	16.4	16.5	17.4	10.8	31.5	26.1	23.0	26.8	29.9	27.7	23.4	15.0	20.4	26.1
Malaysia	4.5	5.2	6.1	7.9	8.8	15.3	17.6	23.3	20.8	33.8	43.2	45.2	47.7	40.7	43.3	38.2	8.0	27.7	43.0
Thailand	7.2	6.9	6.8	6.6	6.6	7.4	7.7	8.8	6.0	10.4	11.6	11.5	12.9	12.1	13.5	12.2	6.9	8.9	12.4
Europe	**0.6**	**0.3**	**0.3**	**0.7**	**1.1**	**0.4**	**0.7**	**0.4**	**0.5**	**1.2**	**1.6**	**1.0**	**1.2**	**1.5**	**1.6**	**1.9**	**0.6**	**0.9**	**1.4**
Czech Republic	—	0.0	—	0.0	0.3	0.4	0.7	1.1	1.2	1.3	1.8	3.1	3.1	3.9	3.8	4.0	0.1	1.2	3.6
Hungary	. . .	. . .	0.3	0.5	0.3	0.2	0.4	0.4	1.5	1.1	1.3	1.5	1.5	1.4	1.2	1.2	0.3	0.9	1.4
Poland	. . .	. . .	. . .	. . .	. . .	. . .	. . .	. . .	. . .	. . .	. . .	. . .	. . .	. . .	. . .	. . .	. . .	. . .	. . .
Russia	. . .	. . .	. . .	. . .	. . .	. . .	. . .	. . .	. . .	. . .	. . .	0.5	0.7	1.0	1.2	1.6	. . .	. . .	1.0
Turkey	0.6	0.3	0.3	0.8	1.4	0.4	0.7	0.1	0.1	0.0	0.0	0.0	0.0	. . .	. . .	. . .	0.6	0.2	0.0
Latin America	**1.2**	**1.0**	**1.2**	**1.5**	**1.8**	**1.3**	**1.3**	**0.7**	**1.0**	**1.1**	**1.3**	**1.4**	**1.7**	**2.0**	**2.4**	**2.8**	**1.4**	**1.1**	**2.1**
Argentina	—	0.1	0.1	0.2	0.8	1.1	1.2	1.3	1.9	2.4	2.6	2.6	2.7	8.6	6.8	6.3	0.4	1.9	5.4
Brazil	. . .	. . .	. . .	. . .	. . .	. . .	. . .	0.1	0.6	0.3	0.4	0.6	0.6	0.4	0.5	0.7	. . .	0.4	0.5
Chile	3.0	3.9	4.7	4.3	4.3	4.4	3.3	3.0	2.3	2.9	3.6	4.8	8.9	11.1	13.5	12.3	4.1	3.0	10.1
Colombia	0.4	0.2	0.2	0.3	0.6	0.7	0.9	0.8	0.7	0.6	0.3	0.1	0.2	0.2	0.4	0.6	0.4	0.7	0.3
Mexico	1.2	1.3	1.7	2.1	2.4	1.3	1.0	0.8	1.1	1.3	1.1	1.4	1.6	1.4	2.0	2.7	1.7	1.1	1.8
Peru	. . .	. . .	. . .	. . .	0.3	0.4	0.6	0.9	1.2	1.6	1.8	2.1	2.2	2.3	3.0	3.2	0.4	1.2	2.6
Mature markets	**12.0**	**11.8**	**11.8**	**11.6**	**12.2**	**12.0**	**11.6**	**12.1**	**12.5**	**14.2**	**14.9**	**15.3**	**16.0**	**16.2**	**16.2**	**15.9**	**11.9**	**13.0**	**15.9**
Euro area[1]	3.5	3.7	3.6	3.0	3.0	3.0	2.7	2.9	2.8	3.2	4.0	5.5	6.7	8.3	10.0	10.9	3.3	3.1	8.3
Japan	8.0	9.1	9.0	8.9	9.3	10.0	9.4	10.5	10.6	15.4	16.0	13.8	14.7	17.2	17.9	16.9	9.1	12.4	16.1
United Kingdom	3.0	2.8	2.6	2.1	2.6	2.8	2.7	2.8	2.4	2.2	2.1	1.9	2.0	1.7	1.7	1.5	2.6	2.4	1.8
United States	22.2	22.3	22.9	23.4	23.6	22.6	22.9	22.7	22.7	24.0	24.2	24.1	24.1	23.1	22.6	22.0	22.8	23.3	23.2

Sources: BIS; Cbonds; MICEX; and IMF staff estimates.
[1]Euro area includes Austria, Belgium, Finland, France, Germany, Greece, Ireland, Italy, the Netherlands, Portugal, and Spain, excluding Luxembourg.

mid-1990s) contributed to the development of securities markets. The relevant measures taken included abolishing the securities transaction tax, deregulating brokerage commission, preparing the legal framework for securitization, allowing banks to issue straight (unsecured) bonds, and introducing a registration system for securities companies. Local corporate bond markets in mature markets grew from about 5 percent of GDP in the early 1980s to an average of 16 percent of GDP during 2000–04. (See Table 4.2 and Figure 4.2 for recent developments.)

Most European corporate bond markets, except for Germany, were relatively small until the introduction of the euro. Pagano and von Thadden (2004) show that it was the corporate sector of the euro area bond market that grew the most in the wake of European Monetary Union, and transformed the euro into a leading currency of denomination for international bond issues. During 2000–04, euro area corporate bond markets increased from about 4 percent to 10 percent of GDP.

Corporate bond issuance in the major EMs has also grown rapidly since the mid-1990s. In Asia, corporate bond markets increased from 4.3 percent of GDP to 8.4 percent, with large variance across countries. Malaysia and Korea's bond markets reached their largest sizes in 2001 (at 48 percent of GDP) and 2002 (at 30 percent of GDP), respectively. The stock of outstanding corporate bonds also doubled in Thailand, reaching 13.5 percent of GDP in 2003. In Latin America, corporate bond markets also more than doubled in size

Figure 4.2. Local Corporate Bonds Outstanding
(In percent of GDP)

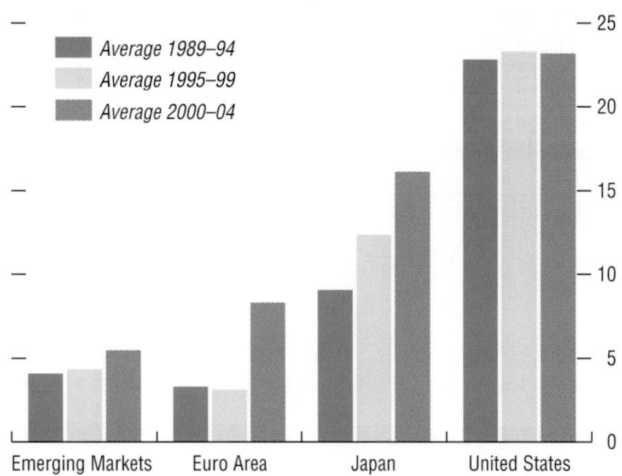

Sources: Bank for International Settlements (BIS); and IMF staff estimates.

Figure 4.3. Corporate Bond Market and Money Market Interest Rates in the Czech Republic

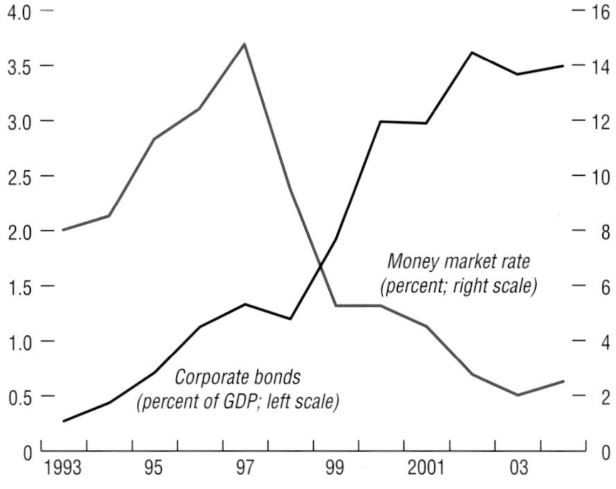

Sources: Bank for International Settlements (BIS); and IMF, *International Financial Statistics*.

between 1997 and 2003, with Chile's bond markets reaching 11 percent of GDP in 2003. The growth of these markets in Central and Eastern Europe has been much less impressive, because of the abundance of bank credit. One exception is the Czech Republic, where the delayed reform of the banking system—which stabilized in 2002 following the completion of privatization and the reduction of impaired assets to below 15 percent of total loans—combined with a sharp fall in local interest rates may have helped spur the growth of the corporate bond market (Figure 4.3).[7] Unlike the pattern observed in the region, increasing bank lending rates in the Czech Republic during 1993–97 may have prompted corporates to look for alternative sources of finance. Likewise, an environment of declining interest rates after 1997 may have skewed investors' choices toward more sophisticated market-based instruments.

The growth of local corporate bond markets did, however, slow in 2004, as the interest rate cycle began to turn, the financing needs of local firms diminished, and the constraints facing new entrants into the bond market became apparent. Most companies are either cash rich and/or are able to access cheap bank funding, as banks are now pursuing aggressive lending strategies following the postcrisis restructuring. Market participants have noted that, despite important structural progress, the takeoff of several EM corporate bond markets has a strong cyclical component. Whether the previous growth spurt in corporate bond issuance is sustainable is subject to debate.

Both cyclical and structural factors have been important drivers of the rapid develop-

[7]The outstanding volume of domestic government securities at the end of 2004 (53.9 percent of GDP) exceeds the latest figure for public debt (27.9 percent of GDP) because of differences in the scope of government definition. Whereas public debt corresponds to a narrow definition of general government, government securities include issuance by a more inclusive nonfinancial public sector.

ment of the domestic corporate bond markets in several emerging market countries. The financing needs of local corporates in the aftermath of financial crises have been a key cause of the domestic corporate bond market development, especially in Asia and Mexico. The easing of inflationary pressures, increased global liquidity, and the sharp decline in domestic interest rates also contributed to the increased issuance of corporate bonds (Figure 4.4). These trends also coincided with corporates' restructuring in EMs (especially in Asia and Latin America), allowing corporates to refinance expensive external debt with local funding. The shift away from international issuance was also supported by the strong growth in assets under the management of such local institutional investors as pension funds, insurance companies, and asset management companies.[8]

The authorities also implemented significant and targeted reforms to facilitate the development of the corporate bond markets. These included establishing rating agencies and benchmark yield curves, permitting issuance of unsecured bonds, and liberalizing market eligibility standards. Reforms and policy initiatives to improve bond market infrastructure have strengthened trading platforms, clearing and settlement systems, and the regulatory environment. In many countries, benchmark yield curves were established through the issuance of government bonds both to fund financial restructuring and infrastructure projects as well as to absorb excess liquidity attributable to the buildup of foreign reserves. However, as discussed later, gaps remain regarding the development of hedging products and derivatives markets, and strengthening the disclosure standards and the framework for creditor rights and investor protection.

[8]See De la Torre and Schmukler (2004) for a discussion on currency denomination of bonds and the link between issuance in domestic and international markets.

Figure 4.4. Domestic Government Bond and Money Market Rates[1]

(In percent)

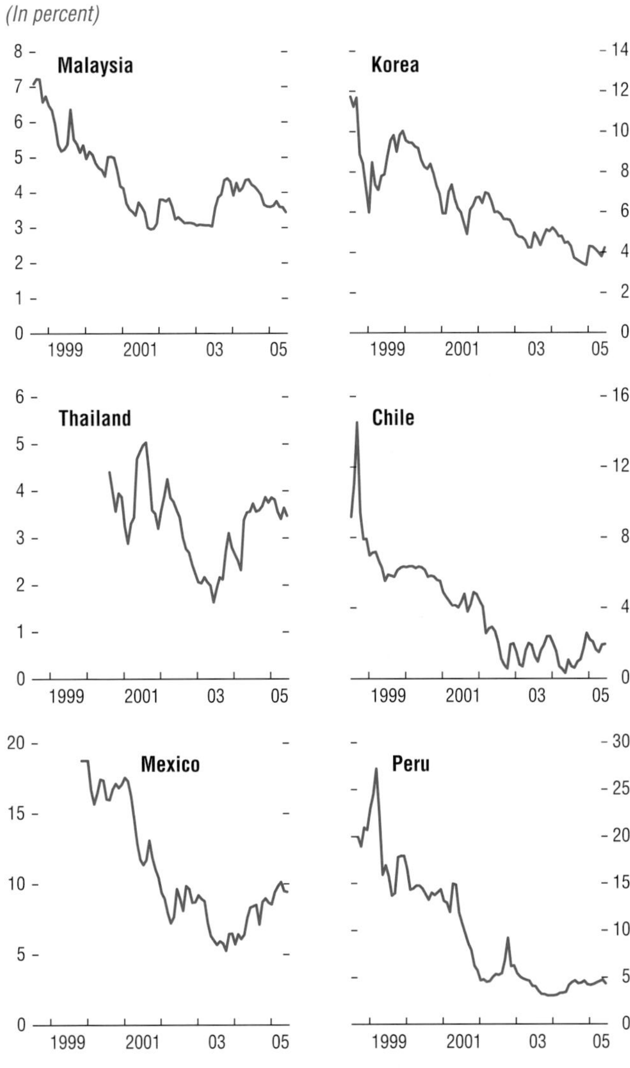

Source: Bloomberg L.P.

[1]For Asia, the rates were for a five-year government bond. For Latin America, one-year money market rates were used.

Table 4.3. Securitization: Selected Emerging Markets
(In millions of U.S. dollars)

	2000	2001	2002	2003	2004
			Domestic Issuance		
Emerging markets	**32,078**	**29,829**	**25,035**	**28,083**	**25,632**
Africa	**0**	**0**	**108**	**0**	**0**
South Africa	0	0	108	0	0
Asia	**32,078**	**29,829**	**24,927**	**26,449**	**18,418**
China	0	0	1,087	0	0
Hong Kong SAR	0	0	256	387	432
Korea	31,078	28,417	23,291	25,776	17,598
Malaysia	969	1,412	151	266	350
Thailand	31	0	141	20	38
Latin America	**0**	**0**	**0**	**1,635**	**7,214**
Argentina	0	0	0	2	161
Brazil	0	0	0	0	0
Chile	0	0	0	343	775
Mexico	0	0	0	1,290	6,279
			International Issuance		
Emerging markets	**2,827**	**3,668**	**5,344**	**2,935**	**5,113**
Africa	**250**	**0**	**0**	**0**	**0**
South Africa	250	0	0	0	0
Asia	**855**	**1,813**	**4,092**	**623**	**2,243**
China	0	0	0	0	0
Hong Kong SAR	142	0	0	43	594
Korea	713	1,813	3,492	580	1,649
Malaysia	0	0	600	0	0
Thailand	0	0	0	0	0
Europe	**222**	**0**	**0**	**287**	**1,800**
Poland	0	0	0	87	0
Russia	0	0	0	0	1,475
Turkey	222	0	0	200	325
Latin America	**1,500**	**1,855**	**1,252**	**2,025**	**1,070**
Argentina	0	234	0	0	0
Brazil	300	1,050	1,150	2,025	1,070
Chile	0	421	40	0	0
Mexico	1,200	150	62	0	0

Sources: Dealogic; and IMF staff estimates.

Since the binding constraint often appears to be on the availability of sound credits, some issuers and arrangers have resorted to credit enhancements and structured products to enhance credit quality and appeal to a wider investor base (Table 4.3). In Latin America, structured finance transactions in local markets have continued to grow steadily; in 2004, they surpassed for the first time the volume of cross-border structured finance issuance. In Korea, the asset-backed securities market—which spurred the development of the corporate bond market following the Asian crisis—declined following the problems with credit card companies in 2003. Meanwhile, after a decline in 2002–03, the structured finance market in Malaysia continued to develop in 2004. That said, conditions have proved challenging for the securitization market. Banks have little incentive to securitize their assets, given the abundance of liquidity in the banking system and strong capital adequacy ratios within the industry.

To analyze the main drivers of these recent trends, and the obstacles to further development of the corporate bond markets, the remainder of this chapter focuses on two groups of issues:

- the main causes of the growth of the demand for and supply of corporate bonds, as well as the role played by intermediaries; and
- aspects of the microstructure of the primary and secondary markets, as well as regulatory issues that help promote the growth of corporate bond markets.

Demand and Supply Factors Driving Corporate Bond Markets

The engines of growth of corporate bond markets have varied across countries. The growth of institutional investors' assets under management has been a major reason for the growth of some corporate bond markets, while the collapse of other sources of funding has been the main cause of the growth in the supply of corporate bonds in other markets. To identify the main obstacles to a deeper and broader market, we need to focus on whether the main driving force of growth has been on the demand or supply side of the market.

The exponential growth of corporate bond markets in the euro area over the last decade illustrates the forces underlying the growth of these markets. Monetary unification, globalization, and efforts to develop government bond markets gave the initial push to bond markets in the euro area that resulted in a sharp increase in corporate bond issuance (Pagano and von Thadden, 2004). These initial triggers operated through changes in the behavior of investors and issuers alike, as well as through ongoing changes in the banking industry. On the demand side, duration and diversification needs of institutional investors were a major force behind the growth in the market, supported by the elimination of currency risks. Asset managers in the euro area countries moved rapidly to reap the diversification gains of cross-border investing, and pension funds' and insurance companies' moves toward diversification were also aided by the relaxation of a number of regulatory restrictions on the matching of their assets and liabilities. The changes in the investment strategies of institutional investors resulted in a net increase in the demand for corporate bonds in (previously) local markets.[9] Issuers that saw this large pool of investors increased their issuance and took advantage of the opportunity to diversify their sources of funding away from local banks. At the same time, banks faced with increasing disintermediation and the need to strengthen balance sheets and business lines supported the process by competing in the primary market and lowering underwriting costs, and by providing increasingly homogeneous secondary market trading facilities. These forces have also been at play in some emerging market countries.

Table 4.4. Local Institutional Investor Base for Corporate Bonds

(In billions of U.S. dollars, unless indicated otherwise)

	Chile	Mexico	Peru	Thailand
AUM of institutional investors (end-2004)[1]				
Pension funds	61	42	8	14
Mutual funds	13	35	2	13
Insurance companies	20	20	2	12
Total AUM of institutional investors (in percent of GDP)	91	16	18	23
Corporate bonds market[2]				
Shares held by:				
Pension funds (in percent)	32	34	36	12
Mutual funds (in percent)	10	30	21	8
Insurance companies (in percent)	50	28	15	7
Other investors (in percent)[3]	8	8	28	73

Sources: Thai Bond Dealing Center; and IMF staff estimates.
Note: AUM = assets under management.
[1]Not including the banking sector.
[2]Includes securitizations.
[3]Includes banks and retail investors.

Demand Factors

The rapid growth of assets under the management of local institutional investors has been one of the key factors behind the rapid development of domestic corporate bond markets in Latin America and, to a lesser extent, in emerging Asia. Institutional investors' assets under management are growing rapidly in EMs as a result of pension reforms, the low levels of insurance penetration, and the growing popularity of mutual funds. Although these factors have largely benefited government bond markets, in some countries they have also boosted corporate bond markets. Corporate bonds constitute an attractive instrument for institutional investors that need to match assets and liabilities; these investors are also attracted by the pickup in yield provided by some exposure to credit risk. In some Asian EMs, state-run pension funds are increasingly farming out the management of assets to private managers: analysts note that an increasingly commercial orientation may lead to further demand for corporate bonds.

Local institutional investors in Chile, Mexico, and Peru, for instance, hold around 70–90 percent of outstanding corporate bonds, while banks and retail investors hold the largest share in Thailand (Table 4.4). The growth in corporate bonds outstanding in the Latin American countries was associated with the growth of pension fund assets under management (Figure 4.5). In Asia, the growth of insurance companies has been an important source of demand for corporate bonds.

[9]The increased demand did not extend to bonds issued outside the euro area itself, mainly because of currency risk considerations, as investors replaced home bias with "euro area home bias" (Baele and others, 2004).

Figure 4.5. Pension Fund Assets Under Management and Corporate Bonds Outstanding
(In percent of GDP)

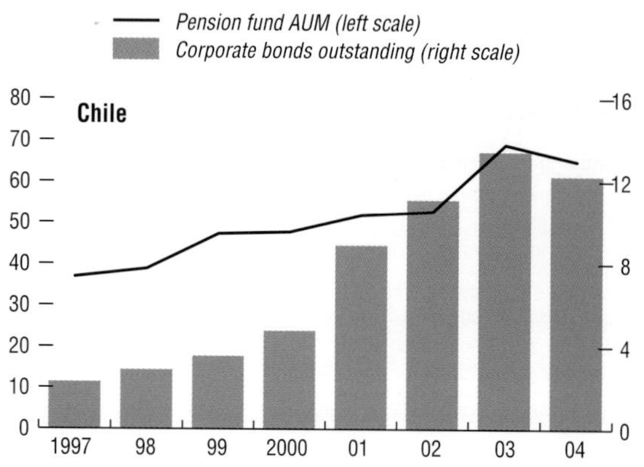

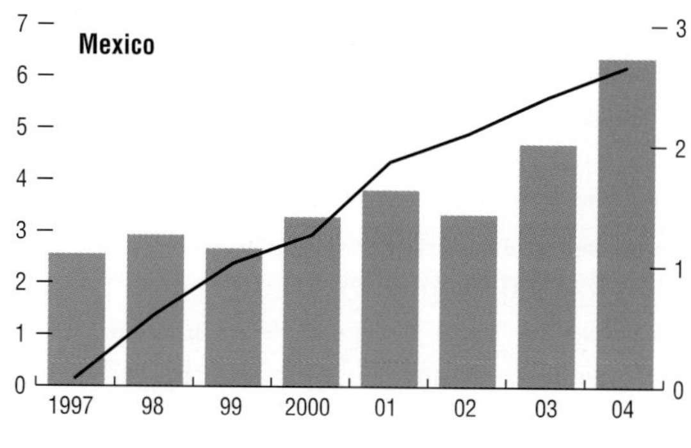

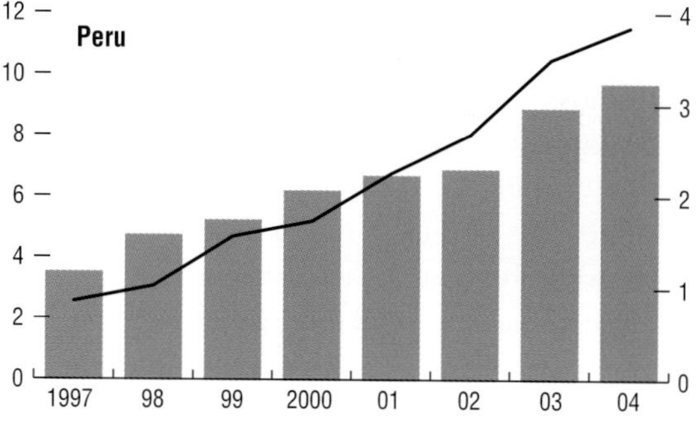

Sources: IMF staff estimates based on FIAP; BIS; and IMF, *International Financial Statistics.*

Table 4.5. Assets Under Management by Insurance Companies
(In percent of GDP)

	1998	1999	2000	2001	2002	2003	2004
Africa							
South Africa	...	...	...	71.7	57.4	57.7	...
Asia							
Korea	14.3	13.6	20.0	19.5	21.0	24.5	...
Malaysia	13.6	15.1	14.9	20.5	20.9	19.3	18.7
Philippines	3.5	3.7	3.8	3.7	4.0	...	...
Singapore	18.5	20.9	21.9	28.9	31.8	36.2	...
Thailand	4.6	5.3	5.5	6.2	7.2	8.3	8.6
Europe							
Hungary	3.3	3.9	4.2	4.5	4.6	5.1	5.7
Poland	3.0	3.6	4.3	5.0	5.9	6.5	5.6
Turkey	1.1	1.6	1.5	1.5	2.1	2.3	...
Latin America							
Argentina	1.8	2.3	2.7	3.2	4.6	4.2	...
Brazil	n.a.	3.7	2.6	2.6	2.8	5.0	...
Chile	13.6	15.8	17.3	18.7	19.7	17.2	18.0
Colombia	0.8	0.8	0.8	0.9	1.0	0.8	0.8
Mexico	1.4	1.4	1.3	1.5	1.6	1.8	1.9
Peru	...	...	...	2.0	2.2	2.7	2.8

Sources: National regulators; and IMF staff estimates.

From a similar level of 14 percent of GDP in 1998, insurance companies' assets under management at end-2003 had grown to 25 percent of GDP in Korea and to 19 percent in Malaysia (Table 4.5). Insurance penetration in Latin America is much lower, with assets under management exceeding 10 percent of GDP only in Chile. In most cases, however, the aggregate exposures of institutional investors to corporate debt are relatively low (see Table 4.6 for a sample of EMs pension funds) and below regulatory limits. This suggests that the potential demand for private debt instruments is significant.

However, the rapid growth in mutual fund assets under management did not have an important impact on corporate bond markets, as these vehicles focus mostly on such liquid assets as money market instruments, government bills and bonds, and equities. Brazil and South Africa have seen mutual fund assets under management (as a percent of GDP) almost triple since 1997 (Table 4.7), while the ratio of corporate bonds outstanding relative to GDP has been stable—albeit at a higher

Table 4.6. Pension Fund Investment in Corporate Fixed-Income Instruments
(In percent of total investment)

	1998	1999	2000	2001	2002	2003	2004
Latin and Central America							
Argentina							
Corporate sector fixed income	**2.50**	**2.13**	**2.80**	**1.69**	**1.06**	**1.54**	**1.97**
Long-term negotiable debt	1.68	1.42	2.50	1.35	0.30	0.90	1.62
Short-term negotiable debt	0.72	0.63	0.31	0.34	0.76	0.64	0.34
Convertible negotiable debt	0.10	0.08	. . .	. . .	. . .	. . .	. . .
Chile							
Corporate sector fixed income	**3.77**	**3.79**	**4.04**	**6.16**	**7.16**	**7.73**	**7.05**
Bonds	3.77	3.79	4.04	6.16	7.16	7.73	7.05
Colombia							
Corporate sector fixed income	**9.16**	**14.78**	**14.51**	**14.89**	**16.60**	**15.42**	**14.80**
Real sector bonds	9.16	14.78	14.51	14.89	16.60	13.80	13.09
Securitization	. . .	. . .	. . .	. . .	. . .	1.62	1.72
Mexico							
Corporate sector fixed income	**3.00**	**2.47**	**5.55**	**8.59**	**15.27**	**15.43**	**14.38**
Private notes	3.00	2.47	5.55	8.59	15.25	15.43	14.38
Indexed term promissory notes	0.13	1.02	3.56	3.24	3.53	5.91	. . .
Nominal term promissory notes	2.87	1.46	1.99	5.35	11.72	9.53	. . .
Peru							
Corporate sector fixed income	**19.21**	**15.50**	**18.68**	**16.36**	**13.12**	**13.31**	**11.64**
Promissory and commercial notes	0.45	0.28	1.08	2.01	1.64	1.12	0.28
Company bonds	18.76	15.21	17.61	14.36	10.86	11.68	9.09
Investment fund bonds	. . .	. . .	. . .	. . .	0.04	. . .	. . .
Bonds for new projects	. . .	. . .	. . .	. . .	0.57	0.50	2.26

Source: International Federation of Pension Funds Administrators (FIAP).

level in South Africa.[10] Similarly, the rapid growth of mutual funds in Poland, Turkey, and Thailand has been associated with the growth of government rather than corporate bond markets.

Participation by foreign investors in local corporate bond markets remains very low relative to participation in equity and government bond markets. For instance, foreign investors hold a large share of long duration government bonds in Malaysia, Mexico, and South Africa, but they rarely invest in local corporate bonds.[11] In Korea, the share of foreign investors in equity markets is about 40 percent, but foreign participation in both corporate and government bond market is very small, as foreign investors see much more upside in equity markets. The general lack of interest from foreign investors in the EM local corporate bond markets has also been attributed to the tightness of spreads, general unfamiliarity with these markets, and the lack of hedging instruments.

Supply Factors

Corporates consider several factors in deciding whether to use bank funding or bond funding. These include cost considerations, access to long-term funding, disclosure

[10]The relatively higher level of corporate bonds in South Africa is because of bond issuance by parastatal enterprises. However, market participants estimate that the corporate bond market is likely to grow steadily in the near term, as South African corporates have growth opportunities and are relatively underleveraged.

[11]Market participants reported that more than 50 percent of Mexico's 10-year local bonds and more than 80 percent of the 20-year local bonds are held by foreign investors.

Table 4.7. Emerging Market Mutual Funds: Total Net Assets[1]

	1997	1998	1999	2000	2001	2002	2003	2004
				(In billions of U. S. dollars)				
Emerging markets	**207.11**	**329.94**	**376.75**	**352.62**	**374.20**	**380.04**	**477.87**	**611.90**
Africa	**12.69**	**12.16**	**18.24**	**16.92**	**14.56**	**20.98**	**34.46**	**54.01**
South Africa	12.69	12.16	18.24	16.92	14.56	20.98	34.46	54.01
Asia	**74.36**	**186.69**	**195.21**	**139.01**	**150.66**	**189.08**	**180.90**	**245.91**
India	9.35	8.69	13.07	13.51	15.28	20.36	29.80	32.85
Korea	53.11	165.03	167.18	110.61	119.44	149.54	121.28	177.42
Malaysia	8.66	10.19	11.39	11.39	12.46	14.13	18.44	22.99
Thailand	3.24	2.78	3.58	3.50	3.47	5.04	11.38	12.66
Europe	**1.66**	**2.57**	**4.14**	**5.67**	**7.31**	**19.13**	**31.60**	**41.30**
Czech Republic	0.36	0.56	1.47	1.99	1.78	3.30	4.08	4.86
Hungary	0.71	1.48	1.73	1.95	2.26	3.99	3.94	4.97
Poland	0.54	0.51	0.76	1.55	2.97	5.47	8.58	12.01
Russia	0.04	0.03	0.18	0.18	0.30	0.37	0.85	1.35
Turkey	n.a.	n.a.	n.a.	n.a.	n.a.	6.00	14.16	18.11
Latin America	**118.40**	**128.53**	**159.17**	**191.02**	**201.68**	**150.84**	**230.91**	**270.69**
Argentina	5.25	6.93	6.99	7.43	3.75	1.02	1.92	2.36
Brazil	108.61	118.69	117.76	148.54	148.19	96.73	171.60	220.59
Chile	4.55	2.91	4.09	4.60	5.09	6.71	8.55	12.59
Colombia	n.a.	n.a.	10.87	11.97	12.92	15.63	16.89	. . .
Mexico	n.a.	n.a.	19.47	18.49	31.72	30.76	31.95	35.16
				(In percent of GDP)				
Emerging markets	**5.34**	**9.39**	**11.31**	**9.60**	**10.44**	**10.57**	**11.74**	**12.79**
Africa	**8.52**	**9.06**	**13.70**	**12.73**	**12.28**	**18.94**	**20.83**	**25.37**
South Africa	8.52	9.06	13.70	12.73	12.28	18.94	20.83	25.37
Asia	**6.27**	**19.82**	**18.01**	**11.75**	**13.02**	**14.95**	**12.66**	**15.14**
India	2.30	2.12	2.99	2.95	3.24	4.11	5.17	4.97
Korea	10.07	47.36	37.52	21.61	24.78	27.30	20.03	26.03
Malaysia	8.65	14.12	14.39	12.62	14.16	14.85	17.78	19.52
Thailand	2.15	2.49	2.92	2.85	3.01	3.97	7.96	7.74
Europe	**0.19**	**0.34**	**0.62**	**0.77**	**0.96**	**2.22**	**3.00**	**3.10**
Czech Republic	0.63	0.90	2.47	3.57	2.92	4.47	4.52	4.54
Hungary	1.54	3.11	3.60	4.21	4.36	6.15	4.75	5.00
Poland	0.35	0.30	0.46	0.93	1.60	2.86	4.09	4.97
Russia	0.01	0.01	0.09	0.07	0.10	0.11	0.20	0.23
Turkey	n.a.	n.a.	n.a.	n.a.	n.a.	3.25	5.90	6.04
Latin America	**7.00**	**7.64**	**11.00**	**11.76**	**13.00**	**11.10**	**16.22**	**17.08**
Argentina	1.79	2.32	2.47	2.61	1.40	1.01	1.51	1.55
Brazil	13.44	15.11	22.47	24.76	29.12	21.00	33.95	36.78
Chile	5.49	3.67	5.60	6.11	7.44	9.95	11.87	13.44
Colombia	n.a.	n.a.	12.61	14.28	15.76	19.17	21.30	. . .
Mexico	n.a.	n.a.	4.05	3.18	5.08	4.74	5.00	5.20

Sources: Bloomberg; Federation of Malaysian Unit Trust Managers; Investment Company Institute; Monetary Authority of Singapore; Security and Exchange Commission of Thailand; Superintendencia de Bancaria and Superintendencia de Valores, Colombia.

[1]Funds of funds are not included; home-domiciled funds except for Hong Kong, Korea, New Zealand, and Singapore, which include home- and foreign-domiciled funds.

requirements, and the desire to diversify funding sources. In some EMs, corporates have found strong incentives to issue bonds when faced with increasing costs of bank lending or when they were rationed out of the loan market—as a result of banking distress. However, even when bond issuance was advantageous—including in terms of maturities and covenants—some corporates were reluctant to issue bonds to avoid the disclosure implicit in securing market funding.

The growth in Asian corporate bond markets has been driven mainly by corporates' need for alternative sources of funding in the face of a collapse in bank lending.[12] Korea and Malaysia had already developed corporate bond markets in the mid-1990s, but both markets more than doubled, relative to GDP, between 1997 and 1999. In Korea, the issuance of nonguaranteed corporate bonds increased sharply after the financial crisis of 1997, aided by the fact that conglomerates owned the investment trust companies (ITCs) that bought the new bonds. However, the mid-1999 collapse of Daewoo Group, the third largest conglomerate, triggered a sharp withdrawal of funds and liquidity problems in the ITCs, which were the main holders of the bonds issued by the group. The Korean experience also demonstrates the potential problems associated with increased issuance of corporate bonds during a period of intensive corporate restructuring, as well as how poor credit risk management by investment trust companies contributed to and further magnified the turmoil in the corporate bond market.[13]

Another clear example of supply-driven growth in corporate bonds is the Russian experience. Ruble-denominated corporate bonds grew from less than 1 percent of GDP in the year 2000 to 2.8 percent in 2004, as a result of the large financing needs of the corporate sector and the inability of the banking system to recover from the crisis of 1998–99. Interestingly, the local corporate bond market in Russia took off despite the absence of a well-developed benchmark yield curve, a strong institutional investor base, or a "credit culture" (Box 4.1). Also, it is one of the few EMs where foreign investors participate on a meaningful scale in the local corporate bond market.

Imbalances Between Demand and Supply of Corporate Bonds

As noted in the April 2004 GFSR, the inability of the local supply of securities to respond to the rapid growth of the demand (derived from the growth in assets under management) may lead to mispricing and eventually to asset price bubbles. This has become an issue in some EMs, both in the sovereign and corporate bond markets, as well as in some equity markets. For instance, in Peru, local corporates have been able to issue local bonds denominated in U.S. dollars at lower costs than the sovereign or similarly rated companies that borrow in international markets. Similarly, some analysts believe that the strong run-up in the Santiago stock exchange is due in part to the shift of pension fund investors toward more aggressive funds that are allowed larger allocations to equities.[14] Also, in Malaysia and Thailand, five-year domestic government bonds were trading at sub-Libor levels in April 2005, compared with Libor plus 20–30 basis points for the five-year offshore bonds.[15]

Moreover, herding behavior and excessive concentration in a few market participants could magnify the asset price effects of portfolio relocations, especially in smaller markets. The experience of several Latin American countries' pension fund industries demonstrates that concentration of demand in a few

[12]Davis and Stone (2004) provide evidence that bond issuance reduces corporate sector vulnerabilities by offsetting bank credit crunches.

[13]The Korean authorities implemented various measures to address these problems. These included the establishment of a bond stabilization fund, the introduction of new instruments to attract redeemed funds back into ITCs and of a scheme to provide funding to allow the rollover of maturing bonds issued by larger firms with temporary liquidity problems, and the implementation of structural reforms to restructure and recapitalize the ailing ITCs. These measures helped improve market sentiment and, together with the sharp decline of interest rates, led to another mild boom in the corporate bond market during March 2002–February 2003.

[14]In 2002, Chilean pension funds were permitted to offer five different funds, from the most conservative to the most aggressive, with increasing allocations to equities. Mexico also allowed a second, more aggressive fund to be introduced early this year, and 90 percent of investors shifted to the new funds—seeking more exposure to equities.

[15]Griffiths (2005).

Box 4.1. Corporate Bond Market in Russia

The corporate bond market in Russia, which came into existence in 1999, experienced rapid growth in the past five years. The total value of all outstanding corporate bonds rose from 39 billion rubles ($1.4 billion) at end-2000 to 267 billion rubles ($9.6 billion) at end-2004 (see first figure below). During 1999–2004, Russia experienced a positive term-of-trade shock (rising oil prices), which resulted in strong capital inflows and higher liquidity in the domestic financial system. The concurrent expansion of the aggregate demand led to an increase in the financing needs of local firms. However, given a slow recovery of Russian banks from the 1998 crisis, the bank lending channel could not serve as an efficient mechanism for reallocating financial resources to meet the funding needs of firms outside the energy sector. At the same time, the "veksel" market (an "informal" commercial paper market) was available only to the largest corporates and banks. Against this background, the corporate bond market emerged as a natural alternative mechanism to channel excess liquidity into the broader nonfinancial sector.

Compared to collateralized domestic bank loans, corporate bonds offered several advantages: a possibility of noncollateralized borrowing, larger size (because of the larger number of creditors), longer tenors (achieved, at least initially, through embedding put options into the longer-term corporate bonds), and often lower borrowing costs. For medium-sized firms, ruble bonds represented an opportunity to build public credit history and to diversify funding sources away from bank loans. For private domestic banks, many of which had access only to short-term funding and had been investing primarily in government bonds before the 1998 crisis, corporate bonds represented an opportunity to have an exposure to credit risk through traded instruments rather than through nontraded loans. Thus, banks were initially the main investors in ruble corporate bonds.

What makes the Russian case interesting is that the local corporate bond market took off despite the absence of certain institutional features that are generally seen as "preconditions" for the existence of a well-functioning corporate bond market. Although there is no general agreement on which conditions are "necessary," multiple studies document that a country with a well-functioning corporate bond market typically has (1) a reliable regulatory framework; (2) a developed market infrastructure; (3) adequate corporate governance and reporting standards; (4) a well-functioning government bond market that provides corporate issuers with a stable and liquid benchmark curve in local currency; (5) a developed "credit culture;" (6) a sound and well-regulated banking system; (7) a broad investor base; and (8) a well-functioning market for derivative instruments for hedging interest rate and credit risks. Many examples, however, show that a subset of these conditions (arguably (1)–(5)) may be sufficient for the *emergence* of the corporate bond market. However, in the case of Russia, despite significant progress in the development of a legal framework for and infrastructure of the securities markets, some key elements of an institutional framework, such as a risk-free benchmark, a broad investor base, and a developed credit culture, are still missing.

Domestic Bond Markets in Russia: Amounts Outstanding
(In billions of dollars)

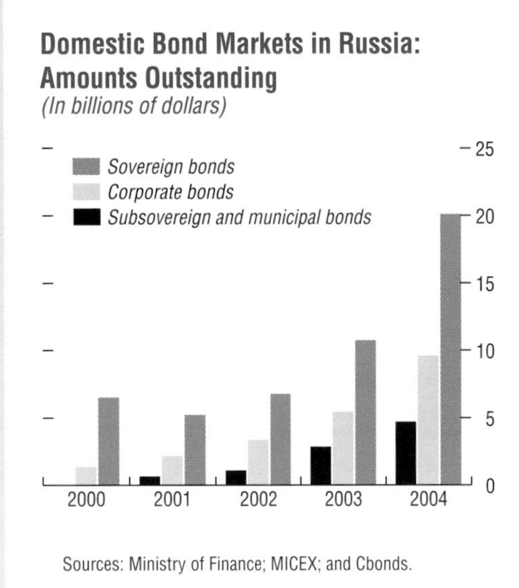

Sources: Ministry of Finance; MICEX; and Cbonds.

Benchmark Yield Curve

The collapse of the government bond market following the 1998 sovereign default left local corporates without a risk-free local currency benchmark. Despite the recent increase in the sovereign ruble bond issuance, secondary market liquidity remains low, in part due to the dominant position of the state-owned Sberbank. Because of low liquidity and pricing inefficiencies, local borrowers prefer not to use the sovereign curve as a benchmark. Instead, they use the synthetic zero-coupon yield curve derived from the yields on bonds issued by the City of Moscow. The latter is viewed as a natural substitute benchmark provider because of its quasi-sovereign status and its well-developed yield curve (10 issues ranging from 6 months to 6 years). However, yields on the Moscow bonds do contain a quasi-sovereign risk premium and, therefore, are not the ideal risk-free local currency benchmark.

In addition, given that the average size of the City of Moscow bonds is comparable to the average size of bonds issued by the "blue chip" corporates, the Moscow benchmark bonds may not be liquid enough to absorb large negative shocks without transmitting volatility to the rest of the ruble bond market. One example of such a negative shock is a potential unexpected change in the foreign investors' appetite for ruble bonds. Indeed, foreign purchases of ruble bonds rose substantially in recent years and were largely driven by the continued nominal appreciation of the ruble, with foreigners focusing mainly on the City of Moscow bonds. According to market sources, foreign investors currently dominate the short segment of the City of Moscow curve and own a significant amount of paper in the long segment.[1] Thus, turnaround of the ruble-dollar rate could trigger capital outflows, which would affect the Moscow benchmark bonds and the rest of the ruble corporate bond market. In contrast, with a deeper and more liquid government bond market, the impact of such shocks on broader markets is likely to be less severe.

Credit Culture

In contrast with many other countries, credit rating agencies do not play a major role in the Russian corporate bond market. Although all three major international credit rating agencies are present in Russia, public credit ratings were so far awarded to about 40 nonfinancial firms out of 200 local bond issuers. Most Russian companies do not have incentives to seek credit ratings, because the regulatory investment restrictions for local institutional investors are not linked to credit ratings. Instead, investment restrictions typically refer to the "quotation lists" of the Moscow stock exchange (MICEX).[2] The majority of rated firms are active participants in the international capital markets, where spreads are closely related to credit quality (as reflected in credit ratings) and maturity of bonds. In contrast, in the ruble bond market, there is no clear relationship between credit ratings and bond prices, although the second figure seems to suggest that higher-rated firms are able to borrow in longer tenors.

Because the pricing is not always aligned with credit fundamentals, and current yields are at historic lows, analysts believe that any major (not necessarily systemically important) credit event can trigger a "re-pricing" of risks across the entire credit spectrum. The reduction in corporate bond yields during 2003–05 was

[1]The unremunerated reserve requirement on foreign purchases of subsovereign bonds is 2 percent, compared with 15 percent for the sovereign bonds, which makes the subsovereign and municipal bonds, for example, the City of Moscow bonds, more attractive for foreigners than the sovereign bonds.

[2]The inclusion in the "quotation lists" is based on the fulfillment of certain formal requirements (with regard to the firm's financial performance, quality of information disclosure, total amount of issue, and market liquidity), rather than on the analysis of credit risk.

Box 4.1 *(concluded)*

Russian Corporate Eurobond and Credit-Linked Note Spreads
(In basis points over the relevant benchmark, June 2005)

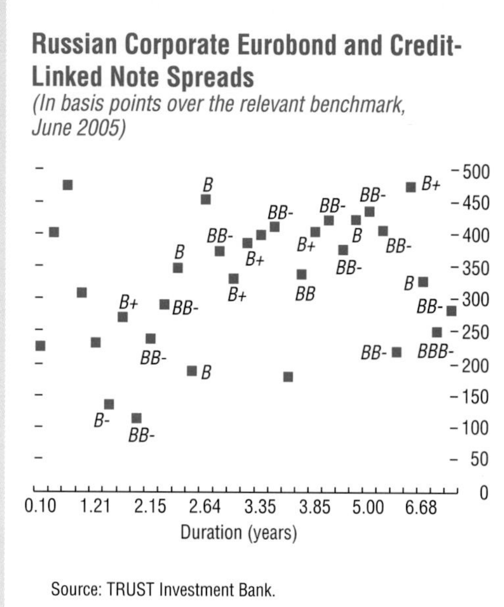

Source: TRUST Investment Bank.

Corporate Ruble Bond Spreads
(In basis points over the relevant benchmark)

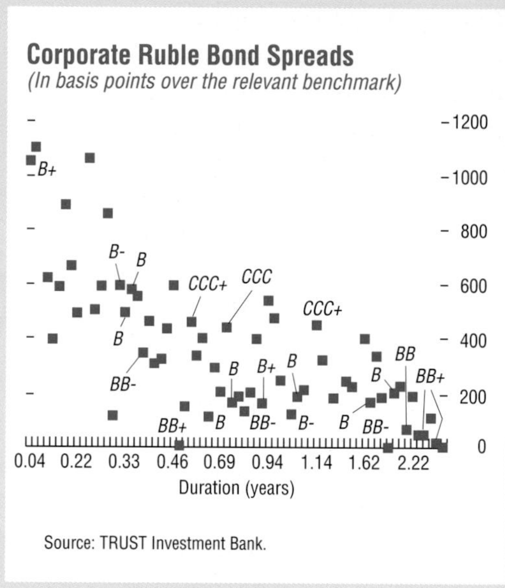

Source: TRUST Investment Bank.

indeed dramatic, with the average yield on the top-tier corporate bonds falling from 14 percent in January 2003 to around 7 percent in April 2005. This decline was mainly driven by high liquidity in the banking sector and by the continued nominal appreciation of the ruble. Also, during 2003–04, many medium-sized and smaller firms (mostly unrated and often not very transparent) entered the bond market, creating the "junk" bond segment at the short-end (see third figure).

Investor Base

While the investor base for Russian corporate bonds is gradually becoming more diverse, local demand is still mainly driven by banks and remains very sensitive to changes in commodity prices. Local banks and brokerage houses currently account for around 50–60 percent of the market (compared with 70–80 percent in 2003); local institutional investors, 20–30 percent; and foreign investors, 10–25 percent. The majority of private banks in Russia have to rely primarily on short-term corporate deposits, rather than on longer-term retail funds. Thus, their liquidity is heavily dependent on corporate flows and, as a result, is highly sensitive to changes in commodity prices. In addition, a large part of funds managed by asset management companies comes from wealthy individuals, who often tend to have a short-term opportunistic approach toward investing in local markets. At the same time, the asset base of the traditional long-term investors, such as pension funds and insurance companies, remains fairly narrow. Lack of long-term money in the corporate bond market implies higher volatility and lower pricing efficiency.

Thus, it can be argued that, in the case of Russia, it was the funding needs of local firms rather than the demand of domestic institutional investors (as was the case in Latin America) that provided a strong impetus for the development of the domestic corporate bond market. Although the corporate bond market in Russia experienced rapid growth in the absence of a well-developed government bond market, a long-term institutional investor base, or a developed credit culture, these elements are needed to ensure its stability and efficiency going forward, and will have to be gradually established as the market continues to mature.

players can lead to pricing distortions at issuance and limited trading in secondary markets. Regulatory limits on exposures to an individual issuer may become binding when a large pension fund faces the option to invest in a bond issued by a relatively small company.

Thus, while the growth in institutional investors' assets under management is contributing to the deepening of the corporate bond markets, the lack of reasonable credits to invest in may lead to distortions and potential financial instability. The preference of institutional investors in these markets to hold high-grade paper has limited the investible universe of corporates to large firms with strong credit fundamentals. Even in countries where institutional investors are not tightly regulated, self-imposed credit-based restrictions by individual companies constrain holdings of subinvestment-grade debt. However, this is not an EM-specific issue (Figure 4.6): in the Group of Seven (G-7) countries, more than 90 percent of corporate bond issuance is in investment-grade categories (Box 4.2).[16]

Given these constraints, pension funds and insurance regulators in some countries are studying how to change the regulatory regimes to allow more freedom to invest, including in corporate bonds. There is a general trend to try to move toward a risk-based rather than an investment-limit-by-instrument regulatory regime. However, regulators are finding it difficult to define a regime that incorporates the many risks—market, credit, operational, and longevity—involved in pension fund management. In the meantime, and recognizing the limitations of the local markets, both the Chilean and Mexican authorities have increased the limits to investments in foreign assets to 30 and 20 percent, respectively, while

Figure 4.6. G-7 Corporate Bond Issuance by S&P Rating
(In percent of total bond issuance per region, 1997–2004)

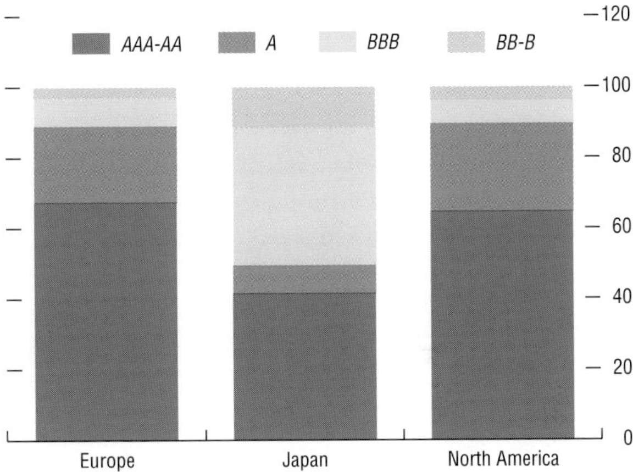

Sources: Dealogic; and IMF staff estimates.

[16]A higher percentage of Japanese corporations with lower credit ratings were able to issue bonds, compared with other G-7 counterparts, largely because of strong demand for assets with higher fixed returns from institutional investors in the very low domestic interest rate environment.

Box 4.2. High-Yield Bonds

A number of theoretical and empirical studies have established the existence of a causal link between financial development and economic growth.[1] Corporate bonds are particularly important in this regard, as borrowing proceeds generally flow directly into investment in the real economy. High-yield bonds potentially have an important role to play as a subset of the corporate bond market, as they can be a vehicle for financing new, or small, enterprises or funding the expansion of weak credits that might otherwise lack a substitute source of funds. In this way, the high-yield market may promote incremental economic growth by providing financing that might not otherwise be available from alternate sources.[2]

The potential contribution of the high-yield market is not inconsequential. In the United States, high-yield bonds peaked as a percentage of the market in the 1980s, before dropping back to sustainable levels of around 6 percent of the market. In Europe, including the United Kingdom, high-yield issuance has been growing rapidly, particularly after the EMU, helped in part by the transfer of knowledge of U.S. investment banks, and investment banks' ability to replicate concepts pioneered in the development of the U.S. high-yield market. However, the high-yield debt market share still remains below that in the United States. In Japan, the abolition of issue standards in 1996 made possible the issuance of high-yield debt. However, relatively few corporations have taken advantage of this type of financing.

High-yield bonds have specific characteristics that differentiate them from other sources of finance. First, high-yield bonds generally have more liberal financial covenants and a wider range of investment conditions than are available in bank loans, and thus provide issuers with a greater degree of financial and operational flexibility. Second, high-yield bonds funnel investment funds into high-growth companies that have outperformed the average for companies in industrial countries in terms of employment growth, productivity, and capital investment.[3]

The question of why high-yield bond markets have failed to develop in emerging markets is puzzling when two of the necessary conditions for their existence—fast-growing corporations and companies with weak credit quality—are present. Information relevant to resolving this apparent contradiction is contained in a recent paper that identifies five macroeconomic variables that determine the structure of the high-yield bond market.[4] These include the following:

- A positive correlation between leveraged buyouts and high-yield bond issuance.
- A negative correlation between mergers and acquisitions (M&A) activity and high-yield bond issuance.
- Industrial production has opposing effects on the financing activities of high-yield borrowers, depending on their type. With many growing faster than the rest of the economy, high-yield borrowers have increased funding needs to finance working capital and investment.[5] Alternatively, declining industrial production is conducive to credit rating downgrades and expansion of the "Fallen Angels," or companies that were formerly investment grade and have been downgraded to high-yield status.
- Equity price movements are positively correlated with the high-yield bond market. Higher stock prices imply increasing corporate values (enhancing bond collateral), plus increasing investor confidence in the path of the economy, both of which encourage a movement of funds into higher-risk investments.
- The high-yield bond market expansion is correlated with the spread between yields on

[1]Herring and Chatusripitak (2001).

[2]High-yield bonds can play this role, particularly when the banking sector is reluctant to increase its risk assets (e.g., the late 1990s in Japan).

[3]Rajan and Zingales (1998).

[4]De Bondt and Marqués-Ibáñez (2004).

[5]Yago and Trimbath (2003).

speculative grade paper and debt issued by investment-grade-rated corporates (or the risk-free rate on government securities).

Viewed through this perspective, analysis of the high-yield corporate bond market in the United States and EU provides valuable input that helps explain the arrested development of high-yield bond markets in emerging market countries. For example, it is relevant that the origins of the high-yield corporate bond market can be traced to the "Fallen Angel" phenomena, and not new issues sold to raise cash.[6] The high-yield market only emerged as a source of finance in the 1980s when it was transformed into a source of finance for highly leveraged (or start-up) companies that were unable to raise funds from banks or raise bank funding on a basis that allowed them sufficient operational flexibility.

A contributing factor in the failure of high-yield bond markets to take hold in emerging markets may relate to patterns of corporate development in these countries. In the United States, growth of the high-yield market was fostered by corporate restructurings, particularly leveraged buyouts. In most of the emerging market economies, there has been little in the way of leveraged buyouts, large-scale acquisitions, and other types of corporate reorganizations potentially requiring large amounts of debt financing—except following large-scale, systemic financial crises. The contrast is important, in that much of high-yield financing completed in the United States has been done in connection with business combinations involving large, low-rated corporations.

Industrial production, economic growth, and financing cost variables (e.g., stock market returns and the spread between the yield on speculative-grade bonds and the risk-free rate) also have an important impact on high-yield bond markets with implications for the development of high-yield financing activity,[7] particularly in the emerging markets. For example, many of the large companies in emerging market countries are solidly profitable, possessing strong balance sheets and open to a wide range of financing alternatives. As a result, there are relatively few "Fallen Angels" with the need to execute high-yield financing transactions.[8] Moreover, as local bond rating scales are adjusted for the credit rating of the sovereign, companies that would not qualify for investment-grade credit ratings in developed economies do qualify as investment grade in emerging market economies. Meanwhile, many companies that would be rated at subinvestment-grade levels according to local scales are privately held or insufficiently large to qualify for public debt financing or to have sufficient needs to justify the expense of a public offering. Given the substantial presence of family-run companies (especially in Latin America) and other factors limiting reorganizations and changes in corporate control, the number of leveraged buyouts and other transactions that could potentially give rise to substantial transactions involving a preponderance of debt securities is very limited.

Finally, given strong returns in the emerging equity markets over the last few years, there has been little incentive for institutional investors to "reach" for the additional return offered through high-yield bond holdings while assuming the accompanying risk. Equity market returns (in excess of the risk-free rate) have been sufficient so that investors have not seen the need to diversify into high-yield credits.[9]

[6]Taggart (1988).

[7]De Bondt and Marqués-Ibáñez (2004).

[8]Recent downgrades of Ford Motor Company and General Motors to junk status according to international credit rating scales may alter this situation, as both have local subsidiaries that are large-scale issuers in the Mexican corporate bond market. However, to date, local ratings for their subsidiaries have remained at investment-grade levels.

[9]In Korea, there are a lot of investors, including overseas investors, participating in equity markets, while far fewer invest in high-yield corporate bonds.

Peru's limit remains at 10.5 percent. Similarly, the Korean authorities have increased the investment limit of insurance companies in foreign assets from 20 to 30 percent, to circumvent the shortage of appropriate instruments in local markets. In Malaysia, there is a 5 percent limit on foreign investment by life insurance companies, while investment-linked funds are subject to a 30 percent limit. Where limits on foreign investment are binding, as in Peru, market participants have developed new domestic instruments to provide foreign exposure to circumvent them.

Role of Financial Intermediaries

Banks and other financial intermediaries in general have played an important role in the development of corporate bond markets, but they have at times been reluctant to support the emergence or growth of corporate bond markets. In several countries, banks and other intermediaries have been important bond issuers—mainly of subordinated debt—as well as buyers of bonds (especially in Russia and some Asian countries). However, their main role is to provide underwriting capabilities to corporates and making secondary markets work adequately (Hawkins, 2002). In some cases, banks have preferred to keep their lending relationships with corporates, rather than provide corporates with alternative instruments such as corporate bonds—especially when bank lending spreads are high. Increasing competition is likely to force banks to change this behavior.

Some analysts have suggested that, in several European countries and in Japan, the market power of banks actually impeded the development of securities markets until the late 1980s. Banks can do this by controlling access to the payment system or distribution networks, or by encouraging regulations that increase the cost of issuance and underwriting of securities.[17]

The last two decades, however, have witnessed an expansion of securities markets everywhere (Rajan and Zingales, 2003). Moreover, the recent growth of corporate bond markets in the European Union and Canada demonstrate that banks and markets can grow in tandem and actually support and complement each other, in particular through investment banking activities. The growth in the EU was aided by the introduction of the euro and a substantial decrease in underwriting fees. In Canada, corporations became increasingly dependent on market-based financing during the 1980s and 1990s as banking legislation changes allowed banks to become more involved in such financial market activities as underwriting and brokerage services.[18]

Reflecting in part some of the obstacles behind the demand and supply of corporate bonds, the level of investment banking activity in many emerging markets is seen as one constraint on local firms' financing via capital markets. Issuing corporate securities typically involves the services of an investment bank (rather than a commercial bank or a securities broker). These services usually include advising the issuers on the terms and timing of the offer and on terms of underwriting the issue (see next section). Investment banking expertise is difficult and slow to develop within a country on its own and is typically costly to purchase from abroad. This may be changing, however, given the increasing role of foreign banks in EMs, together with the increasing move toward universal banking.[19]

In sum, the growth of corporate bond markets has been supported by both demand and supply factors. Further expansion of the local corporate bond markets, however, depends critically on access of new, medium-sized com-

[17]Schinasi and Smith (1998); and Rajan and Zingales (2003).
[18]Calmès (2004).
[19]See IMF (2000 and 2001) and BIS (2004) on recent trends in banking in EMs.

panies to the market. As discussed earlier, although institutional investors' assets under management are growing rapidly, these investors generally invest in investment-grade bonds, which in most EMs limits the universe of corporate names that can issue bonds to about 20–30 large firms with strong credit fundamentals. Similarly, foreign investors would have to move further down the credit spectrum to obtain sufficiently attractive yields commensurate with the risk exposure. They are not prepared to do so, however, because of the nonexistence or illiquidity of suitable corporates in these countries. Thus, to satisfy institutional investors' demand, potential issuers will have to improve their credit fundamentals. This, in turn, requires an improvement in the legal and regulatory framework for these markets and their participants, and it involves, among other things, improvements in corporate governance and transparency (IMF, 2005).

As discussed in earlier issues of the GFSR, the existence of a regulatory framework that ensures investor protection, market integrity, and contains systemic risks is essential for the development of securities markets in general and the corporate bond market in particular.[20] Unlike banks, individual bondholders typically have much smaller stakes in private firms and less bargaining power in the event of default or debt restructuring. Therefore, bankruptcy laws—which clearly define creditors' rights and borrowers' responsibilities, as well as the required enforcement mechanisms—are essential for establishing the legitimacy and credibility of corporate bond instruments. Adequate corporate governance practices and a timely and accurate public disclosure of financial information are important for maintaining credibility and stability of the corporate bond market.

Both market participants and the authorities in EMs with relatively large corporate bond markets are aware of the constraints to further development of the markets and are working to overcome the main obstacles. The Mexican Congress is about to finalize approval of a new capital markets law that aims to change corporate structures and governance to make them more investor friendly, and the pension fund regulatory agency is studying ways to make fund managers less risk averse. In Chile, a new law that creates a modern framework for the development of a venture capital industry is about to be approved. In Peru, pension fund regulators and the securities commission are trying to remove constraints to the emergence of new instruments, allowing pension funds to invest, among others, in private equity and bonds. In Brazil, a new bankruptcy regime that was approved in December 2004 is expected to speed up restructurings, improve investor's collection rights, and boost corporate bond markets. In Korea, in an effort to strengthen corporate governance, the Bankruptcy Law has been strengthened by the integration of all existing "sporadic" laws, with the aim of removing confusion and promoting greater consistency in implementation. The new law is also expected to revitalize the repo market. In Malaysia, several developmental initiatives and reforms, including recommendations from the National Bond Market Committee, Capital Market Masterplan, Finance Committee Report on Corporate Governance, and Corporate Law Reform Committee, have been implemented to improve various aspects of the legal, regulatory, and institutional frame-

[20]Issues related to the architecture of the regulation of corporate bond markets—such as whether regulation is fragmented or centralized (with a single entity responsible for the supervision of the entire financial sector, including the capital market), whether there is a dedicated regulator for the capital market, and whether it also oversees the clearing, settlement, and custody of the bond market—are likely to affect the cost-effectiveness of regulations. Most countries with relatively deeper corporate bond markets have adopted regulation of the corporate bond market concentrated in a single agency and have centralized the regulatory authority over both the primary and secondary markets in a single regulatory body.

works for the development of the corporate bond market.

Market Structure and Obstacles to Growth of Corporate Bond Markets

We now turn to those elements of microstructure that are critical for broadening and deepening corporate bond markets. In addition to demand and supply constraints, and the legal and regulatory framework, elements of the microstructure of primary and secondary markets—such as auctions, trading mechanisms, dissemination of transaction information, and the role of intermediaries—are important for market development. This section focuses on the main determinants of the cost of bond issuance and secondary market liquidity by examining the experiences of the EMs with large corporate bond markets and relevant mature markets.

Primary Markets and Issuance Costs

Key features of the corporate bond issuance process are the structuring, pricing, and distribution of bond issues to end-investors. The cost of issuance also depends on the type of instruments and the nature of bond contracts used in different jurisdictions. Furthermore, these market factors interact with credit ratings, registration, and other regulatory requirements to determine the all-in cost of financing.

Types of Instruments and Bond Contracts

The types of instruments issued by EM corporates vary, reflecting regional trends, and inflation and devaluation experiences. Most corporate debt securities in the largest Asian EMs are plain vanilla fixed coupon bonds. Maturities range from short-term (less than one year) commercial paper sold on a discount basis to 3–10 year corporate bonds, with the majority under five years. Convertible bonds were popular before the bursting of the technology bubble. In contrast, several different structures are used in Latin America, including floating rate notes (paying interest at a spread over the applicable government instrument), bonds with interest and principal indexed to U.S. dollars, and inflation-indexed bonds with adjustable coupons and principal payments. Latin American corporates issue coupon bonds for maturities extending to 30 years, which, in some cases, is longer than the maximum tenor of local government securities. Latin America's comparative success in selling long-term corporate bonds is a result of the widespread use of indexation or capital preservation mechanisms, a consequence in part of a history of high inflation and repeated currency devaluations.

Bond contracts show substantial homogeneity across the major EMs. While no overriding body of law, or regulations, force standardization of bond contracts, this may be the result of concentration in the securities industries similar to the standardization in the unregulated Eurobond market. However, in contrast with the generalized trend toward structuring bonds as "promissory notes" (i.e., in essence "promises to pay" with a minimum of covenants), EM corporate bonds feature terms and conditions that include covenants on leverage, interest coverage, liquidity, negative pledge, cross default, and minimum levels of shareholders' equity.

Mexico's experience clearly illustrates the importance of a standard and flexible instrument that accommodates issuers and investors' needs. The corporate bond market in Mexico was marginal until the introduction of a new instrument—Certificados Bursatiles (CBs)—in the 2001 securities law. The CBs contributed to the takeoff of the market for corporate bonds and has become the dominant debt instrument for corporates—accounting for about 99 percent of 2004 issuance. The CBs combined the attractive features of earlier debt instruments (medium-term notes (MTNs) and debentures).[21] They offer the speed and ease of issuance characteristic of MTNs and the flexible amortization schedules and covenants of debentures.

In some countries, credit enhancements and securitization have broadened investor appeal. Credit guarantees have enabled low-credit-quality borrowers to issue corporate bonds, especially in some Asian EMs.[22] Several EM local markets have increased issuance of securitized and/or structured products, such as asset-backed securities (ABS) and collateralized bond obligations.[23] Owing to the credit enhancements, these instruments normally receive better credit ratings than nonstructured transactions (usually by one or two notches), allowing regulated pension funds to invest in bonds from weaker credits. Structured transactions are also used to circumvent investment limits.[24] However, investors in EMs are not always familiar with the risks associated with these products. In Chile, for instance, the rapid decline in local interest rates during 2004 led to a sharp increase in mortgage prepayments, and several mortgage-backed securities (MBS) were downgraded and some of them defaulted on their obligations. In Korea, investment trust companies suffered losses after March 2003 as the liquidity problems of the credit card companies and the SK Corporation accounting scandal triggered large withdrawals.

In other markets, new instruments are used to attract new investors and broaden the investor base. The recent growth of Islamic bonds in Malaysia has been spurred by the successful establishment of a government yield curve and their popularity among issuers who want to tap a wider investor base in local and regional markets. The issuance of Islamic bonds outstripped that of conventional bonds in Malaysia in 2002, and currently the outstanding stock of Islamic bonds amounts to almost 30 percent of GDP (Box 4.3).

Issuance Process and Costs

The issuance process and associated costs constitute an important determinant of the decision of a corporate to access the local corporate bond market. Low issuance costs are likely to facilitate the development of local corporate bond markets, with positive implications for small enterprise creation (indirectly), large corporation development, and overall economic growth.[25] A reduction in these costs could contribute to increased access for lower-tier credits and further deepen and broaden the corporate bond market.

Issuance costs can be classified into five main categories. Some of these costs are directly linked to issuance methods and other institutional arrangements.

Management Fees

Management fees are paid for advice in structuring the transaction, preparing disclosure documentation for credit rating agencies, issuing registration and other offering documents, as well as in underwriting costs. Such fees are typically the largest single cost of a corporate bond issue; however, highly competitive underwriting business environments in both Asia and Latin America, combined with the structural undersupply of corporate bonds,

[21]Medium-term notes are a schedule of notes, with maturities usually ranging from 1 to 10 years, that are offered either continuously or intermittently over time. Debentures are debt securities that are not secured by a specific pledge of property, but instead represent a general claim on all assets of the firm.

[22]Providers of credit guarantees have been private (monoline) companies, government agencies, or international financial institutions. See Tran and Roldos (2004) for further issues on Asian bond market securitization and guarantees.

[23]The main transactions include mortgage-backed securities, credit cards, construction bridge loans, bonds with partial guarantees, and future flow receivables (including trade receivables, and toll road and tax revenues).

[24]In Peru, for example, structured products backed by local bonds but whose returns are linked to foreign market indices are being sold to pension funds to circumvent the limit on foreign investments.

[25]Levine and Zervos (1998); Beck and Levine (2003).

Box 4.3. Islamic Bonds in Malaysia

Islamic bonds have played an increasingly important role in Malaysia's financial market. Over the past 10 years, the issuance of Islamic bonds in Malaysia has been growing at a compounded rate of 31 percent, outgrowing the issuance of bonds in total, which were growing at the rate of 13 percent over the same period. Islamic bonds issued in 2004 amounted to 9.1 billion Malaysian ringgit ($2.4 billion), accounting for 32 percent of the total bonds issued (see first figure below). The total Islamic bonds outstanding is approximately 107 billion Malaysian ringgit ($28 billion) or about one quarter of the size of the total bond market in Malaysia. It is estimated that about 85 percent of Islamic bonds issued were issued by Malaysia, making Malaysia one of the world's largest Islamic bond markets.[1]

The issuers of Islamic bonds in Malaysia range from the government, government agencies, and private corporation to international development organizations. The government has played an important role in the development of the Islamic bond market by issuing Islamic bonds to use as a benchmark. Currently, Islamic private debt securities are the largest segment of the Malaysian Islamic bond market, accounting for about 70 percent of the market. Recently, Malaysia has allowed multilateral development banks and multinational corporations to issue ringgit denominated bonds in Malaysia. Since then, the International Bank for Reconstruction and Development (IBRD) and the International Finance Corporation (IFC) have issued Islamic bonds in Malaysia.

Despite the impressive growth of new Islamic bond issuance in Malaysia, there is a still a large demand for Islamic instruments. It is estimated that $39 billion worth of assets of Malaysian Muslims are not invested in the Islamic financial system.[2] Together with the much larger amount of Muslim funds from overseas, the largely untapped demand for Islamic financial products presents potential opportunities for Malaysia to develop itself as a center for an Islamic bond market.

Islamic bonds (*Sukuk*) must comply to the *Shariah* principles. The *Shariah* principles are Islamic laws and rules that govern religious, cultural, social, political, and economic aspects of Islamic societies. An important financial aspect of *Shariah* principles is the prohibition of interest (*riba*) on borrowing. Therefore, a fixed or predetermined rate of return is prohibited, whereas the earning of profits or returns from underlying assets is encouraged. Moreover, exchanging money for debt is also prohibited under Islamic finance. To issue an Islamic bond, there must be underlying transactions backed by existing or future assets. In addition, the proceedings from Islamic bonds can only be invested in activities not prohibited by *Shariah*.

Common types of *Shariah* principles used in Islamic bonds in Malaysia can be classified into debt-based, asset-based, and equity-based instru-

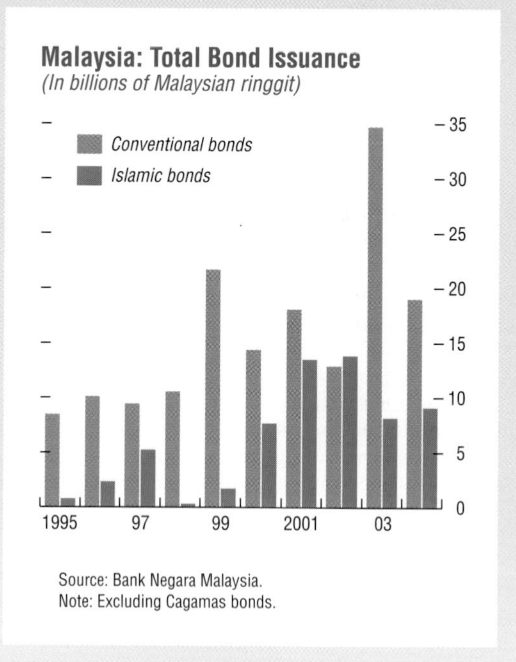

Source: Bank Negara Malaysia.
Note: Excluding Cagamas bonds.

[1]Other countries that have been issuing Islamic bonds include Saudi Arabia, United Arab Emirates, Bahrain, and Indonesia. Recently, Pakistan was successful in issuing its first sovereign Islamic bond of $600 in January 2005.

[2]Nik Jaafar (2005).

ments. *Murabahah* (cost-plus sale), *bai bithaman ajil* (BBA; deferred payment sale), and *istisna* (project finance) bonds can be considered as debt-based bonds because they are issued in exchange for debt created by the repurchase of an underlying asset. These principles effectively limit debt creation to the issuer's (current or future) assets. *Ijarah* (leasing) bonds are backed by an asset under a leasing contract. *Mudharabah* and *musharakah* are profit-sharing contracts between the issuer and investors.

The majority of Islamic bonds in Malaysia are debt-based instruments. As shown in the second figure, about 90 percent of Islamic bonds issued in 2004 were based on *murabahah*, BBA, and *istisna* principles. These debt-based bonds involve the purchase of an asset by investors (lenders) and the simultaneous sale of the asset back to the issuer with a markup (i.e., a profit margin) agreed upon by both parties. The title to the asset is transferred back to the issuer who, as a result of the transactions, is indebted to the investors. The issuer's obligation is securitized via the issuance of debt certificates, which can be traded in the secondary market.[3] *Murabahah* and BBA are similar except that BBA bonds are used for longer-term financing and the seller is not required to disclose the profit margin in the selling price.[4] Similarly, an issuer can also use a working project as an asset to issue Islamic bonds if the project is undertaken with the

Malaysia: Issuance of Islamic Bonds in 2004, by *Shariah* Principle

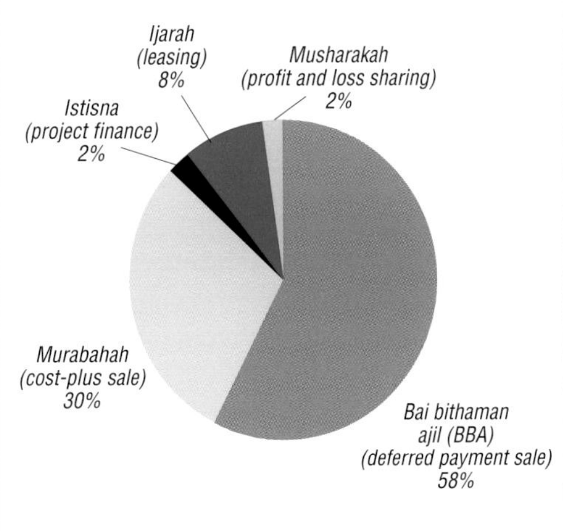

Source: Islamic Finance Information Services.

istisna principle.[5] Once the issuer enters into the *istisna* contract with a contractor to undertake the project, the issuer can use the project as an asset in the sell-and-buyback transactions (similar to what is described above) to issue *istisna* bonds even though the project has not yet been completed.

Islamic bonds can also be backed by an asset. Under the *ijarah* principle, an issuer sells an asset (e.g., plants, equipments, machines, and vehicles) to investors. The investors will then lease them back to the issuer via the *ijarah* contract. The title of the asset will remain with the investors throughout the tenure of the contract. Upon the completion of the contract, the title will be returned to the issuer, unless it is agreed otherwise. *Ijarah* bonds are in effect bonds backed by the receipts from the leasing contract.

[3]While *Shariah* scholars and the Securities Commission in Malaysia have approved the trading of these debt-based bonds in the secondary market, these bonds are not traded in the secondary market in many other countries. Because it is not permissible to sell a deferred debt at the price below its par value as it would result in *riba* (interest), some Islamic jurists prohibit the trading of *murabahah* and similar credit transactions in the secondary market. In Malaysia, Islamic bonds are commonly traded in the secondary market. The annual trading volume of Islamic debt securities (government and PDS) exceeds 126 billion Malaysian ringgit in 2004.

[4]The government of Malaysia has issued Islamic bonds based on these principles. These bonds are considered benchmarks for Islamic bonds.

[5]*Istisna* is a purchase contract of an asset to be constructed in the future. The buyer requires a seller or contractor to construct the asset that will be complete in the future according to the specifications given in the contract.

Box 4.3 *(concluded)*

Some Islamic bonds are based on profit sharing schemes. *Mudharabah* is an agreement between an investor who provides 100 percent of the capital required to complete a project and an entrepreneur who solely manages the project. Profits from the project will be distributed according to a predetermined ratio between the capital provider and the entrepreneur. Any loss will be borne solely by the investor, unless the loss is due to negligence of the entrepreneur. Under *musharakah,* both the entrepreneur and the investors contribute resources to the project, either in the form of capital or in kind. Any profits will be shared at an agreed-upon ratio, but a loss will be shared on the basis of equity participation.

Many market participants in Malaysia perceive Islamic bonds as being similar to conventional bonds in terms of underlying risks. Islamic bonds are widely traded by Islamic investors and are viewed as a perfect substitute for conventional bonds by non-Islamic investors. Because of the relatively small supply of Islamic bonds relative to the larger investor base, Islamic bonds are often traded at higher prices compared with conventional bonds.

However, investor protection mechanisms of Islamic bonds have not yet been tested. In principle, Islamic bonds share the same criteria as (unsecured) conventional bonds in the matter of late payments or default proceedings. However, because there have not been many default cases for Islamic debt securities in Malaysia, the bankruptcy process and dispute resolution mechanism for Islamic securities are largely untested. Its functionality remains to be seen.

have resulted in a dramatic compression in the fees that lead managers charge issuers.

The use of underwriting and auctions for corporate bond issues differ by region. Bond issues in Asia are underwritten and distributed by an investment bank or a syndicate of brokerage houses, similar to the traditional process used in the U.S. domestic and Eurobond markets.[26] Historically, the issuance process was similar in Latin America, but has now migrated to an auction-based system, patterned after government bond auctions. Under this procedure, corporations choose a lead manager (placement agent) for the offering, and institutional investors make direct bids for specific amounts of bonds at various prices. Under a "Dutch auction" mechanism, all bonds are awarded to bidders at a single cut-off price that gives the borrower its desired volume of issuance. Under these auction-based systems, there is no need to form syndicates to spread underwriting risk or to assist the lead manager in the selling effort. Lead managers have been forced to accept this issuance methodology by a concentrated, powerful group of institutional investors who want to ensure that corporate bond offerings are executed in a fair, open, and transparent manner.

Registration, Listing, and Legal Fees

Registration, listing, and other legal mechanisms provide issuers and investors common standards (e.g., business description, financial statements, terms and conditions, public disclosure) both to assess the investment merits of bonds and to provide market and legal safeguards.

In most EMs, shelf registration can be used to increase issuer flexibility, reduce issuance cost, and improve market timing. Corporate bonds can be registered either as a single issue or under a program umbrella, structured

[26]Although the period to complete a bond issue varies across the three regions, the issuance process is similar: companies first offer the indicative spread and terms and conditions to underwriters, and then choose the offer from underwriters that best meet current investors' needs.

along the lines of shelf registration rules in the United States. Shelf registration allows corporations to prepare their bond offering documentation on a regular basis, reducing the workload surrounding preparation of an issue for market, and allowing the spreading of fixed issuance costs over a larger number of instruments.

Most corporate debt issues are either registered with the local securities and exchange commission (SEC) or a similar body (based on the U.S. model), or may also be listed on a stock exchange (as is customary in the Eurobond market).[27] The practice in Latin America is for both SEC-style registration *and* stock exchange listing; however, regulators and stock exchanges have largely come to "gentlemen's agreements" on a division of oversight duties to avoid duplication of effort. There are, however, subtle differences in how the registration process works in practice across countries that affect the cost of issuance.[28]

A corporate bond offering will also entail other fees, including those of trustees or fiscal agents. Typically a trustee or fiscal agent is needed to make interest and principal payments and is compensated through a flat "up-front" fee and additional charges for each payment made on behalf of the issuer. The fiscal agency structure is common in U.S. domestic and Eurobond markets because of its low cost and the fiscal agents' subordinate role (where a fiscal agent acts as the agent of the issuer). Bonds issued under trust deeds are common in most EMs. Because of the trustee's authority to initiate legal proceedings on behalf of bondholders, the trustee can help resolve disputes between issuers and bondholders.[29]

Legal fees are not typically calculated according to the value of the note. Instead, they tend to be calculated on the basis of time-based professional costs, and they tend to be higher for an initial issue and lower thereafter. These costs are relatively low in most EMs. Legal costs connected with an initial corporate debt offering are substantially higher (as much as five times greater) than an update of existing documents for corporates that are frequent issuers. The initial high legal costs can act as a powerful disincentive for potential new corporate debt issuers.

Credit Ratings

Obtaining a credit rating can be an additional expense of a corporate bond transaction. The cost of a credit rating is based on several factors; the most relevant is the issue amount. However, a credit rating is valuable to an issuer and a high credit rating can lower the interest costs on its corporate bond. Ratings, like legal fees, are an area in which frequent issuers have cost advantages. For example, most rating agencies charge an "up-front" fee to recover the incremental costs of preparing the initial credit ratings for a corporation about to issue its first public bond. While the authorities in some jurisdictions do

[27]Registration is the system for complying with laws for offering and selling securities to the public within a jurisdiction (subject to certain exceptions). It is mandatory in some jurisdictions, whereas listing is typically voluntary for the issuer, and is undertaken to facilitate secondary transactions in a security on an exchange (as opposed to over the counter), and is commonly self-regulated (i.e., by the exchange).

[28]In Chile, before corporate bonds can be sold to the pension funds, they must be reviewed by the securities commission and accepted for listing on the stock exchange. In addition to these requirements, corporate bond offerings must be approved by the Risk Classification Commission (CCR), which is composed of representatives from government regulatory agencies and independent experts. The CCR reviews the investment merits of the relevant security to determine its appropriateness for pension fund portfolios, and may require a third credit rating opinion.

[29]Bonds issued under trust deeds typically provide a mechanism for qualified majority bondholders to agree to modify the terms of the bonds. Under local laws, most trustees can call bondholder meetings relatively easily to vote on modifications or changes in the bond indenture. This mechanism functions in much the same way as "collective action" clauses, that is, it eliminates the need for unanimous approval for changes to the bond agreement.

Table 4.8. Cost of Domestic and International Bond Issues

	Face Value *(in U.S. dollars)*					
	Brazil		Chile		Mexico	
	17 million	100 million	15 million	100 million	18 million	91 million
Local bonds total cost (in percent of face value)	**4.6**	**2.4**	**4.6**[1]	**2.7**	**2.0**	**1.2**
Composition of total cost (in percent of total cost)						
Management fees	65.0	86.6	45.6	36.6	50.3	67.7
Registration listing and legal fees	8.8	3.9	10.8	2.7	33.2	23.6
Credit ratings	14.3	5.8	4.3	1.3	12.7	7.4
Marketing costs	11.8	3.7	2.6	0.6	3.8	1.3
Taxes	—	—	36.7	58.8	—	—
International bonds total cost (in percent of face value)	. . .	**2.2**	. . .	**2.2**	. . .	**2.2**

Source: Zervos (2004).
[1]Average of $10 and $20 million bonds.

not require any ratings for public bond issues (or alternatively, require only one), market practice is to have two ratings (three is becoming more common).[30]

Marketing Costs

Marketing costs depend on the location of the investor base, regulatory requirements, investors' needs, and frequency of issuance. Issue documentation, particularly the prospectus/offering circular, must be distributed to all bond purchasers. Unless the borrower is well known or has recently issued, there may also be the need for investor presentations in key financial cities, including group presentations and individual meetings with significant institutional investors. These costs are far less for domestic transactions.

Taxes

Taxes are also a major cost of issuance and influence the structure of corporate bond markets in many ways. A certain minimum level of taxation is acceptable to all parties in corporate debt transactions. However, large-scale levies against corporate borrowers do much to discourage borrowing or move it to tax-free jurisdictions such as the Euromarkets. A powerful example is Chile's stamp tax, which is levied on all loans and debt instruments.[31] A change in the Chilean regulations in 2002, which spread the cost of the tax through several issues, led to a recovery of the commercial paper market in Chile.

In sum, issuance processes and costs vary significantly across countries, and high costs have been one of the obstacles that reduced issuance by corporates (Box 4.4), in particular by smaller and lower-rated companies. Zervos (2004) shows that for a standard size ($100 million) bond, issuance costs in Mexico are roughly half of those in Brazil and Chile (Table 4.8). The higher costs are related to higher disclosure costs in Brazil and the

[30]In Malaysia, companies must obtain credit ratings from at least one agency, while ratings from at least two agencies are required in Korea—as well as in most countries in Latin America. Ratings are not required in Russia.

[31]This tax is charged at a rate of 0.134 percent a month of borrowing, with a maximum rate of 1.608 percent. For many years this tax put corporate bond issuance at a disadvantage to domestic bank loans, for while both type of transactions required payment of the stamp tax, extensions or renegotiations of bank loans were not subject to this tax while bond refinancings were. However, in recognition of the anticompetitive nature of this tax, in 2002, the Chilean authorities changed the regulations to allow corporations to file shelf-style registration statements. Extending for up to 10 years, these registration statements allowed corporations to pay the stamp tax once for a set amount of debt securities; subsequent refinancing issues done under this statement would not be subject to the tax. While shelf-style registration does much to ameliorate the effect of the stamp tax on frequent issuers in Chile, the tax remains onerous for corporations doing debut offerings or small-sized issues. It thus discourages issuance by new borrowers needed to expand the base of the domestic corporate bond market.

stamp tax in Chile, which makes issuance in local markets costlier than issuance in international markets. The study also shows the importance of issue size: the costs of issuing a \$10–\$20 million bond is double the cost of issuing a \$100 million bond—reaching, in the cases of Brazil and Chile, a 4.6 percent level. Although some countries have seen issuance sizes under \$10 million (e.g., Peru where about one-third of corporate bonds are under \$10 million), it is unclear whether these smaller sizes would be reasonable for issuers and investors alike. Indeed, the fraction of issues under \$10 million is much lower in Malaysia, Mexico, and Thailand (Figure 4.7). High issuance costs may explain the reluctance of smaller companies to issue bonds in some local markets.

Figure 4.7. Distribution by Size of the Corporate Bond Issues

(In percent of total)

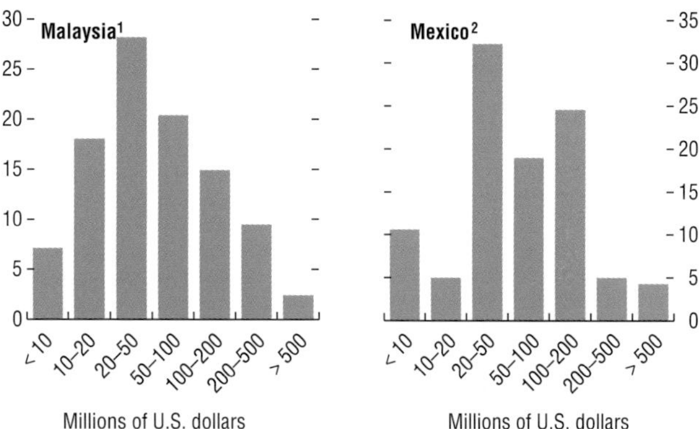

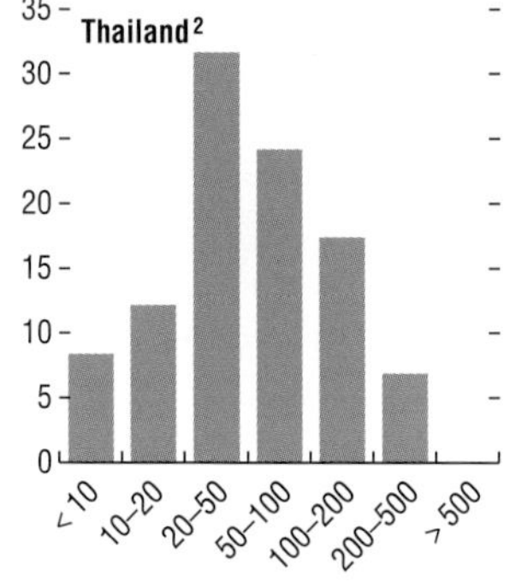

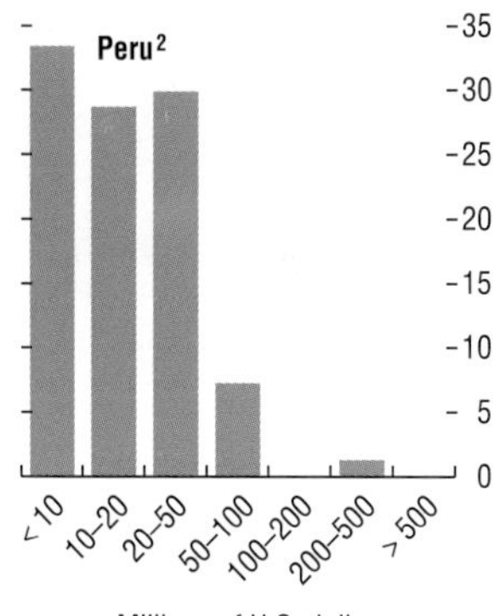

Sources: Bloomberg L.P.; and Malaysia's Securities Commission.

[1]New issuance in 2004.

[2]Outstanding bonds in June 2005.

Secondary Market and Pricing Issues

Secondary markets provide liquidity and facilitate price discovery as well as asset reallocation. These functions are important for the operation of the corporate bond market. This section discusses the importance of well-functioning secondary corporate bond markets as well as some market microstructure issues related to the liquidity of the secondary market.

Market liquidity is an elusive concept and difficult to measure, and many different measures are possible.[32] Generally speaking, liquidity is a measure of how easy it is to trade securities.[33] Liquidity is important for the efficient functioning of securities markets because it ensures that investors can trade securities whenever they wish, making them more willing to invest in the securities in the first place. Important dimensions of market

[32]See, for example, Houweling, Mentink, and Vorst (2005).

[33]Market liquidity is defined in various ways. For example, a market is considered to be liquid when bid-ask prices are regularly quoted, the spreads are small enough, and small trades can be immediately executed with minimal effect on prices.

Box 4.4. Demand and Supply Factors Driving Corporate Bond Markets in China and India

The financial systems of China and India rely heavily on the banking sector for corporate financing, while debt markets have historically been dominated by the government sector—including public banks. The steady increase of sovereign borrowing has outpaced GDP growth over the last 15 years, and, even though financial reforms have removed some regulatory impediments to efficient financial sector development, both countries still show a lack of deep and liquid corporate bond markets.

While the government bond markets in China and India are fairly well developed, the corporate bond markets remain relatively underdeveloped. The size of the total bond market in China was 42 percent of GDP at the end of 2004, whereas the size of the corporate bond markets only amounted to 0.75 percent of GDP (or 3.5 percent of total debt markets; see first figure). Chinese banks increased corporate lending to the private sector from 86.6 percent of GDP in 1990 to 149 percent of GDP in 2004. In India, the credit cycle has been less expansive than in China, with credit to the private sector reaching 37 percent of GDP. The total outstanding volume of corporate bonds amounted to only 1.4 percent of GDP while the total debt market reached 38 percent of GDP: $257 billion (see second figure).

The relatively underdeveloped local institutional investors, as well as the centralized government supervision over capital markets, are the major factors contributing to the underdevelopment of corporate bond markets in China. Because of the troubled history of sizable corporate bond defaults in the 1990s, the government has adopted a merit-based selection system for issuing corporate bonds,[1] ceilings on corporate bond interest rates, and mandatory credit guarantees (by state banks) to protect investors from possible bond defaults. These systems have created a highly segmented, over-regulated issuance process that restricts corporate access to capital markets and permits only the best companies and infrastructure projects to issue bonds. They also limit incentives to develop corporate governance, disclosure, and transparency standards for bond issuance. Moreover, the absence of a comprehensive trading platform and a sound operational infrastructure inhibits efficient information dissemination and price discovery across capital market segments.[2]

In India, high issuance costs, the lack of transparency of the bond issuance process, and the barriers to domestic and foreign institutional investment are the main obstacles to the development of corporate bond markets. The procedures for corporate bond registration and approval are time-consuming and involve several agencies, making issuance costs so high that companies resort to private placements, which are not subject to the strict regulatory provisions and disclosure requirements of public issues. As a result, the proportion of total bond issuance done through private placements has grown from 29.8 percent in 1990 to more than 85 percent in 2004. The heterogeneous tax treatments across different debt securities (issued by the same corporate) create financial distortions and make it difficult for investors to price different instruments. Moreover, the current barriers to institutional investors (e.g., the corporate bond ceiling for foreign institutional investors and the investment restrictions for mutual funds) pose further constraints for the growth of the corporate bond market.

National governments in both countries have taken an active role to encourage the further development of the debt markets over the recent past. In China, a special working group was created by the government in February 2004

[1]It can take 12–15 months or longer to get an approval to issue corporate bonds.

[2]There are three markets for bond trading: the interbank, the exchange, and the over-the-counter (OTC) markets. While all types of financial institutions are allowed to participate directly in the interbank market, commercial banks and credit unions are excluded from trading in the exchange, creating market segmentation, and restricting some trade flows. Moreover, there are no regulations and reporting requirements governing the OTC market, making it difficult to trade across the markets.

Bond Market in China
(In percent of total)

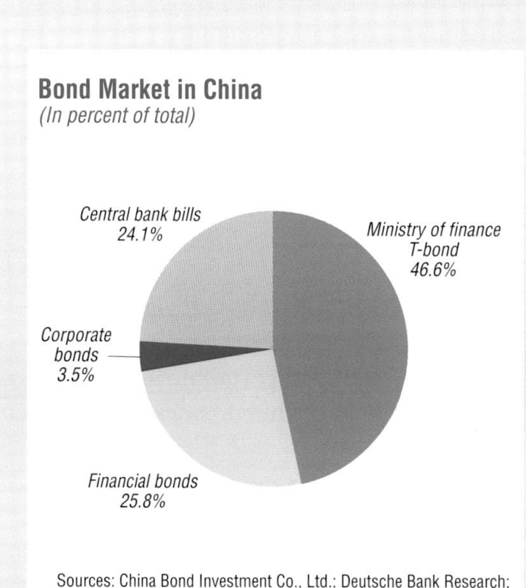

Sources: China Bond Investment Co., Ltd.; Deutsche Bank Research; National Debt Association of China; and IMF staff estimates.
Note: Total outstanding volume (April 2005): 5.8 trillion yuan ($700 billion).

Bond Market in India
(In percent of total)

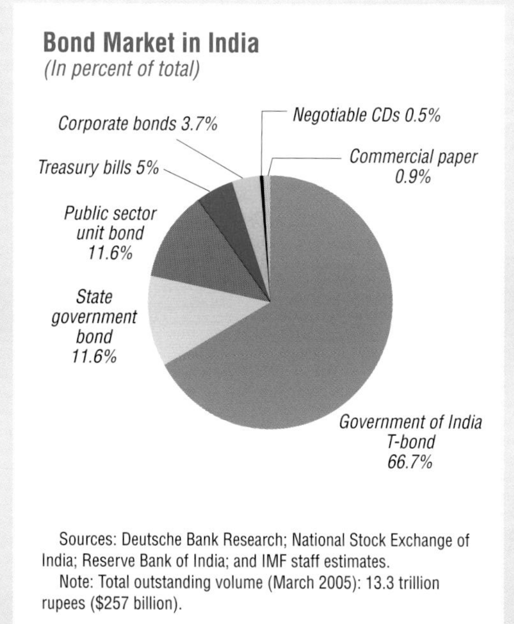

Sources: Deutsche Bank Research; National Stock Exchange of India; Reserve Bank of India; and IMF staff estimates.
Note: Total outstanding volume (March 2005): 13.3 trillion rupees ($257 billion).

to improve regulation in areas of granting nongovernment enterprises access to the corporate bond market, relaxing approval limits on corporate bond issues, and easing interest rate controls. In India, several policy measures, such as the removal of technical impediments to competitive pricing of government securities, the promotion of central bank open market operations via the repo market, and the extension of a liquid zero-bond yield curve up to 30 years are likely to help the corporate bond market.

A number of reforms could further the development of the corporate bond markets in both countries. In China, authorities could further promote fair market competition for funds among government and nongovernment issuers. The reforms ought to seek a sequenced and time-bound transition from the "merit review system" to a system of full disclosures and unified regulatory supervision. Investor protection in bond markets can be promoted through disclosure, legal enforceability, and assessments by independent rating institutions. Moreover, enhancing the development of domestic and foreign institutional investors, and removing barriers to trading between different markets, would improve liquidity in the corporate bond market. In India, the authorities could consider measures to improve regulatory practices by (1) ensuring homogeneity across different debt securities; (2) putting regulation of the corporate debt market under a single regulator, and streamlining disclosure and issuance practices for public debt issues in order to reduce transaction costs, time lags, and uncertainty; and (3) liberalizing restrictions on investments by institutional investors and gradually lifting the existing foreign investment ceiling on corporate bonds.

liquidity include *tightness* and *depth*.[34] *Tightness* provides information about general costs incurred by market participants in executing transactions; it is often measured by the bid-ask spread, the number of bids-offers, or the number of missing bids or offers. *Depth* refers to the ability to execute transactions without

[34]See Mohanty (2002) and BIS (1999) for extended discussions on market liquidity.

Table 4.9. Annual Turnover Ratios of Listed Bonds and Equities on Exchanges, 2004
(In percent)

		Turnover Ratio			
		Listed bonds			
	Exchanges	Total[1]	Private sector	Public sector	Equities
Mature markets					
United States	NYSE[2]	0.2	...	...	91.4
Canada	TSX Group	42.3	—	42.3	55.3
United Kingdom	London SE	110.3	2.3	446.4	180.4
Australia	Australian SE	2.2	...	...	67.4
Japan	Tokyo SE	0.1	19.9	—	90.5
	Osaka SE	—	6.0	—	5.9
Hong Kong SAR	Hong Kong Exchanges	—	0.0	—	51.0
Latin America					
Argentina	Buenos Aires SE	28.1	7.5	30.9	11.9
Colombia	Colombia SE	541.9	157.4	726.7	8.2
Peru	Lima SE	16.5	15.9	18.6	8.7
Mexico	Mexican Exchange	0.6	...	...	26.4
Chile	Santiago SE	...	...	...	10.4
Brazil	Sao Paulo SE	6.8	6.8	—	31.5
Europe					
Hungary	Budapest SE	3.6	12.1	2.5	46.7
Turkey	Istanbul SE	310.2	—	310.2	149.1
Poland	Warsaw SE	1.5	44.1	1.4	22.7
Asia					
China	Shanghai SE	36.5	17.8	37.8	102.7
	Shenzhen SE	12.7	—	12.7	145.8
India	BSE, the SE Mumbai	5.9	—	8.2	30.6
	National Stock Exchange of India	63.3	42.1	63.9	71.7
Malaysia	Bursa Malaysia	21.7	21.7	—	33.9
Korea	Korea Exchange	52.8	0.8	63.8	125.4
Thailand	Thailand SE	0.3	0.3	—	100.9

Source: World Federation of Exchanges.
[1]Total includes domestic and foreign listed bonds.
[2]2003 data for bond turnover.

causing sharp changes in prevailing market prices and is usually measured by quote sizes, volatility, trading volumes, and turnover ratio. Although these are imperfect measures for tightness and depth, they provide quantitative benchmarks of market liquidity.

Although market liquidity is hard to measure, the liquidity of corporate bonds in both mature and emerging markets is relatively low. In many countries the majority of bonds are traded on over-the-counter (OTC) markets[35] and the trading data are often unavailable,[36] which makes it difficult to compare the liquidity of secondary bond markets across countries. Chakravarty and Sarkar (1999) compare the liquidity between corporate and government bonds in the United States and find that the average bid-ask spread for corporate bonds between 1995 and 1997 was 21 cents per $100, compared with 11 cents in the government bond market. They also find that the spreads for AA-rated bonds are lower than noninvestment-grade corporate bonds. Hattori, Koyama, and Yonetani (2001) find that the turnover ratio of the Japanese corporate bond market was about one-fifth of that in the United States. Table 4.9 shows the turnover ratio[37] of listed bonds as well as equities traded on the exchange markets in a sample of both mature and emerging markets.[38] In most countries, corporate bond markets are relatively less liquid compared with equities and public bonds markets. Moreover, liquidity is usually centered on a few quality issues and easily "dries up" as market conditions change. However, in some countries such as Peru and Colombia, where equity market are less active, corporate bond markets are

[35]Over-the-counter (OTC) market refers to a decentralized market where securities are typically traded over the telephone, facsimile, or electronic platform, as opposed to an exchange, which is an organized market and may be either floor-based or electronic. Organized markets usually have more disclosure requirements.

[36]Exceptions include the United States where trading data of all OTC transactions are collected and disseminated through National Association of Securities Dealers's (NASD's) centralized reporting system known as TRACE (Transaction Reporting and Compliance Engine). The information is available to the public on the Bond Market Association's website: *http://www.investinginbonds.com.*

[37]Turnover ratio may be defined in different ways. Here, we define turnover ratio as the ratio between annual trading volume and amount outstanding.

[38]This table should be interpreted with caution because the proportion of bonds listed and traded on the exchanges may differ across the countries. For example, most corporate bonds in the United Kingdom and Japan were listed but rarely traded on the exchanges, whereas only a small fraction of corporate bonds in Thailand and Malaysia were listed. In Peru, most corporate bonds are reportedly listed and traded on the exchange.

relatively more liquid. (See Table 4.10 for Asian country experiences.)

Investors require additional returns to hold securities that are illiquid, to compensate for the risks of not being able to get out of the position when needed or of incurring a large cost to do so. This additional return is known as the *liquidity premium* and is an important component of corporate bond spreads.[39] Spreads on corporate bonds are often found to be wider than justified by historical default losses, most likely reflecting liquidity risks and tax effects.[40] Using corporate bond data for the U.S. market, Longstaff, Mithal, and Neis (2004) find that the default component accounts for most corporate spreads across all credit ratings and the nondefault component of a spread is strongly related to such measures of illiquidity as the size of bid-ask spreads and the principal amount outstanding.

Many factors contribute to the increasing pervasiveness of the illiquidity of secondary markets in EMs.

- Corporate bond markets in many EMs are dominated by large buy-and-hold pension funds and insurance companies. Combined with the underdevelopment of other institutional investors, their buy-and-hold behavior undermines the active trading of corporate bonds. This problem is worsened by the imbalance between the growth of assets under management and the availability of securities.
- Investors in corporate bonds are often concentrated and sometimes behave similarly. Their "herding" behavior tends to make markets one sided and to limit active trading.
- The small issue size of corporate bonds contributes to illiquidity. The size of corporate bond issues in EMs are generally small relative to government bonds and other securities. Moreover, because of their heterogeneous nature (coupon and maturity), bonds issued by the same issuer may not be substitutable.
- The lack of hedging instruments also contributes to the low liquidity of corporate bond markets in many emerging markets. Investing in corporate bonds exposes investors to market, credit, and liquidity risks. Repo and derivative markets that allow investors to hedge such risks and broker dealers to manage their inventory more effectively are underdeveloped in many EMs. Without hedging instruments, some investors are unwilling to buy corporate bonds, exacerbating the lack of liquidity. Moreover, it is uncommon to short sell corporate bonds in some of these countries either because of regulation or because of investors' unwillingness to lend the securities for short selling.[41]

In addition, corporate bond market microstructure plays an important role in determining market liquidity. The market microstructure includes trade execution systems, trading venues, trading commissions,

Table 4.10. Annual Bond Turnover, 2004
(In billions of U.S. dollars)

	Government Bonds		Corporate Bonds	
	Trading volume	Turnover ratio *(in percent)*	Trading volume	Turnover ratio *(in percent)*
China	568.4	224.0	1.42	1.4
Hong Kong SAR	541.0	3471.6	. . .	. . .
Indonesia	28.7	65.0	0.88	15.1
Japan	28,554.5	537.9	1,086.01	88.7
Korea	860.6	331.9	345.39	100.8
Malaysia	84.3	182.3	38.07	77.7
Singapore	126.0	314.9	. . .	. . .
Thailand	68.4	202.9	5.47	27.7

Source: Asianbondonline.

[39]Corporate bond spreads are defined as the difference between the yields on a corporate bond issue and the yields on a relevant (sovereign) benchmark issue.

[40]See, for instance, Elton and others (2001); and Krainer (2004).

[41]Some institutional investors do not want to lend their securities because they are afraid that by lending their securities to be shorted, their net asset value would be adversely affected.

disclosure of contracted price and volume information, and market regulations. Robust and efficient trading, as well as proper data dissemination systems, promote market integrity and improve the liquidity and efficiency of the price discovery process.[42] In most EMs, information about transactions on the exchange are well disseminated. Transparency requirements for listed bonds traded on the OTC market differ across countries. With some exceptions, information is made publicly available with delays ranging from minutes to a day.[43]

A number of countries are trying to encourage more exchange-based trading of bonds through tax incentives. As exchange trading is seen as more transparent, more effective, and allowing a wider range of investors better access to the market, some countries encourage investors to trade bonds on the exchange to promote competition in the secondary market. For example, in Peru, the government encourages trading on the exchange by exempting interest income tax for fixed-income securities traded there.[44] In some countries, institutional investors (e.g., private pension funds) are restricted to trading securities only on the exchange because of the better transparency.

The existence of a large number of illiquid corporate bonds poses a challenge to institutional investors that are required to mark-to-market their portfolios. Some securities are not traded for extended periods of time. In Mexico and Korea, the systems of "price vendors" are established. Institutional investors "purchase" the price quotes from these price vendors who provide price quotes for all securities using their pricing methodologies.[45] In Chile and Peru, the pension fund regulators produce their own "price vectors" for the valuation of portfolios, and there are increasing pressures to have a standardized methodology that can also be applied to mutual funds. In other countries, institutional investors use either prices supplied by their regulators, self-regulatory organizations (Thailand), or average quotes from securities companies (Malaysia).

In sum, more liquid markets would certainly help support the broadening and deepening of corporate bond markets by conveying more pricing information and facilitating trades.

Challenges and Policy Issues

This chapter has analyzed some of the recent experiences of corporate bond market development in selected emerging markets. Building up the institutions needed to deepen and broaden these markets poses a number of challenges and policy issues. We discuss these challenges and policy issues next, drawing a distinction between issues related to the development of the markets and those related to financial stability.

Market Development Issues

Although there is no general agreement on which conditions are "necessary" for corporate bond market development, and there is certainly no "one-size-fits-all" recipe, this chapter as well as other studies on the issue have documented a number of institutional features of a well-functioning corporate bond market. Macroeconomic stability is often mentioned as a precondition for the development of local securities markets, and this is no less relevant for corporate bond markets. Indeed,

[42]See Madhavan (2000) for a review of theoretical and empirical literature on market microstructure.

[43]Information is provided to regulators in the case of Malaysia; to the stock exchange and subsidiaries in the case of Mexico; and to self-regulatory organizations in the cases of Korea (KSDA), Thailand (Thai BDC), Japan (JSDA), and the United States (NASD). See IOSCO (2002 and 2004).

[44]Some transactions, however, are reportedly matched on the OTC market and cleared on the exchange only for tax purposes.

[45]For Information on pricing services in mature markets, see the Bond Market Association (2005).

the achievement of macroeconomic stability by a number of EMs suggests that the time is right to press ahead with other measures that contribute to the development of corporate bond markets. In particular, substantial fiscal consolidation has reduced the crowding-out effect of government issues in local bond markets, despite their useful presence in providing a pricing benchmark. Also, the enhanced credibility of inflation-targeting regimes has contributed to low domestic yields and the attractiveness of local corporate bonds.[46] Among the measures aimed at further developing the local corporate bond market, the more substantive ones would ensure sustainable growth of the demand and supply for bond issues—and market intermediaries—while others would strengthen the microstructure of these markets.

Demand Factors

Emerging markets need to develop a relatively large and diversified institutional investor base, including pension funds, insurance companies, and mutual funds. Although the institutionalization of savings has been a trend in the mature markets for decades, and it is already taking hold in the major emerging markets, authorities in EMs have to ensure that conditions to facilitate the growth of these investors, such as by protecting investors without unduly restricting the growth of alternative saving instruments, are in place. They also must ensure that the regulations needed to preserve the soundness of these intermediaries, such as those that prevent excessive credit concentrations, do not hinder the growth of the corporate bond market.

Supply Factors

A growing and diverse set of issuers with both the size and credit quality necessary to appeal to institutional investors is necessary for the sustained growth of the corporate bond market. Medium-sized and small corporates should adopt high standards of transparency and corporate governance to facilitate market access. Credit enhancements and structured products could also help lower rated corporates to access, or reaccess, bond markets.

Role of Intermediaries

Competitive pressures are likely to force banks and other financial intermediaries to develop diverse instruments to address the needs of investors and issuers. Increased emphasis on better risk management and the adoption of the new Basel accord over the medium term are likely to cause EM banks to economize their capital by providing instruments other than extending and warehousing loans. Measures that facilitate banks' move to the investment banking and brokerage business are likely to both help improve banks' profitability and contribute to the development of securities markets, in particular, corporate bond markets.

Legal and Regulatory Issues

For the effective functioning of securities markets, the authorities must adopt a regulatory framework that ensures investor protection and market integrity, and contains systemic risks. Key elements of the required legal framework include the adoption and enforcement of bankruptcy laws that clearly define creditors' rights and borrowers' responsibilities, the promotion of adequate corporate governance practices, and a timely and accurate public disclosure of financial information. The authorities should also aim to remove legal and other impediments to securitization and the inclusion of credit enhancements.

Improvements in the Microstructure of Primary and Secondary Markets

Financial intermediaries need to be careful in tailoring bond contracts. For example, con-

[46]Disintermediation of the banking system may, however, change the monetary transmission mechanism and reduce the effectiveness of monetary policy.

tracts that benefit the issuer but do not allow for covenants that protect investors may hinder market growth. However, contracts that cater to a specific investor base, as in the case of Islamic bonds, can certainly satisfy a niche demand and provide a boost to the markets.

Measures to reduce issuance costs have proven to be rather effective in promoting the corporate bond market, but some EMs could make further progress in this area. Shelf registration and other measures that reduce the approval time and cost of issuance are unquestionably useful. Similarly, the removal of discriminatory taxation that benefits other securities should be avoided. Rating requirements do add to the cost of issuance but they are necessary for adequate pricing and development of a credit culture. Further reductions in issuance costs could allow reductions in the minimum issuance size and improve access for medium-sized and small enterprises.

A well-developed secondary market certainly helps the development of the primary market, by improving price discovery and liquidity. However, only a few countries have achieved this goal. Measures that require or induce trading to be channeled through the stock (or other) exchanges do increase transparency, but they may remove incentives for market makers to support trading activities—especially during periods of excessive volatility, which are so frequent in emerging markets.

Ancillary markets, such as liquid government bond and derivative markets, are not necessary for the development of corporate bond markets, but they are important supports. The development of an adequate mechanism for pricing credit risk generally requires the existence of a well-developed local currency benchmark yield curve, as well as a credible and transparent mechanism for credit risk assessments. The government is often a natural provider of benchmark interest rates, because of high liquidity, relatively low default risk, and a wide range of maturities of local-currency-denominated sovereign bonds, relative to nonsovereign issues. Similarly, a well-developed market for derivative instruments for hedging interest rate and credit risk exposures is often needed to improve the secondary market liquidity of corporate bond markets. Banks and/or dealers may have limited incentives to "make markets" in corporate bonds if they are unable to hedge the associated risk exposures. Also, the existence of a liquid repo market in government bonds could allow market participants to take on credit risk, without taking on the interest rate risk as well.

Sequencing and Local Versus Regional Markets

Experience to date suggests that there is no uniform formula for the development of a corporate bond market or for the sequencing of the above-mentioned reforms. For instance, although developing the commercial paper market could pave the way for the longer-term corporate bond market, the Chilean experience—where the stamp tax delayed the development of the former without impeding the growth of the latter—provides a clear counter example.

Regional cooperation may help promote the development of bond markets for the countries that lack the minimum efficient scale needed for a deep and liquid bond market. Recently, a number of cooperative efforts to foster the development of the regional and local financial markets have been adopted in Asia and Europe. These regional cooperative efforts range from the financial market integration under European Monetary Union to the Asian Bond Market Initiatives by ASEAN+3,[47] and Asian Bond Funds (ABF) by

[47]ASEAN+3 includes the members of ASEAN (Brunei Darussalam, Cambodia, Indonesia, Lao P.D.R., Malaysia, Myanmar, the Philippines, Singapore, Thailand, and Vietnam) as well as China, Japan, and Korea. Under the Asian Bond Market Initiatives, six working groups have been set up to address a broad range of issues related to local bond market development.

EMEAP.[48] The immediate goals of these regional initiatives are to address impediments in local currency bond markets, which should contribute to the broadening and deepening of the bond markets in the region over time. Because segmentation along national boundaries is perhaps one of the major obstacles to deep and liquid bond markets, these regional cooperative efforts are, to different degrees, expected to overcome the impediments to the development of more integrated bond markets in the region—which may include legal and regulatory constraints, different currency denomination, and capital controls on cross-border investments.[49] However, market participants acknowledge that practical obstacles would most likely make this a long-term option, most easily accomplished in the context of monetary unions or other regional economic integration initiatives (with the agenda going beyond the creation of corporate bond markets).

Financial Stability Issues

Finally, two main issues of financial stability are associated with the development of corporate bond markets. The first, of a macroeconomic nature, is the role of these markets as an alternative funding source for corporates, which could act as a buffer in the face of sudden interruptions in bank credit or international capital flows. The main policy issues associated with the development of these markets have been discussed in previous issues of the GFSR (see also Mathieson and others, 2004). In particular, the importance of corporate sector vulnerabilities associated with balance sheet mismatches calls for a greater diversity of funding sources for corporates, including bonds of different maturities and currency denominations.

The second issue is linked to corporate bond market imbalances, the potential instability of the corporate bond market per se, and potential spillovers to other financial markets and/or the banking system. Market imbalances could arise as a result of the rapid growth in either the demand or the supply of bonds. Although the growth of institutional investors is a positive factor in corporate bond market development, rapid growth in assets under management—relative to the supply of instruments available for investment—combined with excessive concentration in a few market participants that are likely to exhibit herding behavior could fuel asset price bubbles and cause financial market instability. These considerations reinforce the importance of measures to avoid such imbalances, in particular the ones described above for the development of corporate bond markets. Also, regulatory limits on exposures to an individual issuer may become binding when a large pension fund seeks to invest in a bond issued by a relatively small company. Thus, measures to prevent excessive concentration among institutional investors should be considered together with prudential limits on individual exposures. Finally, better risk management practices in the asset management industry could contain the potential instabilities associated with these types of imbalances.

There are few examples of imbalances associated with the rapid growth of the supply of corporate bonds in EMs, but Korea's bond market crisis of 1998 highlights the risks of hastily expanding a market that lacks some of

[48]The Executives' Meeting of East Asia-Pacific Central Banks (EMEAP) is a cooperative organization of central banks and monetary authorities in the East Asia and Pacific region. It includes the central banks of 11 economies: Australia, China, Hong Kong SAR, Indonesia, Japan, Korea, Malaysia, New Zealand, the Philippines, Singapore, and Thailand. The ABFs, which involve the actual creation of bond funds, have been set up to jump-start the development of regional bond markets.

[49]The ABF2 initiative has already led to some improvements in market infrastructure and the regulatory environment, and to some discussions among different countries about coordinating tax and regulatory reforms (see the EMEAP press statement issued on May 12, 2005).

the requisite institutional features. In particular, years of operation under credit guarantees have prevented the development of a "credit culture" and solid institutions to sustain the growth of such a market under the stress conditions created by the bankruptcy of large players. Also, instability in the corporate bond market may also complicate monetary policy implementation if central banks intervene in bond markets in an effort to stabilize bond yields and avoid rollover pressures. This brings into question the balance between the goals of maintaining price stability versus financial stability. A balanced development of the required institutions, intermediaries, and market microstructure described above would go a long way toward reducing these risks.

References

Baele, Lieven, Annalisa Ferrando, Peter Hördahl, Elizaveta Krylova, and Cyril Monnet, 2004, "Measuring Financial Integration in the Euro Area," European Central Bank, *Occasional Paper No. 14* (Frankfurt: European Central Bank).

Bank for International Settlements (BIS), 1999, "Market Liquidity: Research Findings and Selected Policy Implications," Report of a Study Group Established by the Committee on the Global Financial System (CGFS) of the Central Banks of the Group of Ten Countries, CGFS Publications No. 11 (Basel, Switzerland: BIS, May).

———, 2004, "Foreign Direct Investment in the Financial Sector of Emerging Market Economies," Report of a Working Group Established by the Committee on the Global Financial System (CGFS) of the Central Banks of the Group of Ten Countries, CGFS Publications No. 22 (Basel, Switzerland: BIS, March).

Beck, Thorsten, and Ross Levine, 2003, "Legal Institutions and Financial Development," NBER Working Paper No. 10126 (Cambridge, Massachusetts: National Bureau of Economic Research).

Bond Market Association, 2005, "European Bond Pricing Sources and Services: Implications for Price Transparency in the European Bond Market" (European Primary Dealers Association, April). Available via the Internet: *http://www.bondmarkets.com/assets/files/PriceTransparencyStudy_april05.pdf.*

Calmès, Christian, 2004, "Regulatory Changes and Financial Structure: The Case of Canada," Working Paper No. 2004–26 (Ottawa: Bank of Canada).

Chakravarty, Sugato, and Asani Sarkar, 2003, "Trading Costs in Three U.S. Bond Markets," *Journal of Fixed Income,* Vol. 13, pp. 39–48.

Davis, E. Philip, and Mark R. Stone, 2004, "Corporate Financial Structure and Financial Stability," *Journal of Financial Stability,* Vol. 1, No. 1, pp. 65–91.

De Bondt, Gabe, and David Marqués-Ibáñez, 2004, "The High-Yield Segment of the Corporate Bond Market: A Diffusion Modelling Approach for the United States, the United Kingdom, and the Euro Area," Working Paper No. 313 (Frankfurt: European Central Bank, February).

De la Torre, Augusto, and Sergio Schmukler, 2004, "Coping with Risks Through Mismatches: Domestic and International Financial Contracts for Emerging Economies," *International Finance,* Vol. 7 (December), pp. 349–90.

Eichengreen, Barry J., and Pipat Luengnaruemitchai, 2004, "Why Doesn't Asia Have Bigger Bond Markets?" NBER Working Paper No. 10576 (Cambridge, Massachusetts: National Bureau of Economic Research).

Elton, Edwin J., Martin J. Gruber, Deepak Agrawal, and Christopher Mann, 2001, "Explaining the Rate Spread on Corporate Bonds," *The Journal of Finance,* Vol. 56, No. 1, pp. 247–77.

EMEAP, 2005, "The Asian Bond Fund 2 Has Moved into Implementation Phase," Executives' Meeting of East Asia Pacific Central Banks Press Statement (May12). Available via the Internet: *http://www.emeap.org/press/12may05.htm.*

Griffiths, James, 2005, "Another US$40bn Plus Year," *Debt Capital Markets,* Thomson International Financing Review, Special Report (April 23), pp. 16–17.

Hattori, Masazumi, Koji Koyama, and Tatsuya Yonetani, 2001, "Analysis of Credit Spread in Japan's Corporate Bond Market," in *The Changing Shape of Fixed Income Markets: A Collection of Studies by Central Bank Economists,* BIS Papers No. 5 (Basel, Switzerland: Bank for International Settlements, October).

Hawkins, John, 2002, "Bond Markets and Banks in Emerging Economies," in *The Development of Bond Markets in Emerging Economies*, BIS Papers No. 11 (Basel, Switzerland: Bank for International Settlements, June).

Herring, Richard J., and Nathporn Chatusripitak, 2001, "The Case of the Missing Market: The Bond Market and Why It Matters for Financial Development," Center for Financial Institution Working Paper No. 01–08 (Philadelphia: University of Pennsylvania, Wharton School).

Houweling, Patrick, Albert Mentink, and Ton Vorst, 2005, "Comparing Possible Proxies of Corporate Bond Liquidity," *Journal of Banking & Finance*, Vol. 29, No. 6, pp. 1331–58.

International Monetary Fund, 2000, *International Capital Markets: Developments, Prospects, and Key Policy Issues*, World Economic and Financial Surveys (Washington, September).

———, 2001, *International Capital Markets: Developments, Prospects, and Key Policy Issues*, World Economic and Financial Surveys (Washington, August).

———, 2004, *Global Financial Stability Report,* World Economic and Financial Surveys (Washington, April).

———, 2005, *Global Financial Stability Report,* World Economic and Financial Surveys (Washington, April).

IOSCO, 2002, "The Development of Corporate Bond Markets in Emerging Market Countries," Report of the Technical Committee of the International Organization of Securities Commissions (Madrid, Spain: IOSCO, May).

———, 2004, "Transparency of Corporate Bond Markets," Report of the Technical Committee of the International Organization of Securities Commissions (Madrid, Spain: IOSCO, May).

Krainer, John, 2004, "What Determines the Credit Spread?" *FRBSF Economic Letter No. 2004–36* (San Francisco: Federal Reserve Bank of San Francisco, December).

Levine, Ross, and Sara Zervos, 1998, "Stock Markets, Banks, and Economic Growth," *American Economic Review*, Vol. 88, No. 3, pp. 537–58.

Longstaff, Francis, Sanjay Mithal, and Eric Neis, 2004, "Corporate Yield Spreads: Default Risk or Liquidity? New Evidence from the Credit-Default Swap Market," NBER Working Paper No. 10418 (Cambridge, Massachusetts: National Bureau of Economic Research).

Madhavan, Ananth, 2000, "Market Microstructure: A Survey," *Journal of Financial Markets*, Vol. 3, No. 3, pp. 205–58.

Mathieson, Donald J., Jorge E. Roldos, Ramana Ramaswamy, and Anna Ilyina, 2004, *Emerging Local Securities and Derivatives Markets: Recent Development and Policy Issues*, World Economic and Financial Surveys (Washington: International Monetary Fund).

Mohanty, M.S., 2002, "Improving Liquidity in Government Bond Markets: What Can Be Done?" in *The Development of Bond Markets in Emerging Economies*, BIS Papers No. 11 (Basel, Switzerland: Bank for International Settlements, June).

Nik Jaafar, Nik Ruslin, 2005, "Development and Regulation of Islamic Funds," presentation at the World Islamic Funds Conference, Kingdom of Bahrain, May.

Pagano, Marco, and Ernst-Ludwig von Thadden, 2004, "The European Bond Markets Under EMU," *Oxford Review of Economic Policy*, Vol. 20, No. 4, pp. 531–54.

Rajan, Raghuram G., and Luigi Zingales, 1998, "Financial Dependence and Growth," *American Economic Review*, Vol. 88, No. 3, pp. 559–86.

———, 2003, "Banks and Markets: The Changing Character of European Finance," NBER Working Paper No. 9595 (Cambridge, Massachusetts: National Bureau of Economic Research).

Schinasi, Garry, and Todd Smith, 1998, "Fixed-Income Markets in the United States, Europe, and Japan: Some Lessons for Emerging Markets," IMF Working Paper No. 98/173 (Washington: International Monetary Fund).

Taggart, Robert A. Jr., 1988, "The Growth of the 'Junk' Bond Market and Its Role in Financing Takeovers," in *Mergers and Acquisitions*, ed. by A.J. Auerbach, NBER Research Project Report Series (Chicago: University of Chicago Press), pp. 5–24.

Tran, Hung Q., and Jorge Roldos, 2004, "The Role of Securitization and Credit Guarantees," in *Developing Asian Bond Markets*, ed. by Takatoshi Ito and Yung Chul Park (Australia: Asia Pacific Press), pp. 129–44.

Yago, Glenn, and Susanne Trimbath, 2003, *Beyond Junk Bonds: Expanding High Yield Markets* (New York: Oxford University Press).

Zervos, Sara, 2004, "The Transaction Costs of Primary Market Issuance: The Case of Brazil, Chile, and Mexico," Working Paper No. 3424 (Washington: World Bank).

GLOSSARY

401(k)	U.S. tax-deferred retirement plan that allows workers to contribute a percentage of their pre-tax salary for investment in stocks, bonds, or other securities. The employer may match all or part of employees' contributions.
Accrued benefit	Amount of accumulated pension benefits of a pension plan member.
Accumulated benefit obligation (ABO)	Present value of pension benefits promised by a company to its employees, at a particular date and based on current salaries.
Actuarial gain/loss	An actuarial gain (loss) appears when actual experience is more (less) favorable than the actuary's estimate.
Annuity	A contract that provides an income for a specified period of time, such as a number of years or for life.
Asset-backed security (ABS)	A security that is collateralized by loans, leases, receivables, installment contracts on personal property, on real estate. Mortgage-backed securities, collateralized by commercial or residential mortgages, are a type of ABS.
Asset-liability management (ALM)	The management of assets to ensure that liabilities are sufficiently covered by suitable assets as and when the liabilities are due.
Assets under management (AUM)	The market value of assets that a financial institution (i.e., pension fund, insurance company, mutual fund, hedge fund, etc.) manages for itself or on behalf of investors.
Balance sheet mismatch	A balance sheet is a financial statement showing a company's assets, liabilities, and equity on a given date. Typically, a mismatch in a balance sheet implies that the maturities, currency, or interest rate structure of the liabilities differ from those of the assets.
Beneficiary	Individual who is entitled to a pension benefit (including the pension plan member and dependants).
Brady bonds	Bonds issued by emerging market countries as part of a restructuring of defaulted commercial bank loans. These bonds are named after former U.S. Treasury Secretary Nicholas Brady and the first bonds were issued in March of 1990.
Carry trade	A leveraged transaction in which borrowed funds are used to buy a security whose yield is expected to exceed the cost of the borrowed funds.
Cash securitization	The creation of securities from a pool of pre-existing assets and receivables that are placed under the legal control of investors through a special intermediary created for this purpose. This compares with a "synthetic" securitization where the securities are created out of derivative instruments.

Collateralized debt obligations (CDOs)	A structured debt security backed by a portfolio of securities or loans. Securitized interests in the pool of assets are divided into tranches with differing repayment and interest earning streams. In the event of nonpayment or default, the higher-risk "equity" tranches absorb the first loss from anywhere in the portfolio, but up to a limit. After the equity tranche loss limit has been reached, the next least-secured tranche then suffers the additional principal loss, and so on. Interest earnings are typically redistributed toward the high-risk tranche from the more senior or secured tranches. Rating agencies provide separate ratings for each tranche.
Collective action clause	A clause in bond contracts that includes provisions allowing a qualified majority of lenders to amend key financial terms of the debt contract and bind a minority to accept these new terms.
Credit default swap	A financial contract under which an agent buys or sells risk protection against credit risk for a periodic fee in return for a payment by the protection seller contingent on the occurrence of a credit/default event.
Credit enhancement	The process of reducing credit risk by requiring collateral, insurance, or other agreements to provide bondholders with reassurance that principal and interest payments will continue if the borrower defaults.
Credit spreads	The spread between benchmark securities and other debt securities that are comparable in all respects except for credit quality (e.g., the difference between yields on U.S. Treasuries and those on single A-rated corporate bonds of a certain term to maturity).
Debenture	An unsecured bond whose holder has the claim of a general creditor on all assets of the issuer not pledged specifically to secure other debt. A debenture is documented in an indenture.
Defined benefit plan	Pension plan in which benefits are determined by such factors as salary history and duration of employment. The sponsor company is responsible for the investment risk and portfolio management.
Defined contribution plan	Pension plan in which benefits are determined by returns on the plan's investments. Beneficiaries bear the investment risk.
Dependency ratio	Ratio of pensioners to those of working age in a given population.
Derivatives	Financial contracts whose value derives from underlying securities prices, interest rates, foreign exchange rates, market indexes, or commodity prices.
Dollarization	The widespread domestic use of another country's currency (typically the U.S. dollar) to perform the standard functions of money—that of a unit of account, medium of exchange, and store of value.
EMBI	The acronym for the JPMorgan *Emerging Market Bond Index* that tracks the total returns for traded external debt instruments in the emerging markets.

Exchange market	An organized place or organization for trading securities and commodities, usually involving an auction process. Examples include the New York Stock Exchange (NYSE) and the American Stock Exchange (AMEX).
Exchange-traded funds	A type of an investment company whose objective is to achieve the same return as a particular market index or basket of securities. Shares issued by ETFs trade on a secondary market, like a stock, thus experiencing price changes throughout the day as they are bought and sold.
Fallen Angel	Bonds that at the time of issue carried investment grade credit ratings, but whose ratings have fallen over time to subinvestment-grade levels.
Fiscal agent	A bank or trust company that handles fiscal matters for a bond issuer, including paying coupons, redeeming bonds at maturity, and paying any relevant taxes. Unlike the trustee, the fiscal agent acts as a representative of the borrower.
Foreign direct investment	The acquisition abroad (i.e., outside the home country) of physical assets, such as plant and equipment, or of a controlling stake in a company, enterprise, or other entity.
Forward price-earnings ratio	The multiple of future expected earnings at which a stock sells. It is calculated by dividing the current stock price (adjusted for stock splits) by the estimated earnings per share for a future period (typically the next 12 months).
Funded pension plan	Pension plan that has accumulated dedicated assets to pay for the pension benefits.
Funding gap	The difference between the discounted value of accumulating future pension obligations and the present value of assets.
Funding ratio	Ratio of the amount of assets accumulated by a defined benefit pension plan to the sum of promised benefits.
Hedge funds	Investment pools, typically organized as private partnerships and often resident offshore for tax reasons. These funds face few restrictions on their portfolios and transactions. Consequently, they are free to use a variety of investment techniques, including short positions, transactions in derivatives, and leverage.
Hedging	Offsetting an existing exposure by taking an opposite position in the same or a similar risk, for example, by buying derivatives contracts.
High-yield bonds	Bonds with a speculative credit rating [below BB (S&P) or Ba (Moody's) or lower]. High-yield bonds offer investors higher yields than bonds of financially sound companies. High-yield bonds are also known as "junk" bonds.
Hybrid pension plan	Retirement plan that has characteristics typical of both defined benefit and defined contribution plans.

Indenture	Agreement between the issuer and bondholders that details specific terms of the bond issuance. It specifies legal obligations of the bond issuer and rights of bondholders. An indenture spells out the specific terms of a bond, as well as the rights and responsibilities of both the issuer of the security and the holder.
Individual retirement account (IRA)	In the United States, tax-deferred retirement plan permitting all individuals to set aside a fraction of their wages.
Interest rate swaps	An agreement between counterparties to exchange periodic interest payments on some predetermined principal value, which is called the notional principal amount. For example, one party will make fixed-rate and receive variable-rate interest payments.
Investment-grade issues (Subinvestment-grade issues)	A bond that is assigned a rating in the top four categories by commercial credit rating agencies. S&P classifies investment-grade bonds as BBB, or higher, and Moody's classifies investment grade bonds as Baa or higher. (Subinvestment-grade bond issues are rated bonds that are below investment grade.)
Large complex financial institution (LCFI)	A large financial institution that is involved in a diverse range of financial activities and/or in a diverse range of geographical areas.
Leverage	The proportion of debt to equity. Leverage can be built up by direct borrowing (on-balance-sheet leverage, commonly measured by debt-to-equity ratios) or by using off-balance-sheet transactions.
Life-cycle funds	Diversified mutual funds designed to adjust over time with an investor's assumed risk tolerance throughout a variety of life circumstances or savings goals.
Medium-term note (MTN)	A corporate debt instrument that is continuously offered to investors over a period of time by an agent of the issuer. Investors can select from maturity bands of 6 months to 1 year, more than 1 year to 18 months, more than 18 months to 2 years, etc., typically extending to 10-year maturities.
Lump sum payment	Withdrawal of accumulated benefits all at once, as opposed to in regular installments.
Mark-to-market	The valuation of a position or portfolio by reference to the most recent price of a financial instrument. The mark-to-market value might equal the current market value—as opposed to historic accounting or book value—or the present value of expected future cash flows.
Market microstructure	The institutional and behavioral aspects of securities trading process: how information arrives and is disseminated; arrival and execution of orders; impact of market makers and other intermediaries; role of market participants such as individual and institutional investors. Issues concerning market structure include transparency, liquidity, consolidation of order flow, price discovery, trading protocols, clearing and settlement, transaction costs, and regulation.

Mutual fund	A fund operated by an investment company that raises money from shareholders and invests in a group of assets, in accordance with a stated set of objectives. Mutual funds may generally fall under the classification of "open-ended funds" that sell and redeem shares at any time directly to shareholders.
Occupational pension scheme	Pension plan set up and managed by a sponsor company for the benefit of its employees.
Overfunded plan	Pension plan in which assets accumulated are greater than the sum of promised benefits.
Over-the-counter market	A decentralized market where securities are typically traded over the telephone, facsimile, or electronic network. Also referred to as the "OTC market."
(Pair-wise) correlations	A statistical measure of the degree to which the movements of two variables (for example asset returns) are related.
Pay-as-you-go basis (PAYG)	Arrangement under which benefits are paid out of revenue each period.
Pension contribution	Payment made to a pension plan by the sponsor company or by plan participants.
Primary market	The market where a newly issued security is first offered/sold to the public.
Private pension plan	Pension plan where a private entity receives pension contributions and administers the payment of pension benefits.
Projected benefit obligation (PBO)	Present value of pension benefits promised by a company to its employees at a particular date, and including assumption about future salary increases (i.e., assuming that the plan will not terminate in the foreseeable future).
Proprietary trading desk	Investment bank or dealer trading operation, using its own capital, in which direct gains are sought, rather than fee or commission income.
Public pension plan	Pension plan where a government body administers the payment of pension benefits (e.g., social security and similar schemes).
Put (call) option	A financial contract that gives the buyer the right, but not the obligation, to sell (buy) a financial instrument at a set price on or before a given date.
Reinsurance	Insurance placed by an underwriter in another company to cut down the amount of the risk assumed under the original insurance contract.
Secondary markets	Markets in which securities are traded after they are initially offered/sold in the primary market.
Self-regulatory organization	Nongovernment organization that has statutory responsibility to regulate its own members through the adoption and enforcement of rules of conduct for fair, ethical, and efficient practices.

Short sell	Selling a security that the seller does not own but is committed to repurchasing eventually. It is used to capitalize on an expected decline in the security's price.
Solvency	Generally defined as the ability of an insurer to meet its obligations (liabilities) as and when they fall due.
Sponsor company	Company that designs, negotiates, and normally helps to administer an occupational plan for its employees and members.
Spread	See "credit spreads" above (the word credit is sometimes omitted). Other definitions include the gap between bid and ask prices of a financial instrument.
Stop loss order	Order to sell a security when it reaches a certain price.
Syndicated loans	Loans made jointly by a group of banks to one borrower. Usually, one or several lead banks take a larger percentage of the loan (often with a commitment to hold an agreed percentage), and they partition (syndicate) the balance to other banks.
Tail events	The occurrence of large or extreme movements (e.g., price, volatility, correlation, longevity) that, in terms of their probability of occurring, lie within the tail region of the normal distribution of possible outcomes.
Trustee	Person or organization with a duty to receive, manage, and disburse the assets of a plan.
Underfunded plan	Pension plan in which assets accumulated are smaller than the sum of promised benefits.
Unfunded benefit liability	Amount of promised pension benefits that exceeds a plan's assets.
Underwriting	The process whereby a firm, usually an investment bank, purchases an issue of securities from a company and resells it to investors. In general, the underwriter guarantees the proceeds of a security sale to the issuer, thereby in effect taking ownership of the securities.
Value at Risk ("VaR")	An estimate of the loss, over a given horizon, that is unlikely to be exceeded at a given probability level.
Vesting	Right of an employee, on termination of employment, to obtain part or all of his accrued benefits.
Yield curve	A chart that plots the yield to maturity at a specific point in time for debt securities with equal or similar credit risk but different maturity dates.

ANNEX SUMMING UP BY THE CHAIRMAN

The following remarks by the Chairman were made at the conclusion of the Executive Board's discussion of the Global Financial Stability Report *on August 29, 2005.*

General Remarks on the GFSR

Executive Directors took the opportunity of the Board discussion to take stock of the *Global Financial Stability Report* (GFSR) after three years in existence. They noted that the GFSR has become an important instrument of multilateral financial sector surveillance by the Fund, complementing the *World Economic Outlook* (WEO). It has established the IMF as a leader in global financial stability work and has made the IMF a major contributor to international regulatory debates. At the same time, many Directors saw scope for improving the GFSR by making it more concise, sharply focused, and policy-oriented. They also called for reduced overlap between the GFSR and the WEO where possible, and for the Fund's operational work to better integrate the GFSR's findings.

Global Financial Market Surveillance

Directors welcomed the continued improvement in global financial stability. The current configuration of solid growth, low inflation, low bond yields, flat yield curves, and tight credit spreads has supported international financial markets, helping to strengthen the resilience of the global financial system. Furthermore, the much improved balance sheets of the sovereign, corporate, and household sectors, together with structural changes such as the growing importance and diversity of institutional investors and their behaviors, have provided an important cushion to financial markets. However, Directors agreed that while the benign configuration just mentioned has reduced risk in the near term, it has stored up potential vulnerabilities for the medium term, mainly in the form of larger global imbalances and higher debt levels, particularly by the household sector.

Directors agreed that the search for yield remains a dominant theme in financial markets, leading to further narrowing of credit spreads and a greater investor focus on employing leverage and alternative investments to enhance returns. The search for yield continues to stem from low long-term interest rates in mature markets, which have been caused by a variety of reasons. These include the low level of investment that has resulted in an excess supply of global saving, a reduction in inflation risk premia due to greater central bank credibility, reserve accumulation by Asian central banks, and an ongoing shift in institutional investor portfolio preferences from equities to bonds. In part reflecting this last factor, equity earnings yields remain relatively high compared to risk-free government bond yields. The search for yield has also been stimulated by continued subdued volatility across most financial markets.

Directors noted the impact of the search for yield in credit and mortgage markets. Given the compression of spreads in credit markets, investors have increasingly turned to using leverage in various ways to enhance returns, including through a proliferation of structured credit products. They noted that the market quickly stabilized following disturbances in the credit derivatives market in April and May related to developments in the

U.S. auto sector, and the corporate credit market functioned surprisingly smoothly in absorbing downgrades in this sector. Directors observed that this likely reflected the relatively isolated nature of the difficulties as the corporate sector remains broadly healthy, with strong balance sheets and low default rates. However, they considered that the corporate credit cycle appears to be peaking as corporations have begun to increase balance sheet leverage in a variety of ways. This has increased the risk of specific corporate credit events causing corrections in credit derivative and collateralized debt obligation (CDO) markets in the period ahead.

Directors noted that the dollar rebounded against major international currencies despite the widening U.S. current account deficit, as investors focused on interest rate and growth differentials in favor of the United States. In this connection, the global appetite for U.S. assets has to date remained strong. However, the risk of increased exchange rate volatility and a related spike in U.S. bond yields due to a reduction in capital flow to the United States—while being a low probability event given the current economic and financial outlook—cannot be dismissed, and would carry large costs to economic growth and financial markets. Directors welcomed the initial moves by the Chinese and Malaysian authorities to make their currencies more flexible.

Many Directors expressed concern that low mortgage financing costs have induced substantial increases in household debt, particularly in the United States. Relaxation in credit standards and products such as interest-only and negative amortization mortgages may be adding to risks in mortgage markets, allowing households to take on larger levels of debt and giving increased access to marginal borrowers. However, household net worth has also risen due to increases in asset prices, particularly in the housing sector, though marginal borrowers remain particularly vulnerable to possible rises in interest rates and/or declines in housing prices.

Directors welcomed the evidence that emerging financial markets have become increasingly resilient to market disturbances, while cautioning that the positive global economic environment may to some extent be masking underlying vulnerabilities in some countries. Indeed, in recent months, political risks and market volatility have increased in a number of emerging market countries that bear watching. Nonetheless, it is encouraging that many emerging market countries have continued to build cushions against possible adverse developments, including by accumulating reserves, undertaking early financing of external needs, and improving debt structures. Directors took note of the ongoing broadening of the investor base for emerging markets and the extension of investor interest into local instruments. While the increased interest in local markets has to some extent been fostered by cyclical developments, there are also signs that local-currency bonds in particular are becoming an interesting asset class for foreign investors. This should, in turn, help deepen local markets and reduce emerging market vulnerabilities to currency risk. Overall, Directors considered that these developments have kept emerging bond markets resilient in the face of mature credit market disturbances and specific country problems.

Directors also welcomed recent improvements in the balance sheets of key sectors in mature market economies. Moreover, indicators of market and credit risk and financial strength underscore the resilience of the banking and insurance sectors in both mature and emerging markets. A number of Directors, however, stressed the need to guard against the potentially destabilizing effect of hedge fund operations and of the growing use of structured products, while preserving the benefits of these innovations in terms of market efficiency and liquidity.

While considering policy measures to mitigate risks, Directors stressed that ongoing risk management by individual financial institutions and supervisory scrutiny by regulators are the most important lines of defense. In particular, given the risk of corrections in credit derivative and CDO markets, regulators must ensure that financial institutions maintain robust counterparty risk management practices, not least to contain the spillover effect of market corrections should they occur. Directors also stressed the importance of disclosure and transparency to enhance the flow of information, of the Standards and Codes work to help improve regulatory frameworks, and of improving basic financial education especially among individual investors. In the context of rising household indebtedness, mainly in the mortgage market, Directors welcomed the warnings that regulators in some major countries have given to their lending institutions to tighten credit standards. For the medium term, the risk of growing global imbalances has to be addressed by a cooperative effort by the major countries, with each adopting policies appropriate to its circumstances.

Aspects of Global Asset Allocation

Directors welcomed the work undertaken by staff on global asset allocation and the increasing role of institutional investors in financial markets. They noted that a better understanding of the investment patterns of pension funds, insurance companies, mutual funds, and, increasingly, hedge funds would help anticipate the potential for abrupt changes in capital flows across borders and asset classes, with direct relevance to financial stability and to policymakers.

Directors considered the diversity of procedures followed by various institutional investors when allocating assets, reflecting their different time horizons, liability structures, and "cultural backgrounds," as well as external influences, such as accounting and financial reporting standards, tax rules, rating agencies, and the availability of financial instruments needed for adequate risk management. In this context, most Directors agreed that the increasing dominance of strategic asset allocations driven more by long-term economic fundamentals, including risk management objectives, was a positive development, as it helps reduce the volatility and "noise" in financial markets, and makes some asset classes, such as emerging market debt, less prone to boom and bust cycles. In particular, the continued growth of institutions with long-term liabilities, such as pension funds, brings benefits from the point of view of financial stability. Some Directors, however, noted that shifts in asset allocations by such institutions might unsettle emerging markets with relatively shallow financial markets, or amplify long swings and hinder market price discovery.

Directors noted the sustained decline in "home bias" on the part of institutional investors throughout mature economies over the past 15 years, particularly with regard to equity holdings. Directors agreed that major factors cited in the shift toward more internationalized portfolios included less strict investment restrictions, reduced information costs, and the spread of modern portfolio management practices. By raising average returns while reducing portfolio volatility, these developments have bolstered financial stability. However, Directors noted that the decline in home bias has also increased cross-border capital flows and has probably led to greater cross-border correlations among asset markets. Accordingly, Directors underscored that Fund surveillance has taken on even greater importance in a world in which institutional portfolios have become increasingly international. A few Directors expressed doubt about the report's findings that investors from major economies, like the United States and the United Kingdom, would have little to gain from further international diversification of portfolios.

Directors discussed the implications for financial stability of proposals and potential changes in accounting policy. They recognized the importance of international efforts to improve accounting principles in order to enhance the comparability and transparency of accounts and to strengthen market discipline. However, views differed on the impact of changes in accounting principles on financial market stability. A number of Directors agreed that accounting and financial reporting standards may influence market behavior and asset allocations by key institutional investors, including by potentially encouraging long-term investors to adopt short-term time horizons, or by reducing the diversity of market behaviors across institutional investor categories, particularly as it relates to their long-term, stable investment behavior. These Directors encouraged ongoing international efforts to preserve both the measurement benefits of using market or fair values, wherever possible, and secular gains in financial stability. A number of other Directors suggested that, while some issues exist as to fair valuation of assets and liabilities with thin markets, fair value accounting would strengthen transparency in financial markets, and would not lead to a shift to short-run strategies by major institutional investors.

Corporate Bond Markets in Emerging Market Countries

Directors welcomed the detailed study on corporate bond markets in emerging market countries. They observed that the achievement of macroeconomic stability by a number of emerging market countries suggests that the time may be right to press ahead with measures that contribute to the development of corporate bond markets. Directors called for continued efforts by emerging markets to facilitate the growth of institutional investors, and noted that medium- and small-sized corporations should adopt high standards of transparency and corporate governance to facilitate market access. Directors stressed that for the effective functioning of securities markets, the authorities should adopt a regulatory framework that ensures investor protection and market integrity and contains systemic risks.

Directors noted that emerging market countries should take measures that reduce the approval time and cost of issuance, including costs associated with discriminatory taxation. Directors stressed the importance of a well-developed secondary market in improving price discovery and liquidity while at the same time acknowledging that only a few industrial countries were able to achieve this goal. Directors also noted the complementary role of the development of a government bond market, and that regional cooperation may help promote the development of bond markets for countries that lack the minimum efficient scale needed for a deep and liquid bond market.

Directors stressed the role of corporate bond markets as an alternative funding source for corporations, noting that such markets could act as a buffer in the face of sudden interruptions in bank credit or international capital flows. However, several Directors cautioned against too rapid a growth of corporate bond markets in countries that lack the supporting financial infrastructure. In particular, the rapid growth in assets under management of institutional investors combined with excessive concentration in a few market participants could fuel asset price bubbles and cause financial market instability. Directors encouraged countries to take measures to prevent excessive concentration as well as to improve risk management practices and underscored the need for a balanced development of the required institutions, intermediaries, and market microstructure to reduce risks.

Directors offered several suggestions to take the GFSR to the next level of development after three years of publication, which staff will consider carefully going forward.

STATISTICAL APPENDIX

This statistical appendix presents data on financial developments in key financial centers and emerging markets. It is designed to complement the analysis in the text by providing additional data that describe key aspects of financial market developments. These data are derived from a number of sources external to the IMF, including banks, commercial data providers, and official sources, and are presented for information purposes only; the IMF does not, however, guarantee the accuracy of the data from external sources.

Presenting financial market data in one location and in a fixed set of tables and charts, in this and future issues of the GFSR, is intended to give the reader an overview of developments in global financial markets. Unless otherwise noted, the statistical appendix reflects information available up to July 22, 2005.

Mirroring the structure of the chapters of the report, the appendix presents data separately for key financial centers and emerging market countries. Specifically, it is organized into three sections:

- Figures 1–14 and Tables 1–9 contain information on market developments in key financial centers. This includes data on global capital flows, and on markets for foreign exchange, bonds, equities, and derivatives, as well as sectoral balance sheet data for the United States, Japan, and Europe.
- Figures 15 and 16, and Tables 10–21 present information on financial developments in emerging markets, including data on equity, foreign exchange, and bond markets, as well as data on emerging market financing flows.
- Tables 22–27 report key financial soundness indicators for selected countries, including bank profitability, asset quality, and capital adequacy.

List of Tables and Figures

Key Financial Centers

Figures

1. Major Net Exporters and Importers of Capital in 2004 155
2. Exchange Rates: Selected Major Industrial Countries 156
3. United States: Yields on Corporate and Treasury Bonds 157
4. Selected Spreads 158
5. Nonfinancial Corporate Credit Spreads 159
6. Equity Markets: Price Indexes 160
7. Implied and Historical Volatility in Equity Markets 161
8. Historical Volatility of Government Bond Yields and Bond Returns for Selected Countries 162
9. Twelve-Month Forward Price/Earnings Ratios 163
10. Flows into U.S.-Based Equity Funds 163
11. United States: Corporate Bond Market 164
12. Europe: Corporate Bond Market 165
13. United States: Commercial Paper Market 166
14. United States: Asset-Backed Securities 167

Tables

1. Global Capital Flows: Inflows and Outflows 168
2. Global Capital Flows: Amounts Outstanding and Net Issues of International Debt Securities by Currency of Issue and Announced International Syndicated Credit Facilities by Nationality of Borrower 170
3. Selected Indicators on the Size of the Capital Markets, 2004 171
4. Global Over-the-Counter Derivatives Markets: Notional Amounts and Gross Market Values of Outstanding Contracts 172
5. Global Over-the-Counter Derivatives Markets: Notional Amounts and Gross Market Values of Outstanding Contracts by Counterparty, Remaining Maturity, and Currency 173
6. Exchange-Traded Derivative Financial Instruments: Notional Principal Amounts Outstanding and Annual Turnover 174
7. United States: Sectoral Balance Sheets 176
8. Japan: Sectoral Balance Sheets 177
9. Europe: Sectoral Balance Sheets 178

Emerging Markets

Figures

15. Emerging Market Volatility Measures 179
16. Emerging Market Debt Cross-Correlation Measures 180

Tables

10. Equity Market Indices 181
11. Foreign Exchange Rates 184
12. Emerging Market Bond Index: EMBI Global Total Returns Index 186
13. Emerging Market Bond Index: EMBI Global Yield Spreads 188
14. Emerging Market External Financing: Total Bonds, Equities, and Loans 190
15. Emerging Market External Financing: Bond Issuance 192
16. Emerging Market External Financing: Equity Issuance 193
17. Emerging Market External Financing: Loan Syndication 194
18. Equity Valuation Measures: Dividend-Yield Ratios 196
19. Equity Valuation Measures: Price-to-Book Ratios 197
20. Equity Valuation Measures: Price-Earnings Ratios 198
21. United States: Mutual Fund Flows 199

Financial Soundness Indicators

22. Bank Regulatory Capital to Risk-Weighted Assets 200
23. Bank Capital to Assets 202
24. Bank Nonperforming Loans to Total Loans 204
25. Bank Provisions to Nonperforming Loans 206
26. Bank Return on Assets 208
27. Bank Return on Equity 210

Figure 1. Major Net Exporters and Importers of Capital in 2004

Countries That Export Capital[1]

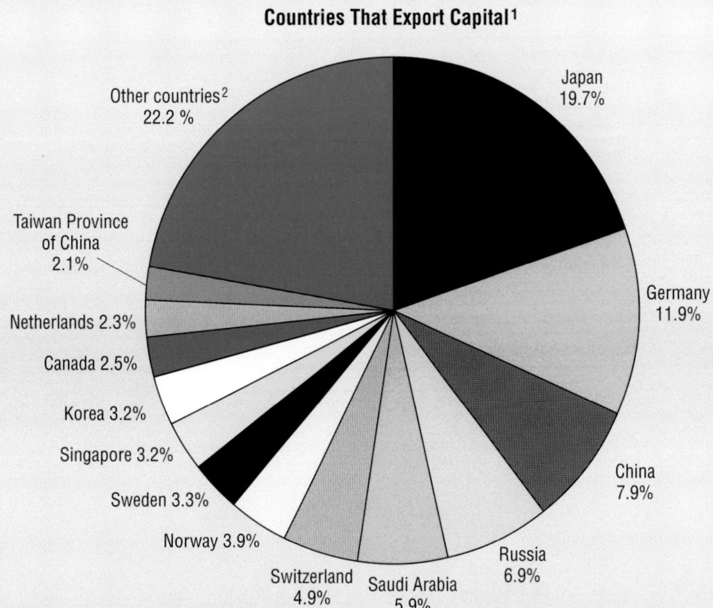

Countries That Import Capital[3]

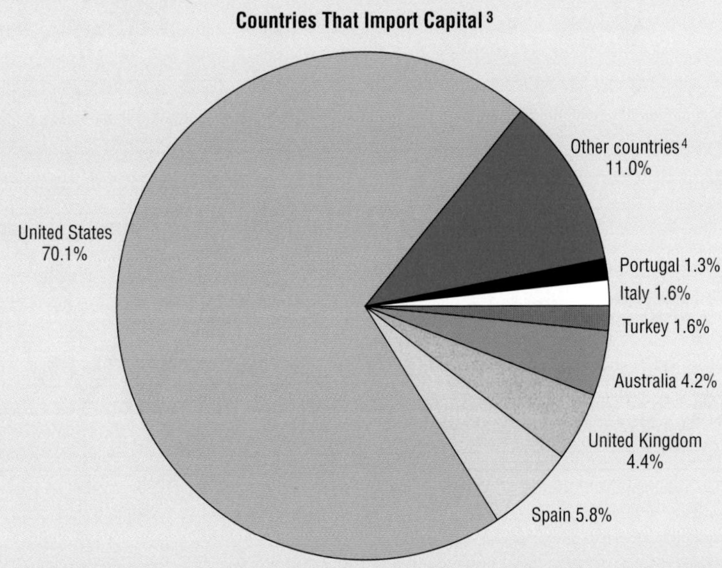

Source: International Monetary Fund, *World Economic Outlook* database as of August 30, 2005.

[1]As measured by countries' current account surplus (assuming errors and omissions are part of the capital and financial accounts).

[2]Other countries include all countries with shares of total surplus less than 2.1 percent.

[3]As measured by countries' current account deficit (assuming errors and omissions are part of the capital and financial accounts).

[4]Other countries include all countries with shares of total deficit less than 1.3 percent.

Figure 2. Exchange Rates: Selected Major Industrial Countries

Sources: Bloomberg L.P.; and the IMF Competitive Indicators System.

Note: In each panel, the effective and bilateral exchange rates are scaled so that an upward movement implies an appreciation of the respective local currency.

[1]Local currency units per U.S. dollar except for the euro area and the United Kingdom, for which data are shown as U.S. dollars per local currency.

[2]1995 = 100; constructed using 1989–91 trade weights.

Figure 3. United States: Yields on Corporate and Treasury Bonds
(Weekly data)

Sources: Bloomberg L.P.; and Merrill Lynch.

Figure 4. Selected Spreads
(In basis points)

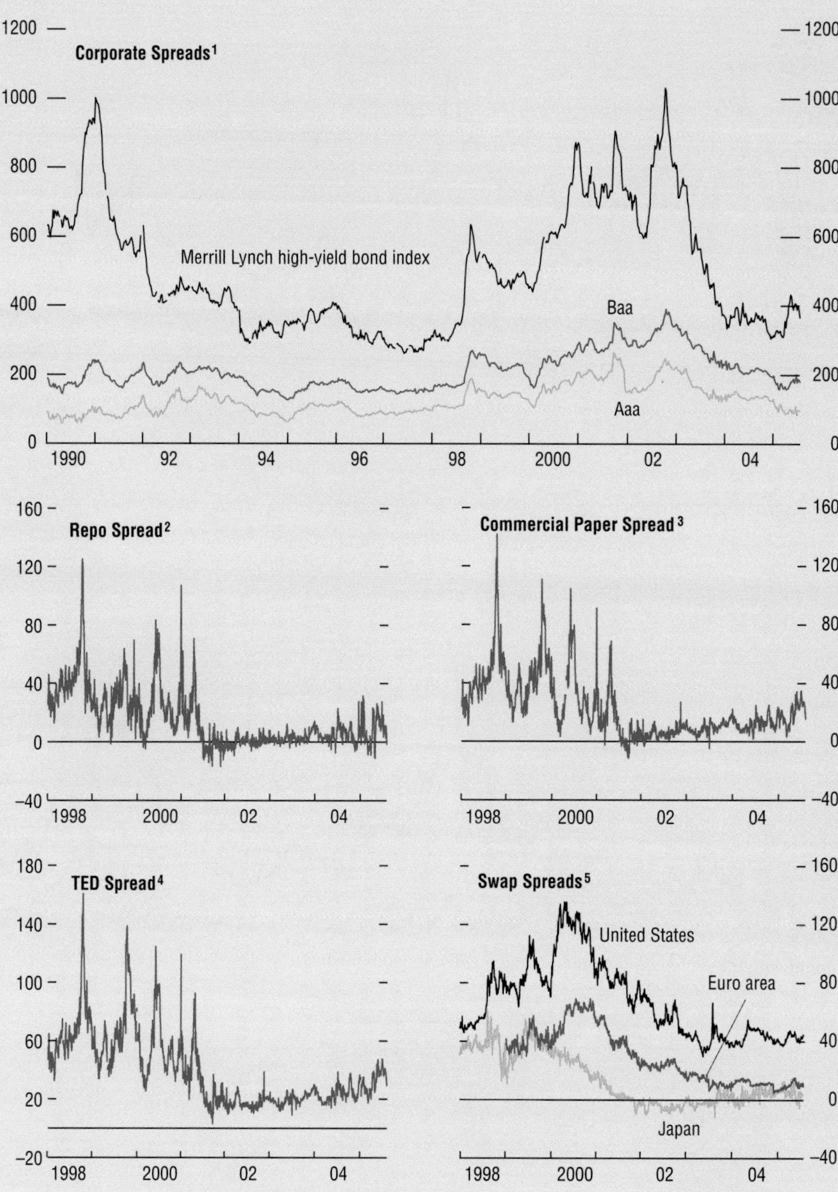

Sources: Bloomberg L.P.; and Merrill Lynch.
[1]Spreads over 10-year U.S. treasury bond; weekly data.
[2]Spread between yields on three-month U.S. treasury repo and on three-month U.S. treasury bill.
[3]Spread between yields on 90-day investment-grade commercial paper and on three-month U.S. treasury bill.
[4]Spread between three-month U.S. dollar LIBOR and yield on three-month U.S. treasury bill.
[5]Spread over 10-year government bond.

Figure 5. Nonfinancial Corporate Credit Spreads
(In basis points)

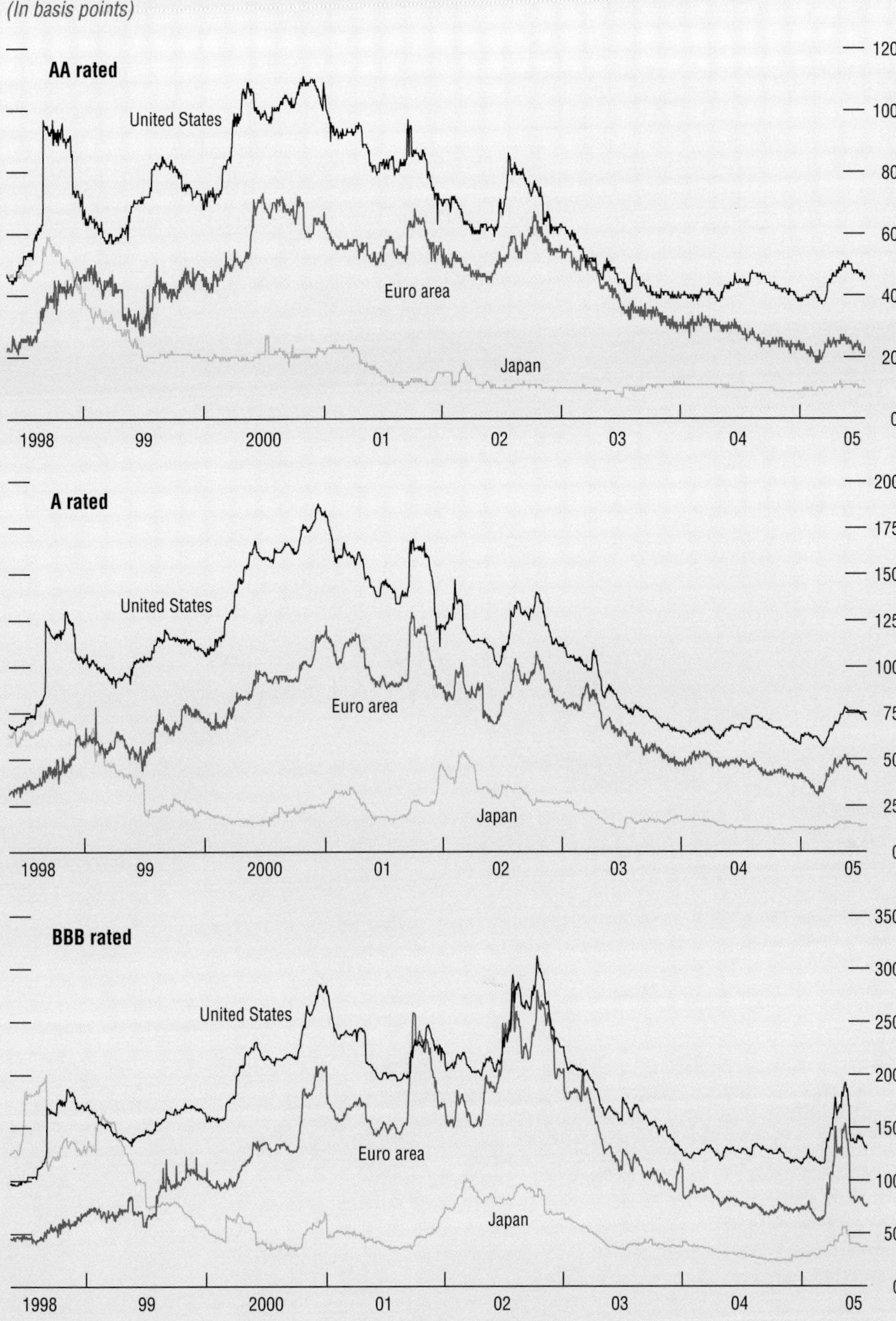

Source: Merrill Lynch.

Figure 6. Equity Markets: Price Indexes
(January 1, 1990 = 100; weekly data)

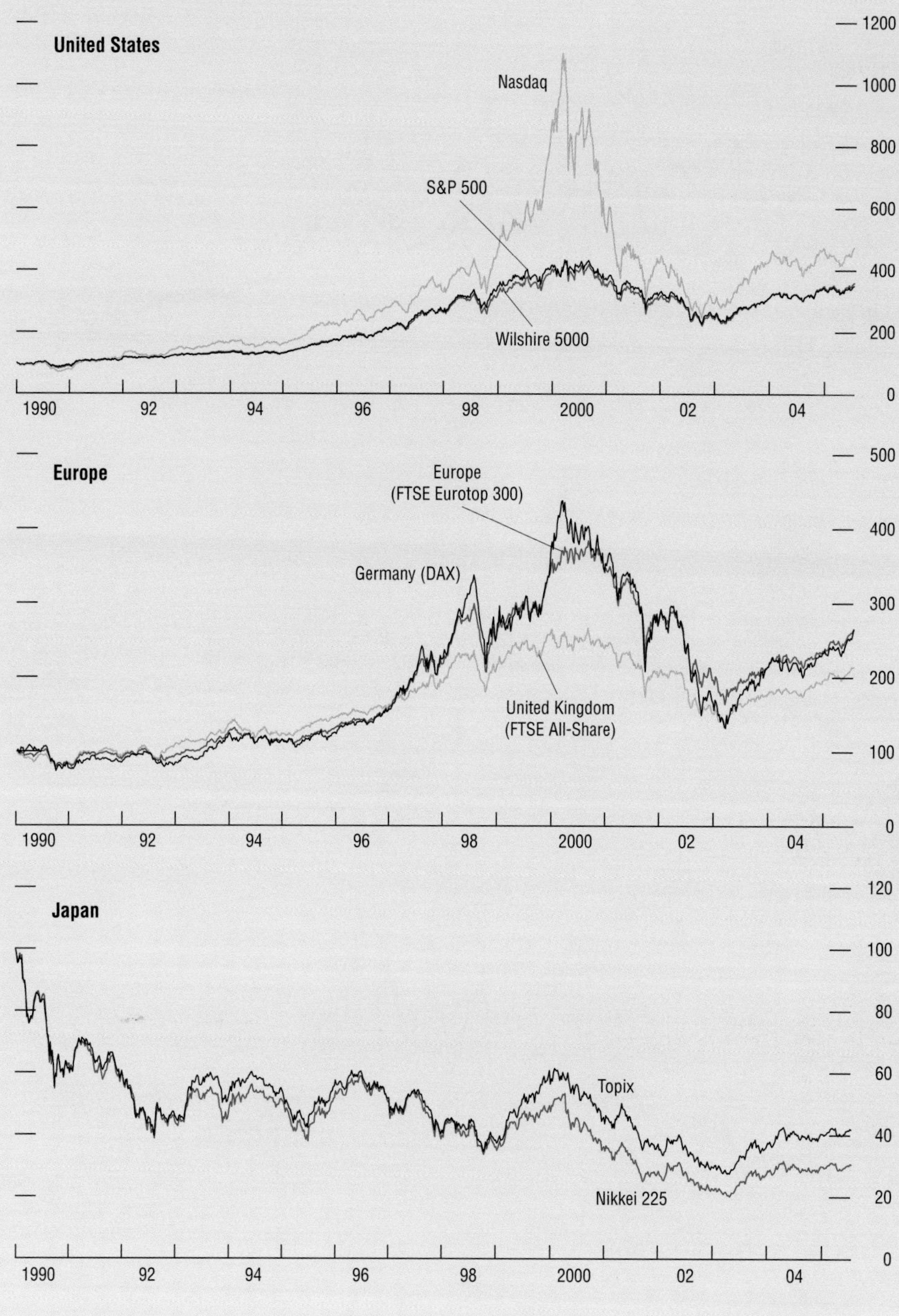

Source: Datastream.

Figure 7. Implied and Historical Volatility in Equity Markets

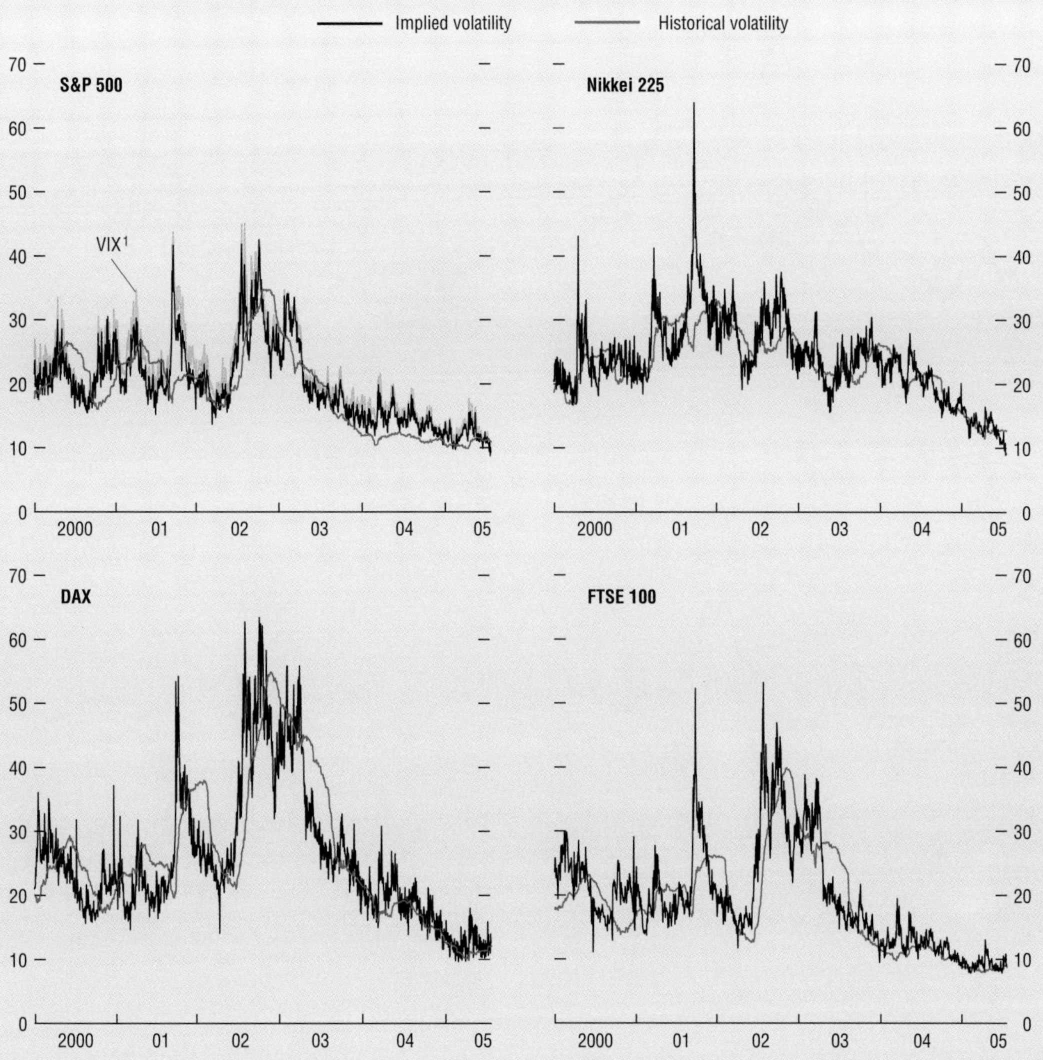

Sources: Bloomberg L.P.; and IMF staff estimates.

Note: Implied volatility is a measure of the equity price variability implied by the market prices of call options on equity futures. Historical volatility is calculated as a rolling 100-day annualized standard deviation of equity price changes. Volatilities are expressed in percent rate of change.

[1]VIX is the Chicago Board Options Exchange volatility index. This index is calculated by taking a weighted average of implied volatility for the eight S&P 500 calls and puts.

Figure 8. Historical Volatility of Government Bond Yields and Bond Returns for Selected Countries[1]

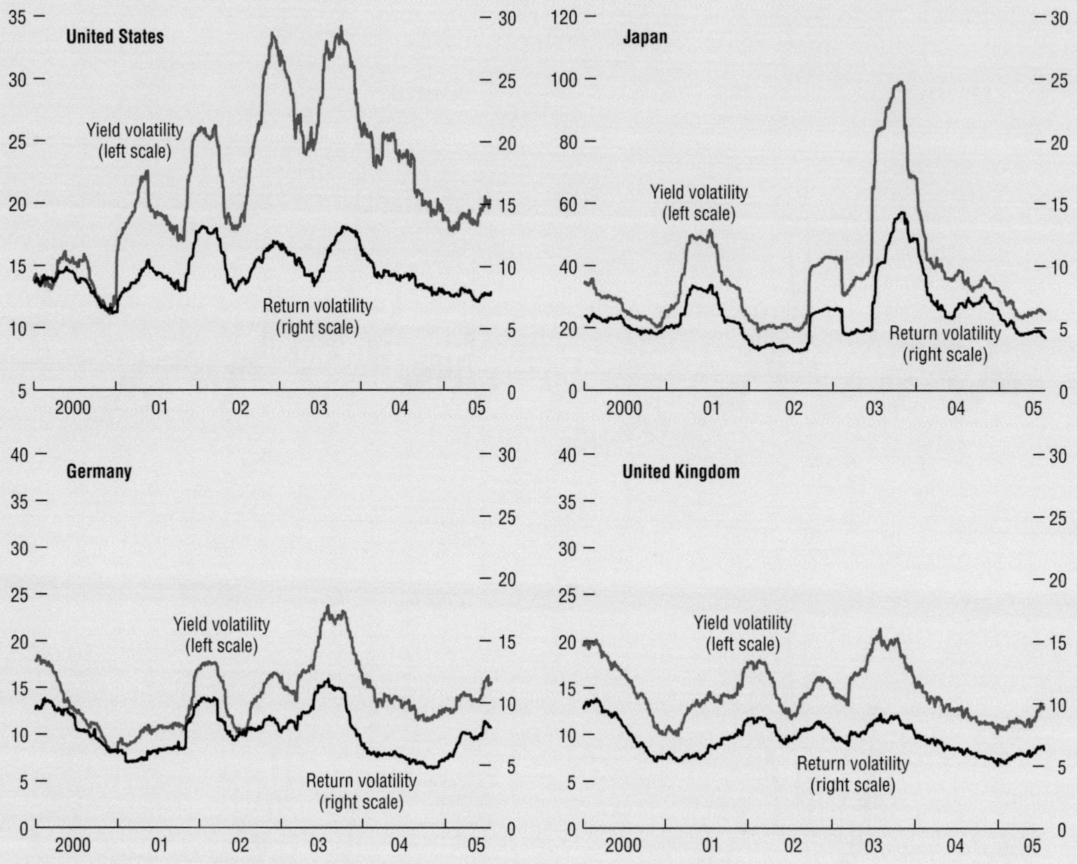

Sources: Bloomberg L.P.; and Datastream.

[1]Volatility calculated as a rolling 100-day annualized standard deviation of changes in yield and returns on 10-year government bonds. Returns are based on 10-plus year government bond indexes.

Figure 9. Twelve-Month Forward Price/Earnings Ratios

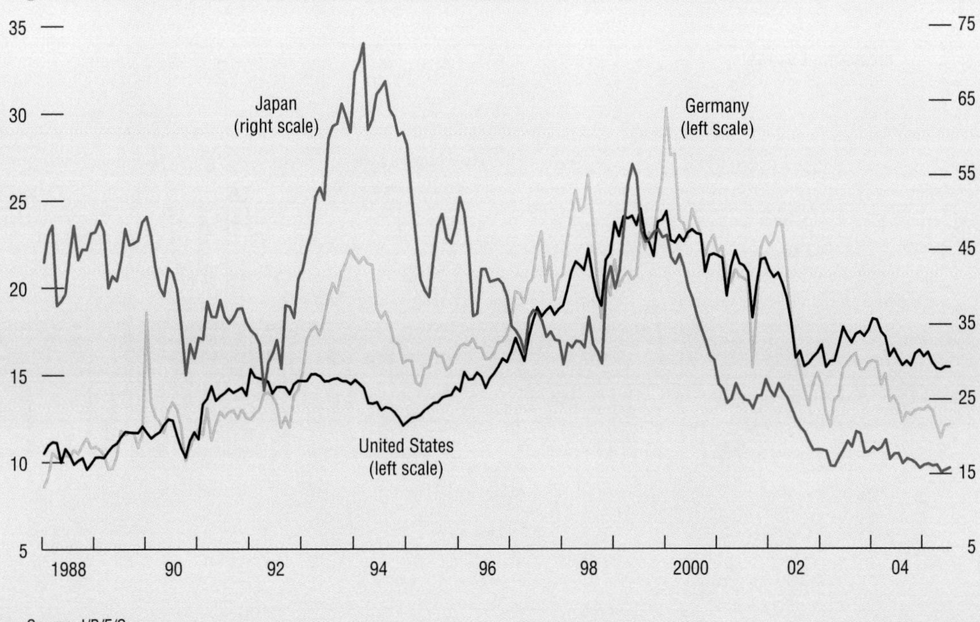

Source: I/B/E/S.

Figure 10. Flows into U.S.-Based Equity Funds

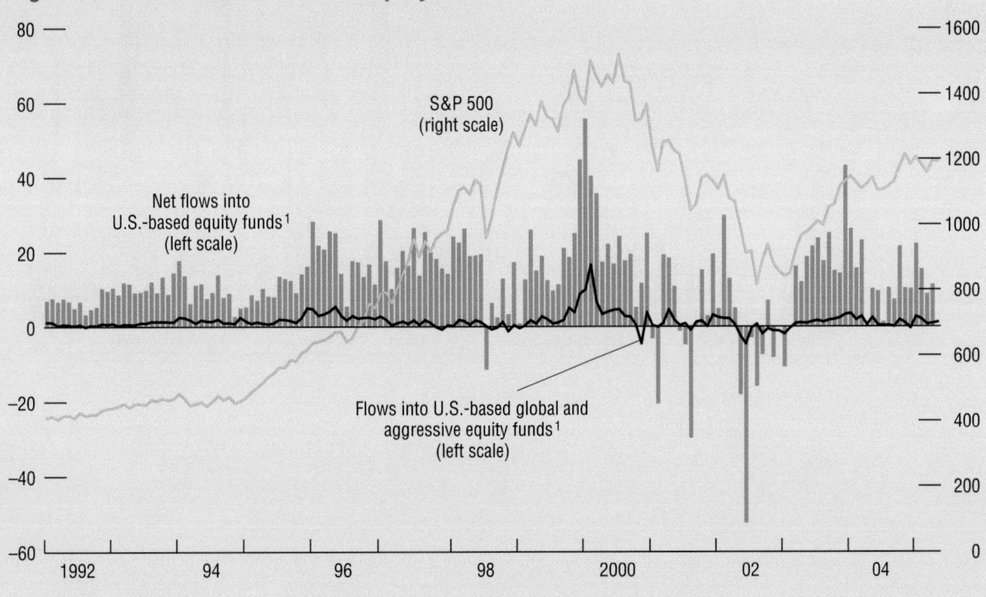

Sources: AMG Data Services; Investment Company Institute; and Datastream.
[1]In billions of U.S. dollars.

Figure 11. United States: Corporate Bond Market

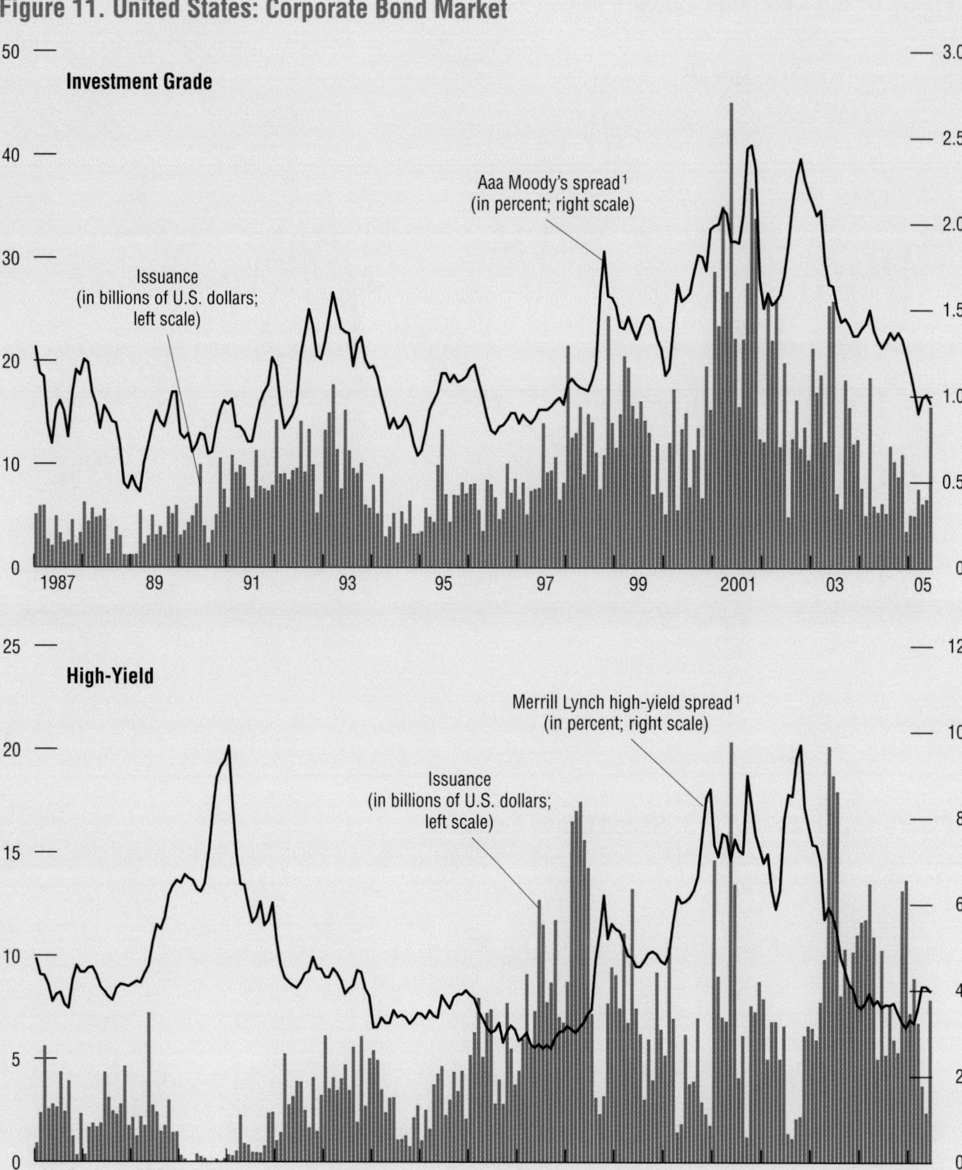

Sources: Board of Governors of the Federal Reserve System; and Bloomberg L.P.
[1]Spread against yield on 10-year U.S. government bonds.

Figure 12. Europe: Corporate Bond Market[1]

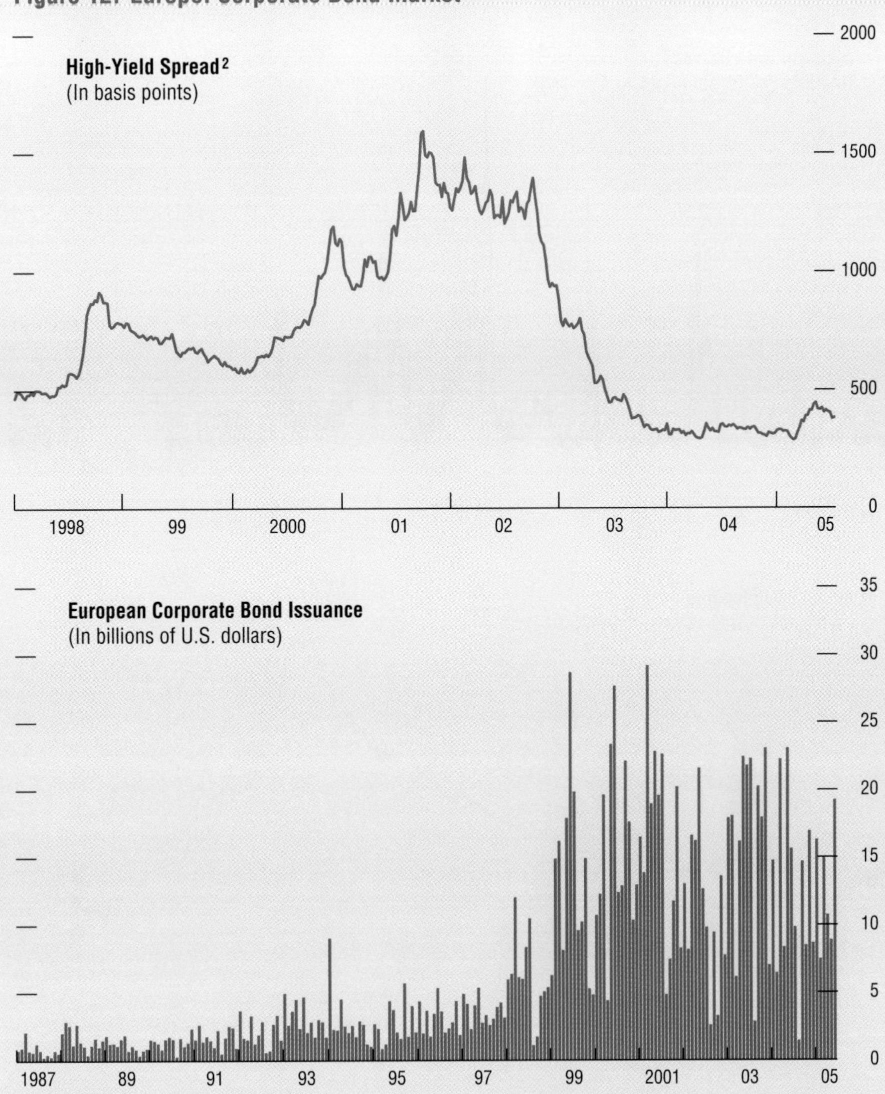

Sources: Bondware; and Datastream.
[1]Nonfinancial corporate bonds.
[2]Spread between yields on a Merrill Lynch High-Yield European Issuers Index bond and a 10-year German government benchmark bond.

Figure 13. United States: Commercial Paper Market[1]

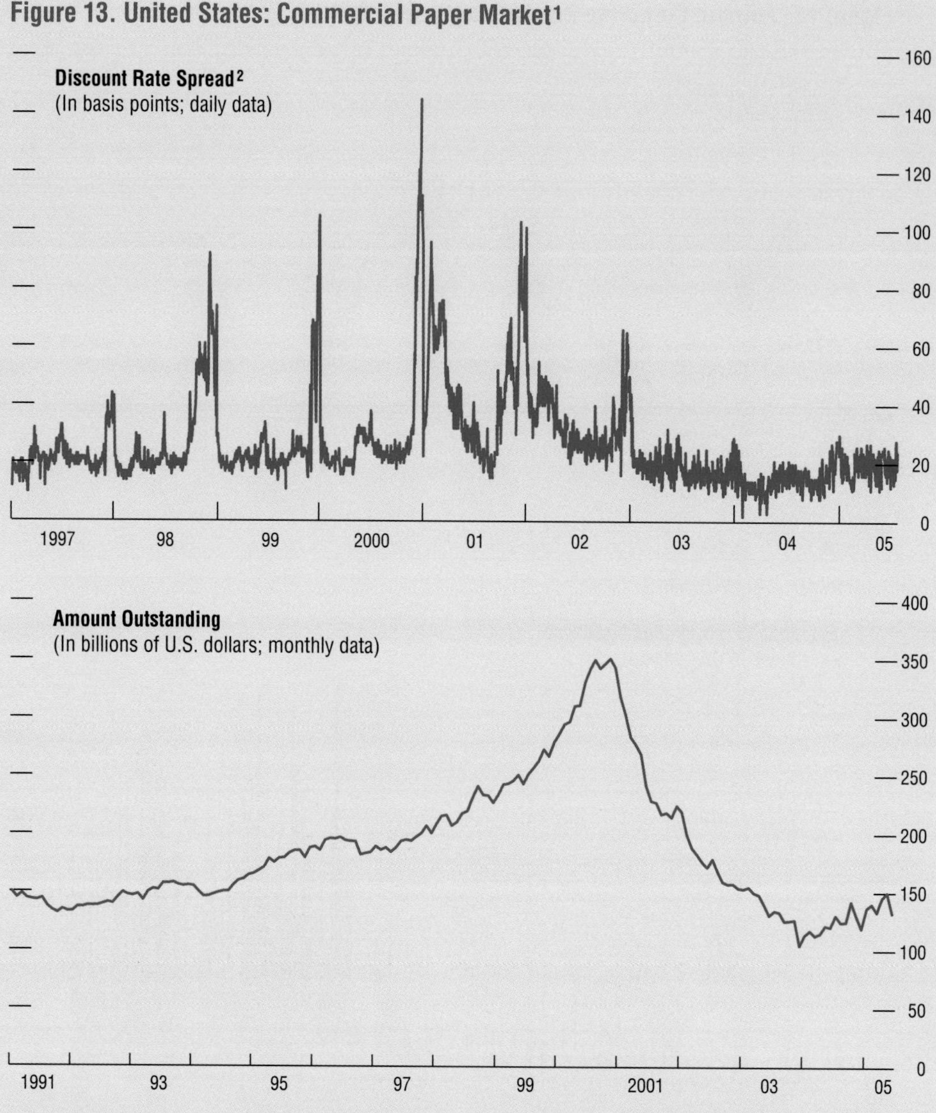

Source: Board of Governors of the Federal Reserve System.
[1]Nonfinancial commercial paper.
[2]Difference between 30-day A2/P2 and AA commercial paper.

Figure 14. United States: Asset-Backed Securities

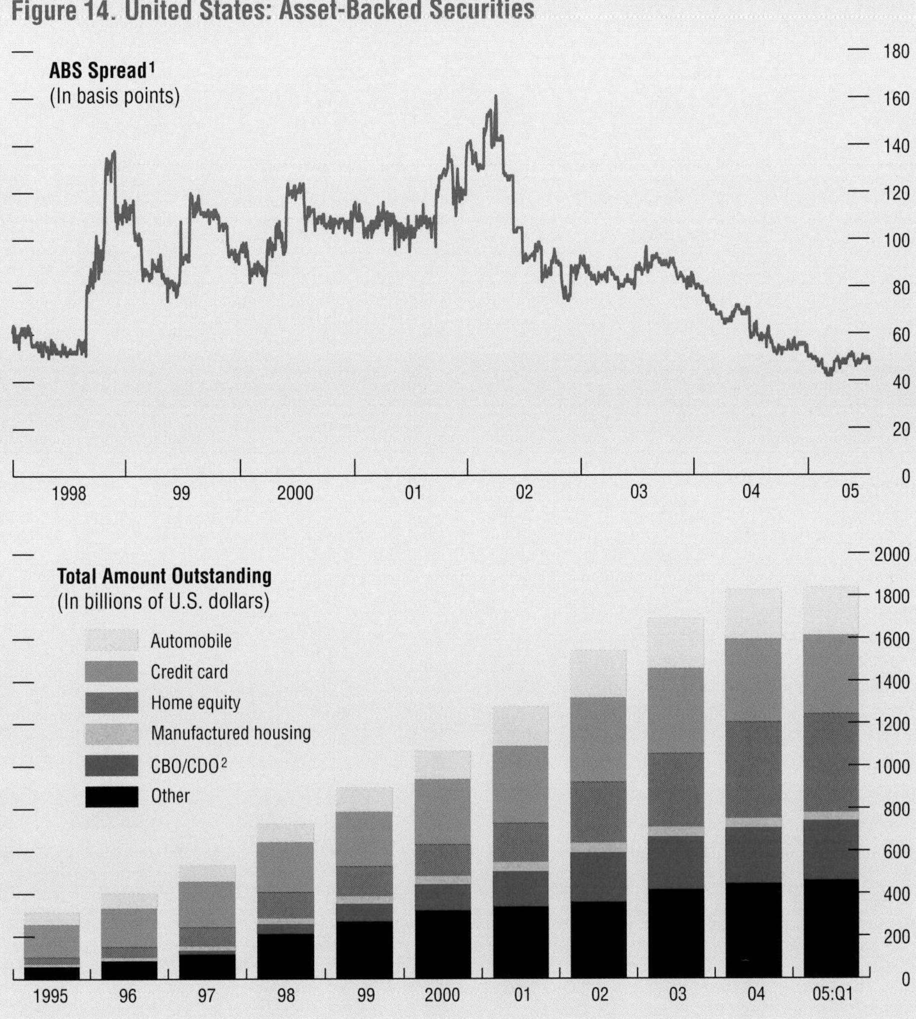

Sources: Merrill Lynch; Datastream; and the Bond Market Association.
[1]Merrill Lynch AAA Asset-Backed Master Index (fixed rate) option-adjusted spread.
[2]Collateralized bond/debt obligations.

Table 1. Global Capital Flows: Inflows and Outflows[1]

(In billions of U.S. dollars)

	Inflows										
	1994	1995	1996	1997	1998	1999	2000	2001	2002	2003	2004
United States											
Direct investment	46.1	57.8	86.5	105.6	179.0	289.4	321.3	167.0	72.4	39.9	115.5
Portfolio investment	139.4	210.4	332.8	333.1	187.6	285.6	436.6	428.3	427.9	544.5	794.4
Other investment	120.5	170.4	131.8	268.1	57.0	165.2	289.0	187.5	268.0	244.8	523.3
Reserve assets	n.a.	n.a.	n.a.	n.a.	n.a.	n.a.	n.a.	n.a.	n.a.	n.a.	n.a.
Total capital flows	306.0	438.6	551.1	706.8	423.6	740.2	1,046.9	782.9	768.2	829.2	1,433.2
Canada											
Direct investment	8.2	9.3	9.6	11.5	22.7	24.8	66.1	27.7	21.4	6.1	6.3
Portfolio investment	17.2	18.4	13.7	11.7	16.6	2.7	10.3	24.2	13.4	14.5	42.5
Other investment	16.0	−3.9	15.7	28.0	5.4	−10.8	0.8	7.8	5.4	11.7	−6.0
Reserve assets	n.a.	n.a.	n.a.	n.a.	n.a.	n.a.	n.a.	n.a.	n.a.	n.a.	n.a.
Total capital flows	41.4	23.9	39.1	51.2	44.8	16.6	77.2	59.7	40.2	32.3	42.8
Japan											
Direct investment	0.9	0.0	0.2	3.2	3.3	12.3	8.2	6.2	9.1	6.2	7.8
Portfolio investment	64.5	59.8	66.8	79.2	56.1	126.9	47.4	60.5	−20.0	81.2	196.7
Other investment	−5.6	97.3	31.1	68.0	−93.3	−265.1	−10.2	−17.6	26.6	34.1	68.3
Reserve assets	n.a.	n.a.	n.a.	n.a.	n.a.	n.a.	n.a.	n.a.	n.a.	n.a.	n.a.
Total capital flows	59.8	157.1	98.1	150.4	−34.0	−125.9	45.4	49.1	15.7	121.5	272.8
United Kingdom											
Direct investment	10.7	21.7	27.4	37.5	74.7	89.3	122.2	53.8	25.5	20.7	72.6
Portfolio investment	47.0	58.8	68.0	43.7	35.1	183.8	255.8	69.6	76.2	156.8	171.0
Other investment	−10.8	106.2	251.8	322.2	110.5	90.0	414.6	327.0	109.1	409.6	720.5
Reserve assets	n.a.	n.a.	n.a.	n.a.	n.a.	n.a.	n.a.	n.a.	n.a.	n.a.	n.a.
Total capital flows	46.9	186.7	347.2	403.4	220.3	363.2	792.5	450.4	210.8	587.1	964.0
Euro area											
Direct investment	. . .	. . .	. . .	. . .	. . .	209.7	404.8	175.7	171.2	158.2	97.1
Portfolio investment	. . .	. . .	. . .	. . .	. . .	282.9	270.7	316.5	286.2	363.2	444.1
Other investment	. . .	. . .	. . .	. . .	. . .	208.3	337.2	237.8	60.7	188.1	349.2
Reserve assets	n.a.	n.a.	n.a.	n.a.	n.a.	n.a.	n.a.	n.a.	n.a.	n.a.	n.a.
Total capital flows	. . .	. . .	. . .	. . .	. . .	700.8	1,012.7	730.1	518.0	709.4	890.5
Emerging Markets and Developing Countries[2]											
Direct investment	96.0	122.1	144.0	187.2	184.9	207.9	206.0	219.3	170.2	183.1	250.0
Portfolio investment	93.8	78.0	165.7	155.1	50.4	125.1	92.6	5.6	−1.6	71.8	170.1
Other investment	10.1	138.3	96.6	173.3	−99.2	−66.8	7.5	−34.5	25.3	120.5	153.6
Reserve assets	n.a.	n.a.	n.a.	n.a.	n.a.	n.a.	n.a.	n.a.	n.a.	n.a.	n.a.
Total capital flows	199.8	338.3	406.4	515.6	136.1	266.2	306.1	190.4	193.8	375.4	573.6

Sources: International Monetary Fund, *World Economic Outlook* database as of August 30, 2005, and *International Financial Statistics.*

[1]The total net capital flows are the sum of direct investment, portfolio investment, other investment flows, and reserve assets. “Other investment” includes bank loans and deposits.

[2]This aggregate comprises the group of Other Emerging Market and Developing Countries defined in the World Economic Outlook, together with Hong Kong SAR, Israel, Korea, Singapore, and Taiwan Province of China.

Outflows										
1994	1995	1996	1997	1998	1999	2000	2001	2002	2003	2004
−80.2	−98.8	−91.9	−104.8	−142.6	−224.9	−159.2	−142.4	−134.8	−173.8	−248.5
−63.2	−122.4	−149.3	−116.9	−124.2	−116.2	−121.9	−84.6	15.9	−72.3	−90.8
−40.9	−121.4	−178.9	−262.8	−74.2	−171.2	−288.4	−134.9	−75.4	−38.8	−481.1
5.3	−9.7	6.7	−1.0	−6.7	8.7	−0.3	−4.9	−3.7	1.5	2.8
−178.9	−352.3	−413.4	−485.5	−347.8	−503.7	−569.8	−366.8	−198.0	−283.4	−817.7
−9.3	−11.5	−13.1	−23.1	−34.1	−17.3	−44.5	−36.2	−26.8	−22.1	−47.0
−6.6	−5.3	−14.2	−8.6	−15.1	−15.6	−43.0	−24.4	−17.0	−11.4	−14.4
−20.4	−8.3	−21.1	−16.2	9.4	10.2	−4.2	−10.7	−8.1	−17.0	−5.0
0.4	−2.7	−5.5	2.4	−5.0	−5.9	−3.7	−2.2	0.2	3.3	2.8
−35.9	−27.9	−53.9	−45.4	−44.8	−28.5	−95.4	−73.4	−51.7	−47.3	−63.5
−18.1	−22.5	−23.4	−26.1	−24.6	−22.3	−31.5	−38.5	−32.0	−28.8	−31.0
−92.0	−86.0	−100.6	−47.1	−95.2	−154.4	−83.4	−106.8	−85.9	−176.3	−173.8
−35.1	−102.2	5.2	−192.0	37.9	266.3	−4.1	46.6	36.4	149.9	−48.0
−25.3	−58.6	−35.1	−6.6	6.2	−76.3	−49.0	−40.5	−46.1	−187.2	−160.9
−170.4	−269.4	−154.0	−271.6	−75.8	13.4	−168.0	−139.2	−127.7	−242.3	−413.6
−34.9	−45.3	−34.8	−62.4	−122.1	−201.6	−245.4	−59.7	−49.5	−64.1	−80.2
31.5	−61.7	−93.4	−85.0	−53.2	−34.3	−97.2	−124.7	1.2	−58.4	−262.0
−42.4	−74.9	−214.7	−277.9	−23.0	−96.8	−426.2	−255.0	−150.7	−421.3	−585.3
−1.5	0.9	0.7	3.9	0.3	1.0	−5.3	4.5	0.6	2.6	−0.4
−47.4	−181.0	−342.2	−421.5	−198.0	−331.7	−774.1	−434.9	−198.3	−541.2	−928.0
...	...	...	...	...	−338.2	−404.9	−284.7	−170.2	−153.4	−196.1
...	...	...	...	...	−330.5	−385.2	−254.6	−162.9	−313.8	−353.4
...	...	...	...	...	−31.0	−166.2	−244.3	−218.9	−269.8	−362.8
...	...	...	...	...	11.6	16.2	16.5	−2.6	35.2	15.4
...	...	...	...	...	−688.1	−940.1	−767.1	−554.6	−701.9	−896.9
−15.6	−21.8	−29.3	−41.0	−26.2	−34.7	−39.0	−40.8	−27.4	−29.6	−61.0
−12.1	−53.0	−87.1	−112.8	−7.0	−49.8	−105.3	−105.0	−88.5	−130.9	−179.8
−65.3	−49.2	−95.6	−141.5	29.4	−77.4	−139.6	20.8	0.7	−118.7	−182.7
−67.3	−130.0	−94.6	−105.2	−34.8	−93.4	−113.2	−116.0	−185.8	−364.8	−517.2
−160.3	−253.9	−306.6	−400.6	−38.7	−255.3	−397.2	−240.9	−301.0	−644.0	−940.7

Table 2. Global Capital Flows: Amounts Outstanding and Net Issues of International Debt Securities by Currency of Issue and Announced International Syndicated Credit Facilities by Nationality of Borrower

(In billions of U.S. dollars)

	1997	1998	1999	2000	2001	2002	2003	2004	2005 Q1
Amounts outstanding of international debt securities by currency of issue									
U.S. dollar	1,432.9	1,832.6	2,356.3	2,905.0	3,607.3	4,042.6	4,484.6	4,864.3	4,961.8
Japanese yen	444.2	462.5	497.4	452.1	411.1	433.1	487.9	530.7	521.2
Pound sterling	266.7	322.4	391.1	452.7	506.1	618.7	778.3	984.2	1,006.7
Canadian dollar	67.2	55.5	56.4	51.5	47.5	51.5	79.3	112.4	120.1
Swedish krona	4.1	7.5	7.2	7.7	8.2	11.1	15.8	20.9	20.6
Swiss franc	138.5	153.5	135.5	132.0	123.6	159.1	195.6	228.6	219.4
Euro[1]	848.5	1,133.3	1,450.8	1,767.8	2,287.4	3,280.6	4,830.3	6,222.2	6,228.3
Other	78.8	84.1	98.3	97.1	110.1	151.9	216.9	286.3	302.0
Total	3,280.9	4,051.4	4,993.0	5,865.9	7,101.3	8,748.6	11,088.7	13,249.6	13,380.1
Net issues of international debt securities by currency of issue									
U.S. dollar	320.3	399.6	524.2	548.7	702.3	435.4	442.0	379.7	97.4
Japanese yen	34.0	–32.8	–23.4	10.6	18.6	–17.4	3.7	27.2	3.8
Pound sterling	46.4	53.9	77.8	92.1	65.7	52.3	85.7	134.2	47.6
Canadian dollar	–6.2	–7.5	–2.3	–2.8	–1.1	3.6	15.6	25.4	8.5
Swedish krona	–0.4	3.6	0.1	1.2	1.4	1.1	2.0	3.5	0.9
Swiss franc	–1.6	6.3	4.0	–0.2	–5.2	8.0	15.8	13.2	2.9
Euro[1]	130.0	214.5	506.9	423.1	623.7	492.3	785.2	923.6	310.1
Other	23.3	8.6	14.5	9.1	18.9	30.7	38.3	53.2	21.2
Total	545.8	646.2	1,101.8	1,081.8	1,424.3	1,006.0	1,388.3	1,560.0	492.4
Announced international syndicated credit facilities by nationality of borrower									
All countries	1,080.6	905.3	1,025.2	1,450.0	1,381.4	1,296.9	1,241.4	1,807.3	420.7
Industrial countries	903.8	820.3	959.5	1,316.1	1,269.8	1,198.0	1,130.0	1,634.1	387.0
Of which:									
United States	606.1	575.5	622.6	793.0	844.1	737.1	608.8	898.8	188.1
Japan	6.1	11.4	15.4	17.5	23.8	19.5	18.2	27.6	5.1
Germany	23.6	15.5	34.0	42.4	35.8	84.0	97.1	115.5	15.7
France	38.7	19.8	33.7	72.9	50.1	63.9	65.8	151.6	49.6
Italy	10.1	6.0	16.1	34.9	36.0	22.9	45.3	22.4	21.6
United Kingdom	101.3	79.8	109.0	132.2	105.7	109.3	104.1	148.4	37.0
Canada	37.6	41.4	22.8	37.8	39.2	34.9	28.4	38.8	7.4

Source: Bank for International Settlements.
[1]For 1997–98, the euro includes euro area currencies.

Table 3. Selected Indicators on the Size of the Capital Markets, 2004

(In billions of U.S. dollars unless noted otherwise)

	GDP	Total Reserves Minus Gold[1]	Stock Market Capitalization	Debt Securities			Bank Assets[2]	Bonds, Equities, and Bank Assets[3]	Bonds, Equities, and Bank Assets[3] (in percent of GDP)
				Public	Private	Total			
World	40,890.5	3,856.3	37,168.4	23,065.1	34,897.0	57,962.1	49,577.9	144,708.5	353.9
European Union	12,271.7	281.1	9,270.3	7,265.9	11,996.0	19,261.9	22,145.9	50,678.0	413.0
Euro area	9,550.1	174.5	5,873.0	6,272.0	9,544.3	15,816.3	16,127.5	37,978.8	397.7
North America	12,727.7	110.3	17,501.0	6,175.9	17,419.7	23,595.6	9,138.3	50,234.9	394.7
Canada	993.4	34.4	1,177.5	646.4	408.9	1,055.3	1,329.4	3,562.2	358.6
United States	11,734.3	75.9	16,323.5	5,529.5	17,010.8	22,540.3	7,808.9	46,672.7	397.7
Japan	4,671.2	833.9	5,844.7	6,840.0	2,322.6	9,162.6	7,239.9	22,247.3	476.3
Memorandum items:									
EU countries									
Austria	294.7	7.9	87.8	180.3	248.5	428.8	339.5	856.1	290.5
Belgium	352.3	10.4	268.7	432.7	355.5	788.2	1,219.2	2,276.1	646.1
Denmark	241.7	39.1	155.2	127.0	389.7	516.7	530.6	1,202.6	497.6
Finland	186.2	12.3	183.8	127.0	86.7	213.7	162.0	559.4	300.5
France	2,046.3	35.3	1,435.7	1,198.2	1,867.4	3,065.6	4,689.3	9,190.6	449.1
Germany	2,754.7	48.8	1,194.5	1,379.2	3,178.0	4,557.2	3,469.1	9,220.8	334.7
Greece	205.5	1.2	121.9	291.2	35.8	327.0	225.3	674.2	328.1
Ireland	181.9	2.8	114.1	44.6	197.6	242.2	708.7	1,065.0	585.6
Italy	1,680.1	27.9	789.6	1,693.6	1,360.9	3,054.5	2,305.9	6,149.9	366.0
Luxembourg	31.7	0.3	50.1	0.0	46.8	46.8	643.1	740.1	2,334.5
Netherlands	607.5	10.1	612.2	294.0	1,068.3	1,362.3	1,150.4	3,124.9	514.4
Portugal	167.9	5.2	73.9	126.2	151.1	277.3	179.6	530.8	316.1
Spain	1,041.3	12.4	940.7	505.0	947.7	1,452.7	1,197.4	3,590.8	344.8
Sweden	346.9	22.1	376.8	189.1	296.0	485.1	351.5	1,213.4	348.9
United Kingdom	2,133.0	45.3	2,865.2	677.8	1,766.0	2,443.8	4,974.2	10,283.3	482.1
Emerging market countries[4]	9,868.6	1,937.1	5,143.0	2,322.4	1,336.2	3,658.6	8,115.6	16,917.2	171.4
Of which:									
Asia	4,453.9	1,248.6	3,509.8	971.2	1,009.1	1,980.3	5,673.5	11,163.6	250.6
Latin America	2,005.0	195.7	849.7	753.7	215.1	968.8	920.9	2,739.4	136.6
Middle East	945.6	149.5	132.8	12.6	18.3	30.9	627.3	791.0	83.6
Africa	685.6	91.9	442.5	91.5	35.7	127.2	411.4	981.1	143.1
Europe	1,778.5	251.5	208.2	493.4	58.0	551.4	482.6	1,242.2	69.8

Sources: World Federation of Exchanges; Bank for International Settlements; International Monetary Fund, *International Financial Statistics* (IFS) and *World Economic Outlook* database as of August 30, 2005; and ©2003 Bureau van Dijk Electronic Publishing-Bankscope.

[1]Data are from the IFS.

[2]Assets of commercial banks; data refer to 2003.

[3]Sum of the stock market capitalization, debt securities, and bank assets.

[4]This aggregate comprises the group of Other Emerging Market and Developing Countries defined in the *World Economic Outlook*, together with Hong Kong SAR, Israel, Korea, Singapore, and Taiwan Province of China.

Table 4. Global Over-the-Counter Derivatives Markets: Notional Amounts and Gross Market Values of Outstanding Contracts[1]

(In billions of U.S. dollars)

	Notional Amounts					Gross Market Values				
	End-Dec. 2002	End-June 2003	End-Dec. 2003	End-June 2004	End-Dec. 2004	End-Dec. 2002	End-June 2003	End-Dec. 2003	End-June 2004	End-Dec. 2004
Total	**141,665**	**169,658**	**197,167**	**220,058**	**248,288**	**6,360**	**7,896**	**6,987**	**6,395**	**9,133**
Foreign exchange	**18,448**	**22,071**	**24,475**	**26,997**	**29,575**	**881**	**996**	**1,301**	**867**	**1,562**
Outright forwards and forex swaps	10,719	12,332	12,387	13,926	15,242	468	476	607	308	643
Currency swaps	4,503	5,159	6,371	7,033	8,217	337	419	557	442	761
Options	3,226	4,580	5,717	6,038	6,115	76	101	136	116	158
Interest rate[2]	**101,658**	**121,799**	**141,991**	**164,626**	**187,340**	**4,266**	**5,459**	**4,328**	**3,951**	**5,306**
Forward rate agreements	8,792	10,271	10,769	13,144	12,805	22	20	19	29	20
Swaps	79,120	94,583	111,209	127,570	147,366	3,864	5,004	3,918	3,562	4,793
Options	13,746	16,946	20,012	23,912	27,169	381	434	391	360	492
Equity-linked	**2,309**	**2,799**	**3,787**	**4,521**	**4,385**	**255**	**260**	**274**	**294**	**501**
Forwards and swaps	364	488	601	691	759	61	67	57	63	81
Options	1,944	2,311	3,186	3,829	3,626	194	193	217	231	420
Commodity[3]	**923**	**1,040**	**1,406**	**1,270**	**1,439**	**86**	**100**	**128**	**166**	**170**
Gold	315	304	344	318	369	28	12	39	45	32
Other	608	736	1,062	952	1,070	58	88	88	121	138
Forwards and swaps	402	458	420	503	554	...	...	...	...	...
Options	206	279	642	449	516	...	...	...	...	...
Other	**18,328**	**21,949**	**25,508**	**22,644**	**25,549**	**871**	**1,081**	**957**	**1,116**	**1,594**
Memorandum items:										
Gross credit exposure[4]	n.a.	n.a.	n.a.	n.a.	n.a.	1,511	1,750	1,969	1,478	2,076
Exchange-traded derivatives	18,448	22,071	24,475	26,997	29,575	...	...	...	...	...

Source: Bank for International Settlements.

[1]All figures are adjusted for double-counting. Notional amounts outstanding have been adjusted by halving positions vis-à-vis other reporting dealers. Gross market values have been calculated as the sum of the total gross positive market value of contracts and the absolute value of the gross negative market value of contracts with nonreporting counterparties.

[2]Single-currency contracts only.

[3]Adjustments for double-counting are estimated.

[4]Gross market values after taking into account legally enforceable bilateral netting agreements.

Table 5. Global Over-the-Counter Derivatives Markets: Notional Amounts and Gross Market Values of Outstanding Contracts by Counterparty, Remaining Maturity, and Currency[1]

(In billions of U.S. dollars)

	Notional Amounts					Gross Market Values				
	End-Dec. 2002	End-June 2003	End-Dec. 2003	End-June 2004	End-Dec. 2004	End-Dec. 2002	End-June 2003	End-Dec. 2003	End-June 2004	End-Dec. 2004
Total	**141,665**	**169,658**	**197,167**	**220,058**	**248,288**	**6,360**	**7,896**	**6,987**	**6,395**	**9,133**
Foreign exchange	**18,448**	**22,071**	**24,475**	**26,997**	**29,575**	**881**	**996**	**1,301**	**867**	**1,562**
By counterparty										
With other reporting dealers	6,842	7,954	8,660	10,796	11,664	285	284	395	247	485
With other financial institutions	7,597	8,948	9,450	10,113	11,640	377	427	535	352	665
With nonfinancial customers	4,009	5,168	6,365	6,088	6,271	220	286	370	267	412
By remaining maturity										
Up to one year[2]	14,522	17,543	18,840	21,252	23,115	...	...	...	...	...
One to five years[2]	2,719	3,128	3,901	3,912	4,386	...	...	...	...	...
Over five years[2]	1,208	1,399	1,734	1,834	2,073	...	...	...	...	...
By major currency										
U.S. dollar[3]	16,500	19,401	21,429	24,551	25,998	813	891	1,212	808	1,441
Euro[3]	7,794	9,879	10,145	10,312	11,936	429	526	665	380	751
Japanese yen[3]	4,791	4,907	5,500	6,516	7,083	189	165	217	178	257
Pound sterling[3]	2,462	3,093	4,286	4,614	4,349	98	114	179	130	220
Other[3]	5,349	6,862	7,590	8,001	9,783	233	296	329	238	454
Interest rate[4]	**101,658**	**121,799**	**141,991**	**164,626**	**187,340**	**4,266**	**5,459**	**4,328**	**3,951**	**5,306**
By counterparty										
With other reporting dealers	46,722	53,622	63,579	72,550	82,190	1,848	2,266	1,872	1,606	2,146
With other financial institutions	43,607	53,133	57,564	70,219	86,256	1,845	2,482	1,768	1,707	2,655
With nonfinancial customers	11,328	15,044	20,847	21,857	18,894	573	710	687	638	505
By remaining maturity										
Up to one year[2]	36,938	44,927	46,474	57,157	62,185	...	...	...	...	...
One to five years[2]	40,137	46,646	58,914	66,093	76,444	...	...	...	...	...
Over five years[2]	24,583	30,226	36,603	41,376	48,711	...	...	...	...	...
By major currency										
U.S. dollar	34,399	40,110	46,178	57,827	59,724	1,917	2,286	1,734	1,464	1,508
Euro	38,429	50,000	55,793	63,006	75,443	1,499	2,178	1,730	1,774	2,920
Japanese yen	14,650	15,270	19,526	21,103	23,276	378	405	358	324	336
Pound sterling	7,442	8,322	9,884	11,867	15,166	252	315	228	188	237
Other	6,738	8,097	10,610	10,823	13,732	220	275	278	201	304
Equity-linked	**2,309**	**2,799**	**3,787**	**4,521**	**4,385**	**255**	**260**	**274**	**294**	**501**
Commodity[5]	**923**	**1,040**	**1,406**	**1,270**	**1,439**	**86**	**100**	**128**	**166**	**170**
Other	**18,328**	**21,949**	**25,508**	**22,644**	**25,549**	**871**	**1,081**	**957**	**1,116**	**1,594**

Source: Bank for International Settlements.

[1]All figures are adjusted for double-counting. Notional amounts outstanding have been adjusted by halving positions vis-à-vis other reporting dealers. Gross market values have been calculated as the sum of the total gross positive market value of contracts and the absolute value of the gross negative market value of contracts with nonreporting counterparties.

[2]Residual maturity.

[3]Counting both currency sides of each foreign exchange transaction means that the currency breakdown sums to twice the aggregate.

[4]Single-currency contracts only.

[5]Adjustments for double-counting are estimated.

Table 6. Exchange-Traded Derivative Financial Instruments: Notional Principal Amounts Outstanding and Annual Turnover

	1988	1989	1990	1991	1992	1993	1994	1995
				(In billions of U.S. dollars)				
Notional principal amounts outstanding								
Interest rate futures	895.4	1,201.0	1,454.8	2,157.4	2,913.1	4,960.4	5,807.6	5,876.2
Interest rate options	279.0	386.0	595.4	1,069.6	1,383.8	2,361.4	2,623.2	2,741.8
Currency futures	12.1	16.0	17.0	18.3	26.5	34.7	40.4	33.8
Currency options	48.0	50.2	56.5	62.9	71.6	75.9	55.7	120.4
Stock market index futures	27.0	41.1	69.1	76.0	79.8	110.0	127.7	172.2
Stock market index options	42.7	70.2	93.6	136.8	163.1	231.6	242.7	337.7
Total	1,304.1	1,764.5	2,286.4	3,521.0	4,637.9	7,774.1	8,897.2	9,282.1
North America	951.2	1,153.5	1,264.4	2,152.8	2,698.1	4,359.9	4,823.5	4,852.3
Europe	177.4	250.9	461.4	710.7	1,114.4	1,777.9	1,831.8	2,241.3
Asia-Pacific	175.5	360.1	560.5	657.0	823.5	1,606.0	2,171.8	1,990.2
Other	0.0	0.0	0.1	0.5	1.9	30.3	70.1	198.3
				(In millions of contracts traded)				
Annual turnover								
Interest rate futures	156.4	201.0	219.1	230.9	330.1	427.0	628.5	561.0
Interest rate options	30.5	39.5	52.0	50.8	64.8	82.9	116.6	225.5
Currency futures	22.5	28.2	29.7	30.0	31.3	39.0	69.8	99.6
Currency options	18.2	20.7	18.9	22.9	23.4	23.7	21.3	23.3
Stock market index futures	29.6	30.1	39.4	54.6	52.0	71.2	109.0	114.8
Stock market index options	79.1	101.7	119.1	121.4	133.9	144.1	197.6	187.3
Total	336.3	421.2	478.2	510.4	635.6	787.9	1,142.9	1,211.6
North America	252.3	288.0	312.3	302.6	341.4	382.4	513.5	455.0
Europe	40.8	64.3	83.0	110.5	185.1	263.4	398.1	354.7
Asia-Pacific	34.3	63.6	79.1	85.8	82.9	98.5	131.7	126.4
Other	8.9	5.3	3.8	11.5	26.2	43.6	99.6	275.5

Source: Bank for International Settlements.

1996	1997	1998	1999	2000	2001	2002	2003	2004	2005 Q1
(In billions of U.S. dollars)									
5,979.0	7,586.7	8,031.4	7,924.8	7,907.8	9,269.5	9,955.6	13,123.7	18,164.9	20,449.6
3,277.8	3,639.9	4,623.5	3,755.5	4,734.2	12,492.8	11,759.5	20,793.8	24,604.1	34,328.6
37.7	42.3	31.7	36.7	74.4	65.6	47.0	80.1	104.2	87.5
133.4	118.6	49.2	22.4	21.4	27.4	27.4	37.9	60.7	60.0
195.9	210.9	291.5	340.3	371.5	333.9	325.5	501.9	634.3	712.4
394.5	808.7	907.4	1,510.2	1,148.3	1,574.9	1,700.8	2,202.3	3,023.9	3,768.9
10,018.1	12,407.1	13,934.7	13,589.9	14,257.7	23,764.1	23,815.7	36,739.7	46,592.1	59,406.8
4,841.2	6,347.9	7,355.1	6,930.6	8,167.9	16,203.2	13,693.8	19,503.9	27,609.0	35,851.5
2,828.1	3,587.4	4,397.1	4,008.5	4,197.4	6,141.3	8,800.4	15,406.1	16,307.0	20,818.3
2,154.0	2,235.7	1,882.5	2,401.3	1,606.2	1,308.5	1,192.4	1,613.1	2,426.9	2,402.0
194.8	236.1	300.0	249.5	286.2	111.1	129.1	216.6	249.2	335.0
(In millions of contracts traded)									
612.2	701.6	760.0	672.7	781.2	1,057.5	1,152.0	1,576.8	1,902.6	533.8
151.1	116.7	129.6	117.9	107.6	199.6	240.3	302.2	361.0	109.7
73.6	73.5	54.6	37.2	43.6	49.1	42.7	58.7	83.8	28.3
26.3	21.1	12.1	6.8	7.1	10.5	16.1	14.3	13.1	4.5
93.9	115.9	178.0	204.8	225.2	337.1	530.2	725.7	804.4	198.9
172.3	178.2	195.1	322.5	481.4	1,148.2	2,235.4	3,233.9	2,980.1	679.6
1,129.3	1,207.2	1,329.4	1,361.9	1,646.1	2,802.0	4,216.8	5,911.7	6,144.7	1,554.8
428.4	463.6	530.2	463.0	461.3	675.7	912.2	1,279.7	1,633.6	465.5
391.8	482.8	525.9	604.5	718.5	957.8	1,074.8	1,346.4	1,412.6	398.5
115.9	126.8	170.9	207.8	331.3	985.1	2,073.1	3,111.5	2,847.6	626.7
193.2	134.0	102.4	86.6	135.0	183.4	156.7	174.1	250.9	64.1

Table 7. United States: Sectoral Balance Sheets
(In percent)

	1998	1999	2000	2001	2002	2003	2004
Corporate sector							
Debt/net worth	51.3	51.1	48.6	51.6	50.8	48.4	46.0
Short-term debt/total debt	40.3	38.8	39.3	33.5	30.0	27.3	27.1
Interest burden[1]	12.6	13.4	15.8	17.7	15.7	13.2	12.1
Household sector							
Net worth/assets	85.7	86.1	85.0	83.7	82.0	82.2	81.9
Equity/total assets	31.5	35.1	31.1	26.6	20.9	24.2	24.2
Equity/financial assets	45.0	49.8	45.7	40.8	33.8	38.4	39.2
Net worth/disposable personal income	585.7	632.3	583.3	549.2	503.6	543.7	560.5
Home mortgage debt/total assets	9.4	9.1	9.8	10.8	12.3	12.3	12.8
Consumer credit/total assets	3.3	3.2	3.5	3.8	4.1	3.8	3.6
Total debt/financial assets	20.5	19.7	22.0	24.9	29.2	28.2	29.3
Debt-service burden[2]	12.1	12.3	12.6	13.1	13.3	13.2	13.2
Banking sector[3]							
Credit quality							
Nonperforming loans[4]/total loans	1.0	1.0	1.1	1.4	1.5	1.2	0.9
Net loan losses/average total loans	0.7	0.6	0.7	1.0	1.1	0.9	0.6
Loan-loss reserve/total loans	1.8	1.7	1.7	1.9	1.9	1.8	1.6
Net charge-offs/total loans	0.7	0.6	0.7	1.0	1.1	0.9	0.6
Capital ratios							
Total risk-based capital	12.2	12.2	12.1	12.7	12.8	12.8	12.6
Tier 1 risk-based capital	9.5	9.5	9.4	9.9	10.0	10.1	10.0
Equity capital/total assets	8.5	8.4	8.5	9.1	9.2	9.1	10.1
Core capital (leverage ratio)	7.5	7.8	7.7	7.8	7.9	7.9	7.8
Profitability measures							
Return on average assets (ROA)	1.3	1.3	1.2	1.2	1.4	1.4	1.4
Return on average equity (ROE)	14.8	15.7	14.8	14.2	14.9	15.2	14.6
Net interest margin	4.0	4.0	3.9	3.9	4.1	3.7	3.6
Efficiency ratio[5]	61.0	58.7	58.4	57.7	55.8	56.5	58.0

Sources: Board of Governors of the Federal Reserve System, *Flow of Funds;* Department of Commerce, Bureau of Economic Analysis; Federal Deposit Insurance Corporation; and Federal Reserve Bank of St. Louis.

[1]Ratio of net interest payments to pre-tax income.

[2]Ratio of debt payments to disposable personal income.

[3]FDIC-insured commercial banks.

[4]Loans past due 90+ days and nonaccrual.

[5]Noninterest expense less amortization of intangible assets as a percent of net interest income plus noninterest income.

Table 8. Japan: Sectoral Balance Sheets[1]

(In percent)

	FY1998	FY1999	FY2000	FY2001	FY2002	FY2003	FY2004
Corporate sector							
Debt/shareholders' equity (book value)	189.3	182.5	156.8	156.0	146.1	121.3	121.5
Short-term debt/total debt	39.0	39.4	37.7	36.8	39.0	37.8	36.8
Interest burden[2]	46.5	36.3	28.4	32.3	27.8	22.0	18.4
Debt/operating profits	1,813.8	1,472.1	1,229.3	1,480.0	1,370.0	1,079.2	965.9
Memorandum items:							
Total debt/GDP[3]	106.8	108.3	102.0	100.4	99.3	89.4	95.1
Household sector							
Net worth/assets	85.1	85.5	85.4	85.1	85.1	85.0	. . .
Equity	3.1	5.6	4.9	4.4	4.9	6.3	. . .
Real estate	39.5	37.5	36.7	35.5	34.3	32.7	. . .
Net worth/net disposable income	723.1	747.2	747.8	745.5	728.1	718.9	. . .
Interest burden[4]	5.3	5.0	5.1	5.0	4.9	4.7	. . .
Memorandum items:							
Debt/equity	477.0	258.8	299.5	335.3	300.9	240.2	. . .
Debt/real estate	37.7	38.5	40.0	41.9	43.4	45.9	. . .
Debt/net disposable income	126.7	126.3	128.3	130.2	127.3	127.1	. . .
Debt/net worth	17.5	16.9	17.2	17.5	17.5	17.7	. . .
Equity/net worth	3.7	6.5	5.7	5.2	5.8	7.4	. . .
Real estate/net worth	46.4	43.9	42.9	41.7	40.3	38.5	. . .
Total debt/GDP[3]	77.3	77.5	76.4	77.1	76.4	75.8	. . .
Banking sector							
Credit quality							
Nonperforming loans[5]/total loans	6.2	5.9	6.3	8.4	7.4	5.8	4.0
Capital ratio							
Stockholders' equity/assets	4.4	4.8	4.6	3.9	3.3	3.9	4.2
Profitability measures							
Return on equity (ROE)[6]	−12.5	2.6	−0.5	−14.3	−19.5	−2.7	4.1

Sources: Ministry of Finance, *Financial Statements of Corporations by Industries;* Cabinet Office, Economic and Social Research Institute, *Annual Report on National Accounts;* Japanese Bankers Association, *Financial Statements of All Banks;* and Financial Services Agency, *The Status of Nonperforming Loans.*

[1]Data are for fiscal years beginning April 1. Data on household nonfinancial assets and disposable income are only available through FY2003.

[2]Interest payments as a percent of operating profits.

[3]Revised due to the change in GDP figures.

[4]Interest payments as a percent of disposable income.

[5]Nonperforming loans are based on figures reported under the Financial Reconstruction Law.

[6]Net income as a percentage of stockholders' equity (no adjustment for preferred stocks, etc.).

Table 9. Europe: Sectoral Balance Sheets[1]

(In percent)

	1998	1999	2000	2001	2002	2003	2004
Corporate sector							
Debt/equity[2]	84.0	84.9	82.7	83.9	84.4	82.8	. . .
Short-term debt/total debt	36.8	37.5	41.9	39.9	38.1	36.1	. . .
Interest burden[3]	16.8	17.1	18.9	19.8	19.1	18.6	. . .
Debt/operating profits	260.8	289.0	315.7	322.4	337.2	331.2	. . .
Memorandum items:							
Financial assets/equity	1.8	2.1	2.0	1.9	1.6	1.6	. . .
Liquid assets/short-term debt	93.7	90.2	83.7	87.9	92.1	91.4	. . .
Household sector							
Net worth/assets	85.3	85.7	85.4	84.7	84.4	84.5	. . .
Equity/net worth	15.9	18.6	17.5	16.6	13.1	12.8	. . .
Equity/net financial assets	39.5	43.9	43.3	43.1	37.4	36.2	. . .
Interest burden[4]	6.8	6.4	6.6	6.3	6.2	6.1	. . .
Memorandum items:							
Nonfinancial assets/net worth	58.9	56.8	58.7	60.9	65.0	64.6	
Debt/net financial assets	44.0	41.5	43.0	45.5	51.1	49.5	. . .
Debt/income	91.8	94.8	95.5	95.6	99.4	102.7	. . .
Banking sector[5]							
Credit quality							
Nonperforming loans/total loans	3.7	3.8	3.5	3.4	3.7	3.7	3.7
Loan-loss reserve/nonperforming loans	77.1	72.5	78.5	81.1	76.9	76.1	76.1
Loan-loss reserve/total loans	2.8	2.8	2.8	2.7	2.9	2.8	2.8
Loan-loss provisions/total operating income[6]	12.8	10.2	7.4	10.1	13.1	11.1	11.1
Capital ratios							
Equity capital/total assets	3.9	3.9	4.1	4.0	4.0	4.1	4.1
Capital funds/liabilities	6.3	6.3	6.6	6.5	6.6	6.6	6.6
Profitability measures							
Return on assets, or ROA (after tax)	0.5	0.5	0.7	0.4	0.3	0.4	0.4
Return on equity, or ROE (after tax)	11.7	12.5	17.6	10.3	8.2	9.4	9.4
Net interest margin	1.8	1.5	1.5	1.5	1.6	1.6	1.6
Efficiency ratio[7]	68.0	67.8	68.9	70.3	71.0	66.9	66.9

Sources: ©2003 Bureau van Dijk Electronic Publishing-Bankscope; and IMF staff estimates.
[1]GDP-weighted average for France, Germany, and the United Kingdom, unless otherwise noted.
[2]Corporate equity adjusted for changes in asset valuation.
[3]Interest payments as a percent of gross operating profits.
[4]Interest payments as percent of disposable income.
[5]Fifty largest European banks. Data availability may restrict coverage to fewer than 50 banks for specific indicators.
[6]Includes the write-off of goodwill in foreign subsidiaries by banks with exposure to Argentina.
[7]Cost-to-income ratio.

Figure 15. Emerging Market Volatility Measures

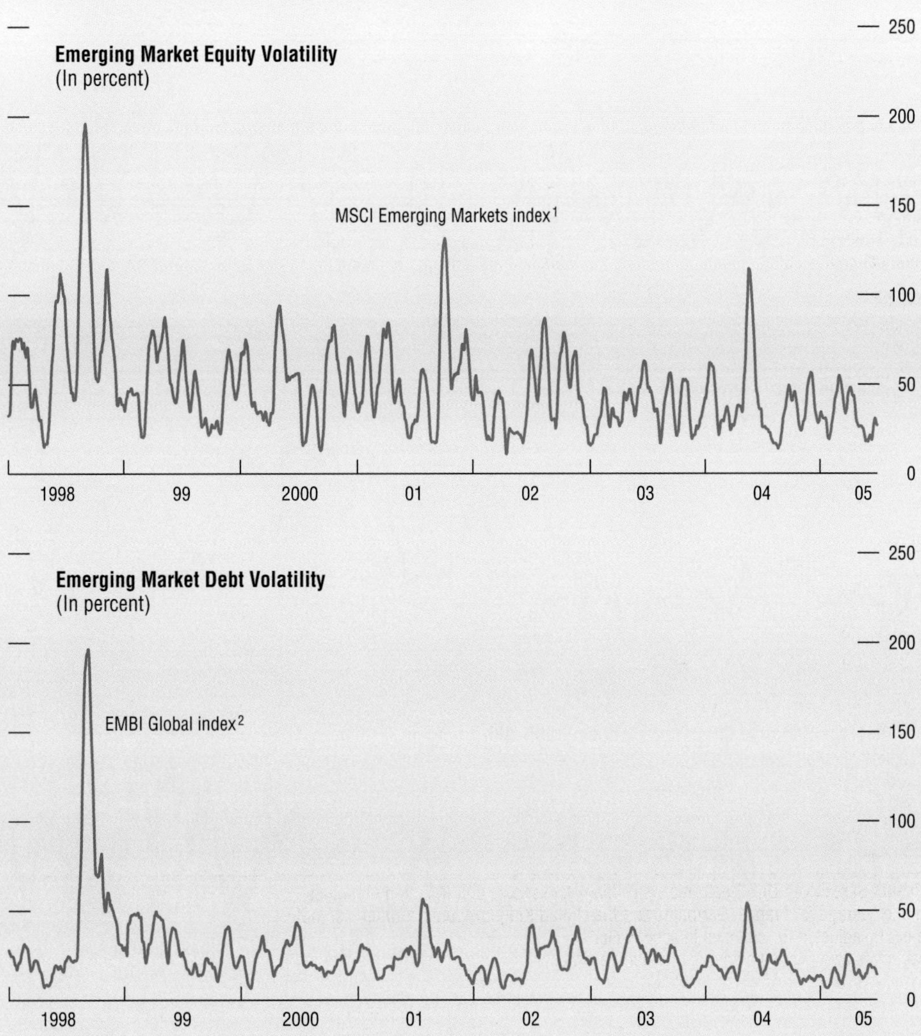

Sources: For "Emerging Market Equity Volatility," Morgan Stanley Capital International (MSCI); and IMF staff estimates. For "Emerging Market Debt Volatility," JPMorgan Chase & Co.; and IMF staff estimates.

[1]Data utilize the Emerging Markets index in U.S. dollars to calculate 30-day rolling volatilities.

[2]Data utilize the EMBI Global total return index in U.S. dollars to calculate 30-day rolling volatilities.

Figure 16. Emerging Market Debt Cross-Correlation Measures

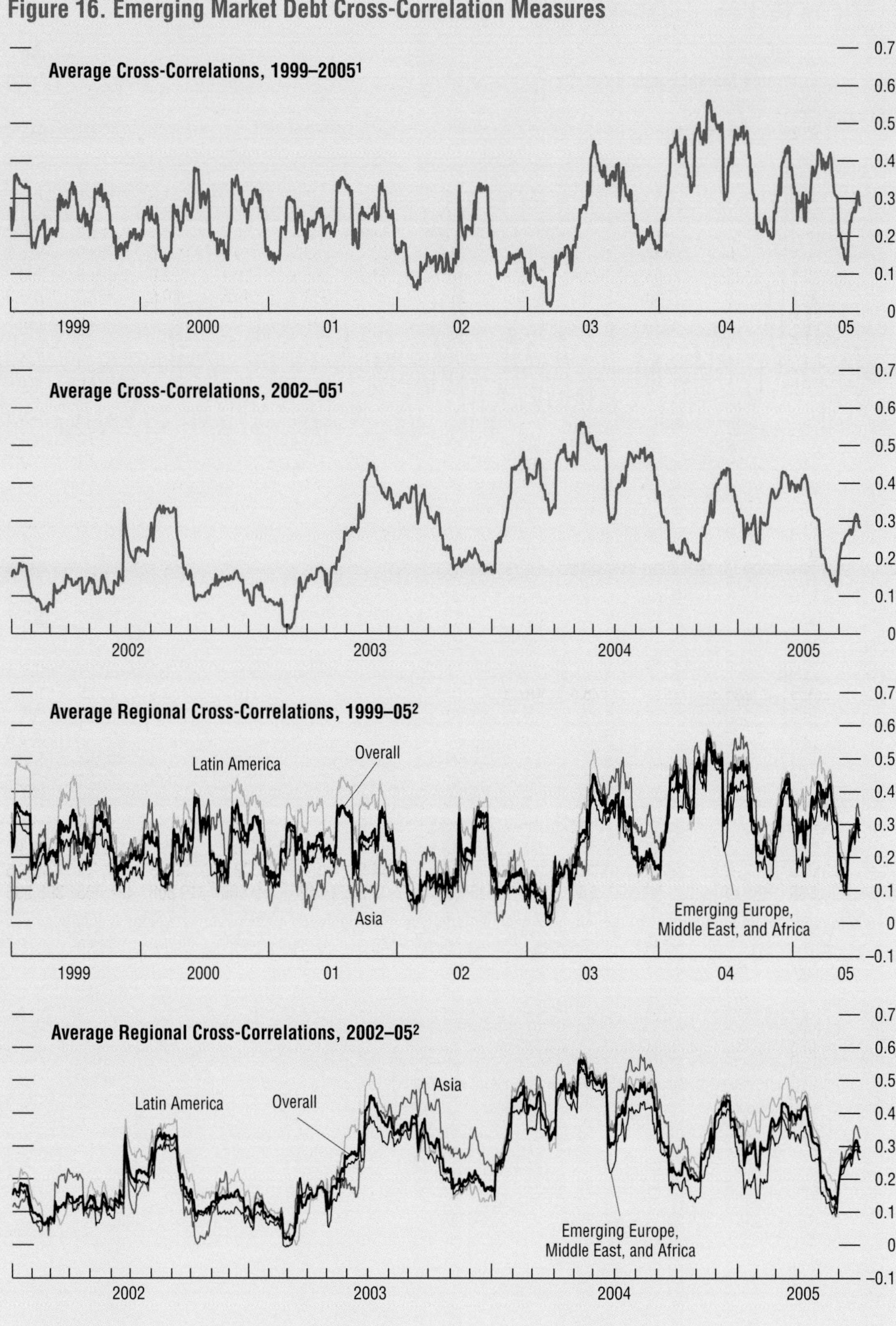

Sources: JPMorgan Chase & Co.; and IMF staff estimates.

[1]Thirty-day moving simple average across all pair-wise return correlations of 20 constituents included in the EMBI Global.

[2]Simple average of all pair-wise correlations of all markets in a given region with all other bond markets, regardless of region.

Table 10. Equity Market Indices

	2005 End of Period		2004 End of Period				End of Period					12-Month High	12-Month Low	All-Time High[1]	All-Time Low[1]
	Q1	Q2	Q1	Q2	Q3	Q4	2000	2001	2002	2003	2004				
World	**1,151.2**	**1,148.8**	**1,059.2**	**1,062.5**	**1,047.9**	**1,169.3**	**1,221.3**	**1,003.5**	**792.2**	**1,036.3**	**1,169.3**	**997.7**	**1,193.0**	**1,448.8**	**423.1**
Emerging Markets															
Emerging Markets	**548.7**	**565.2**	**482.1**	**432.2**	**464.2**	**542.2**	**333.8**	**317.4**	**292.1**	**442.8**	**542.2**	**418.5**	**588.7**	**588.7**	**175.3**
EM Latin America	**1,510.5**	**1,617.0**	**1,169.5**	**1,062.4**	**1,238.3**	**1,483.6**	**915.6**	**876.2**	**658.9**	**1,100.9**	**1,483.6**	**1,056.8**	**1,669.0**	**1,669.0**	**185.6**
Argentina	1,316.4	1,440.5	1,034.6	847.8	1,073.7	1,163.0	1,232.7	959.6	470.3	933.6	1,163.0	856.3	1,486.3	2,052.2	152.6
Brazil	1,090.5	1,145.9	786.9	686.4	862.9	1,046.6	763.2	597.1	395.4	802.0	1,046.6	690.5	1,217.7	1,306.4	84.1
Chile	1,027.3	1,078.5	779.6	762.0	870.5	997.3	604.7	568.7	445.5	800.6	997.3	765.3	1,096.2	1,119.6	183.0
Colombia	236.5	277.6	152.8	145.8	184.6	245.0	42.1	57.7	68.3	108.6	245.0	142.8	277.6	275.7	41.2
Mexico	2,643.4	2,940.3	2,241.1	2,114.1	2,222.4	2,715.6	1,464.9	1,698.2	1,442.8	1,873.1	2,715.6	2,011.1	2,981.9	2,975.8	308.9
Peru	355.9	349.8	364.7	308.8	340.5	343.4	125.0	144.1	182.7	344.1	343.4	295.1	381.6	381.6	73.5
Venezuela	127.6	121.7	123.0	131.7	149.4	151.0	106.1	95.4	77.7	103.8	151.0	119.6	166.4	278.4	56.1
EM Asia	**236.4**	**243.0**	**222.1**	**195.0**	**203.2**	**231.6**	**143.6**	**149.7**	**140.4**	**206.4**	**231.6**	**185.2**	**250.5**	**433.0**	**104.1**
China	25.3	26.1	24.7	22.5	24.1	25.3	22.8	16.8	14.1	25.5	25.3	21.1	26.7	136.9	12.9
India	267.7	296.3	230.8	201.6	232.1	273.1	173.4	141.2	148.8	246.2	273.1	202.7	296.3	323.9	77.7
Indonesia	1,422.8	1,518.7	892.4	927.3	1,060.5	1,324.0	456.4	437.2	519.6	831.1	1,324.0	925.3	1,562.5	1,504.1	280.0
Korea	276.0	281.1	276.1	237.3	245.9	256.4	125.6	190.4	184.7	246.0	256.4	215.7	290.5	292.9	59.5
Malaysia	322.3	324.6	342.6	306.5	316.8	335.9	245.2	250.7	244.0	300.4	335.9	299.1	348.3	465.7	88.3
Pakistan	266.5	270.4	200.7	192.4	188.2	211.7	99.1	67.4	146.0	188.2	211.7	177.3	327.2	327.2	54.4
Philippines	405.1	396.8	296.1	331.8	364.7	381.1	352.6	292.2	210.1	303.7	381.1	318.2	453.5	917.3	132.6
Taiwan Province of China	247.5	260.8	277.0	248.3	243.8	257.7	222.2	255.6	189.5	259.1	257.7	224.3	267.0	483.5	103.9
Thailand	266.0	265.5	240.8	245.3	247.4	263.9	102.5	107.5	130.2	280.5	263.9	225.7	292.8	669.4	72.0
EM Europe, Middle East, & Africa	**220.6**	**221.7**	**185.6**	**171.8**	**185.3**	**222.7**	**. . .**	**103.5**	**108.4**	**163.9**	**222.7**	**165.1**	**243.4**	**243.4**	**80.8**
Czech Republic	269.3	286.3	191.1	178.4	197.3	234.8	107.6	97.5	116.2	152.9	234.8	171.3	292.2	291.4	62.8
Egypt	750.6	973.8	282.6	284.2	422.1	505.3	154.9	101.9	97.4	234.6	505.3	284.2	997.4	849.7	89.9
Hungary	1,238.1	1,322.6	782.7	812.9	888.9	1,057.0	582.9	507.9	535.5	646.9	1,057.0	800.6	1,360.3	1,360.3	77.1
Israel	168.7	163.9	156.5	167.5	139.0	167.4	196.0	132.7	90.8	141.4	167.4	135.2	180.0	236.2	67.6
Jordan	474.6	592.8	250.2	252.5	284.0	379.2	116.1	149.5	153.5	238.3	379.2	253.7	609.0	502.4	103.1
Morocco	181.0	191.7	188.3	189.4	190.6	189.1	198.9	180.1	138.5	171.4	189.1	158.5	196.4	302.1	99.6
Poland	1,486.4	1,529.1	1,251.6	1,218.3	1,264.7	1,419.3	1,307.9	891.9	861.0	1,118.3	1,419.3	1,144.1	1,579.9	1,792.9	99.6
Russia	503.4	526.0	596.7	470.5	508.7	479.9	155.2	237.8	270.7	461.1	479.9	408.2	558.3	626.8	30.6
South Africa	358.3	378.5	302.7	278.9	327.8	352.4	244.8	309.3	272.7	296.8	352.4	270.6	380.4	374.6	99.7
Turkey	426,533	441,094	336,724	303,284	369,472	425,008	163,012	234,490	169,900	319,808	425,008	305,535	475,282	475,282	426
EM Sectors															
Energy	376.0	414.8	324.4	277.8	324.5	349.0	148.5	162.1	163.1	287.4	349.0	276.2	415.8	406.9	81.7
Materials	275.3	260.6	253.1	222.3	262.0	265.0	140.8	173.9	182.8	250.1	265.0	220.0	295.7	295.7	98.5
Industrials	129.7	129.2	107.2	99.2	106.8	128.0	73.4	63.8	61.8	98.9	128.0	97.0	139.1	276.8	52.6
Consumer discretionary	283.2	289.0	250.9	218.7	241.9	292.3	126.0	130.6	138.8	233.8	292.3	213.1	308.4	308.4	74.1
Consumer staple	150.0	161.9	124.4	117.1	126.4	147.0	103.1	94.6	88.2	118.6	147.0	116.8	162.2	157.1	80.4
Health care	293.5	301.8	286.6	291.6	251.4	290.8	173.9	146.5	169.8	272.5	290.8	243.0	313.2	302.0	83.3
Financials	187.1	188.2	151.0	138.8	149.5	187.9	112.6	107.7	98.6	138.8	187.9	134.1	204.6	204.6	74.6
Information technology	167.0	173.6	174.5	149.5	141.6	161.5	130.9	134.2	103.9	149.6	161.5	130.8	179.2	300.0	73.1
Telecommunications	127.5	133.9	108.9	104.1	106.9	131.6	113.8	91.9	72.7	100.8	131.6	97.9	138.0	211.5	62.9
Utilities	147.2	164.3	127.7	114.3	132.4	149.8	95.7	91.5	72.4	127.2	149.8	114.4	167.6	247.8	63.1

Table 10. Equity Market Indices *(continued)*

	Period on Period Percent Change														
	2005 End of period		2004 End of period				End of period					12-Month High	12-Month Low	All-Time High[1]	All-Time Low[1]
	Q1	Q2	Q1	Q2	Q3	Q4	2000	2001	2002	2003	2004				
World	**−1.6**	**−0.2**	**2.2**	**0.3**	**−1.4**	**11.6**	**−14.1**	**−17.8**	**−21.1**	**30.8**	**12.8**	. . .	. . .	. . .	. . .
Emerging Markets															
Emerging Markets	**1.2**	**3.0**	**8.9**	**−10.3**	**7.4**	**16.8**	**−31.8**	**−4.9**	**−8.0**	**51.6**	**22.4**	. . .	. . .	. . .	. . .
EM Latin America	**1.8**	**7.1**	**6.2**	**−9.2**	**16.6**	**19.8**	**−18.4**	**−4.3**	**−24.8**	**67.1**	**34.8**	. . .	. . .	. . .	. . .
Argentina	13.2	9.4	10.8	−18.1	26.7	8.3	−26.1	−22.2	−51.0	98.5	24.6	. . .	. . .	. . .	. . .
Brazil	4.2	5.1	−1.9	−12.8	25.7	21.3	−14.2	−21.8	−33.8	102.9	30.5	. . .	. . .	. . .	. . .
Chile	3.0	5.0	−2.6	−2.2	14.2	14.6	−17.0	−6.0	−21.7	79.7	24.6	. . .	. . .	. . .	. . .
Colombia	−3.5	17.3	40.7	−4.5	26.6	32.7	−41.2	37.1	18.3	59.0	125.7	. . .	. . .	. . .	. . .
Mexico	−2.7	11.2	19.7	−5.7	5.1	22.2	−21.5	15.9	−15.0	29.8	45.0	. . .	. . .	. . .	. . .
Peru	3.6	−1.7	6.0	−15.3	10.3	0.9	−26.7	15.3	26.8	88.4	−0.2	. . .	. . .	. . .	. . .
Venezuela	−15.5	−4.6	18.5	7.0	13.5	1.1	0.8	−10.0	−18.6	33.6	45.4	. . .	. . .	. . .	. . .
EM Asia	**2.1**	**2.8**	**7.6**	**−12.2**	**4.2**	**14.0**	**−42.5**	**4.2**	**−6.2**	**47.1**	**12.2**	. . .	. . .	. . .	. . .
China	0.0	3.0	−3.0	−9.1	7.3	5.1	−32.0	−26.0	−16.0	80.3	−0.7	. . .	. . .	. . .	. . .
India	−2.0	10.7	−6.3	−12.6	15.1	17.7	−17.2	−18.6	5.3	65.5	11.0	. . .	. . .	. . .	. . .
Indonesia	7.5	6.7	7.4	3.9	14.4	24.8	−49.3	−4.2	18.9	60.0	59.3	. . .	. . .	. . .	. . .
Korea	7.6	1.8	12.2	−14.1	3.6	4.3	−44.6	51.6	−3.0	33.2	4.2	. . .	. . .	. . .	. . .
Malaysia	−4.1	0.7	14.0	−10.5	3.4	6.0	−17.3	2.3	−2.7	23.1	11.8	. . .	. . .	. . .	. . .
Pakistan	25.9	1.5	6.6	−4.1	−2.2	12.5	−4.3	−32.0	116.7	28.9	12.5	. . .	. . .	. . .	. . .
Philippines	6.3	−2.0	−2.5	12.1	9.9	4.5	−32.1	−17.1	−28.1	44.5	25.5	. . .	. . .	. . .	. . .
Taiwan Province of China	−3.9	5.4	6.9	−10.4	−1.8	5.7	−42.3	15.0	−25.8	36.7	−0.6	. . .	. . .	. . .	. . .
Thailand	0.8	−0.2	−14.1	1.9	0.9	6.7	−50.0	4.9	21.1	115.4	−5.9	. . .	. . .	. . .	. . .
EM Europe, Middle East, & Africa	**−1.0**	**0.5**	**13.2**	**−7.4**	**7.8**	**20.2**	. . .	. . .	**4.7**	**51.2**	**35.8**	. . .	. . .	. . .	. . .
Czech Republic	14.7	6.3	25.0	−6.6	10.6	19.0	5.5	−9.4	19.2	31.6	53.6	. . .	. . .	. . .	. . .
Egypt	48.6	29.7	20.5	0.5	48.5	19.7	−38.4	−34.2	−4.4	140.8	115.4	. . .	. . .	. . .	. . .
Hungary	17.1	6.8	21.0	3.9	9.3	18.9	−19.6	−12.9	5.4	20.8	63.4	. . .	. . .	. . .	. . .
Israel	0.8	−2.8	10.7	7.0	−17.0	20.4	24.7	−32.3	−31.6	55.7	18.4	. . .	. . .	. . .	. . .
Jordan	25.2	24.9	5.0	0.9	12.5	33.5	−24.7	28.8	2.6	55.3	59.1	. . .	. . .	. . .	. . .
Morocco	−4.3	5.9	9.8	0.6	0.6	−0.8	−20.2	−9.5	−23.1	23.8	10.4	. . .	. . .	. . .	. . .
Poland	4.7	2.9	11.9	−2.7	3.8	12.2	−4.8	−31.8	−3.5	29.9	26.9	. . .	. . .	. . .	. . .
Russia	4.9	4.5	29.4	−21.2	8.1	−5.7	−30.4	53.2	13.9	70.3	4.1	. . .	. . .	. . .	. . .
South Africa	1.7	5.6	2.0	−7.9	17.5	7.5	−1.2	26.3	−11.8	8.8	18.7	. . .	. . .	. . .	. . .
Turkey	0.4	3.4	5.3	−9.9	21.8	15.0	−33.5	43.8	−27.5	88.2	32.9	. . .	. . .	. . .	. . .
EM Sectors															
Energy	7.7	10.3	12.9	−14.4	16.8	7.6	−24.7	9.2	0.6	76.2	21.4	. . .	. . .	. . .	. . .
Materials	3.9	−5.3	1.2	−12.2	17.9	1.2	−21.0	23.5	5.2	36.8	6.0	. . .	. . .	. . .	. . .
Industrials	1.3	−0.3	8.4	−7.4	7.7	19.8	−41.7	−13.1	−3.2	60.1	29.5	. . .	. . .	. . .	. . .
Consumer discretionary	−3.1	2.0	7.3	−12.8	10.6	20.8	−41.6	3.6	6.3	68.4	25.0	. . .	. . .	. . .	. . .
Consumer staple	2.0	8.0	4.9	−5.8	7.9	16.3	−20.2	−8.2	−6.7	34.4	24.0	. . .	. . .	. . .	. . .
Health care	0.9	2.8	5.2	1.7	−13.8	15.7	0.7	−15.8	15.9	60.5	6.7	. . .	. . .	. . .	. . .
Financials	−0.4	0.6	8.8	−8.1	7.7	25.7	−24.3	−4.3	−8.4	40.7	35.4	. . .	. . .	. . .	. . .
Information technology	3.4	3.9	16.7	−14.3	−5.3	14.0	−44.9	2.6	−22.6	43.9	8.0	. . .	. . .	. . .	. . .
Telecommunications	−3.1	5.0	8.0	−4.4	2.7	23.1	−31.1	−19.2	−20.9	38.7	30.5	. . .	. . .	. . .	. . .
Utilities	−1.7	11.6	0.4	−10.5	15.8	13.2	−25.0	−4.4	−20.9	75.7	17.8	. . .	. . .	. . .	. . .

Table 10. Equity Market Indices *(concluded)*

	Period on Period Percent Change														
	2005 End of period		2004 End of period				End of period					12-Month High	12-Month Low	All-Time High[1]	All-Time Low[1]
	Q1	Q2	Q1	Q2	Q3	Q4	2000	2001	2002	2003	2004				
Developed Markets															
Australia	816.1	853.6	680.5	700.6	725.2	797.9	640.1	690.8	604.4	655.5	797.9	639.6	539.9	712.9	250.2
Austria	196.7	221.2	141.1	150.7	156.9	185.3	96.9	94.6	91.8	118.0	185.3	105.4	79.7	105.4	96.2
Belgium	83.1	83.2	63.6	66.3	72.2	77.9	85.8	78.6	55.3	60.1	77.9	65.0	38.1	53.9	51.2
Canada	1,188.2	1,228.1	1,062.0	1,058.7	1,072.3	1,139.3	1,156.4	965.8	818.3	1,019.7	1,139.3	886.4	705.8	1,511.4	338.3
Denmark	2,317.1	2,510.2	1,909.4	2,011.5	2,092.1	2,115.9	2,333.3	2,060.1	1,448.8	1,772.7	2,115.9	1,752.8	1,245.8	2,776.6	556.5
Finland	98.2	110.0	113.1	91.6	88.1	93.9	267.5	171.8	100.3	97.4	93.9	126.0	78.8	383.1	78.8
France	107.1	111.5	95.3	98.0	96.0	100.6	152.0	123.1	81.3	93.2	100.6	95.3	63.4	178.6	63.4
Germany	80.7	83.5	73.0	75.4	72.6	79.2	124.0	100.1	56.0	74.6	79.2	78.4	42.9	163.6	41.4
Greece	86.0	92.1	67.0	68.5	68.7	83.3	106.1	76.8	46.8	63.6	83.3	61.9	38.2	197.2	38.2
Hong Kong SAR	7,336.6	7,779.1	6,747.8	6,349.0	6,956.4	7,668.5	7,690.1	6,058.0	4,808.4	6,341.3	7,668.5	5,553.6	4,305.4	10,165.3	1,995.5
Ireland	78.2	86.0	71.0	76.4	78.4	85.2	92.1	93.1	56.8	65.9	85.2	67.1	51.9	107.3	51.9
Italy	97.9	97.5	79.8	83.1	83.1	93.2	119.9	91.2	69.6	78.1	93.2	78.4	58.7	132.1	58.7
Japan	708.3	707.3	709.2	714.6	665.9	699.1	808.2	650.3	524.3	637.3	699.1	628.7	462.1	1,655.3	462.1
Netherlands	73.8	78.1	67.4	69.2	65.2	69.3	124.5	100.4	66.0	68.4	69.3	80.9	47.4	134.9	47.4
New Zealand	123.5	129.1	112.8	115.6	119.9	127.0	83.9	94.2	90.0	107.6	127.0	101.4	86.6	141.0	56.7
Norway	1,841.8	1,988.6	1,407.3	1,475.8	1,603.2	1,690.3	1,458.0	1,278.4	898.3	1,240.9	1,690.3	1,116.3	762.2	1,599.1	455.9
Portugal	75.9	72.3	74.1	72.7	72.7	74.7	97.9	79.5	57.0	66.1	74.7	64.6	48.1	123.1	48.1
Singapore	1,181.3	1,228.6	1,048.3	1,041.3	1,110.7	1,148.1	1,173.4	936.8	764.9	1,005.1	1,148.1	922.1	687.3	1,624.2	508.2
Spain	105.8	111.5	92.0	92.8	91.7	104.3	107.7	99.0	69.9	89.6	104.3	81.9	61.1	133.7	27.4
Sweden	5,998.2	6,467.4	5,238.6	5,385.2	5,451.9	5,785.4	7,735.0	6,178.8	3,517.4	4,675.2	5,785.4	4,173.8	2,914.9	12,250.4	787.2
Switzerland	778.4	820.6	734.4	735.8	717.5	747.1	1,017.0	813.4	603.2	714.3	747.1	716.9	481.4	1,032.8	158.1
United Kingdom	1,478.7	1,539.5	1,321.9	1,349.4	1,376.6	1,453.0	1,841.4	1,586.2	1,179.2	1,348.7	1,453.0	1,336.7	986.4	1,974.2	585.4
United States	1,109.3	1,122.6	1,055.9	1,068.9	1,044.5	1,137.4	1,249.9	1,084.5	824.6	1,045.4	1,137.4	950.4	726.5	1,493.0	273.7
Developed Markets															
Australia	2.3	4.6	3.8	3.0	3.5	10.0	3.7	7.9	–12.5	8.5	21.7	...	...	...	...
Austria	6.1	12.5	19.6	6.8	4.1	18.1	–7.6	–2.4	–3.0	28.5	57.0	...	...	...	...
Belgium	6.7	0.1	5.8	4.3	8.8	7.9	–13.1	–8.3	–29.7	8.7	29.5	...	...	...	...
Canada	4.3	3.4	4.1	–0.3	1.3	6.3	8.1	–16.5	–15.3	24.6	11.7	...	...	...	...
Denmark	9.5	8.3	7.7	5.3	4.0	1.1	9.9	–11.7	–29.7	22.4	19.4	...	...	...	...
Finland	4.6	12.1	16.2	–19.1	–3.8	6.5	–8.9	–35.8	–41.6	–2.9	–3.6	...	...	...	...
France	6.5	4.1	2.3	2.9	–2.0	4.7	1.4	–19.0	–34.0	14.6	7.9	...	...	...	...
Germany	2.0	3.5	–2.2	3.4	–3.8	9.1	–10.8	–19.3	–44.0	33.2	6.1	...	...	...	...
Greece	3.2	7.1	5.4	2.2	0.4	21.2	–38.6	–27.6	–39.1	35.8	31.1	...	...	...	...
Hong Kong SAR	–4.3	6.0	6.4	–5.9	9.6	10.2	–16.7	–21.2	–20.6	31.9	20.9	...	...	...	...
Ireland	–8.1	9.9	7.7	7.5	2.6	8.6	–8.5	1.1	–39.0	16.0	29.2	...	...	...	...
Italy	5.1	–0.4	2.3	4.0	—	12.1	3.9	–24.0	–23.6	12.2	19.3	...	...	...	...
Japan	1.3	–0.1	11.3	0.8	–6.8	5.0	–20.3	–19.5	–19.4	21.6	9.7	...	...	...	...
Netherlands	6.6	5.7	–1.5	2.8	–5.8	6.2	1.0	–19.4	–34.3	3.6	1.3	...	...	...	...
New Zealand	–2.7	4.5	4.8	2.5	3.8	5.9	–24.9	12.2	–4.4	19.6	18.0	...	...	...	...
Norway	9.0	8.0	13.4	4.9	8.6	5.4	7.1	–12.3	–29.7	38.1	36.2	...	...	...	...
Portugal	1.6	–4.8	12.1	–1.9	—	2.7	–6.2	–18.8	–28.3	15.9	13.1	...	...	...	...
Singapore	2.9	4.0	4.3	–0.7	6.7	3.4	–25.7	–20.2	–18.4	31.4	14.2	...	...	...	...
Spain	1.4	5.4	2.6	0.8	–1.1	13.8	–11.2	–8.0	–29.5	28.3	16.4	...	...	...	...
Sweden	3.7	7.8	12.1	2.8	1.2	6.1	–13.8	–20.1	–43.1	32.9	23.7	...	...	...	...
Switzerland	4.2	5.4	2.8	0.2	–2.5	4.1	6.2	–20.0	–25.8	18.4	4.6	...	...	...	...
United Kingdom	1.8	4.1	–2.0	2.1	2.0	5.5	–6.7	–13.9	–25.7	14.4	7.7	...	...	...	...
United States	–2.5	1.2	1.0	1.2	–2.3	8.9	–13.6	–13.2	–24.0	26.8	8.8	...	...	...	...

Source: Data are provided by Morgan Stanley Capital International. Regional and sectoral compositions conform to Morgan Stanley Capital International definitions.
[1]From 1990 or initiation of the index.

Table 11. Foreign Exchange Rates

(Units per U.S. dollar)

	2005 End of Period		2004 End of Period				End of Period					12-Month High	12-Month Low	All-Time High[1]	All-Time Low[1]
	Q1	Q2	Q1	Q2	Q3	Q4	2000	2001	2002	2003	2004				
Emerging Markets															
Latin America															
Argentina	2.92	2.89	2.86	2.96	2.98	2.97	1.00	1.00	3.36	2.93	2.97	2.86	3.06	0.98	3.86
Brazil	2.68	2.33	2.90	3.09	2.86	2.66	1.95	2.31	3.54	2.89	2.66	2.33	3.08	0.00	3.95
Chile	586.10	577.75	612.40	636.00	610.75	555.75	573.85	661.25	720.25	592.75	555.75	555.75	644.25	295.18	759.75
Colombia	2,374	2,327.25	2,679.55	2,693.2	2,618.9	2,354.75	2,236	2,277.50	2,867	2,780	2,354.75	2305	2680.2	689.21	2980
Mexico	11.17	10.75	11.13	11.49	11.38	11.15	9.62	9.16	10.37	11.23	11.15	10.74	11.59	2.68	11.67
Peru	3.26	3.25	3.46	3.47	3.34	3.28	3.53	3.44	3.51	3.46	3.28	3.25	3.47	1.28	3.65
Venezuela	2,147	2,145	1,918	1,918	1,918	1,918	700	758	1,389	1,598	1,918	1,918	2,148	45.0	2,148
Asia															
China	8.28	8.28	8.28	8.28	8.28	8.28	8.28	8.28	8.28	8.28	8.28	8.28	8.28	4.73	8.80
India	43.75	43.49	43.6	46.06	45.95	43.46	46.68	48.25	47.98	45.63	43.46	43.29	46.47	16.92	49.05
Indonesia	9,465	9,760	8,564	9,400	9,155	9,270	9,675	10,400	8,950	8,420	9,270	8,800	9,760	1,977	16,650
Korea	1,015	1,035	1,147	1,155	1,152	1,035	1,265	1,314	1,186	1,192	1,035	997	1,170	684.00	1,963
Malaysia	3.8	3.80	3.80	3.80	3.80	3.80	3.80	3.80	3.80	3.80	3.80	3.80	3.80	2.44	4.71
Pakistan	59.4	59.70	57.39	58.08	59.19	59.43	57.6	59.9	58.25	57.25	59.43	58.05	61.33	21.18	64.35
Philippines	54.8	55.98	56.20	56.12	56.28	56.23	50.00	51.60	53.60	55.54	56.23	53.95	56.46	23.10	56.46
Taiwan Province of China	31.53	31.62	33.02	33.78	33.98	31.74	33.08	34.95	34.64	33.96	31.74	30.79	34.2	24.48	35.19
Thailand	39.12	41.33	39.29	40.93	41.4	38.92	43.38	44.21	43.11	39.62	38.92	38.24	41.65	23.15	55.5
Europe, Middle East, & Africa															
Czech Republic	23.18	24.85	26.67	26.17	25.37	22.42	37.28	35.6	30.07	25.71	22.42	21.91	26.51	21.91	42.17
Egypt	5.80	5.79	6.20	6.19	6.24	6.09	3.89	4.58	4.62	6.17	6.09	5.79	6.25	3.29	6.25
Hungary	190.82	204.04	201.68	205.61	198.21	181.02	282.34	274.81	224.48	208.70	181.02	180.05	208.09	90.20	317.56
Israel	4.36	4.58	4.53	4.50	4.48	4.32	4.04	4.40	4.74	4.39	4.32	4.30	4.58	1.96	5.01
Jordan	0.71	0.71	0.71	0.71	0.71	0.71	0.71	0.71	0.71	0.71	0.71	0.71	0.71	0.64	0.72
Morocco	11.19	10.69	10.38	10.73	10.56	11.09	9.45	9.61	9.80	10.08	11.09	10.39	11.28	7.75	11.28
Poland	3.16	3.34	3.86	3.69	3.51	3.01	4.13	3.96	3.83	3.73	3.01	2.92	3.72	1.72	4.71
Russia	27.86	28.63	28.52	29.07	29.22	27.72	28.16	30.51	31.96	29.24	27.72	27.45	29.28	0.98	31.96
South Africa	6.24	6.65	6.29	6.14	6.45	5.67	7.58	11.96	8.57	6.68	5.67	5.62	6.92	2.50	12.45
Turkey	1.35	1.33	1.31	1.48	1.51	1.34	0.67	1.45	1.66	1.41	1.34	1.26	1.52	0.00	1.77
Developed Markets															
Australia[2]	0.77	0.76	0.77	0.70	0.73	0.78	0.56	0.51	0.56	0.75	0.78	0.69	0.80	0.84	0.48
Canada	1.21	1.23	1.31	1.33	1.26	1.20	1.50	1.59	1.57	1.30	1.20	1.18	1.33	1.12	1.61
Denmark	5.75	6.15	6.05	6.09	5.98	5.49	7.92	8.35	7.08	5.91	5.49	5.45	6.19	5.34	9.00
Euro[2]	1.30	1.21	1.23	1.22	1.24	1.36	0.94	0.89	1.05	1.26	1.36	1.20	1.36	1.36	0.83
Hong Kong SAR	7.80	7.77	7.79	7.80	7.80	7.77	7.80	7.80	7.80	7.76	7.77	7.77	7.80	7.70	7.82
Japan	107.15	110.92	104.22	108.77	110.05	102.63	114.41	131.66	118.79	107.22	102.63	102.05	111.99	80.63	159.9
New Zealand[2]	0.71	0.70	0.67	0.64	0.68	0.72	0.44	0.42	0.52	0.66	0.72	0.63	0.74	0.74	0.39
Norway	6.34	6.53	6.84	6.93	6.71	6.08	8.80	8.96	6.94	6.67	6.08	6.05	7.04	5.51	9.58
Singapore	1.65	1.69	1.67	1.72	1.68	1.63	1.73	1.85	1.73	1.70	1.63	1.62	1.73	1.39	1.91
Sweden	7.07	7.81	7.54	7.51	7.27	6.66	9.42	10.48	8.69	7.19	6.66	6.60	7.83	5.09	11.03
Switzerland	1.20	1.28	1.27	1.25	1.25	1.14	1.61	1.66	1.38	1.24	1.14	1.13	1.28	1.12	1.82
United Kingdom[2]	1.89	1.79	1.85	1.82	1.81	1.92	1.49	1.45	1.61	1.79	1.92	1.77	1.95	2.01	1.37

Table 11 *(concluded)*

	Period on Period Percent Change														
	2005 End of period		2004 End of period				End of period					12-Month High	12-Month Low	All-Time High[1]	All-Time Low[1]
	Q1	Q2	Q1	Q2	Q3	Q4	2000	2001	2002	2003	2004				
Emerging Markets															
Latin America															
Argentina	1.9	1.1	2.6	–3.4	–0.8	0.3	0.2	–0.2	–70.2	14.7	–1.4	. . .	. . .	. . .	. . .
Brazil	–0.9	14.9	–0.1	–6.1	7.8	7.7	–7.7	–15.6	–34.7	22.4	8.9	. . .	. . .	. . .	. . .
Chile	–5.2	1.4	–3.2	–3.7	4.1	9.9	–7.8	–13.2	–8.2	21.5	6.7	. . .	. . .	. . .	. . .
Colombia	–0.8	2.0	3.7	–0.5	2.8	11.2	–16.3	–1.8	–20.6	3.1	18.1	. . .	. . .	. . .	. . .
Mexico	–0.2	3.9	0.9	–3.1	0.9	2.1	–1.2	5.1	–11.7	–7.6	0.7	. . .	. . .	. . .	. . .
Peru	0.6	0.2	0.1	–0.3	3.9	1.8	–0.5	2.4	–2.0	1.5	5.6	. . .	. . .	. . .	. . .
Venezuela	–10.7	0.1	–16.7	—	—	—	–7.3	–7.7	–45.5	–13.1	–16.7	. . .	. . .	. . .	. . .
Asia															
China	—	—	—	—	—	—	—	—	—	—	—	. . .	. . .	. . .	. . .
India	–0.7	0.6	4.6	–5.3	0.2	5.7	–6.7	–3.3	0.6	5.2	5.0	. . .	. . .	. . .	. . .
Indonesia	–2.1	–3.0	–1.7	–8.9	2.7	–1.2	–26.6	–7.0	16.2	6.3	–9.2	. . .	. . .	. . .	. . .
Korea	1.9	–1.8	3.9	–0.7	0.3	11.3	–9.9	–3.7	10.8	–0.5	15.2	. . .	. . .	. . .	. . .
Malaysia	—	—	—	—	—	—	—	—	—	—	—	. . .	. . .	. . .	. . .
Pakistan	—	–0.5	–0.2	–1.2	–1.9	–0.4	–10.1	–3.8	2.8	1.7	–3.7	. . .	. . .	. . .	. . .
Philippines	2.6	–2.1	–1.2	0.1	–0.3	0.1	–19.5	–3.1	–3.7	–3.5	–1.2	. . .	. . .	. . .	. . .
Taiwan Province of China	0.7	–0.3	2.8	–2.2	–0.6	7.1	–5.1	–5.3	0.9	2.0	7.0	. . .	. . .	. . .	. . .
Thailand	–0.5	–5.3	0.8	–4.0	–1.1	6.4	–13.6	–1.9	2.6	8.8	1.8	. . .	. . .	. . .	. . .
Europe, Middle East, & Africa															
Czech Republic	–3.3	–6.7	–3.6	1.9	3.1	13.2	–3.9	4.7	18.4	16.9	14.7	. . .	. . .	. . .	. . .
Egypt	5.0	0.1	–0.5	0.1	–0.7	2.4	–11.5	–15.1	–0.9	–25.1	1.3	. . .	. . .	. . .	. . .
Hungary	–5.1	–6.5	3.5	–1.9	3.7	9.5	–10.6	2.7	22.4	7.6	15.3	. . .	. . .	. . .	. . .
Israel	–0.9	–4.7	–3.0	0.6	0.4	3.6	2.7	–8.1	–7.3	8.0	1.6	. . .	. . .	. . .	. . .
Jordan	—	0.1	–0.1	0.1	—	0.0	–0.3	0.2	–0.1	0.1	—	. . .	. . .	. . .	. . .
Morocco	–0.9	4.6	–2.9	–3.3	1.6	–4.8	–1.1	–1.7	–1.9	–2.7	–9.2	. . .	. . .	. . .	. . .
Poland	–4.7	–5.4	–3.3	4.7	5.0	16.6	0.4	4.2	3.5	2.6	24.0	. . .	. . .	. . .	. . .
Russia	–0.5	–2.7	2.5	–1.9	–0.5	5.4	–2.2	–7.7	–4.5	9.3	5.5	. . .	. . .	. . .	. . .
South Africa	–9.2	–6.2	6.2	2.5	–4.9	13.9	–18.8	–36.6	39.6	28.2	18.0	. . .	. . .	. . .	. . .
Turkey	–0.6	1.5	7.0	–11.4	–1.4	12.1	–18.6	–53.9	–12.4	17.7	4.7	. . .	. . .	. . .	. . .
Developed Markets															
Australia	–0.9	–1.4	2.0	–8.8	4.1	7.2	–14.9	–8.8	10.2	33.9	3.8	. . .	. . .	. . .	. . .
Canada	–0.7	–1.2	–0.9	–1.8	5.7	4.9	–3.5	–5.9	1.3	21.2	7.9	. . .	. . .	. . .	. . .
Denmark	–4.5	–6.6	–2.2	–0.8	1.8	9.1	–6.7	–5.1	17.9	19.8	7.8	. . .	. . .	. . .	. . .
Euro	–4.4	–6.6	–2.2	–0.9	1.9	9.0	–6.3	–5.6	18.0	20.0	7.6	. . .	. . .	. . .	. . .
Hong Kong SAR	–0.3	0.4	–0.4	–0.1	—	0.3	–0.3	—	0.0	0.4	–0.1	. . .	. . .	. . .	. . .
Japan	–4.2	–3.4	2.9	–4.2	–1.2	7.2	–10.4	–13.1	10.8	10.8	4.5	. . .	. . .	. . .	. . .
New Zealand	–0.9	–2.0	2.0	–4.8	6.5	6.0	–14.9	–6.1	25.9	25.0	9.5	. . .	. . .	. . .	. . .
Norway	–4.1	–3.0	–2.6	–1.2	3.3	10.3	–8.9	–1.8	29.2	4.1	9.6	. . .	. . .	. . .	. . .
Singapore	–1.1	–2.1	1.5	–2.5	2.0	3.2	–4.0	–6.0	6.4	2.1	4.2	. . .	. . .	. . .	. . .
Sweden	–5.9	–9.4	–4.6	0.3	3.3	9.2	–9.5	–10.2	20.6	20.9	8.0	. . .	. . .	. . .	. . .
Switzerland	–4.7	–6.6	–2.1	1.4	0.2	9.3	–1.3	–3.0	20.0	11.7	8.7	. . .	. . .	. . .	. . .
United Kingdom	–1.4	–5.2	3.4	–1.4	–0.5	5.9	–7.7	–2.6	10.7	10.9	7.4	. . .	. . .	. . .	. . .

Source: Bloomberg L.P.

[1]High value indicates value of greatest appreciation against the U.S. dollar; low value indicates value of greatest depreciation against the U.S. dollar. "All Time" refers to the period since 1990 or initiation of the currency.

[2]U.S. dollars per unit.

Table 12. Emerging Market Bond Index: EMBI Global Total Returns Index

	2005 End of Period		2004 End of Period				End of Period					12-Month High	12-Month Low	All-Time High[1]	All-Time Low[1]
	Q1	Q2	Q1	Q2	Q3	Q4	2000	2001	2002	2003	2004				
Composite	**312**	**332**	**292**	**276**	**301**	**316**	**196**	**199**	**225**	**283**	**316**	**332**	**277**	**332**	**63**
Latin America															
Argentina	77	76	74	70	74	81	183	61	57	67	81	81	71	194	47
Brazil	431	467	387	364	418	446	222	238	230	390	446	467	366	467	68
Chile	170	177	168	164	170	172	116	129	150	162	172	177	164	177	98
Colombia	221	240	216	199	216	228	115	149	169	201	228	240	199	240	70
Dominican Republic	134	148	97	85	112	126	. . .	102	117	99	126	148	85	148	83
Ecuador	580	562	523	437	519	562	177	241	230	464	562	613	436	613	61
El Salvador	124	131	119	111	119	123	. . .	. . .	98	110	123	131	111	131	95
Mexico	305	323	299	282	300	308	192	219	254	284	308	323	283	323	58
Panama	502	550	475	449	478	511	300	353	395	452	511	550	450	550	56
Peru	477	507	440	408	452	485	244	307	341	431	485	509	408	509	52
Uruguay	126	136	106	94	116	129	. . .	105	62	97	129	136	95	136	38
Venezuela	471	501	398	390	451	484	224	236	281	393	484	501	392	501	59
Asia															
China	251	261	249	240	249	253	179	203	230	241	253	261	240	261	98
Malaysia	204	214	200	191	203	207	133	150	175	194	207	214	192	214	64
Philippines	288	301	265	262	276	280	157	201	230	261	280	303	263	303	81
Thailand	187	190	188	184	188	188	138	153	174	184	188	190	184	190	75
Europe, Middle East, & Africa															
Bulgaria	626	648	594	592	616	630	372	468	525	578	630	648	593	648	80
Côte d'Ivoire	65	69	65	56	65	65	42	54	43	58	65	69	56	100	29
Egypt	149	155	145	142	147	150	. . .	103	122	140	150	155	142	155	87
Hungary	142	151	144	142	144	144	111	122	137	142	144	151	142	151	97
Lebanon	191	197	184	185	192	195	122	130	148	177	195	197	185	197	99
Morocco	272	276	264	265	268	268	199	222	237	262	268	276	265	276	73
Nigeria	653	712	618	595	638	656	267	364	376	586	656	712	597	712	66
Pakistan	106	108	160	100	105	107	. . .	122	160	160	107	109	100	160	91
Poland	312	328	306	292	309	312	221	245	280	290	312	329	292	329	71
Russia	479	523	446	417	441	475	164	256	348	426	475	523	412	523	26
South Africa	317	336	312	298	315	323	190	220	271	297	323	336	298	336	99
Tunisia	136	145	134	127	135	138	. . .	. . .	112	127	138	145	127	145	98
Turkey	300	318	290	261	294	307	144	176	213	279	307	318	263	318	91
Ukraine	317	328	295	281	294	310	127	199	241	289	310	328	279	328	100
Latin	279	298	259	244	271	285	202	177	189	252	285	298	245	298	62
Non-Latin	373	397	355	337	359	374	186	240	291	342	374	397	338	397	72

Table 12 *(concluded)*

	Period on Period Percent Change														
	2005 End of period		2004 End of period				End of period					12-Month High	12-Month Low	All-Time High[1]	All-Time Low[1]
	Q1	Q2	Q1	Q2	Q3	Q4	2000	2001	2002	2003	2004				
Composite	**−1.3**	**6.5**	**3.4**	**−5.5**	**9.0**	**4.9**	**14.4**	**1.4**	**13.1**	**25.7**	**11.7**	. . .	. . .	. . .	. . .
Latin America															
Argentina	−5.3	−0.7	9.2	−4.9	5.0	9.8	7.8	−66.9	−6.4	19.1	19.8	. . .	. . .	. . .	. . .
Brazil	−3.4	8.2	−0.9	−5.8	14.9	6.7	13.0	7.3	−3.6	69.8	14.3	. . .	. . .	. . .	. . .
Chile	−1.1	4.0	3.5	−2.6	3.7	1.3	12.2	11.7	15.8	8.3	6.0	. . .	. . .	. . .	. . .
Colombia	−3.1	8.7	7.1	−7.6	8.5	5.3	3.0	29.5	13.3	19.4	13.2	. . .	. . .	. . .	. . .
Dominican Republic	6.4	10.4	−2.0	−11.9	31.7	11.8	. . .	. . .	13.9	−15.3	27.2	. . .	. . .	. . .	. . .
Ecuador	3.3	−3.1	12.9	−16.4	18.7	8.2	53.9	36.1	−4.7	101.5	21.1	. . .	. . .	. . .	. . .
El Salvador	1.4	5.1	7.9	−6.3	6.6	3.4	. . .	. . .	. . .	11.9	11.5	. . .	. . .	. . .	. . .
Mexico	−1.0	6.1	5.3	−5.6	6.4	2.7	17.5	14.3	16.1	11.6	8.6	. . .	. . .	. . .	. . .
Panama	−1.6	9.5	5.2	−5.5	6.4	6.8	8.3	17.6	11.9	14.4	13.0	. . .	. . .	. . .	. . .
Peru	−1.8	6.3	2.0	−7.1	10.7	7.4	0.2	26.2	10.8	26.6	12.6	. . .	. . .	. . .	. . .
Uruguay	−2.5	8.0	10.2	−11.9	24.2	11.2	. . .	. . .	−40.6	55.6	34.0	. . .	. . .	. . .	. . .
Venezuela	−2.7	6.3	1.4	−2.1	15.6	7.3	16.0	5.6	18.9	39.9	23.2	. . .	. . .	. . .	. . .
Asia															
China	−0.8	4.0	3.3	−3.6	4.0	1.4	12.1	13.3	13.6	4.5	5.1	. . .	. . .	. . .	. . .
Malaysia	−1.5	4.8	3.2	−4.5	5.9	2.1	11.6	12.9	16.9	10.7	6.6	. . .	. . .	. . .	. . .
Philippines	2.9	4.6	1.4	−0.9	5.2	1.3	−2.9	27.6	14.6	13.4	7.1	. . .	. . .	. . .	. . .
Thailand	−0.2	1.6	2.2	−2.2	1.9	0.2	14.3	11.3	13.5	5.9	2.0	. . .	. . .	. . .	. . .
Europe, Middle East, & Africa															
Bulgaria	−0.6	3.5	2.6	−0.3	4.0	2.2	5.1	25.7	12.2	10.2	8.9	. . .	. . .	. . .	. . .
Côte d'Ivoire	−1.4	7.2	12.9	−14.3	16.7	. . .	−20.2	30.5	−20.7	34.8	12.9	. . .	. . .	. . .	. . .
Egypt	−0.3	3.6	3.8	−2.2	3.2	1.9	. . .	. . .	18.5	14.4	6.8	. . .	. . .	. . .	. . .
Hungary	−1.2	6.1	1.4	−1.5	1.5	−0.1	9.8	10.4	12.3	3.7	1.2	. . .	. . .	. . .	. . .
Lebanon	−2.0	3.2	3.8	0.8	3.8	1.3	8.9	6.2	14.1	19.5	9.9	. . .	. . .	. . .	. . .
Morocco	1.3	1.6	0.7	0.4	1.1	0.1	5.5	11.1	7.2	10.2	2.4	. . .	. . .	. . .	. . .
Nigeria	−0.5	9.1	5.4	−3.6	7.2	2.8	5.3	36.3	3.3	55.8	11.9	. . .	. . .	. . .	. . .
Pakistan	−0.3	2.0	. . .	−37.7	5.0	1.9	. . .	. . .	31.3	−0.2	−33.3	. . .	. . .	. . .	. . .
Poland	. . .	5.3	5.4	−4.5	5.9	1.0	15.9	10.6	14.2	3.7	7.5	. . .	. . .	. . .	. . .
Russia	0.9	9.2	4.7	−6.5	5.8	7.6	54.9	55.8	35.9	22.4	11.5	. . .	. . .	. . .	. . .
South Africa	−1.8	5.9	4.9	−4.4	5.5	2.8	8.5	16.2	22.9	9.6	8.8	. . .	. . .	. . .	. . .
Tunisia	−1.4	6.2	5.1	−4.7	5.8	2.7	. . .	. . .	. . .	13.3	8.7	. . .	. . .	. . .	. . .
Turkey	−2.3	6.0	4.2	−10.1	12.7	4.3	1.1	22.5	21.1	30.8	10.0	. . .	. . .	. . .	. . .
Ukraine	2.3	3.5	2.2	−5.0	4.8	5.3	. . .	57.1	21.0	19.8	7.2	. . .	. . .	. . .	. . .
Latin	−2.1	6.6	3.1	−5.9	10.9	5.4	12.5	−12.4	6.8	33.0	13.4	. . .	. . .	. . .	. . .
Non-Latin	−0.1	6.3	3.8	−5.0	6.5	4.1	18.2	28.8	21.0	17.7	9.2	. . .	. . .	. . .	. . .

Source: JPMorgan Chase & Co.
[1]From 1990 or initiation of the index.

Table 13. Emerging Market Bond Index: EMBI Global Yield Spreads

	2005 End of Period		2004 End of Period				End of Period					12-Month	12-Month	All-Time	All-Time
	Q1	Q2	Q1	Q2	Q3	Q4	2000	2001	2002	2003	2004	High	Low	High[1]	Low[1]
Composite[2]	**374**	**297**	**414**	**482**	**409**	**347**	**735**	**728**	**725**	**403**	**347**	**483**	**297**	**1,631**	**297**
Latin America															
Argentina[2]	5,075	462	4,840	5,087	5,389	4,527	770	5,363	6,342	5,485	4,527	6,194	462	7,222	381
Brazil	458	409	554	646	466	376	748	864	1,460	459	376	644	372	2,451	372
Chile	71	60	91	83	78	64	220	175	176	90	64	87	57	260	57
Colombia	407	331	379	483	407	332	755	508	633	427	332	491	323	1,076	261
Dominican Republic	679	441	1,338	1,730	1,079	824	...	446	499	1,141	824	1,750	433	1,750	304
Ecuador	677	808	701	952	778	690	1,415	1,233	1,801	799	690	960	592	4,764	592
El Salvador	242	261	255	274	276	245	...	...	411	284	245	299	221	434	217
Mexico	191	181	184	218	189	174	391	306	329	201	174	217	152	1,149	152
Panama	301	258	334	365	351	274	501	404	446	324	274	369	236	769	236
Peru	288	252	355	450	340	239	687	521	609	325	239	456	229	1,061	229
Uruguay	430	406	576	710	497	388	...	284	1,228	636	388	705	340	1,982	251
Venezuela	454	460	647	643	490	403	958	1,130	1,131	586	403	640	388	2,658	388
Asia															
China	53	54	65	67	75	57	160	99	84	58	57	76	47	364	39
Malaysia	95	86	113	129	104	78	237	207	212	100	78	129	76	1,141	76
Philippines	431	450	480	448	456	457	644	466	522	415	457	508	385	993	300
Thailand	48	48	69	76	64	61	173	132	128	67	61	98	31	951	31
Europe, Middle East, & Africa															
Bulgaria	87	84	165	137	115	77	772	433	291	177	77	138	62	1,679	62
Côte d'Ivoire	3,158	3,218	2,798	3,273	2,955	3,121	2,443	2,418	3,195	3,013	3,121	3,408	2,941	3,408	582
Egypt	63	79	133	130	127	101	...	360	325	131	101	150	47	646	47
Hungary	61	60	29	44	10	32	136	93	52	28	32	69	–2	196	–29
Lebanon	297	379	400	346	332	334	338	645	776	421	334	415	292	1,082	111
Morocco	186	144	164	168	165	170	584	518	390	160	170	201	131	1,606	128
Nigeria	501	389	504	591	491	457	1,807	1,103	1,946	499	457	598	389	2,937	389
Pakistan	204	229	289	313	270	233	...	1,115	271	289	233	323	197	2,225	0
Poland	48	58	72	72	64	69	241	195	185	76	69	78	39	410	17
Russia	209	162	256	304	298	213	1,172	669	478	257	213	330	160	7,063	160
South Africa	126	93	135	168	143	102	418	319	250	152	102	172	85	757	85
Tunisia	107	67	132	144	115	91	...	...	273	146	91	155	48	394	48
Turkey	311	295	316	465	323	264	803	702	696	309	264	457	236	1,196	236
Ukraine	214	204	294	358	333	255	1,953	940	671	258	255	393	167	2,314	167
Latin	463	337	531	600	492	415	702	888	981	518	415	599	337	1,532	337
Non-Latin	246	234	257	316	289	239	791	523	444	248	239	322	209	1,812	209

Table 13 *(concluded)*

	Period on Period Percent Change														
	2005 End of period		2004 End of period				End of period					12-Month	12-Month	All-Time	All-Time
	Q1	Q2	Q1	Q2	Q3	Q4	2000	2001	2002	2003	2004	High	Low	High[1]	Low[1]
Composite[2]	**27**	**−77**	**11**	**68**	**−73**	**−62**	**−16**	**−7**	**−3**	**−322**	**−56**	**. . .**	**. . .**	**. . .**	**. . .**
Latin America															
Argentina[2]	548	−4,613	−645	247	302	−862	237	4,593	979	−857	−958	. . .	. . .	. . .	. . .
Brazil	82	−49	95	92	−180	−90	110	116	596	−1,001	−83	. . .	. . .	. . .	. . .
Chile	7	−11	1	−8	−5	−14	81	−45	1	−86	−26	. . .	. . .	. . .	. . .
Colombia	75	−76	−48	104	−76	−75	339	−247	125	−206	−95	. . .	. . .	. . .	. . .
Dominican Republic	−145	−238	197	392	−651	−255	. . .	. . .	53	642	−317	. . .	. . .	. . .	. . .
Ecuador	−13	131	−98	251	−174	−88	−1,938	−182	568	−1,002	−109	. . .	. . .	. . .	. . .
El Salvador	−3	19	−29	19	2	−31	. . .	. . .	. . .	−127	−39	. . .	. . .	. . .	. . .
Mexico	17	−10	−17	34	−29	−15	30	−85	23	−128	−27	. . .	. . .	. . .	. . .
Panama	27	−43	10	31	−14	−77	91	−97	42	−122	−50	. . .	. . .	. . .	. . .
Peru	49	−36	30	95	−110	−101	244	−166	88	−284	−86	. . .	. . .	. . .	. . .
Uruguay	42	−24	−60	134	−213	−109	. . .	. . .	944	−592	−248	. . .	. . .	. . .	. . .
Venezuela	51	6	61	−4	−153	−87	90	172	1	−545	−183	. . .	. . .	. . .	. . .
Asia															
China	−4	1	7	2	8	−18	35	−61	−15	−26	−1	. . .	. . .	. . .	. . .
Malaysia	17	−9	13	16	−25	−26	65	−30	5	−112	−22	. . .	. . .	. . .	. . .
Philippines	−26	19	65	−32	8	1	334	−178	56	−107	42	. . .	. . .	. . .	. . .
Thailand	−13	0	2	7	−12	−3	9	−41	−4	−61	−6	. . .	. . .	. . .	. . .
Europe, Middle East, & Africa															
Bulgaria	10	−3	−12	−28	−22	−38	146	−339	−142	−114	−100	. . .	. . .	. . .	. . .
Côte d'Ivoire	37	60	−215	475	−318	166	1,051	−25	777	−182	108	. . .	. . .	. . .	. . .
Egypt	−38	16	2	−3	−3	−26	. . .	. . .	−35	−194	−30	. . .	. . .	. . .	. . .
Hungary	29	−1	1	15	−34	22	19	−43	−41	−24	4	. . .	. . .	. . .	. . .
Lebanon	−37	82	−21	−54	−14	2	119	307	131	−355	−87	. . .	. . .	. . .	. . .
Morocco	16	−42	4	4	−3	5	204	−66	−128	−230	10	. . .	. . .	. . .	. . .
Nigeria	44	−112	5	87	−100	−34	770	−704	843	−1,447	−42	. . .	. . .	. . .	. . .
Pakistan	−29	25	0	24	−43	−37	. . .	. . .	−844	18	−56	. . .	. . .	. . .	. . .
Poland	−21	10	−4	0	−8	5	29	−46	−10	−109	−7	. . .	. . .	. . .	. . .
Russia	−4	−47	−1	48	−6	−85	−1,260	−503	−191	−221	−44	. . .	. . .	. . .	. . .
South Africa	24	−33	−17	33	−25	−41	141	−99	−69	−98	−50	. . .	. . .	. . .	. . .
Tunisia	16	−40	−14	12	−29	−24	. . .	. . .	. . .	−127	−55	. . .	. . .	. . .	. . .
Turkey	47	−16	7	149	−142	−59	360	−101	−6	−387	−45	. . .	. . .	. . .	. . .
Ukraine	−41	−10	36	64	−25	−78	. . .	−1,013	−269	−413	−3	. . .	. . .	. . .	. . .
Latin	48	−126	13	69	−108	−77	104	186	93	−463	−103	. . .	. . .	. . .	. . .
Non-Latin	7	−12	9	59	−27	−50	−222	−268	−79	−196	−9	. . .	. . .	. . .	. . .

Source: JPMorgan Chase & Co.
[1]From 1990 or initiation of the index.
[2]With the completion of Argentina's debt restructuring, JPMorgan Chase & Co. rebalanced its family of emerging market bond indices in June; defaulted Argentine securities were replaced by performing ones.

Table 14. Emerging Market External Financing: Total Bonds, Equities, and Loans
(In millions of U.S. dollars)

							2004		2005	
	1999	2000	2001	2002	2003	2004	Q3	Q4	Q1	Q2
Total	**163,569.6**	**216,402.7**	**162,137.7**	**147,295.6**	**199,265.6**	**290,820.1**	**65,767.3**	**84,662.4**	**69,352.9**	**81,107.3**
Africa	**4,707.2**	**9,382.8**	**6,992.3**	**7,019.0**	**12,306.3**	**11,608.1**	**5,441.1**	**1,332.4**	**950.4**	**1,999.0**
Algeria	. . .	. . .	50.0	150.0	75.0	271.7	105.9	. . .	. . .	. . .
Angola	. . .	. . .	455.0	350.0	1,542.0	2,900.0	2,350.0	. . .	8.7	. . .
Botswana	. . .	. . .	22.5	. . .	. . .	. . .	. . .	. . .	. . .	. . .
Burkina Faso	. . .	. . .	. . .	. . .	. . .	. . .	. . .	. . .	11.0	. . .
Cameroon	. . .	. . .	53.8	. . .	100.0	. . .	. . .	. . .	. . .	. . .
Chad	. . .	. . .	400.0	. . .	. . .	. . .	. . .	. . .	. . .	. . .
Congo, Dem. Rep. of	. . .	20.8	. . .	. . .	. . .	. . .	. . .	. . .	. . .	. . .
Côte d'Ivoire	179.0	. . .	15.0	. . .	. . .	100.0	100.0	. . .	. . .	. . .
Djibouti	. . .	. . .	. . .	. . .	. . .	40.0	. . .	40.0	. . .	. . .
Ethiopia	. . .	. . .	. . .	. . .	. . .	40.0	40.0	. . .	. . .	. . .
Gabon	. . .	. . .	. . .	. . .	. . .	22.0	. . .	22.0	. . .	. . .
Ghana	30.0	320.0	300.0	420.0	650.0	870.0	870.0	. . .	. . .	. . .
Guinea	. . .	. . .	. . .	. . .	. . .	70.0	70.0	. . .	. . .	. . .
Kenya	. . .	7.5	80.2	. . .	134.0	135.1	61.5	73.5	. . .	. . .
Malawi	. . .	. . .	. . .	. . .	. . .	4.8	. . .	. . .	. . .	. . .
Mali	. . .	. . .	. . .	150.4	287.6	288.9	. . .	288.9	. . .	. . .
Mauritius	160.0	. . .	. . .	. . .	. . .	. . .	. . .	. . .	. . .	. . .
Morocco	322.2	56.4	136.1	. . .	474.7	1,615.3	464.5	. . .	. . .	580.6
Mozambique	. . .	. . .	200.0	. . .	35.5	222.4	. . .	. . .	. . .	. . .
Namibia	. . .	. . .	. . .	. . .	35.0	. . .	. . .	. . .	. . .	50.0
Niger	. . .	. . .	. . .	. . .	27.0	. . .	. . .	. . .	. . .	. . .
Nigeria	90.0	. . .	100.0	960.0	593.0	225.0	195.0	. . .	77.2	. . .
Senegal	. . .	. . .	. . .	40.0	. . .	. . .	. . .	. . .	. . .	. . .
Seychelles	. . .	50.0	. . .	150.0	. . .	80.0	. . .	. . .	. . .	. . .
South Africa	3,423.4	8,698.8	4,646.7	4,058.1	7,837.4	3,798.5	1,184.2	558.1	762.3	877.5
Sudan	. . .	. . .	. . .	. . .	. . .	. . .	. . .	. . .	. . .	. . .
Tanzania	. . .	135.0	. . .	. . .	. . .	. . .	. . .	. . .	. . .	. . .
Tunisia	352.6	94.3	533.0	740.5	485.2	924.4	. . .	349.9	91.2	490.9
Zambia	. . .	. . .	. . .	. . .	30.0	. . .	. . .	. . .	. . .	. . .
Zimbabwe	150.0	. . .	. . .	. . .	. . .	. . .	. . .	. . .	. . .	. . .
Asia	**55,958.6**	**85,881.0**	**67,483.4**	**67,201.3**	**87,968.3**	**136,609.3**	**29,516.9**	**40,141.7**	**29,912.3**	**35,416.2**
Bangladesh	. . .	. . .	. . .	. . .	. . .	176.8	. . .	176.8	. . .	. . .
Brunei	. . .	. . .	. . .	129.0	. . .	. . .	. . .	. . .	. . .	. . .
China	3,461.8	23,063.4	5,567.3	8,891.6	13,589.8	23,881.9	3,104.5	6,023.7	3,760.3	9,003.2
Hong Kong SAR	11,488.3	21,046.4	18,307.3	12,602.1	9,055.7	19,142.0	4,246.4	8,737.7	5,376.0	3,477.7
India	2,376.2	2,224.2	2,382.2	1,380.8	4,094.1	12,921.9	2,951.9	3,396.5	3,887.9	4,240.1
Indonesia	1,465.3	1,283.1	964.9	974.0	5,109.9	3,636.1	175.0	1,208.0	172.5	1,157.9
Korea	13,542.3	14,230.4	17,021.0	14,693.5	17,237.0	26,469.9	7,399.9	7,591.7	7,708.5	8,865.2
Lao P.D.R.	. . .	. . .	. . .	71.4	. . .	210.0	. . .	140.0	. . .	1,000.0
Macao SAR	. . .	29.5	. . .	. . .	. . .	357.0	357.0	. . .	. . .	. . .
Malaysia	5,177.2	4,506.4	4,432.4	5,597.3	5,729.2	7,731.0	1,190.6	2,055.9	1,770.9	1,258.6
Marshall Islands	. . .	. . .	. . .	34.7	. . .	. . .	. . .	. . .	. . .	. . .
Mongolia	. . .	. . .	. . .	. . .	. . .	. . .	. . .	. . .	30.0	. . .
Pakistan	. . .	. . .	182.5	289.1	9.3	800.0	. . .	. . .	286.2	417.8
Papua New Guinea	232.4	. . .	. . .	. . .	153.7	. . .	. . .	. . .	. . .	. . .
Philippines	7,181.7	5,021.9	3,658.8	5,458.1	5,453.5	6,227.0	2,136.6	293.2	2,385.8	750.0
Singapore	4,338.7	6,079.7	10,383.6	3,810.0	6,792.7	9,971.1	3,221.1	3,457.4	1,147.6	1,414.5
Sri Lanka	23.0	100.0	105.0	. . .	186.0	135.0	. . .	100.0	. . .	. . .
Taiwan Province of China	4,019.9	6,703.5	3,794.0	10,959.3	18,149.3	20,952.9	4,095.2	5,717.7	2,654.4	2,229.8
Thailand	2,551.7	1,572.5	684.4	1,927.0	2,357.2	3,882.7	524.7	1,243.1	732.2	1,556.1
Vietnam	100.0	20.0	. . .	383.5	51.0	114.0	114.0	. . .	. . .	45.3
Europe	**26,191.5**	**37,021.7**	**22,787.7**	**29,566.9**	**47,854.8**	**68,105.3**	**11,592.2**	**23,591.5**	**13,677.7**	**20,863.9**
Azerbaijan	77.2	. . .	16.0	. . .	. . .	2,070.4	997.0	18.2	41.0	20.7
Belarus	. . .	. . .	. . .	. . .	36.0	21.4	. . .	. . .	. . .	21.4
Bulgaria	53.9	8.9	242.3	1,260.8	381.3	1,667.6	19.7	788.4	29.5	318.4
Croatia	1,504.9	1,498.7	1,766.0	1,425.4	2,026.0	1,267.7	149.2	439.3	570.8	506.1
Cyprus	288.5	86.3	633.0	547.9	648.2	. . .	. . .	. . .	. . .	. . .
Czech Republic	540.3	127.1	564.6	453.4	4,349.5	1,322.0	346.9	355.7	235.9	292.6
Estonia	289.2	412.7	202.1	292.6	507.7	257.8	. . .	128.9	. . .	66.4
Georgia	. . .	. . .	. . .	. . .	6.0	. . .	. . .	. . .	. . .	. . .
Gibraltar	65.0	80.0	. . .	. . .	. . .	. . .	. . .	. . .	. . .	. . .
Hungary	3,471.2	1,308.8	1,364.7	1,040.2	3,774.8	4,196.2	442.1	1,658.0	. . .	1,698.9

Table 14 *(concluded)*

	1999	2000	2001	2002	2003	2004	2004 Q3	2004 Q4	2005 Q1	2005 Q2
Europe *(continued)*										
Kazakhstan	417.0	429.6	573.5	743.5	1,535.0	3,897.2	906.0	997.2	1,164.8	1,453.0
Kyrgyz Republic	. . .	. . .	. . .	95.0	. . .	. . .	. . .	. . .	. . .	. . .
Latvia	288.9	23.0	212.1	74.6	70.7	706.4	145.0	208.3	235.9	275.9
Lithuania	959.7	683.8	247.3	374.3	431.7	155.0	. . .	72.5	386.1	72.5
Macedonia	. . .	. . .	. . .	. . .	47.6	110.1	10.3	17.4	. . .	82.5
Malta	57.0	. . .	85.0	. . .	114.7	392.7	150.0	242.7	. . .	. . .
Moldova	40.0	. . .	. . .	. . .	. . .	7.0	. . .	. . .	2.0	5.0
Poland	3,780.7	5,252.9	4,836.6	5,913.2	7,818.1	1,948.6	443.8	831.7	136.8	752.0
Romania	176.0	594.4	1,347.2	1,442.2	1,828.2	1,693.9	404.4	345.3	781.4	123.0
Russia	166.8	3,950.7	3,200.1	8,496.0	12,081.2	29,116.7	4,227.9	11,316.1	6,237.1	9,727.8
Serbia and Montenegro	. . .	. . .	. . .	19.4	10.9	. . .	. . .	. . .	. . .	. . .
Slovak Republic	994.7	1,466.7	219.9	143.1	940.6	247.3	30.5	86.5	30.5	135.2
Slovenia	687.7	672.7	827.2	309.3	394.8	2,756.3	717.7	658.3	807.5	204.4
Tajikistan	. . .	. . .	. . .	. . .	. . .	1.2	. . .	. . .	1.2	. . .
Turkey	11,900.0	20,385.4	6,405.1	6,376.0	9,413.0	15,830.1	2,538.8	5,350.0	2,667.1	4,936.9
Ukraine	290.7	. . .	15.0	514.0	1,400.0	411.8	63.0	66.9	346.6	156.8
Uzbekistan	142.0	40.0	30.0	46.0	38.7	28.0	. . .	10.0	3.6	14.3
Middle East	**15,387.4**	**14,999.7**	**11,020.3**	**10,685.4**	**8,368.1**	**21,434.1**	**3,092.0**	**6,500.1**	**7,491.3**	**11,546.5**
Bahrain	361.1	1,391.0	207.0	665.0	1,800.0	1,767.0	442.0	1,075.0	220.0	1,539.7
Egypt	1,533.7	919.4	2,545.0	670.0	155.0	1,138.7	. . .	221.0	150.0	217.3
Iran, I.R. of	692.0	757.7	887.0	2,666.4	700.0	1,942.7	39.9	225.9	1,255.2	. . .
Iraq	. . .	. . .	. . .	. . .	. . .	. . .	. . .	. . .	107.8	. . .
Israel	3,719.0	2,908.5	1,602.6	344.4	750.0	3,514.0	341.1	1,150.1	954.6	81.8
Jordan	. . .	60.0	. . .	80.9	. . .	199.4	. . .	199.4	. . .	. . .
Kuwait	147.5	250.0	770.0	750.0	365.0	1,282.5	157.5	825.0	220.0	3,325.0
Lebanon	1,421.4	1,752.4	3,300.0	990.0	160.0	3,263.5	620.5	1,375.0	. . .	500.0
Libya	. . .	50.0	. . .	. . .	. . .	. . .	. . .	. . .	. . .	. . .
Oman	356.8	685.0	. . .	2,332.0	907.8	1,328.6	175.0	455.0	753.0	1,460.0
Qatar	2,000.0	1,980.0	913.0	1,536.7	880.8	2,042.7	. . .	198.7	. . .	722.0
Saudi Arabia	4,374.8	2,200.9	275.0	280.0	569.5	2,214.0	816.0	600.0	950.0	2,004.0
United Arab Emirates	781.0	2,045.0	520.7	370.0	2,080.0	2,741.0	500.0	175.0	2,880.7	1,696.7
Latin America	**61,324.9**	**69,117.6**	**53,854.0**	**32,823.0**	**42,768.1**	**53,063.4**	**16,125.1**	**13,096.7**	**17,321.2**	**11,281.7**
Argentina	17,844.4	16,648.5	3,423.9	824.2	160.0	1,771.4	. . .	506.0	150.0	135.0
Bolivia	. . .	. . .	20.0	90.0	. . .	116.0	. . .	116.0	100.0	. . .
Brazil	12,951.9	23,238.2	19,532.9	10,925.6	12,001.2	15,593.6	5,062.5	2,625.8	4,509.8	3,380.6
Chile	8,031.7	5,782.5	3,935.3	2,959.6	4,699.0	6,439.8	1,535.9	3,134.7	396.1	1,098.5
Colombia	3,555.8	3,093.2	4,895.0	2,096.0	1,911.3	1,543.8	500.0	543.8	517.1	335.0
Costa Rica	300.0	250.0	400.0	250.0	490.0	310.0	. . .	. . .	. . .	25.5
Dominican Republic	. . .	74.0	500.0	. . .	600.0	69.8	. . .	. . .	1.9	. . .
Ecuador	. . .	. . .	31.1	258.0	70.4	140.5	101.0	. . .	9.1	. . .
El Salvador	223.0	50.0	1,263.5	1,261.5	348.5	286.5	286.5	. . .	25.0	375.0
Grenada	166.5	110.0	135.0	. . .	32.5	180.5	140.5	40.0	. . .	. . .
Guadeloupe	. . .	. . .	. . .	17.4	. . .	. . .	. . .	. . .	. . .	. . .
Guatemala	222.0	505.0	325.0	44.0	300.0	439.3	330.0	50.0	. . .	. . .
Honduras	. . .	. . .	. . .	. . .	. . .	169.0	169.0	. . .	. . .	. . .
Jamaica	. . .	421.0	726.5	345.0	49.6	903.2	344.1	186.2	208.1	500.0
Mexico	14,099.5	15,313.4	13,823.5	10,040.6	16,992.3	18,788.2	6,040.6	4,114.4	9,576.6	3,327.9
Nicaragua	. . .	. . .	. . .	. . .	. . .	22.0	. . .	. . .	. . .	. . .
Paraguay	55.0	. . .	70.0	. . .	. . .	. . .	. . .	. . .	. . .	. . .
Peru	1,618.4	465.4	137.5	1,993.0	1,375.0	1,475.7	. . .	805.7	400.0	. . .
St. Lucia	. . .	. . .	. . .	. . .	20.0	. . .	. . .	. . .	. . .	. . .
Trinidad and Tobago	230.0	301.0	70.0	303.0	46.0	415.0	115.0	200.0	100.0	. . .
Uruguay	465.0	602.1	1,147.4	400.0	. . .	. . .	. . .	. . .	. . .	500.0
Venezuela	1,561.7	2,263.3	3,417.5	1,015.0	3,672.5	4,399.1	1,500.0	774.1	1,327.5	1,604.2

Source: Data provided by the Bond, Equity and Loan database of the International Monetary Fund sourced from Dealogic.

Table 15. Emerging Market External Financing: Bond Issuance

(In millions of U.S. dollars)

							2004		2005	
	1999	2000	2001	2002	2003	2004	Q3	Q4	Q1	Q2
Developing Countries	**82,359.4**	**80,475.4**	**89,036.9**	**61,647.4**	**98,777.6**	**128,097.8**	**31,415.5**	**34,856.7**	**27,041.7**	**29,073.7**
Africa	**2,345.5**	**1,485.8**	**2,109.6**	**2,161.1**	**5,511.9**	**2,495.4**	**214.7**	**. . .**	**493.2**	**1,368.4**
Mauritius	160.0	. . .	. . .	. . .	. . .	. . .	. . .	. . .	. . .	. . .
Morocco	151.5	. . .	. . .	. . .	464.9	. . .	. . .	. . .	. . .	. . .
South Africa	1,804.7	1,485.8	1,647.7	1,511.1	4,690.0	1,950.9	214.7	. . .	493.2	877.5
Tunisia	229.3	. . .	462.0	650.0	357.0	544.5	. . .	. . .	. . .	490.9
Asia	**23,424.7**	**24,501.4**	**35,869.2**	**22,532.7**	**35,778.8**	**52,425.7**	**13,921.8**	**12,673.5**	**11,138.2**	**10,528.8**
China	1,060.0	1,770.7	2,341.9	602.8	2,034.2	4,575.3	2,442.8	2,093.8	. . .	1,208.3
Hong Kong SAR	7,124.8	7,058.9	10,458.6	1,951.6	2,625.6	4,209.4	1,775.6	1,262.8	2,930.8	471.4
India	100.0	100.0	99.3	153.0	450.0	4,452.1	814.0	1,775.0	1,018.1	605.0
Indonesia	. . .	. . .	125.0	375.0	609.0	1,363.5	. . .	38.2	. . .	1,000.0
Korea	4,905.8	7,653.0	7,756.3	6,705.5	11,531.3	16,965.5	3,490.5	4,233.4	4,238.3	4,161.4
Malaysia	2,062.4	1,419.7	2,150.0	1,880.0	962.5	2,514.5	125.0	414.5	503.1	400.0
Pakistan	. . .	. . .	. . .	. . .	. . .	500.0	. . .	. . .	. . .	. . .
Philippines	4,751.2	2,467.3	1,842.4	4,773.8	3,799.6	4,458.1	1,658.1	. . .	1,750.0	750.0
Singapore	2,147.1	2,333.8	8,664.7	562.1	4,336.8	4,627.6	2,616.8	1,110.1	167.9	435.1
Sri Lanka	. . .	. . .	. . .	. . .	. . .	100.0	. . .	100.0	. . .	. . .
Taiwan Province of China	475.0	1,698.0	2,152.4	5,480.8	9,129.7	7,259.7	599.0	1,645.7	380.0	405.0
Thailand	798.4	. . .	278.6	48.0	300.0	1,400.0	400.0	. . .	150.0	1,092.6
Europe	**13,872.8**	**14,202.5**	**11,558.6**	**14,997.0**	**24,411.4**	**30,785.5**	**8,186.1**	**12,125.0**	**3,443.9**	**6,312.3**
Azerbaijan	. . .	. . .	. . .	. . .	. . .	1,005.0	. . .	8.0	. . .	3.5
Bulgaria	53.9	. . .	223.4	1,247.8	. . .	808.1	19.7	247.9	. . .	29.0
Croatia	601.2	858.0	934.0	847.5	983.6	588.6	149.2	439.3	197.7	200.1
Cyprus	288.5	. . .	480.5	479.8	648.2	. . .	. . .	. . .	. . .	. . .
Czech Republic	421.7	. . .	50.7	428.4	3,168.4	956.5	346.9	355.7	235.9	. . .
Estonia	84.9	335.7	65.5	292.6	323.3	128.9	. . .	. . .	. . .	. . .
Hungary	2,410.5	540.8	1,247.8	70.5	2,211.4	1,498.8	197.8	490.4	. . .	763.1
Kazakhstan	300.0	350.0	250.0	209.0	100.0	1,868.2	766.8	878.2	317.0	530.0
Latvia	236.7	. . .	180.8	. . .	. . .	353.2	145.0	160.0	90.9	115.9
Lithuania	531.5	376.2	222.4	355.6	431.7	72.5	. . .	72.5	376.1	. . .
Macedonia	. . .	. . .	. . .	. . .	. . .	17.4	. . .	17.4	. . .	. . .
Poland	1,652.6	1,553.5	2,773.7	2,679.9	4,301.2	541.4	. . .	36.0	. . .	309.3
Romania	. . .	259.5	908.6	1,062.2	813.6	847.0	159.7	63.8	577.6	6.1
Russia	. . .	75.0	1,352.7	3,391.5	4,005.0	12,937.0	3,480.9	4,719.7	900.8	3,595.0
Slovak Republic	800.2	978.3	219.9	143.1	861.3	117.0	30.5	50.0	. . .	71.9
Slovenia	439.1	384.7	490.0	30.2	. . .	1,364.5	641.5	51.6	153.9	149.1
Turkey	5,761.2	8,490.8	2,158.7	3,259.8	5,253.8	7,561.5	2,185.1	4,477.6	472.4	459.3
Ukraine	290.7	. . .	. . .	499.0	1,310.0	119.9	63.0	56.9	121.6	80.0
Middle East	**4,409.8**	**4,670.6**	**5,920.7**	**3,706.6**	**1,860.0**	**9,035.5**	**620.5**	**2,937.0**	**1,675.0**	**2,399.7**
Bahrain	209.1	188.5	. . .	325.0	750.0	292.0	. . .	42.0	. . .	399.7
Egypt	100.0	. . .	1,500.0	. . .	. . .	. . .	. . .	. . .	. . .	. . .
Iran, I.R. of	. . .	. . .	. . .	986.3	. . .	. . .	. . .	. . .	. . .	. . .
Israel	1,679.2	1,329.7	1,120.7	344.4	750.0	2,520.0	. . .	875.0	. . .	. . .
Jordan	. . .	. . .	. . .	80.9	. . .	145.0	. . .	145.0	. . .	. . .
Kuwait	. . .	. . .	. . .	750.0	200.0	500.0	. . .	500.0	. . .	500.0
Lebanon	1,421.4	1,752.4	3,300.0	990.0	160.0	3,263.5	620.5	1,375.0	. . .	500.0
Oman	. . .	. . .	. . .	. . .	. . .	250.0	. . .	. . .	. . .	. . .
Qatar	1,000.0	1,400.0	. . .	. . .	. . .	665.0	. . .	. . .	. . .	. . .
Saudi Arabia	. . .	. . .	. . .	. . .	. . .	. . .	. . .	. . .	600.0	. . .
United Arab Emirates	. . .	. . .	. . .	230.0	. . .	1,400.0	. . .	. . .	1,075.0	1,000.0
Latin America	**38,306.7**	**35,615.2**	**33,578.8**	**18,250.0**	**31,215.5**	**33,355.7**	**8,472.4**	**7,121.2**	**10,291.4**	**8,464.5**
Argentina	14,182.8	13,024.8	1,500.5	. . .	100.0	1,115.4	. . .	100.0	150.0	. . .
Brazil	8,585.8	11,382.1	12,238.8	6,375.5	10,709.9	9,528.4	3,288.1	1,755.5	3,489.8	2,565.3
Chile	1,763.8	679.7	1,536.0	1,728.9	2,900.0	2,350.0	. . .	1,200.0	. . .	400.0
Colombia	1,675.6	1,547.2	4,263.3	1,000.0	1,765.0	1,543.8	500.0	543.8	447.1	335.0
Costa Rica	300.0	250.0	250.0	250.0	490.0	310.0	. . .	. . .	. . .	. . .
Dominican Republic	. . .	. . .	500.0	. . .	600.0	. . .	. . .	. . .	. . .	. . .
El Salvador	150.0	50.0	353.5	1,251.5	348.5	286.5	286.5	. . .	. . .	375.0
Grenada	. . .	. . .	. . .	100.0	. . .	. . .	. . .	. . .	. . .	. . .
Guatemala	. . .	. . .	325.0	. . .	300.0	380.0	330.0	. . .	. . .	. . .
Jamaica	. . .	421.0	690.7	300.0	. . .	806.9	247.8	186.2	. . .	500.0
Mexico	9,854.0	7,078.4	9,231.7	4,914.1	9,082.1	11,369.0	2,320.0	1,770.0	4,380.0	2,185.0
Peru	. . .	. . .	. . .	1,930.0	1,250.0	1,305.7	. . .	805.7	400.0	. . .
Trinidad and Tobago	230.0	250.0	. . .	. . .	. . .	100.0	. . .	. . .	100.0	. . .
Uruguay	350.0	442.6	1,106.1	400.0	. . .	. . .	. . .	. . .	. . .	500.0
Venezuela	1,214.7	489.4	1,583.2	. . .	3,670.0	4,260.0	1,500.0	760.0	1,324.5	1,604.2

Source: Data provided by the Bond, Equity and Loan database of the International Monetary Fund sourced from Dealogic.

Table 16. Emerging Market External Financing: Equity Issuance

(In millions of U.S. dollars)

							2004		2005	
	1999	2000	2001	2002	2003	2004	Q3	Q4	Q1	Q2
Developing Countries	**23,187.4**	**41,772.8**	**11,245.9**	**16,359.4**	**28,295.7**	**44,941.9**	**5,566.7**	**15,350.6**	**10,532.7**	**15,170.2**
Africa	**658.7**	**103.3**	**150.9**	**340.5**	**977.4**	**1,746.3**	**564.5**	**31.0**	**. . .**	**580.6**
Côte d'Ivoire	. . .	. . .	. . .	. . .	. . .	100.0	100.0	. . .	. . .	. . .
Morocco	. . .	56.4	6.8	. . .	. . .	1,615.3	464.5	. . .	. . .	580.6
South Africa	658.7	46.9	144.1	340.5	977.4	31.0	. . .	31.0	. . .	. . .
Sudan	. . .	. . .	. . .	. . .	. . .	. . .	. . .	. . .	. . .	. . .
Asia	**18,271.8**	**31,567.7**	**9,591.5**	**12,411.4**	**24,679.6**	**35,203.3**	**4,079.0**	**10,763.1**	**7,776.4**	**11,533.3**
China	1,477.4	20,239.7	2,810.4	2,546.0	6,413.2	14,528.3	213.6	2,674.8	1,942.6	7,442.9
Hong Kong SAR	3,370.0	3,088.6	297.1	2,857.7	3,480.1	5,152.6	584.5	3,127.9	892.7	60.4
India	874.4	916.7	467.2	264.8	1,299.7	3,937.6	683.4	688.1	1,761.4	2,053.2
Indonesia	522.2	28.2	347.2	281.0	1,008.4	535.2	. . .	177.4	147.5	74.1
Korea	6,590.6	784.8	3,676.4	1,553.7	1,222.6	3,223.3	2,191.6	. . .	375.5	. . .
Macao SAR	. . .	29.5	. . .	. . .	. . .	. . .	. . .	. . .	. . .	. . .
Malaysia	. . .	. . .	15.4	891.2	618.2	887.2	283.1	131.2	215.2	153.6
Papua New Guinea	232.4	. . .	. . .	. . .	153.7	. . .	. . .	. . .	. . .	. . .
Philippines	221.7	194.6	. . .	11.3	. . .	18.0	. . .	18.0	535.8	. . .
Singapore	1,725.6	2,202.2	625.8	891.6	1,168.7	2,472.7	24.2	1,809.9	444.7	354.5
Taiwan Province of China	2,500.4	3,951.5	1,126.6	3,057.9	8,276.3	3,350.0	98.6	1,256.0	1,404.1	1,170.7
Thailand	757.3	132.0	225.3	56.3	1,038.7	1,098.4	. . .	879.8	56.9	223.9
Europe	**1,411.6**	**3,339.8**	**259.4**	**1,612.4**	**1,811.3**	**5,261.2**	**88.7**	**3,905.0**	**1,856.7**	**1,749.0**
Croatia	. . .	. . .	22.3	. . .	. . .	. . .	. . .	. . .	. . .	. . .
Czech Republic	. . .	. . .	. . .	. . .	824.6	174.4	. . .	. . .	. . .	101.5
Estonia	190.3	. . .	. . .	. . .	. . .	. . .	. . .	. . .	. . .	66.4
Hungary	529.2	19.1	. . .	. . .	13.2	884.7	. . .	535.0	. . .	. . .
Latvia	. . .	. . .	. . .	22.7	. . .	. . .	. . .	. . .	. . .	. . .
Lithuania	. . .	150.5	. . .	. . .	. . .	. . .	. . .	. . .	. . .	. . .
Poland	636.3	358.9	. . .	217.3	604.9	841.4	. . .	734.1	112.4	406.7
Russia	55.8	387.7	237.1	1,301.0	368.7	2,674.4	. . .	2,408.5	1,744.3	1,154.5
Turkey	. . .	2,423.8	. . .	71.4	. . .	686.3	88.7	227.4	. . .	. . .
Ukraine	. . .	. . .	. . .	. . .	. . .	. . .	. . .	. . .	. . .	19.9
Middle East	**2,084.0**	**1,618.1**	**86.8**	**. . .**	**. . .**	**868.6**	**221.1**	**166.1**	**404.6**	**299.1**
Egypt	89.2	319.4	. . .	. . .	. . .	141.0	. . .	141.0	. . .	217.3
Israel	1,994.8	1,298.7	86.8	. . .	. . .	624.0	221.1	25.1	404.6	81.8
Oman	. . .	. . .	. . .	. . .	. . .	23.6	. . .	. . .	. . .	. . .
Saudi Arabia	. . .	. . .	. . .	. . .	. . .	80.0	. . .	. . .	. . .	. . .
Latin America	**761.3**	**5,143.9**	**1,157.2**	**1,995.0**	**827.4**	**1,862.5**	**613.4**	**485.4**	**495.0**	**1,008.2**
Argentina	349.6	393.1	34.4	. . .	. . .	. . .	. . .	. . .	. . .	. . .
Brazil	161.4	3,102.5	1,122.9	1,148.5	287.4	1,455.4	452.5	485.4	495.0	665.3
Chile	. . .	. . .	. . .	. . .	. . .	266.3	160.9	. . .	. . .	. . .
Dominican Republic	. . .	74.0	. . .	. . .	. . .	. . .	. . .	. . .	. . .	. . .
Mexico	162.0	1,574.3	. . .	846.6	540.0	140.8	. . .	. . .	. . .	342.9
Peru	88.4	. . .	. . .	. . .	. . .	. . .	. . .	. . .	. . .	. . .

Source: Data provided by the Bond, Equity and Loan database of the International Monetary Fund sourced from Dealogic.

Table 17. Emerging Market External Financing: Loan Syndication
(In millions of U.S. dollars)

							2004		2005	
	1999	2000	2001	2002	2003	2004	Q3	Q4	Q1	Q2
Total	**58,022.8**	**94,154.5**	**61,854.9**	**69,388.9**	**72,192.3**	**117,780.5**	**28,785.1**	**34,455.1**	**31,778.5**	**36,863.4**
Africa	**1,703.0**	**7,793.7**	**4,731.8**	**4,517.4**	**5,817.1**	**7,366.4**	**4,661.9**	**1,301.4**	**457.2**	**50.0**
Algeria	...	...	50.0	150.0	75.0	271.7	105.9	...	...	...
Angola	...	...	455.0	350.0	1,542.0	2,900.0	2,350.0	...	8.7	...
Botswana	...	...	22.5	...	...	...	...	...	...	...
Burkina Faso	...	...	...	...	...	...	...	...	11.0	...
Cameroon	...	...	53.8	...	100.0	...	...	...	...	...
Chad	...	...	400.0	...	...	...	...	...	...	...
Congo, Dem. Rep. of	...	20.8	...	...	...	...	...	...	...	...
Côte d'Ivoire	179.0	...	15.0	...	...	...	...	...	...	...
Djibouti	...	...	...	...	...	40.0	...	40.0	...	...
Ethiopia	...	...	...	...	...	40.0	40.0	...	...	...
Gabon	...	...	...	...	...	22.0	...	22.0	...	...
Ghana	30.0	320.0	300.0	420.0	650.0	870.0	870.0	...	...	...
Guinea	...	...	...	...	...	70.0	70.0	...	...	...
Kenya	...	7.5	80.2	...	134.0	135.1	61.5	73.5	...	...
Malawi	...	...	...	...	...	4.8	...	...	...	...
Mali	...	...	...	150.4	287.6	288.9	...	288.9	...	...
Morocco	170.6	...	129.3	...	9.8	...	...	...	...	...
Mozambique	...	...	200.0	...	35.5	222.4	...	...	...	...
Namibia	...	...	...	...	35.0	...	...	...	...	50.0
Niger	...	...	...	...	27.0	...	...	...	...	...
Nigeria	90.0	...	100.0	960.0	593.0	225.0	195.0	...	77.2	...
Senegal	...	...	...	40.0	...	...	...	...	...	...
Seychelles	...	50.0	...	150.0	...	80.0	...	...	...	...
South Africa	960.0	7,166.1	2,855.0	2,206.5	2,170.0	1,816.6	969.5	527.1	269.1	...
Tanzania	...	135.0	...	...	...	...	...	...	...	...
Tunisia	123.4	94.3	71.0	90.5	128.2	379.9	...	349.9	91.2	...
Zambia	...	...	...	...	30.0	...	...	...	...	...
Zimbabwe	150.0	...	...	...	...	...	...	...	...	...
Asia	**14,262.0**	**29,812.0**	**22,022.7**	**32,257.3**	**27,509.9**	**48,980.3**	**11,516.1**	**16,705.1**	**10,997.7**	**13,354.1**
Bangladesh	...	...	...	...	...	176.8	...	176.8	...	...
Brunei	...	...	...	129.0	...	...	...	...	...	...
China	924.4	1,053.1	415.0	5,742.8	5,142.4	4,778.3	448.1	1,255.1	1,817.7	352.0
Hong Kong SAR	993.5	10,898.9	7,551.6	7,792.9	2,950.0	9,780.0	1,886.3	4,347.0	1,552.5	2,945.9
India	1,401.8	1,207.6	1,815.7	963.1	2,344.4	4,532.2	1,454.5	933.4	1,108.4	1,581.9
Indonesia	943.1	1,254.9	492.6	318.0	3,492.5	1,737.4	175.0	992.4	25.0	83.8
Korea	2,046.0	5,792.6	5,588.2	6,434.3	4,483.0	6,281.1	1,717.8	3,358.3	3,094.7	4,703.8
Lao P.D.R.	...	...	...	71.4	...	210.0	...	140.0	...	1,000.0
Macao SAR	...	...	...	...	...	357.0	357.0	...	...	...
Malaysia	3,114.8	3,086.7	2,267.0	2,826.1	4,148.6	4,329.3	782.5	1,510.2	1,052.6	705.0
Marshall Islands	...	...	...	34.7	...	...	...	...	...	...
Mongolia	...	...	...	...	...	...	...	...	30.0	...
Pakistan	...	...	182.5	289.1	9.3	300.0	...	...	286.2	417.8
Philippines	2,208.9	2,360.0	1,816.4	673.0	1,653.8	1,750.9	478.5	275.2	100.0	...
Singapore	466.0	1,543.7	1,093.2	2,356.3	1,287.2	2,870.8	580.1	537.4	535.0	624.9
Sri Lanka	23.0	100.0	105.0	...	186.0	35.0	...	...	...	...
Taiwan Province of China	1,044.5	1,054.0	515.0	2,420.5	743.3	10,343.2	3,397.6	2,816.0	870.3	654.1
Thailand	996.0	1,440.5	180.5	1,822.7	1,018.5	1,384.3	124.7	363.3	525.3	239.6
Vietnam	100.0	20.0	...	383.5	51.0	114.0	114.0	...	...	45.3
Europe	**10,907.1**	**19,479.3**	**10,969.7**	**12,957.5**	**21,632.1**	**32,058.6**	**3,317.4**	**7,561.5**	**8,377.1**	**12,802.6**
Azerbaijan	77.2	...	16.0	...	...	1,065.4	997.0	10.2	41.0	17.2
Belarus	...	...	...	...	36.0	21.4	...	...	...	21.4
Bulgaria	...	8.9	18.9	13.0	381.3	859.5	...	540.5	29.5	289.4
Croatia	903.6	640.7	809.8	577.8	1,042.5	679.1	...	...	373.1	306.0
Cyprus	...	86.3	152.5	68.1	...	...	...	...	...	...
Czech Republic	118.6	127.1	513.9	25.0	356.5	191.1	...	...	...	191.1
Estonia	14.0	77.0	136.6	...	184.3	128.9	...	128.9	...	...
Georgia	...	...	...	...	6.0	...	...	...	...	...
Gibraltar	65.0	80.0	...	...	...	...	...	...	...	...

Table 17 *(concluded)*

	1999	2000	2001	2002	2003	2004	2004		2005	
							Q3	Q4	Q1	Q2
Europe *(continued)*										
Hungary	531.6	748.9	116.9	969.7	1,550.2	1,812.7	244.3	632.6	...	935.8
Kazakhstan	117.0	79.6	323.5	534.5	1,435.0	2,029.0	139.2	119.0	847.8	923.0
Kyrgyz Republic	...	...	...	95.0	...	...	...	...	...	...
Latvia	52.2	23.0	31.3	51.9	70.7	353.2	...	48.3	145.0	160.0
Lithuania	428.2	157.2	24.9	18.8	...	82.5	...	...	10.0	72.5
Macedonia	...	...	...	...	47.6	92.7	10.3	...	...	82.5
Malta	57.0	...	85.0	...	114.7	392.7	150.0	242.7	...	...
Moldova	40.0	...	...	...	...	7.0	...	...	2.0	5.0
Poland	1,491.9	3,340.5	2,062.9	3,016.0	2,912.1	565.8	443.8	61.6	24.4	36.0
Romania	176.0	334.9	438.6	380.0	1,014.6	846.9	244.7	281.5	203.8	116.9
Russia	111.0	3,488.1	1,610.3	3,803.5	7,707.5	13,505.3	747.0	4,187.9	3,592.0	4,978.3
Serbia and Montenegro	...	...	...	19.4	10.9	...	...	...	...	...
Slovak Republic	194.5	488.3	...	...	79.3	130.3	...	36.5	30.5	63.3
Slovenia	248.6	288.0	337.2	279.0	394.8	1,391.8	76.2	606.7	653.6	55.3
Tajikistan	...	...	...	...	...	1.2	...	...	1.2	...
Turkey	6,138.8	9,470.9	4,246.4	3,044.8	4,159.2	7,582.3	265.0	645.0	2,194.7	4,477.6
Ukraine	...	...	15.0	15.0	90.0	291.9	...	10.0	225.0	56.9
Uzbekistan	142.0	40.0	30.0	46.0	38.7	28.0	...	10.0	3.6	14.3
Middle East	**8,893.7**	**8,711.0**	**5,012.7**	**6,978.8**	**6,508.1**	**11,530.0**	**2,250.4**	**3,397.0**	**5,411.7**	**8,847.7**
Bahrain	152.0	1,202.5	207.0	340.0	1,050.0	1,475.0	442.0	1,033.0	220.0	1,140.0
Egypt	1,344.5	600.0	1,045.0	670.0	155.0	997.7	...	80.0	150.0	...
Iran, I.R. of	692.0	757.7	887.0	1,680.1	700.0	1,942.7	39.9	225.9	1,255.2	...
Iraq	...	...	...	...	...	...	...	...	107.8	...
Israel	45.0	280.0	395.0	...	...	370.0	120.0	250.0	550.0	...
Jordan	...	60.0	...	...	...	54.4	...	54.4	...	...
Kuwait	147.5	250.0	770.0	...	165.0	782.5	157.5	325.0	220.0	2,825.0
Libya	...	50.0	...	...	...	...	...	...	...	...
Oman	356.8	685.0	...	2,332.0	907.8	1,055.0	175.0	455.0	753.0	1,460.0
Qatar	1,000.0	580.0	913.0	1,536.7	880.8	1,377.7	...	198.7	...	722.0
Saudi Arabia	4,374.8	2,200.9	275.0	280.0	569.5	2,134.0	816.0	600.0	350.0	2,004.0
United Arab Emirates	781.0	2,045.0	520.7	140.0	2,080.0	1,341.0	500.0	175.0	1,805.7	696.7
Latin America	**22,257.0**	**28,358.5**	**19,118.0**	**12,677.9**	**10,725.2**	**17,845.2**	**7,039.3**	**5,490.1**	**6,534.8**	**1,809.0**
Argentina	3,312.1	3,230.6	1,889.0	824.2	60.0	656.0	...	406.0	...	135.0
Bolivia	...	...	20.0	90.0	...	116.0	...	116.0	100.0	...
Brazil	4,204.7	8,753.6	6,171.3	3,401.7	1,003.9	4,609.8	1,321.9	384.9	525.0	150.0
Chile	6,267.9	5,102.8	2,399.3	1,230.7	1,799.0	3,823.5	1,375.0	1,934.7	396.1	698.5
Colombia	1,880.2	1,546.0	631.7	1,096.0	146.3	...	...	...	70.0	...
Costa Rica	...	...	150.0	...	...	...	...	...	...	25.5
Cuba	...	...	...	...	...	69.8	...	...	1.9	...
Dominican Republic	...	...	31.1	258.0	70.4	140.5	101.0	...	9.1	...
Ecuador	73.0	...	910.0	10.0	...	...	...	...	25.0	...
El Salvador	166.5	110.0	135.0	...	32.5	180.5	140.5	40.0	...	...
Guadeloupe	...	...	...	17.4	...	...	...	...	...	...
Guatemala	222.0	505.0	...	44.0	...	59.3	...	50.0	...	...
Honduras	...	...	...	...	...	169.0	169.0	...	...	...
Jamaica	...	...	35.8	45.0	49.6	96.3	96.3	...	208.1	...
Mexico	4,083.6	6,660.7	4,591.8	4,280.0	7,370.2	7,278.4	3,720.6	2,344.4	5,196.6	800.0
Nicaragua	...	...	...	...	...	22.0	...	...	...	...
Paraguay	55.0	...	70.0	...	...	...	...	...	...	...
Peru	1,530.0	465.4	137.5	63.0	125.0	170.0	...	...	...	...
St. Lucia	...	...	...	...	20.0	...	...	...	...	...
Trinidad and Tobago	...	51.0	70.0	303.0	46.0	315.0	115.0	200.0	...	...
Uruguay	115.0	159.5	41.3	...	...	...	...	...	...	...
Venezuela	347.0	1,773.9	1,834.3	1,015.0	2.5	139.1	...	14.1	3.0	...

Source: Data provided by the Bond, Equity and Loan database of the International Monetary Fund sourced from Dealogic.

Table 18. Equity Valuation Measures: Dividend-Yield Ratios

							2004		2005	
	1999	2000	2001	2002	2003	2004	Q3	Q4	Q1	Q2
Argentina	3.29	4.62	5.16	3.42	1.08	1.00	1.08	1.00	0.89	1.45
Brazil	2.95	3.18	4.93	5.51	3.46	4.43	5.02	4.43	3.65	4.05
Chile	1.88	2.33	2.31	2.76	1.76	3.01	1.89	3.01	3.14	2.90
China	3.14	0.95	1.95	2.41	2.19	2.26	2.39	2.26	2.31	2.82
Colombia	6.78	11.12	5.63	4.78	3.92	2.52	2.79	2.52	2.58	2.76
Czech Republic	1.36	0.95	2.28	2.36	6.85	4.29	5.08	4.29	3.56	1.80
Egypt	3.92	5.75	6.48	7.53	4.69	1.98	2.34	1.98	1.44	1.44
Hong Kong SAR	2.31	2.58	3.25	3.85	2.82	2.74	3.00	2.74	3.09	3.11
Hungary	1.14	1.46	1.30	1.40	0.94	1.95	2.30	1.95	1.67	2.36
India	1.25	1.59	2.03	1.81	1.47	1.53	1.79	1.53	1.56	1.54
Indonesia	0.91	3.05	3.65	4.17	3.83	3.23	3.54	3.23	3.05	3.19
Israel	1.87	2.26	2.24	1.47	1.10	1.43	1.30	1.43	1.86	2.04
Jordan	4.24	4.54	3.51	3.77	2.36	1.57	1.91	1.57	1.24	1.15
Korea	0.81	2.05	1.54	1.38	1.82	2.40	2.50	2.40	2.61	2.58
Malaysia	1.15	1.70	1.87	2.04	2.38	2.22	2.28	2.22	2.45	2.77
Mexico	1.27	1.63	1.98	2.30	1.83	1.87	2.14	1.87	1.98	2.03
Morocco	2.49	3.59	3.97	4.84	4.18	3.61	3.54	3.61	3.81	4.64
Pakistan	4.00	5.12	16.01	10.95	8.63	7.04	7.46	7.04	6.11	5.79
Peru	2.86	3.38	3.16	2.37	1.75	3.28	2.58	3.28	3.45	6.10
Philippines	1.08	1.44	1.43	1.97	1.43	1.65	1.61	1.65	1.76	2.15
Poland	0.70	0.68	1.87	1.84	1.28	1.28	1.72	1.28	1.19	3.04
Russia	0.14	0.92	1.11	1.87	2.38	3.12	2.50	3.12	2.16	2.28
Singapore	0.86	1.40	1.80	2.27	2.03	2.25	2.29	2.25	2.26	2.60
South Africa	2.09	2.75	3.47	3.83	3.22	2.63	2.74	2.63	3.01	3.09
Sri Lanka	3.22	5.59	4.79	3.35	2.51	2.63	2.62	2.63	2.02	2.07
Taiwan Province of China	0.97	1.71	1.42	1.60	1.86	2.95	3.13	2.95	3.07	3.51
Thailand	0.70	2.13	2.02	2.48	1.69	3.03	3.12	3.03	3.90	3.84
Turkey	0.76	1.91	1.15	1.35	0.89	1.93	2.22	1.93	2.10	3.11
Venezuela	5.80	5.05	3.89	2.38	3.68	5.75	5.98	5.75	5.60	6.33
Emerging Markets	1.52	2.09	2.30	2.43	2.25	2.61	2.74	2.61	2.65	2.90
EM Asia	1.01	1.71	1.73	1.81	1.96	2.48	2.59	2.48	2.64	2.89
EM Latin America	2.28	2.69	3.37	3.64	2.61	3.30	3.56	3.30	2.98	3.26
EM Europe and Middle East	1.16	1.84	1.69	1.71	1.81	2.15	2.17	2.15	1.95	2.38
ACWI Free	1.27	1.46	1.72	2.25	1.99	2.08	2.15	2.08	2.15	2.17

Data are from Morgan Stanley Capital International. The countries above include the 27 constituents of the Emerging Markets index as well as Hong Kong SAR and Singapore. Regional breakdowns conform to Morgan Stanley Capital International conventions. All indices reflect investible opportunities for global investors by taking into account restrictions on foreign ownership. The indices attempt to achieve an 85 percent representation of freely floating stocks.

Table 19. Equity Valuation Measures: Price-to-Book Ratios

							2004		2005	
	1999	2000	2001	2002	2003	2004	Q3	Q4	Q1	Q2
Argentina	1.47	1.04	0.86	1.20	1.79	2.24	2.16	2.24	2.50	2.44
Brazil	1.24	1.18	1.11	1.24	1.81	1.84	1.82	1.84	1.83	1.82
Chile	1.69	1.49	1.39	1.15	1.55	1.78	1.67	1.78	1.93	2.00
China	0.69	2.75	1.88	1.30	2.16	1.98	1.88	1.98	1.98	1.95
Colombia	0.71	0.49	0.53	1.18	1.34	1.92	1.64	1.92	1.87	1.89
Czech Republic	0.80	1.00	0.81	0.84	1.06	1.64	1.35	1.64	1.89	1.89
Egypt	3.57	2.32	1.39	1.05	2.17	3.89	3.38	3.89	5.37	6.41
Hong Kong SAR	2.27	1.67	1.38	1.10	1.47	1.71	1.56	1.71	1.55	1.63
Hungary	3.35	2.33	2.03	1.91	1.97	2.62	2.43	2.62	2.96	2.79
India	3.55	2.71	2.13	2.15	3.79	3.63	3.13	3.63	3.51	3.61
Indonesia	2.41	1.03	2.72	2.23	2.26	3.10	2.50	3.10	3.28	2.96
Israel	2.53	3.04	2.22	1.74	2.46	2.62	2.23	2.62	2.54	2.45
Jordan	1.03	1.02	1.38	1.26	1.98	3.01	2.31	3.01	3.88	4.89
Korea	1.42	0.82	1.33	1.21	1.52	1.36	1.38	1.36	1.44	1.44
Malaysia	1.98	1.59	1.76	1.54	1.85	1.95	1.86	1.95	1.83	1.88
Mexico	2.31	1.91	1.99	1.77	2.20	2.58	2.38	2.58	2.45	2.48
Morocco	3.53	2.56	1.79	1.40	1.50	2.42	1.91	2.42	2.32	2.52
Pakistan	1.48	1.41	0.88	2.04	2.31	2.39	2.15	2.39	2.70	3.01
Peru	1.92	1.13	1.29	1.84	2.77	2.28	2.39	2.28	2.36	2.22
Philippines	1.64	1.27	1.11	0.85	1.40	1.61	1.56	1.61	1.78	1.90
Poland	2.12	2.10	1.33	1.37	1.72	2.11	1.82	2.11	2.22	2.22
Russia	2.41	0.90	1.27	1.22	1.33	1.11	1.39	1.11	1.39	1.66
Singapore	2.56	2.05	1.63	1.26	1.62	1.70	1.65	1.70	1.71	1.77
South Africa	2.75	2.68	1.81	1.72	1.95	2.43	2.01	2.43	2.48	2.49
Sri Lanka	1.00	0.60	0.83	1.22	1.52	1.43	1.45	1.43	1.62	1.78
Taiwan Province of China	3.46	1.87	1.98	1.53	2.10	1.88	1.82	1.88	1.80	1.81
Thailand	2.04	1.51	1.68	1.83	2.94	2.41	2.34	2.41	2.31	2.20
Turkey	9.21	2.72	3.80	1.76	2.02	1.92	1.66	1.92	1.79	1.87
Venezuela	0.63	0.67	0.48	0.87	1.41	1.63	1.65	1.63	1.56	1.18
Emerging Markets	2.12	1.64	1.59	1.45	1.90	1.91	1.82	1.91	1.94	1.96
EM Asia	2.09	1.53	1.68	1.41	1.95	1.81	1.75	1.81	1.81	1.83
EM Latin America	1.57	1.36	1.35	1.44	1.90	2.05	1.97	2.05	2.03	2.03
EM Europe and Middle East	3.41	2.15	1.70	1.42	1.67	1.78	1.72	1.78	1.97	2.05
ACWI Free	4.23	3.46	2.67	2.07	2.46	2.46	2.34	2.46	2.42	2.45

Data are from Morgan Stanley Capital International. The countries above include the 27 constituents of the Emerging Markets index as well as Hong Kong SAR and Singapore. Regional breakdowns conform to Morgan Stanley Capital International conventions. All indices reflect investible opportunities for global investors by taking into account restrictions on foreign ownership. The indices attempt to achieve an 85 percent representation of freely floating stocks.

Table 20. Equity Valuation Measures: Price-Earnings Ratios

	1999	2000	2001	2002	2003	2004	2004		2005	
							Q3	Q4	Q1	Q2
Argentina	24.82	20.69	19.13	−12.86	13.72	47.24	244.47	47.24	53.16	15.18
Brazil	18.64	12.83	8.49	11.23	10.34	10.80	9.89	10.80	10.24	9.45
Chile	46.40	31.96	18.02	17.16	30.81	23.06	25.04	23.06	23.66	22.55
China	14.97	40.60	14.09	12.14	17.11	13.83	13.15	13.83	13.51	12.66
Colombia	20.30	−103.44	64.91	9.55	8.94	17.67	10.56	17.67	17.16	17.54
Czech Republic	−42.04	16.49	9.21	10.40	12.49	26.64	18.18	26.64	23.20	20.40
Egypt	16.54	9.35	6.28	7.33	10.90	14.23	13.88	14.23	19.67	26.93
Hong Kong SAR	30.81	7.64	20.47	14.91	20.00	19.90	19.50	19.90	18.02	18.37
Hungary	18.50	14.82	19.34	10.06	13.11	11.26	11.89	11.26	13.74	12.15
India	22.84	15.61	13.84	13.56	18.96	17.65	15.63	17.65	16.16	17.05
Indonesia	−48.73	18.68	8.37	7.14	10.37	12.91	11.14	12.91	13.19	12.21
Israel	25.51	23.88	228.84	−46.62	34.05	20.11	17.36	20.11	19.91	18.96
Jordan	13.51	−107.11	15.10	12.39	21.38	32.50	25.04	32.50	41.82	41.29
Korea	23.24	8.12	15.23	11.44	13.93	8.24	9.09	8.24	8.48	8.40
Malaysia	−8.41	20.63	22.62	13.21	16.33	16.05	15.55	16.05	15.18	15.00
Mexico	14.64	13.78	14.23	14.07	15.70	15.02	15.66	15.02	14.20	12.80
Morocco	18.65	9.30	10.77	9.87	22.46	15.55	26.69	15.55	14.88	15.57
Pakistan	17.60	8.39	4.53	8.07	8.68	9.45	8.76	9.45	11.23	11.14
Peru	18.46	15.44	14.08	20.42	26.45	11.88	17.69	11.88	12.27	9.38
Philippines	142.83	−35.06	43.72	18.21	20.18	14.87	14.35	14.87	15.16	14.75
Poland	22.33	14.30	18.32	−261.14	19.50	13.27	12.58	13.27	13.95	13.48
Russia	−126.43	5.69	5.03	7.33	11.13	8.19	9.59	8.19	12.21	12.77
Singapore	41.18	18.94	16.53	21.07	21.38	14.33	14.00	14.33	14.39	14.63
South Africa	18.73	14.87	11.30	10.50	12.75	14.97	14.38	14.97	14.96	14.12
Sri Lanka	7.59	4.24	8.53	14.35	12.69	11.03	10.53	11.03	12.03	13.91
Taiwan Province of China	38.26	14.06	21.08	73.13	25.70	12.40	12.76	12.40	11.80	15.06
Thailand	−8.94	−14.61	16.67	15.52	15.24	11.49	11.33	11.49	10.41	9.91
Turkey	38.60	11.77	25.51	101.33	11.01	13.61	11.85	13.61	13.32	13.53
Venezuela	17.68	21.76	18.43	13.43	24.40	12.44	14.91	12.44	11.88	8.93
Emerging Markets	27.17	14.85	13.99	13.95	15.03	12.15	12.22	12.15	12.11	12.27
EM Asia	40.98	15.47	16.73	14.85	16.72	11.23	11.47	11.23	10.96	11.79
EM Latin America	18.28	14.93	11.67	13.84	13.18	13.10	12.82	13.10	12.48	11.24
EM Europe and Middle East	37.25	14.05	13.10	16.27	14.65	12.64	12.31	12.64	14.99	14.59
ACWI Free	35.70	25.44	26.76	23.18	21.94	17.94	17.41	17.94	17.10	17.17

Data are from Morgan Stanley Capital International. The countries above include the 27 constituents of the Emerging Markets index as well as Hong Kong SAR and Singapore. Regional breakdowns conform to Morgan Stanley Capital International conventions. All indices reflect investible opportunities for global investors by taking into account restrictions on foreign ownership. The indices attempt to achieve an 85 percent representation of freely floating stocks.

Table 21. United States: Mutual Fund Flows
(In millions of U.S. dollars)

	1999	2000	2001	2002	2003	2004	2004		2005	
							Q3	Q4	Q1	Q2
Asia Pacific (ex-Japan)	151.7	−1,207.9	−496.2	−43.0	1,510.8	1,574.3	−42.1	952.7	600.2	78.9
Corporate high yield	−510.1	−6,162.3	5,938.3	8,082.4	20,261.9	−3,259.3	1,490.4	659.4	−4,839.1	−2,345.7
Corporate investment grade	7,136.3	4,253.7	21,692.0	32,688.3	16,660.2	3,339.1	1,677.9	126.4	2,593.2	1,107.5
Emerging markets debt	18.4	−499.9	−447.7	449.7	889.0	211.4	99.9	29.9	34.9	121.5
Emerging markets equity	23.5	−349.9	−1,662.7	−330.7	4,672.7	5,815.8	105.9	3,493.1	2,853.2	1,759.6
European equity	−1,664.9	620.9	−1,790.8	−1,044.8	−947.4	873.2	−118.7	714.5	564.9	−160.2
Global equity	4,673.2	12,626.7	−3,005.5	−5,152.1	−1,995.4	8,373.4	1,453.7	2,735.7	4,410.0	910.5
Growth-Aggressive	15,247.5	46,610.3	17,882.8	5,611.6	11,464.9	9,915.4	−356.3	168.5	−86.4	1,831.3
International and global debt	−1,581.6	−3,272.2	−1,602.2	−823.0	3,225.0	5,143.4	724.0	2,039.3	2,750.8	1,191.3
International equity	2,998.5	13,322.4	−4,488.2	4,240.0	14,650.8	35,441.1	4,211.2	11,688.6	14,882.5	6,962.6
Japanese equity	731.0	−830.6	−269.8	−82.0	1,863.3	3,313.7	422.7	35.1	307.2	−293.7
Latin American equity	−120.9	−94.6	−146.7	32.7	185.7	65.3	−1.6	159.7	221.1	149.3

Data are provided by AMG Data Services and cover net flows of U.S.-based mutual funds. Fund categories are distinguished by a primary investment objective that signifies an investment of 65 percent or more of a fund's assets. Primary sector data are mutually exclusive, but emerging and regional sectors are all subsets of international equity.

Table 22. Bank Regulatory Capital to Risk-Weighted Assets
(In percent)

	2000	2001	2002	2003	2004	2005	Latest
Latin America							
Argentina[1]	10.6	13.3	13.9	11.7	11.2	11.6	February
Bolivia	13.5	14.6	16.1	15.3	14.9	14.9	March
Brazil	13.8	14.8	16.6	18.9	18.2	. . .	
Chile	13.3	12.7	14.0	14.1	13.6	14.2	April
Colombia[2]	13.2	13.0	12.6	13.1	14.0	. . .	September
Costa Rica	16.7	15.1	15.8	16.5	18.1	17.7	March
Dominican Republic	12.1	11.8	12.0	11.4	13.1	. . .	
Ecuador	13.1	13.5	14.4	14.9	14.9	. . .	April
El Salvador	11.5	11.8	12.2	12.8	13.0	. . .	September
Jamaica	25.6	23.6	18.5	16.1	15.9	. . .	
Honduras	12.3	12.7	12.9	13.0	14.5	. . .	
Mexico	13.8	14.7	15.5	14.2	14.1	13.7	March
Nicaragua	14.3	16.4	18.0	14.2	14.3	15.5	February
Panama	13.5	13.6	14.5	17.5	19.6	. . .	September
Paraguay	. . .	16.9	17.9	20.9	20.5	23.0	February
Peru	12.9	13.4	12.5	13.3	14.2	14.3	March
Uruguay[3]	. . .	11.3	–5.0	11.3	29.8	29.4	March
Venezuela	. . .	. . .	. . .	. . .	. . .	. . .	
Emerging Europe							
Belarus	24.4	20.7	24.2	26.0	25.2	. . .	
Bosnia and Herzegovina	26.3	22.4	19.7	19.5	18.0	. . .	
Bulgaria	35.6	31.1	25.2	22.4	16.6	15.4	March
Croatia	21.3	18.5	17.2	15.7	14.1	15.4	March
Czech Republic	17.4	15.0	14.2	14.5	12.6	12.7	March
Estonia	13.2	14.4	15.3	14.5	13.4	12.6	April
Hungary	13.7	13.9	13.0	11.8	11.2	. . .	
Israel	9.2	9.4	9.9	10.3	10.8	. . .	
Latvia	14.0	14.2	13.1	11.7	11.7	. . .	December
Lithuania	16.3	15.7	14.8	13.3	12.3	. . .	
Moldova	48.6	43.1	36.4	31.8	31.9	32.1	March
Poland	12.9	15.1	13.8	13.7	15.6	. . .	
Romania	23.8	28.8	25.0	20.0	18.8	19.1	March
Russia	19.0	20.3	19.1	19.1	17.0	17.6	March
Serbia and Montenegro	. . .	. . .	25.6	31.1	27.9	. . .	
Slovak Republic	12.5	19.8	21.3	21.6	19.0	. . .	
Slovenia	13.5	11.9	11.9	11.5	11.0	. . .	
Turkey	17.3	15.3	25.1	30.9	28.8	. . .	
Ukraine	15.5	20.7	18.0	15.2	16.8	17.1	March
Western Europe							
Austria	13.3	13.7	13.3	14.5	14.7	. . .	
Belgium	12.0	12.9	13.2	12.9	12.3	. . .	September
Finland	11.6	10.5	11.7	19.3	19.1	. . .	June
France	11.9	12.1	12.3	12.6	. . .	. . .	
Germany	11.7	12.0	12.7	13.4	13.2	. . .	
Greece	13.6	12.4	10.5	12.0	11.9	. . .	September
Iceland	9.8	11.4	12.2	12.3	12.8	. . .	
Ireland	10.7	10.6	12.3	13.9	12.6	. . .	
Italy	10.1	10.4	11.2	11.4	11.5	. . .	
Luxembourg	13.1	13.7	15.0	17.1	17.5	. . .	
Netherlands	10.7	11.0	11.5	11.5	11.5	. . .	
Norway	12.1	12.6	12.2	12.4	12.2	. . .	
Portugal	9.2	9.5	9.8	10.0	10.3	. . .	June
Spain	12.4	12.9	12.5	12.5	11.6	. . .	
Sweden	9.9	10.0	10.1	10.1	10.0	. . .	March
Switzerland	12.7	11.8	12.1	11.2	11.0	. . .	
United Kingdom	13.0	13.2	12.2	12.4	12.3	. . .	June

Table 22 *(concluded)*

	2000	2001	2002	2003	2004	2005	Latest
Asia							
Bangladesh	6.7	6.7	7.5	8.4	8.8	...	
China	...	...	...	...	...	...	
Hong Kong SAR	17.8	16.5	15.7	15.3	15.4	15.4	March
India	11.1	11.4	11.9	12.9	13.4	...	June
Indonesia[4]	21.6	18.2	20.1	22.3	20.9	...	
Korea	10.5	10.8	10.5	10.4	11.3	...	
Malaysia	12.5	13.0	13.2	13.8	13.8	14.2	February
Philippines	16.2	14.5	15.5	16.0	16.9	...	September
Singapore	19.6	18.2	16.9	16.0	16.1	15.9	March
Thailand	11.3	13.3	13.0	13.4	11.9	...	
Middle East and Central Asia							
Armenia	25.0	13.6	30.5	33.8	32.3	...	
Azerbaijan	...	...	...	14.7	20.9	...	June
Egypt	10.2	10.2	9.9	11.0	11.1	12.0	March
Jordan[5]	19.4	17.4	16.7	15.9	...	...	
Kazakhstan	25.7	18.6	17.2	16.9	15.9	...	
Kuwait	22.2	22.0	19.7	18.4	17.3	...	September
Lebanon	16.9	18.0	19.4	22.3	22.2	...	June
Morocco	12.8	12.6	12.2	9.3	10.2	...	
Pakistan[6]	11.4	11.3	12.6	11.1	11.4	...	September
Saudi Arabia	21.0	20.3	18.7	19.4	18.0	17.1	March
Tunisia	13.3	10.6	9.8	9.3	11.6	...	
United Arab Emirates	19.5	19.8	19.0	18.6	16.9	...	
Sub-Saharan Africa							
Angola	...	...	20.1	18.1	20.5	...	September
Botswana	27.1	27.6	20.2	21.5	20.6	...	
Gabon	13.2	17.2	17.6	19.9	17.8	...	
Ghana	11.6	14.7	13.4	9.3	13.7	...	
Kenya	17.6	17.3	17.0	17.3	16.5	...	June
Madagascar	14.1	15.7	15.3	14.0	11.6	...	
Mozambique	–2.1	5.5	14.0	17.0	18.7	...	
Nigeria	17.5	16.2	18.1	17.8	14.6	...	
Senegal	20.6	16.8	15.5	11.7	13.0	...	June
Sierra Leone	24.6	29.4	48.4	39.8	37.1	...	
South Africa	14.5	11.4	12.6	12.2	13.3	12.9	March
Uganda	20.5	23.1	20.7	16.7	20.6	...	
Zambia	...	22.0	28.0	23.7	22.0	...	
Zimbabwe	44.0	44.5	30.6	16.2	...	...	
Other							
Australia	9.8	10.5	9.9	10.1	10.5	...	
Canada	11.9	12.3	12.4	13.4	13.3	...	
Japan[7]	11.7	10.8	9.4	11.1	11.6	...	March
United States	12.4	12.9	13.0	13.0	13.2	...	

Sources: National authorities; and IMF staff estimates.
[1]Assets are not risk-weighted.
[2]Includes mortgage institutions.
[3]Private banks. Data in 2002 include suspended banks.
[4]Top 16 banks.
[5]For 2003, the calculations include market risk.
[6]The data refer to commercial banks only, excluding specialized banks.
[7]Ratio for the major banks. Data refer to end-March of the following calendar year.

Table 23. Bank Capital to Assets
(In percent)

	2000	2001	2002	2003	2004	2005	Latest
Latin America							
Argentina	...	...	...	...	...	...	
Bolivia	9.8	10.5	11.9	12.1	11.5	11.1	June
Brazil	12.1	13.6	13.5	16.2	16.0	15.9	May
Chile	7.5	7.2	7.2	7.3	7.0	6.8	May
Colombia	...	11.2	11.0	11.5	12.1	11.9	March
Costa Rica	10.8	12.9	12.6	13.6	11.9	12.2	May
Dominican Republic	9.4	10.0	10.7	7.8	7.4	...	March
Ecuador	12.9	8.8	10.3	10.2	9.9	9.8	March
El Salvador	8.8	8.9	8.5	9.0	8.0	...	September
Jamaica	...	...	...	...	...	...	
Honduras	8.8	9.2	8.1	7.6	8.4	...	
Mexico	9.6	9.4	11.1	11.4	11.5	...	September
Nicaragua	...	...	...	...	...	...	
Panama	9.6	9.6	10.2	12.2	13.2	13.1	April
Paraguay	12.4	12.1	10.9	9.5	10.5	10.6	May
Peru	9.1	9.8	10.1	9.3	9.8	9.5	May
Uruguay	...	...	...	...	...	...	
Venezuela	13.0	14.1	15.9	14.3	12.5	11.0	February
Emerging Europe							
Belarus	...	15.1	18.7	20.4	20.0	...	
Bosnia and Herzegovina	...	18.8	17.9	15.0	13.2	...	
Bulgaria	15.3	13.5	13.3	13.2	11.0	10.1	March
Croatia	11.9	9.3	9.5	9.0	8.5	9.3	March
Czech Republic	5.4	5.2	5.2	5.7	5.6	5.7	March
Estonia	12.6	13.3	12.1	11.3	9.8	9.4	April
Hungary	8.3	8.5	8.7	8.3	8.9	...	
Israel	7.3	7.7	6.5	7.2	7.1	...	
Latvia	8.5	9.1	8.8	8.6	8.2	...	November
Lithuania	10.2	9.8	10.7	10.4	9.5	...	
Moldova	30.6	27.5	23.0	21.1	20.2	19.5	March
Poland	7.1	8.0	8.7	8.2	8.2	...	June
Romania	8.6	12.1	11.6	10.9	8.5	8.1	March
Russia	12.1	12.6	14.4	14.8	14.0	13.5	April
Serbia and Montenegro	...	...	...	...	...	...	
Slovak Republic	4.6	6.3	6.8	7.7	7.2	...	August
Slovenia	10.1	8.8	8.3	8.3	7.5	...	
Turkey	6.1	9.6	11.6	13.6	14.3	13.9	April
Ukraine	16.2	15.6	14.9	12.3	13.1	12.4	March
Western Europe							
Austria	5.2	5.1	5.6	5.8	6.0	5.8	April
Belgium	2.8	2.7	3.0	3.1	3.2	...	September
Finland	6.3	10.2	10.1	9.6	8.2	8.0	April
France	6.7	6.7	6.8	6.7	6.5	6.2	April
Germany	4.2	4.4	4.6	4.6	4.4	4.2	April
Greece	8.9	9.2	9.4	7.6	7.9	7.9	April
Iceland	6.2	6.5	7.2	7.1	7.1	...	
Ireland	6.5	5.9	5.5	5.2	4.9	4.6	April
Italy	7.0	7.1	7.1	7.0	6.9	6.9	April
Luxembourg	4.0	4.0	4.6	4.8	4.8	4.6	April
Netherlands	5.1	4.8	4.7	4.3	3.9	4.0	March
Norway	7.0	6.8	6.3	6.0	6.1	5.9	May
Portugal	5.8	5.5	5.6	5.8	6.1	...	
Spain	8.5	8.4	8.5	8.1	8.5	8.3	April
Sweden	...	6.5	6.2	6.2	6.3	6.6	February
Switzerland	6.0	5.6	5.4	5.2	5.0	...	
United Kingdom[1]	6.5	6.6	6.7	6.8	...	...	

Table 23 *(concluded)*

	2000	2001	2002	2003	2004	2005	Latest
Asia							
Bangladesh	3.5	3.5	4.1	3.2	2.7	. . .	May
China[2]	. . .	. . .	3.8	4.3	3.9	. . .	
Hong Kong SAR	9.0	9.8	10.7	11.5	12.3	. . .	November
India	5.7	5.3	5.5	5.7	5.9	. . .	March
Indonesia	6.0	5.3	7.1	8.7	9.3	9.9	February
Korea	4.6	4.9	4.7	4.4	4.8	4.9	March
Malaysia	8.5	8.5	8.7	8.5	8.1	. . .	
Philippines	13.6	13.6	13.4	13.1	12.8	. . .	June
Singapore	10.0	10.0	11.0	10.7	9.7	10.1	March
Thailand[3]	7.5	8.9	8.9	9.6	8.7	. . .	
Middle East and Central Asia							
Armenia	14.3	8.8	18.4	18.1	17.8	. . .	
Azerbaijan	. . .	19.5	19.8	11.1	11.9	14.2	March
Egypt	5.6	5.2	4.8	5.3	5.1	5.0	March
Jordan	7.0	6.6	6.2	6.4	. . .	. . .	
Kazakhstan[3]	13.6	11.0	9.0	9.0	8.0	. . .	
Kuwait	11.5	11.1	10.4	10.6	11.0	. . .	September
Lebanon	6.4	6.2	6.4	6.1	5.7	5.6	April
Morocco	9.8	8.7	8.5	7.6	7.6	. . .	May
Pakistan[4]	4.9	4.6	6.1	6.0	6.2	. . .	September
Saudi Arabia	9.6	9.3	9.3	8.8	8.0	9.4	March
Tunisia	. . .	. . .	. . .	. . .	. . .	. . .	
United Arab Emirates	12.9	13.0	13.0	12.6	12.1	. . .	
Sub-Saharan Africa							
Angola	10.6	11.1	9.0	11.1	11.3	10.5	April
Botswana	10.3	10.1	9.8	11.1	9.7	. . .	
Gabon	. . .	. . .	. . .	. . .	. . .	. . .	
Ghana	11.8	12.5	12.0	12.0	12.4	. . .	July
Kenya	12.9	13.3	11.6	11.8	11.4	. . .	June
Madagascar	7.1	7.0	6.7	6.8	6.2	. . .	
Mozambique	–2.7	8.2	7.8	5.6	6.5	. . .	
Nigeria	7.4	7.5	10.4	8.6	9.9	. . .	
Senegal	9.9	9.7	10.3	7.8	8.4	. . .	June
Sierra Leone	18.5	20.0	18.0	20.3	11.6	. . .	
South Africa	8.7	7.8	8.2	7.0	7.0	7.4	May
Uganda	9.8	10.0	9.2	8.5	10.1	. . .	September
Zambia	. . .	. . .	. . .	. . .	. . .	. . .	
Zimbabwe	9.4	9.3	9.5	7.6	10.7	. . .	
Other							
Australia[3]	6.9	7.1	6.3	5.8	5.9	6.0	March
Canada	4.7	4.6	4.6	4.7	4.4	4.7	April
Japan[5]	4.6	3.9	3.3	3.9	4.2	. . .	March
United States	8.5	9.0	9.2	9.2	10.3	. . .	

Sources: National authorities; and IMF staff estimates.

[1]Data for U.K. large banks. Data are unavailable on the same basis for 2004. Bankscope data for the balance sheet equity and assets of the top 15 U.K. banks suggest an equity to asset ratio of 5.4 in 2003 and 5.0 in 2004.

[2]Ratio for the state commercial banks.

[3]For Thailand and Australia, tier 1 capital to total assets. For Kazakhstan, tier 1 capital to risk-weighted assets.

[4]The data refer to commercial banks only, excluding specialized banks.

[5]Data refer to end-March of the following calendar year.

Table 24. Bank Nonperforming Loans to Total Loans

(In percent)

	2000	2001	2002	2003	2004	2005	Latest
Latin America							
Argentina	16.0	19.1	38.6	33.6	18.6	13.2	June
Bolivia	10.3	14.4	17.6	16.7	14.0	13.8	June
Brazil***	8.3	5.6	4.8	4.8	3.9	. . .	
Chile	1.7	1.6	1.8	1.6	1.2	1.2	April
Colombia	11.0	9.7	8.7	6.8	3.3	3.5	March
Costa Rica	3.5	2.4	3.2	1.7	2.0	1.8	March
Dominican Republic	2.6	2.6	4.9	8.9	7.3	. . .	
Ecuador	31.0	27.8	8.4	7.9	6.4	7.3	March
El Salvador	. . .	. . .	15.8	12.3	12.0	. . .	September
Jamaica	11.0	6.8	4.6	3.8	3.0	. . .	
Honduras	10.6	11.4	11.3	8.7	6.4	. . .	
Mexico	5.8	5.1	4.6	3.2	2.5	2.4	March
Nicaragua	5.2	9.3	12.6	12.7	9.3	9.6	February
Panama	1.4	3.0	4.6	3.3	2.6	. . .	September
Paraguay	. . .	16.5	19.7	20.6	10.8	10.8	February
Peru	. . .	17.0	14.6	12.2	9.5	9.4	March
Uruguay[1]	. . .	9.3	31.4	6.4	3.6	3.6	March
Venezuela	6.6	7.0	9.2	7.7	2.8	2.6	February
Emerging Europe							
Belarus	10.8	13.4	10.8	6.2	4.6	. . .	
Bosnia and Herzegovina	9.9	5.9	5.3	4.4	3.5	. . .	
Bulgaria[2]	17.3	13.1	8.6	7.3	7.1	6.5	March
Croatia***	9.5	7.3	5.9	5.1	4.5	4.5	March
Czech Republic	29.3	13.7	10.6	4.9	4.1	4.8	March
Estonia	1.0	1.3	0.8	0.4	0.3	0.2	April
Hungary	3.0	2.7	2.9	2.6	2.7	. . .	
Israel	6.9	8.2	9.8	10.5	10.5	. . .	
Latvia	4.6	2.8	2.0	1.4	1.1	1.1	March
Lithuania**	11.3	8.3	6.5	3.0	2.3	. . .	
Moldova	20.6	10.4	7.7	6.2	6.5	6.3	March
Poland**	15.5	18.6	22.0	22.2	15.5	. . .	
Romania	. . .	. . .	. . .	8.3	8.1	8.8	March
Russia	7.7	6.2	5.6	5.0	3.8	3.7	March
Serbia and Montenegro	. . .	. . .	21.6	24.1	22.8	. . .	
Slovak Republic	13.7	12.3	9.2	6.4	5.4	. . .	August
Slovenia	6.5	7.0	7.0	6.5	5.7	. . .	
Turkey	9.2	29.3	17.6	11.5	6.0	. . .	
Ukraine[3]	29.6	25.1	21.9	28.3	30.0	25.3	March
Western Europe							
Austria	2.4	2.3	2.3	2.2	. . .	. . .	
Belgium	2.8	2.9	3.0	2.6	2.2	. . .	September
Finland	0.6	0.6	0.5	0.4	0.4	. . .	June
France	5.0	5.0	5.0	4.8	. . .	. . .	
Germany	4.7	4.6	5.0	5.3	. . .	. . .	
Greece	12.3	8.2	7.3	7.0	7.1	. . .	September
Iceland[4]	1.5	2.0	2.6	2.1	0.9	. . .	
Ireland	1.0	1.0	1.0	0.9	0.8	. . .	
Italy	7.8	6.7	6.5	6.6	6.5	. . .	
Luxembourg[5]	0.5	0.4	0.4	0.3	0.3	. . .	
Netherlands[6]	1.8	1.8	2.3	2.1	1.8	. . .	
Norway	1.2	1.3	1.8	1.6	1.0	. . .	
Portugal	2.2	2.1	2.3	2.4	2.2	. . .	June
Spain	1.2	1.2	1.1	1.0	0.8	0.8	March
Sweden[7]	1.6	1.5	1.2	1.2	0.9	. . .	
Switzerland	4.1	3.6	3.1	2.3	1.6	. . .	
United Kingdom	2.5	2.6	2.6	2.5	2.2	. . .	September

Table 24 ***(concluded)***

	2000	2001	2002	2003	2004	2005	Latest
Asia							
Bangladesh	34.9	31.5	28.0	22.1	17.6	17.5	March
China[8]	22.4	29.8	26.0	20.4	15.6	. . .	
Hong Kong SAR	7.3	6.5	5.0	3.9	2.2	. . .	
India	12.8	11.4	10.4	8.8	6.6	. . .	June
Indonesia[9]	34.4	28.6	22.1	17.9	13.4	. . .	
Korea	8.9	3.3	2.4	2.6	1.9	. . .	
Malaysia	15.4	17.8	15.8	13.9	11.8	11.6	February
Philippines[10]	24.0	27.7	26.5	26.1	24.7	. . .	
Singapore	3.4	3.6	3.4	3.2	2.9	. . .	June
Thailand	17.7	10.5	15.7	12.9	11.9	. . .	
Middle East and Central Asia							
Armenia	17.5	24.4	12.5	9.9	7.2	. . .	
Azerbaijan[11]	. . .	. . .	. . .	15.1	9.5	8.2	March
Egypt	13.6	15.6	16.9	20.2	24.2	27.0	March
Jordan	18.4	19.3	21.0	19.9	. . .	. . .	
Kazakhstan	. . .	. . .	18.3	25.9	29.9	. . .	
Kuwait	19.2	10.3	7.8	6.1	5.4	. . .	September
Lebanon[12]	7.8	10.0	12.4	12.8	10.1	10.4	February
Morocco	17.5	16.8	17.2	18.1	19.4	. . .	
Pakistan[13]	19.5	19.6	17.7	13.7	9.0	. . .	
Saudi Arabia	10.4	10.1	9.2	5.4	3.1	. . .	
Tunisia	21.6	19.2	20.9	24.0	23.7	. . .	
United Arab Emirates	12.7	15.7	15.3	14.3	12.5	. . .	
Sub-Saharan Africa							
Angola	. . .	. . .	10.4	9.0	13.3	. . .	September
Botswana	1.7	4.1	3.5	3.7	2.8	. . .	
Gabon	6.6	8.6	11.4	13.8	15.8	. . .	
Ghana	11.9	19.6	22.7	18.3	16.1	. . .	
Kenya	33.3	30.1	29.8	25.6	22.9	. . .	June
Madagascar	8.6	10.3	19.6	16.7	11.4	. . .	
Mozambique	17.8	23.4	20.8	26.8	6.4	. . .	
Nigeria	22.6	19.7	21.4	19.8	21.6	. . .	
Senegal	18.1	17.8	18.5	13.3	14.2	. . .	June
Sierra Leone	37.9	29.1	17.1	9.9	14.8	. . .	
South Africa	. . .	3.1	2.8	2.4	1.8	1.8	March
Uganda****	9.8	6.5	3.0	7.2	2.2	. . .	
Zambia	. . .	23.6	11.4	5.3	7.6	. . .	
Zimbabwe	19.6	11.4	4.2	4.7	. . .	. . .	
Other							
Australia	0.5	0.7	0.6	0.4	0.3	. . .	
Canada	1.3	1.5	1.6	1.2	0.7	. . .	
Japan[14]	5.3	8.4	7.2	5.2	2.9	. . .	March 2005
United States	1.1	1.3	1.4	1.1	0.8	. . .	

Sources: National authorities; and IMF staff estimates.
[1]Private banks. Data in 2002 include suspended banks.
[2]Loans in categories "watch", "substandard", "doubtful", "loss".
[3]The increase in NPLs in 2003 reflects a revision in the official definition.
[4]NPLs net of specific provisions and excluding appropriated assets.
[5]Value adjustments on credit to total gross credit.
[6]Three largest banks.
[7]Four major banks.
[8]State-owned commercial banks.
[9]Compromised assets include reported NPLs, restructured loans, foreclosed assets. Top 16 banks.
[10]NPLs plus "real and other properties owned or acquired."
[11]NPLs to total assets.
[12]Problem loans net of provisions and unearned interest.
[13]The data refer to commercial banks only, excluding specialized banks.
[14]Ratio for the major banks. Data refer to end-March of the following calendar year.
(**) 30-day NPL classification
(***) 60-day NPL classification
(****) 180-day NPL classification

Table 25. Bank Provisions to Nonperforming Loans

(In percent)

	2000	2001	2002	2003	2004	2005	Latest
Latin America							
Argentina	61.1	66.4	73.8	79.2	102.9	110.6	June
Bolivia	61.4	63.7	63.7	74.0	84.3	78.1	June
Brazil	81.4	126.6	143.6	144.6	161.7	...	
Chile	145.5	146.5	128.1	130.9	165.5	158.0	April
Colombia[1]	56.6	77.5	86.5	98.5	149.2	137.0	March
Costa Rica	100.8	113.2	102.6	145.9	...	...	
Dominican Republic	121.6	112.3	64.9	65.0	...	...	
Ecuador	104.0	102.2	131.4	127.3	119.0	107.0	March
El Salvador	84.9	103.1	115.1	129.8	128.6	...	September
Jamaica	116.8	122.1	110.7	104.1	106.3	...	
Honduras	27.7	27.2	38.7	38.2	64.6	...	
Mexico	115.3	123.8	138.1	167.1	201.8	199.6	March
Nicaragua	109.6	37.6	42.9	36.2	44.2	48.7	February
Panama	158.2	85.5	54.5	72.0	96.5	...	September
Paraguay	...	37.0	46.6	54.8	54.6	55.5	February
Peru	...	63.1	69.3	67.2	68.5	68.4	March
Uruguay[2]	...	45.4	51.7	56.5	56.2	56.4	March
Venezuela	93.6	92.4	97.9	103.7	130.2	139.2	February
Emerging Europe							
Belarus	...	37.7	15.8	29.1	32.4	...	
Bosnia and Herzegovina	64.2	60.6	73.8	79.5	96.1	...	
Bulgaria	51.3	43.0	39.3	40.9	40.6	36.8	March
Croatia	79.9	71.8	68.1	60.8	60.3	60.6	March
Czech Republic	46.8	60.3	77.5	76.7	69.4	61.0	March
Estonia	...	...	...	...	...	...	
Hungary	57.0	42.6	50.8	47.3	51.1	...	
Israel	55.8	57.1	54.7	53.8	...	...	
Latvia	74.1	80.4	95.5	89.4	99.1	...	
Lithuania	34.6	34.2	18.6	21.6	...	...	
Moldova	...	...	...	...	...	...	
Poland	40.5	42.6	46.7	47.3	58.0	...	
Romania	...	...	...	33.5	34.3	33.6	March
Russia[3]	102.6	108.1	112.5	118.0	139.5	137.8	April
Serbia and Montenegro	...	...	...	...	...	...	
Slovak Republic	75.1	79.7	86.1	88.3	89.1	...	August
Slovenia	45.3	44.6	38.0	35.0	34.0	...	
Turkey	59.8	47.1	64.2	88.6	88.1	...	
Ukraine	38.4	39.2	37.0	22.3	21.1	23.8	March
Western Europe							
Austria	...	...	...	...	...	...	
Belgium	57.0	57.0	51.8	52.8	53.7	...	September
Finland	...	...	...	...	...	...	
France	60.8	59.9	58.3	58.4	...		
Germany	...	...	...	...	...	...	
Greece	36.8	43.3	46.9	49.9	...	...	September
Iceland	42.5	42.0	40.0	45.5	58.8	...	
Ireland	106.1	110.8	108.7	97.0	...	...	
Italy	48.6	50.0	53.6	55.1	...	...	
Luxembourg	...	...	...	...	...	...	
Netherlands	73.7	73.3	55.0	59.6	...	...	
Norway	32.0	33.7	29.2	33.1	36.8	...	
Portugal	66.7	66.8	62.8	72.6	...	...	
Spain[1]	134.9	160.4	183.2	209.7	266.2	...	June
Sweden	...	...	...	...	...	...	
Switzerland	...	...	...	...	...	...	
United Kingdom	...	...	...	...	...	...	

Table 25 *(concluded)*

	2000	2001	2002	2003	2004	2005	Latest
Asia							
Bangladesh	59.1	60.5	55.8	40.3	...	...	
China	...	...	...	...	...	...	
Hong Kong SAR	...	...	...	...	...	...	
India	...	...	...	...	...	...	
Indonesia[4]	36.1	35.5	35.9	43.4	43.1	...	
Korea	...	...	...	...	...	...	
Malaysia	41.0	37.7	38.1	38.9	39.9	39.6	February
Philippines	28.6	29.6	30.1	30.9	33.2	...	
Singapore[1]	...	60.1	61.2	64.9	76.6	77.7	March
Thailand	47.2	54.9	61.8	72.8	69.0	...	February
Middle East and Central Asia							
Armenia	83.4	89.3	95.8	103.7	107.4	...	
Azerbaijan	...	...	...	13.7	7.8	7.3	March
Egypt	73.5	69.4	67.5	62.3	57.0	53.2	March
Jordan	34.6	36.4	36.7	38.9	...	...	
Kazakhstan	19.5	15.1	20.6	15.8	15.3	...	
Kuwait	50.1	53.7	64.3	72.4	72.4	...	September
Lebanon	64.6	62.6	62.3	64.6	67.3	...	
Morocco	47.8	52.9	54.7	54.9	59.3	...	
Pakistan[5]	53.9	53.2	58.2	64.7	72.7	...	
Saudi Arabia	99.0	107.0	110.4	136.0	164.0	...	
Tunisia	49.2	47.4	43.9	43.1	45.8	...	
United Arab Emirates	86.0	87.0	87.5	88.5	94.6	...	
Sub-Saharan Africa							
Angola	...	...	...	...	...	...	
Botswana	96.1	118.3	131.8	179.6	55.4	...	
Gabon	64.7	63.0	66.5	78.8	78.4	...	
Ghana	58.6	46.4	63.6	64.4	...	...	
Kenya	...	...	...	...	...	...	
Madagascar	75.0	74.1	56.3	62.2	66.3	...	
Mozambique	...	...	...	...	...	...	
Nigeria	49.7	73.6	60.9	...	...	...	
Senegal	67.6	70.2	70.5	75.3	73.0	...	June
Sierra Leone	95.0	108.6	119.6	92.7	43.1	...	
South Africa	44.0	46.0	54.2	66.1	82.0	...	
Uganda	61.7	70.0	81.5	76.5	87.8	...	September
Zambia	...	...	...	...	...	...	
Zimbabwe	44.4	28.3	52.8	70.1	...	...	
Other							
Australia[1]	132.1	107.1	109.8	138.3	150.8	...	June
Canada	42.8	44.0	41.1	43.5	47.7	48.6	March
Japan[6]	35.5	31.8	36.1	43.6	44.0	...	September
United States	146.4	128.8	123.7	140.4	167.8	...	

Sources: National authorities; and IMF staff estimates.
[1]Includes general provisions.
[2]Private banks. Data in 2002 include suspended banks.
[3]In 2004, change in the definition, not comparable with previous years.
[4]Loan-loss reserve to compromised assets. Top 16 banks.
[5]The data refer to commercial banks only, excluding specialized banks.
[6]Data refer to end-March of the following calendar year.

Table 26. Bank Return on Assets

(In percent)

	2000	2001	2002	2003	2004	2005	Latest
Latin America							
Argentina	0.0	0.0	–8.9	–2.9	–0.5	0.4	June
Bolivia	–0.8	–0.4	0.1	0.3	–0.1	0.1	June
Brazil	1.1	–0.1	1.9	1.5	1.8	. . .	
Chile	1.0	1.3	1.1	1.3	1.2	1.4	April
Colombia[1]	. . .	1.8	2.7	3.5	4.1	4.1	March
Costa Rica[2]	1.7	1.9	1.8	2.1	2.0	1.9	March
Dominican Republic	. . .	2.1	2.3	0.0	1.8	. . .	
Ecuador	–2.8	–6.6	1.5	1.5	1.6	2.1	March
El Salvador	0.3	0.9	1.1	1.1	1.0	. . .	September
Jamaica[2]	1.7	2.4	2.9	3.9	2.7	. . .	
Honduras	0.9	0.9	0.8	1.2	1.2	. . .	
Mexico	0.9	0.8	–1.1	1.7	1.5	2.0	March
Nicaragua	1.9	1.8	1.8	2.1	2.8	2.8	February
Panama[2]	1.6	1.3	2.0	1.9	1.9	. . .	September
Paraguay	1.4	2.2	1.0	0.4	1.7	2.3	February
Peru	0.3	0.4	0.8	1.1	1.2	1.3	March
Uruguay[3]	. . .	–0.1	–35.2	–2.0	–0.2	–0.1	March
Venezuela	2.8	2.8	5.3	6.2	5.9	4.3	February
Emerging Europe							
Belarus	1.0	0.8	1.0	1.5	1.4	. . .	
Bosnia and Herzegovina	–1.3	–0.6	0.4	0.6	0.6	. . .	
Bulgaria	3.1	2.9	2.1	2.4	2.1	2.0	March
Croatia	1.3	0.7	1.3	1.4	1.4	1.4	March
Czech Republic	0.7	0.7	1.1	1.2	1.3	1.8	March
Estonia	1.2	2.7	1.6	1.7	1.6	. . .	March
Hungary	1.3	1.4	1.4	1.5	2.0	. . .	
Israel	0.5	0.2	0.1	0.4	0.6	. . .	
Latvia	2.0	1.5	1.5	1.4	1.7	. . .	
Lithuania	0.5	–0.1	1.0	1.4	1.3	. . .	
Moldova[5]	7.4	4.3	4.3	4.5	3.9	3.2	March
Poland	1.1	1.0	0.5	0.5	1.4	. . .	
Romania	1.8	2.5	2.7	2.7	2.5	2.8	March
Russia.	0.9	2.4	2.6	2.6	2.9	. . .	
Serbia and Montenegro	. . .	. . .	–8.4	–0.3	–1.2	. . .	
Slovak Republic	0.5	1.0	1.2	1.2	1.0	. . .	September
Slovenia[2]	1.1	0.5	1.1	1.0	1.1	. . .	
Turkey	. . .	. . .	1.1	2.3	2.5	. . .	
Ukraine	. . .	1.2	1.2	1.0	1.1	1.5	March
Western Europe							
Austria[4]	0.8	0.8	0.7	1.5	1.5	. . .	
Belgium[5]	0.8	0.5	0.5	0.5	0.7	. . .	September
Finland	1.2	0.7	0.5	0.7	1.0	. . .	June
France	0.5	0.5	0.5	0.4	. . .	. . .	
Germany[6]	0.2	0.1	0.1	–0.1	. . .	. . .	
Greece	1.4	1.0	0.5	0.6	0.8	. . .	September
Iceland	0.7	0.8	1.1	1.3	1.8	. . .	
Ireland	1.2	0.9	1.0	0.9	. . .	. . .	
Italy	0.8	0.6	0.5	0.5	. . .	. . .	
Luxembourg	0.5	0.5	0.4	0.5	0.5	. . .	
Netherlands	0.6	0.4	0.4	0.5	0.5	. . .	
Norway	1.1	0.8	0.4	0.6	0.9	. . .	
Portugal	0.9	0.8	0.7	0.8	0.8	. . .	June
Spain	1.0	1.0	0.9	0.9	1.0	. . .	
Sweden[7]	0.9	0.8	0.6	0.7	. . .	. . .	
Switzerland[5]	1.4	1.1	1.1	0.9	0.9	. . .	
United Kingdom[2]	0.9	0.5	0.9	0.6	0.8	. . .	September

Table 26 *(concluded)*

	2000	2001	2002	2003	2004	2005	Latest
Asia							
Bangladesh	0.0	0.7	0.5	0.5	0.7	. . .	
China[8]	0.1	0.1	0.1	. . .	. . .	. . .	
Hong Kong SAR[9]	. . .	. . .	. . .	1.9	1.7	. . .	
India[2]	0.7	0.5	0.8	1.0	1.2	. . .	June
Indonesia[10]	0.3	0.6	1.4	1.6	2.5	. . .	
Korea[2]	−0.6	0.8	0.6	0.1	0.9	. . .	
Malaysia	1.4	1.0	1.3	1.3	1.4	. . .	
Philippines	0.4	0.4	0.8	1.1	1.2	. . .	
Singapore	1.3	1.0	0.8	1.1	1.0	. . .	
Thailand	−0.2	1.5	0.2	0.7	1.3	. . .	
Middle East and Central Asia							
Armenia	−1.9	−9.1	3.9	2.7	3.2	. . .	. . .
Azerbaijan	. . .	0.5	1.5	1.8	1.9	2.2	March
Egypt	0.9	0.8	0.7	0.5	0.5	0.6	March
Jordan	0.3	0.7	0.5	0.7	. . .	. . .	
Kazakhstan[2]	1.5	0.9	2.0	2.0	1.4	. . .	
Kuwait	2.0	2.0	1.8	2.0	2.3	. . .	September
Lebanon	0.7	0.5	0.6	0.7	0.8	. . .	
Morocco	0.7	0.9	0.3	−0.2	0.8	. . .	
Pakistan[11]	0.0	0.0	0.8	1.2	1.3	. . .	
Saudi Arabia	2.0	2.2	2.3	2.3	2.5	3.0	March
Tunisia	1.2	1.1	0.7	0.6	0.4	. . .	
United Arab Emirates	1.8	1.9	1.9	1.9	2.1	. . .	
Sub-Saharan Africa							
Angola	. . .	. . .	0.7	4.7	3.6	. . .	September
Botswana	4.7	4.6	4.3	4.2	4.0	. . .	
Gabon	6.2	5.6	5.2	4.7	. . .	. . .	
Ghana[2]	9.7	8.7	6.8	6.4	6.2	. . .	
Kenya[2]	0.5	1.6	1.0	2.3	2.1	. . .	June
Madagascar	3.2	2.1	0.9	2.4	3.0	. . .	
Mozambique	0.0	0.1	1.6	1.2	1.4	. . .	
Nigeria	4.0	3.3	2.4	1.7	3.1	. . .	
Senegal	1.7	1.6	1.8	1.8	. . .	. . .	
Sierra Leone	15.9	11.9	10.4	10.7	5.4	. . .	
South Africa[2]	. . .	0.8	0.4	0.8	1.2	1.3	March
Uganda	4.4	4.4	2.7	3.3	4.5	. . .	
Zambia	. . .	2.4	0.0	3.8	2.1	. . .	
Zimbabwe	6.0	5.1	4.0	6.7	. . .	. . .	
Other							
Australia[12]	1.3	1.0	1.2	1.1	1.2	. . .	
Canada	0.7	0.7	0.4	0.7	0.8	. . .	
Japan[2,13]	0.0	−0.8	−0.7	0.1	0.3	. . .	March
United States	1.1	1.1	1.3	1.4	1.3	. . .	

Sources: National authorities; and IMF staff estimates.
[1]Operating margin to assets.
[2]Before tax.
[3]Private banks. Data in 2002 include suspended banks.
[4]Operating profit.
[5]Gross profit.
[6]The 2003 figure is for large banks only.
[7]Ratio for the four major financial groups.
[8]State-owned commercial banks.
[9]Net interest margin.
[10]Top 16 banks.
[11]The data refer to commercial banks only, excluding specialized banks.
[12] Four major banks.
[13]Data refer to end-March of the following calendar year.

Table 27. Bank Return on Equity
(In percent)

	2000	2001	2002	2003	2004	2005	Latest
Latin America							
Argentina	0.0	–0.2	–59.2	–22.7	–4.2	3.3	June
Bolivia	–8.6	–4.1	0.6	2.7	–1.2	0.7	June
Brazil	12.7	–1.2	21.8	17.0	18.7	. . .	
Chile	12.7	17.7	14.4	16.7	16.7	19.0	April
Colombia	–20.7	1.1	9.6	16.9	23.2	23.2	March
Costa Rica[1]	16.3	18.7	17.1	19.5	20.7	19.9	March
Dominican Republic	. . .	21.5	22.0	–0.5	21.3	. . .	
Ecuador	–21.3	–36.0	15.3	12.7	14.2	20.1	March
El Salvador	3.2	10.7	12.2	11.5	9.8	. . .	September
Jamaica[1]	17.0	21.5	24.5	32.3	20.5	. . .	
Honduras	7.6	8.4	8.2	11.8	14.9	. . .	
Mexico	10.4	8.6	–10.4	14.2	12.9	17.9	March
Nicaragua	27.1	28.7	23.9	29.2	34.9	33.3	February
Panama	. . .	. . .	. . .	. . .	. . .	. . .	
Paraguay	12.4	21.2	9.0	4.5	18.3	21.7	February
Peru	3.1	4.5	8.4	10.8	11.3	12.4	March
Uruguay	. . .	. . .	. . .	. . .	. . .	. . .	
Venezuela	23.1	20.3	35.6	44.0	45.2	36.3	February
Emerging Europe							
Belarus	4.8	4.9	4.4	6.4	6.3	. . .	
Bosnia and Herzegovina	–5.8	–3.5	2.5	5.1	5.6	. . .	
Bulgaria	20.3	20.2	14.9	22.7	20.0	19.9	March
Croatia	10.4	6.5	13.7	15.6	16.6	15.8	March
Czech Republic	13.1	16.6	27.4	23.8	23.4	32.1	March
Estonia	8.0	20.7	11.9	14.2	13.8	. . .	March
Hungary	13.4	17.6	16.2	19.5	25.2	. . .	
Israel	10.9	5.6	2.5	8.3	11.4	. . .	
Latvia	18.6	19.0	16.4	16.7	21.4	. . .	
Lithuania	5.0	–1.1	9.8	13.4	13.4	. . .	
Moldova[2]	25.0	14.3	16.7	20.3	18.2	16.6	March
Poland	14.5	12.8	5.2	5.4	17.6	. . .	
Romania	12.3	15.8	18.8	20.0	19.3	21.8	March
Russia	8.0	19.4	18.0	17.8	20.3	. . .	
Serbia and Montenegro	. . .	. . .	–60.6	–1.2	–5.3	. . .	
Slovak Republic	11.2	15.4	17.1	14.9	11.9	. . .	August
Slovenia[1]	11.4	4.8	13.3	12.5	14.2	. . .	
Turkey	–10.5	–69.4	9.3	16.0	17.4	. . .	
Ukraine	–0.5	7.5	8.0	7.6	8.4	11.2	March
Western Europe							
Austria	9.4	9.8	5.4	6.3	9.3	. . .	
Belgium[2]	29.6	19.2	17.1	17.1	24.0	. . .	September
Finland	22.4	13.5	10.7	10.1	12.4	. . .	June
France	9.7	9.6	9.1	8.6	. . .	. . .	
Germany	6.1	4.6	2.9	–1.5	. . .	. . .	
Greece	15.4	12.4	6.8	8.9	11.4	. . .	September
Iceland	10.7	13.5	18.1	22.1	30.9	. . .	
Ireland	22.0	16.0	18.0	17.8	. . .	. . .	
Italy	11.2	8.6	7.1	7.3	. . .	. . .	
Luxembourg	36.7	40.7	36.4	34.9	39.8	. . .	
Netherlands	14.7	10.8	9.2	12.3	13.8	. . .	
Norway	15.6	11.6	6.2	9.6	14.6	. . .	
Portugal	15.1	14.9	11.7	13.9	13.3	. . .	June
Spain	15.5	13.9	12.3	13.7	14.5	. . .	
Sweden[3]	15.7	13.0	10.9	13.1	15.1	. . .	
Switzerland[2]	23.6	17.8	18.3	16.0	16.7	. . .	
United Kingdom[1]	13.5	7.7	12.0*	20.0	22.0	. . .	June

Table 27 ***(concluded)***

	2000	2001	2002	2003	2004	2005	Latest
Asia							
Bangladesh	0.3	15.9	11.6	9.8	13.0	. . .	
China	. . .	. . .	. . .	. . .	. . .	. . .	
Hong Kong SAR	13.5	13.9	13.3	13.5	. . .	. . .	
India	12.8	10.4	15.3	18.8	20.8	. . .	March
Indonesia[4]	. . .	12.0	19.0	19.2	25.7	. . .	
Korea[1]	−11.9	15.9	11.7	2.2	18.0	. . .	
Malaysia	19.3	13.1	16.3	15.3	16.6	. . .	
Philippines	2.6	3.2	5.8	8.5	8.3	. . .	June
Singapore	. . .	9.7	7.6	10.1	10.5	. . .	September
Thailand	−4.8	32.8	4.2	10.5	19.8	. . .	
Middle East and Central Asia							
Armenia	−12.3	−78.6	21.6	14.4	18.4	. . .	
Azerbaijan	. . .	. . .	. . .	13.7	12.9	14.2	March
Egypt	16.1	13.7	12.4	8.8	9.8	10.2	March
Jordan	4.4	10.9	8.7	10.2	. . .	. . .	
Kazakhstan[1]	7.9	5.4	13.8	14.2	11.2	. . .	
Kuwait	17.6	18.2	17.4	18.6	20.4	. . .	September
Lebanon	. . .	8.4	9.4	10.9	10.6	. . .	
Morocco	8.1	10.2	1.9	−2.1	10.9	. . .	
Pakistan[5]	−0.3	−0.3	14.3	20.5	19.8	. . .	September
Saudi Arabia[6]	21.0	21.9	22.2	22.7	31.7	32.2	March
Tunisia	13.7	14.0	8.0	7.6	5.1	. . .	
United Arab Emirates	16.2	15.5	16.2	16.8	18.6	. . .	
Sub-Saharan Africa							
Angola	. . .	. . .	18.3	27.0	20.3	. . .	September
Botswana	45.2	46.7	43.8	44.3	36.0	. . .	
Gabon	60.2	36.8	35.3	30.9	. . .	. . .	
Ghana	65.7	49.7	36.9	54.0	. . .	. . .	
Kenya[1]	4.9	15.7	10.9	23.2	22.7	. . .	June
Madagascar	35.7	27.1	11.8	31.9	38.8	. . .	
Mozambique	. . .	3.5	22.1	16.3	18.7	. . .	
Nigeria	. . .	43.7	28.1	19.8	27.4	. . .	
Senegal	20.3	18.6	21.1	22.1	22.1	. . .	March
Sierra Leone	56.7	39.9	33.3	33.0	29.6	. . .	
South Africa	. . .	8.9	5.2	11.6	16.2	16.9	March
Uganda	53.1	45.8	24.6	33.1	39.0	. . .	September
Zambia	. . .	. . .	. . .	. . .	. . .	. . .	
Zimbabwe	43.2	42.7	57.7	114.8	. . .	. . .	
Other							
Australia[3]	19.4	15.6	18.2	16.4	18.2	. . .	
Canada	15.3	13.9	9.4	14.6	17.3	. . .	
Japan[7]	−0.5	−14.3	−19.5	−2.7	4.1	. . .	March
United States	13.5	13.0	14.1	15.0	13.3	. . .	

Sources: National authorities; and IMF staff estimates.
[1]Before tax.
[2]Gross profit.
[3]Four major banks.
[4]Top 16 banks.
[5]The data refer to commercial banks only, excluding specialized banks.
[6]The return on equity is based on all own funds.
[7]After tax. Data refer to end-March of the following calendar year.
(*) Post-tax return on equity.

World Economic and Financial Surveys

This series (ISSN 0258-7440) contains biannual, annual, and periodic studies covering monetary and financial issues of importance to the global economy. The core elements of the series are the *World Economic Outlook* report, usually published in April and September, and the semiannual *Global Financial Stability Report*. Other studies assess international trade policy, private market and official financing for developing countries, exchange and payments systems, export credit policies, and issues discussed in the *World Economic Outlook*. Please consult the IMF *Publications Catalog* for a complete listing of currently available World Economic and Financial Surveys.

World Economic Outlook: A Survey by the Staff of the International Monetary Fund

The *World Economic Outlook*, published twice a year in English, French, Spanish, and Arabic, presents IMF staff economists' analyses of global economic developments during the near and medium term. Chapters give an overview of the world economy; consider issues affecting industrial countries, developing countries, and economies in transition to the market; and address topics of pressing current interest.

ISSN 0256-6877.
$49.00 (academic rate: $46.00); paper.
2004. (September). ISBN 1-58906-406-2. **Stock #WEOEA2004002.**
2004. (April). ISBN 1-58906-337-6. **Stock #WEOEA200401.**
2003. (April). ISBN 1-58906-212-4. **Stock #WEOEA0012003.**
2002. (Sep.). ISBN 1-58906-179-9. **Stock #WEOEA0022002.**

Global Financial Stability Report: Market Developments and Issues

The *Global Financial Stability Report*, published twice a year, examines trends and issues that influence world financial markets. It replaces two IMF publications—the annual *International Capital Markets* report and the electronic quarterly *Emerging Market Financing* report. The report is designed to deepen understanding of international capital flows and explores developments that could pose a risk to international financial market stability.

$49.00 (academic rate: $46.00); paper.
April 2005 ISBN-1-58906-418-6. **Stock #GFSREA2005001.**
September 2004 ISBN 1-58906-378-3. **Stock #GFSREA2004002.**
April 2004 ISBN 1-58906-328-7. **Stock #GFSREA0012004.**
September 2003 ISBN 1-58906-236-1. **Stock #GFSREA0022003.**
March 2003 ISBN 1-58906-210-8. **Stock #GFSREA0012003.**

Emerging Local Securities and Derivatives Markets

by Donald Mathieson, Jorge E. Roldos, Ramana Ramaswamy, and Anna Ilyna

The volatility of capital flows since the mid-1990s has sparked an interest in the development of local securities and derivatives markets. This report examines the growth of these markets in emerging market countries and the key policy issues that have arisen as a result.

$42.00 (academic rate: $35.00); paper.
2004. ISBN 1-58906-291-4. **Stock #WEOEA0202004.**

Official Financing: Recent Developments and Selected Issues

by a staff team in the Policy Development and Review Department led by Martin G. Gilman and Jian-Ye Wang

This study provides information on official financing for developing countries, with the focus on low-income countries. It updates the 2001 edition and reviews developments in direct financing by official and multilateral sources.

$42.00 (academic rate: $35.00); paper.
2003. ISBN 1-58906-228-0. **Stock #WEOEA0132003.**
2001. ISBN 1-58906-038-5. **Stock #WEOEA0132001.**

Exchange Arrangements and Foreign Exchange Markets: Developments and Issues

by a staff team led by Shogo Ishii

This study updates developments in exchange arrangements during 1998–2001. It also discusses the evolution of exchange rate regimes based on de facto policies since 1990, reviews foreign exchange market organization and regulations in a number of countries, and examines factors affecting exchange rate volatility.

ISSN 0258-7440
$42.00 (academic rate $35.00)
2003 (March) ISBN 1-58906-177-2. **Stock #WEOEA0192003.**

World Economic Outlook Supporting Studies

by the IMF's Research Department

These studies, supporting analyses and scenarios of the *World Economic Outlook*, provide a detailed examination of theory and evidence on major issues currently affecting the global economy.

$25.00 (academic rate: $20.00); paper.
2000. ISBN 1-55775-893-X. **Stock #WEOEA0032000.**

Exchange Rate Arrangements and Currency Convertibility: Developments and Issues

by a staff team led by R. Barry Johnston

A principal force driving the growth in international trade and investment has been the liberalization of financial transactions, including the liberalization of trade and exchange controls. This study reviews the developments and issues in the exchange arrangements and currency convertibility of IMF members.

$20.00 (academic rate: $12.00); paper.
1999. ISBN 1-55775-795-X. **Stock #WEOEA0191999.**

Available by series subscription or single title (including back issues); academic rate available only to full-time university faculty and students. For earlier editions please inquire about prices.

The IMF *Catalog of Publications* is available on-line at the Internet address listed below.

Please send orders and inquiries to:
International Monetary Fund, Publication Services, 700 19th Street, N.W.
Washington, D.C. 20431, U.S.A.
Tel.: (202) 623-7430 Telefax: (202) 623-7201
E-mail: publications@imf.org
Internet: http://www.imf.org